DEPENDENCY, OBLIGATIONS, AND ENTITLEMENTS

a new sociology of aging,
the life course, and the elderly

Judah Matras

Brookdale Institute of Gerontology and Adult Human Development
Jerusalem
Carleton University, Ottawa, Canada
University of Haifa

PRENTICE HALL, Englewood Cliffs, New Jersey 07632

Library of Congress Cataloging-in-Publication Data

Matras, Judah.
  Dependency, obligations, and entitlements : a new sociology of
aging, the life course, and the elderly / by Judah Matras.
    p. cm.
  Bibliography: p.
  Includes index.
  ISBN 0-13-199316-X : $26.00
  1. Aged—Social conditions. I. Title.
HQ1061.M355 1900
305.26—dc20

89-8855
CIP

For ORIT, with love and admiration

Editorial/production supervision: Cyndy Lyle Rymer
Cover Design: 20/20 Services, Inc.
Manufacturing buyer: Carol Bystrom

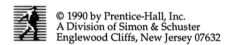
© 1990 by Prentice-Hall, Inc.
A Division of Simon & Schuster
Englewood Cliffs, New Jersey 07632

Printed in the United States of America

10 9 8 7 6 5 4 3 2 1

0-13-199316-X

Prentice-Hall International (UK) Limited, *London*
Prentice-Hall of Australia Pte. Limited, *Sydney*
Prentice-Hall Canada Inc., *Toronto*
Prentice-Hall Hispanoamericana, S.A., *Mexico*
Prentice-Hall of India Private Limited, *New Delhi*
Prentice-Hall of Japan, Inc., *Tokyo*
Simon & Schuster Asia Pte. Ltd., *Singapore*
Editora Prentice-Hall do Brasil, Ltda., *Rio de Janeiro*

CONTENTS

PART IV   The Elderly

9   THE SOCIAL STATUS OF THE ELDERLY
historical and comparative perspectives   *173*

10   SOCIOLOGICAL THEORIES OF AGING IN OLD AGE   *197*

11   ROLE TRANSITIONS IN MIDDLE AND LATE LIFE
the contraction of social networks   *230*

12 DEPENDENCY, OBLIGATIONS, AND ENTITLEMENTS
the changing mix of family, market, and societal responses *260*

PART V Conclusion

13 AFTER THE BABY BOOM
the new aging, life course, and family cycle *296*

REFERENCES *306*
INDEX *320*

PREFACE

In this book I try to present and relate information and ideas about the main historical population trends, about individual life course and family cycles and their transitions, and about the population who are at the close of their life courses and family cycles: the elderly. The book is an outcome of my teaching and research experience at Carleton University, Ottawa, and the University of Haifa, and of my research experience at Brookdale Institute of Gerontology and Adult Human Development in Jerusalem. But, of course, it draws very heavily on the research, teaching, and policy planning and evaluation experiences of my friends and colleagues in these institutions and elsewhere, and it draws on the rapidly expanding literature on these topics in the social scientific disciplines and in social gerontology.

But this book, as well as my teaching of the sociology of aging, the life course, and the elderly, departs from other texts in sociology, social gerontology, and population studies in that I propose an explicit linkage between population trends and societal organization. The linkage resides in the responses to changes engendered in the life course and family cycle, that is in changing patterns of dependency, obligations, and entitlements through the life course. These affect societies generally and the lives and well-being of families and individuals at all ages. But the especially dramatic outcome of these processes in our own century is the growth of the elderly population and the growing social, economic, and political salience of dependency, obligations, and entitlements in the later years of the life course and family cycle.

Studies of population aging have long been dominated by issues of labor force size, composition, and productivity, and of costs of income maintenance and health care for the elderly. Studies of the elderly have, in turn, been dominated by the themes of crises and "adaptation" to "old age," while studies of the life course have similarly been dominated by issues of transitions, for example to adolescence, employment, marriage, parenthood, middle-age, etc., and the individual "adaptations" to them. In this volume population aging is treated not only in terms of growth in the proportions and numbers of elderly persons but also in terms of the changing longevity and total life years, declining fertility and life years devoted to parenting, and changing patterns of kin availability which population aging necessarily entails. The life course is seen not only as the sequences of "crises" and "adaptations" accompanying transitions across physiological and biological "stages," but also in terms of the changing, largely age-graded, social and economic participation and relations at the family, peer-group and community, and societal levels. The elderly are seen not only as a population at risk and in need, and not only as cases requiring intervention and treatment to resolve their own and their families' medical and psychosocial predicaments, but also as a major societal resource and increasingly an economic and political force in modern society. And attention to the elderly population belongs not only in social gerontology and the helping professions but, rather, much more centrally in the traditional social scientific disciplines than has been the case heretofore. It is my hope that this book can make a modest contribution to bringing the intersection of problems and studies of aging, the life course, and the elderly closer to the center of contemporary social scientific inquiry.

My greatest and most immediate debt is to my students at Carleton University, Ottawa, and at the University of Haifa. Their interest in and commitment to the well-being and welfare of individuals and of societies, their curiosity about the underlying demographic, social, economic, and political processes, and their patience and willingness to entertain and follow complex arguments and analyses of correlates and outcomes of such processes have been the main inspiration and source of staying power for me in writing this book. The support of friends, colleagues, staff, and facilities at Brookdale institute of Gerontology and Adult Human Development in Jerusalem has been invaluable at every stage of my thinking and work on this book. The contributions of researchers and scholars, writers and legislators, planners and administrators, and others of many backgrounds and of many professional and public commitments to ideas, information, and analyses presented here will be evident in virtually every part of the book. And I have tried to note credits and make citations whenever appropriate; but I also apologize for any inadvertent slightings or omissions.

My own first involvement in studies of the life course came at the urging and encouragement of David Featherman and was undertaken in collaboration with Yossi Shavit; and I have continued to benefit from their friendship, comment, and encouragement as well as from their own very important contributions to life course studies. Special thanks are due, also, to Karl Ulrich Mayer and to John Myles, who, both in the examples of their own work on the life course, the elderly, and social structure and in private discussions and exchanges, have helped me focus my own analyses of the interfaces between demographic, life course, and socio-political dynamics. The support and encouragement of Edward Stanford were probably critical both for my undertaking to write this book and for its actual completion and realization. My wife, Hagit, has sustained more than her fair share of deprivations as this book has taken shape. Hopefully there will be gratifications as well—both to share and to have as her own—but for the moment there are only my own expressions of thanks.

Judah Matras
Jerusalem, June 1989

PART I   Introduction

1

INTRODUCTION
AND OVERVIEW

concepts and social meanings
of age and aging

Individuals age throughout their lifetimes, indeed even before they are born! Families, organizations, and communities age and undergo change and development over time. Populations may or may not age over any particular time period. However, recent Western sociodemographic history is dominated by declining mortality and declining fertility that have led to the aging of populations and societies.

In this book we shall try to show that aging of the population means not only that more people are living longer and that there are more elderly persons in the population. Rather, that it signals a new framework for organization of the individual life course, and a new framework for family and community interdependency and relationships. It focuses on how the age-related patterns of dependency, family and social obligations, and entitlements and claims on family and community are affected and how they change under the shifting demographic, socioeconomic, and political contingencies of individual and population aging.

Dependency is an individual's inability to carry out the ordinary activities of sustenance and daily life without assistance from some other person or agency. Examples include economic or income support; being dressed or having meals prepared; having arrangements made for admission to schools, transportation to visit friends, or laundry services; but do not include the individual's own *purchase* of services in a private market transaction that he carries out on his own behalf, exchanging his own personal resources. Obligations are requirements of individuals, groups, or societies to respond to needs, or address and resolve dependencies of other individuals, in some given social relationship to them, for example, obligations to parents, children, other kin, neighbors, members of some group or organization, or citizens. Entitlements are legitimate claims that individuals have on other individuals, groups, agencies, or social units to resources or services that can address their needs, dependencies, or simply their wishes. Everywhere and throughout history much of the human condition, and much of social, economic, and political organization, has revolved about matters of dependency, obligations, and entitlements.

The concepts of age and aging have assumed a wide range of meanings, sometimes precise and well-defined, but often obscure or even mystical. Our first concern in this first chapter is to present and illustrate the concepts and social meanings of age and aging that will serve us in addressing our main objective. In subsequent chapters we examine the aging of populations and societies in its macrosocietal dimensions. Then we study the life course: the sequences of events, activities, and role incumbencies and behavior that characterize individuals as they age and develop from birth to death. We next consider the individual and social issues, contingencies, problems, and opportunities associated with the population created and enlarged most dramatically by recent trends in U.S. and world population—the elderly. Finally, in the closing chapter we note recent socioeconomic, demographic, and political trends and their bearing on the aging process.

This is a book on the sociology and social demography of aging, the life course, and the elderly. It will not teach you to be the director of an old age home or senior citizens facility; it will not teach you how to look after your grandparents or your aging parents or relatives; and it will not even teach you how to relax, have fun, and enjoy your own aging—although these are worthy goals, and hopefully, this book will contribute to their realization. The main objective of this book is to expand the reader's understanding of the processes of individual and population aging, their interrelations, and their impact on personal, family, and community well-being and on social organization.

OVERVIEW

The demographic transitions from the historical regime of high fertility offset by high mortality (called the high-balance demographic regime) to the modern conditions of low fertility and low mortality (called the low-balance demographic regime) first give rise to a dependency crunch: Large numbers of surviving children and aging parents place new, sometimes overwhelming, demands for economic and emotional support on adult parents and breadwinners. In contemporary societies, and especially in modern democracies, the dependency crunch in turn creates demands for social or political—typically government—intervention and welfare measures to diminish the hardships and inequities of the new dependency.

The completion or maturing of the demographic transitions subsequently leads to liberation from dependency through (a) controlled fertility, (b) women's employment outside the home, and (c) public assumption of risks and programs for maintenance of income, services, and consumption. That these trends have been occurring at the same time as dramatic technological developments and revolutionary changes in production, storage, and access to knowledge and information has caused them to be even more compelling in their impact on individuals, families, communities, national societies, and the world social, economic, and political community.

All societies and most social organizations and subsystems are characterized by population change and turnover and flows of successive cohorts (those born or entering a population or social setting at about the same historical time) across and through the network of social institutions. The organization of communities and societies is subject to a variety of discontinuities and disequilibria arising from population turnover and cohort flows and succession. The extent and manner in which stability and continuity are effected or in which change is introduced is dependent in large measure upon the social structuring and organization of the *life course*; that is, the physiological, psychological, and social processes and sequence of capacities and age-graded or time- and duration-dependent events, activities, and relationships characterizing the individual from birth through death.

This point has been made in a variety of formulations and in a variety of social scientific contexts. The concepts of socialization, career, intergenerational mobility, class- or strata-culture, life transitions, seniority, rites of passage, inheritance, and social reproduction all concern and address aspects of individual and aggregate life-course patterns of social organization. The general starting point in much of the work on socialization, life transitions, career or intergenerational mobility, and the like is the view that organization and structuring of the life course of individuals and groups are central mechanisms of societal stability or change in the face of population turnover and cohort succession.

Three Major Trends

In the chapters which follow we shall argue that, in advanced democratic industrial societies, three major trends influence the life course, indeed partly revolutionize it. Through their effects on the life course of individuals and successive cohorts, these trends affect also the processes of social status attainment, mobility, and strata formation, as well as the basic axes of social organization, legitimacy, and order and, of course, the well-being and life chances of individuals and families. These major trends and processes are:

1. *Population aging:* The changing demographic regime, in the direction of declining mortality and increased longevity and joint survival of couples, families, or other social units; and subsequently, declining fertility, smaller families, sibships, and kinship units, and compressed or more compact child-rearing time budgets, leading to new personal, family, and societal patterns of activities, social relationships, attitudes and values, and responses to needs and dependency.

2. *Changes in material production, employment, and income distribution mechanisms:* Technological and organizational innovations leading to expanded production of goods and services under diminishing and partially redundant employment, and the growth of nonemployment-based income entitlements.

3. *Enhancement of knowledge and information:* Extension of schooling, revolutions in information and communications, and the enhanced transparency, or mutual visibility, among the various social strata leading to diminishing acceptability of social inequalities of opportunity and condition and to demands and expectations of politicization of distribution of income and services.

A number of important consequences follow. Expressed very briefly, these are:

1. Parenting and demographic viability: Societies can and do survive and flourish without universal parenting, and with only short-term or less intensive parenting required on the part of those becoming parents. More than any other factor diminished fertility has changed the content, structure, and timing features of the individual life course and family cycle as well as the life course pattern of kinship presence, dependencies, and obligations.

2. Work and material welfare: Societies and their individual members can enjoy minimal, and perhaps reasonably high, levels of material welfare and security with short-term and less intensive lifetime employment. Employment remains the central mechanism for allocation of income and the goods and services it buys. Various extra-employment income maintenance measures operate both to assure income to those without employment-based entitlements and to regulate the demand for employment; there remain deep competition and struggle over employment reflected in the various bounds, constraints, and organizational features of the labor market.

3. Visibility, knowledge, and demand: Many individuals and groups in modern societies already have and enjoy the advantages and possibilities of (1) and (2) above; more and more people and organized groups and social strata come to know about them and demand them as well from their elites, leaders, or governments.

4. Age-grading and age-roles: Because of new relationships between the life span and new demographic and economic realities, many of the traditional patterns of age-grading (that is, of the age-related allocation of social roles) and of age-related rules and expectations regarding schooling, family functions, employment, and leisure are anachronistic, obsolete, and indeed oppressive in contemporary societies.

We consider these points in more detail in the following chapters.

AGE STRUCTURE, AGING, AND THE SOCIAL ORGANIZATION
OF DEPENDENCY, OBLIGATIONS, AND ENTITLEMENTS

Societies as a whole, and component social subsystems, must always confront and address the age composition and aging patterns of their populations in at least three crucial ways:

1. *The persons of different ages in the population at any moment in time have different capacities, experience, and potential for social and economic participation as well as different demands and needs.* Societies and their component subsystems must integrate members of different ages, organize their interrelationships, and address their differing needs and capacities. Social scientists have long recognized age differentiation, age-grading of social roles and positions, and age-based division of labor and exchange as central features and processes of social organization that accomplish this.

2. *Each individual and each population subgroup are always experiencing a process of aging, with whatever change in personal and collective capacities, needs, and individual and social experiences that entails.* Societies must allow for such individual and group aging processes and achieve an acceptable or viable mix of societal stability and societal change in its wake. Social scientists have studied the processes and institutions of socialization generally and specific role transitions as the social organizational features that accomplish this.

3. *Each age group, and each population subgroup generally, will depart from its present position, or from the society or subsystem altogether; it will be replaced by a new cohort, a new population subgroup born later.* The new cohort does not identically replace the departing group. Rather, its own historical identity and the period effects it has experienced differ from those of the cohort it replaces. Societies must deal with such turnover while maintaining the level, stability, and integrity of social and economic activity, social and political relationships, and output and allocation of social rewards. Social scientists have studied these processes under various social change rubrics, including industrialization, urbanization, development, or modernization at the societal levels, and organizational change, intergenerational mobility, and political socialization at lower levels. Social scientists writing in the Marxian and neo-Marxian traditions have examined such processes under the heading of social reproduction.

The Demographic Transition, Aging,
and Age-Related Activities, Needs, and Responses

We shall argue in this book that the transformation of the demographic regime from the high balance of high fertility offset by high mortality to the low balance of low mortality offset by low fertility—the process denoted *demographic transition*—entails a chain of developments leading not only to aging of the population, but also to new patterns of individual life course and family-cycle activities, needs, and interpersonal and societal relationships. We will emphasize

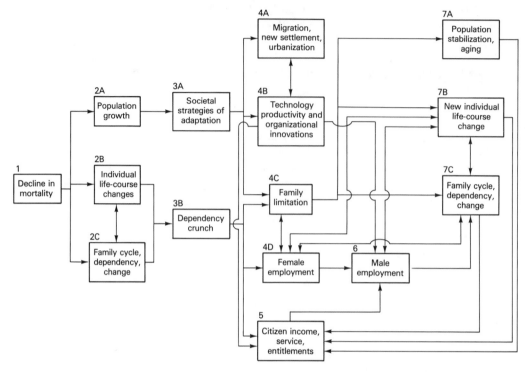

Figure 1.1 Individual, Family, and Societal Responses to the Demographic Transition, Individual and Population Aging, and Changes in Age-Related Dependency and Obligations.

that: there are changes in the lifelong patterns of family and interpersonal dependency, obligations, and entitlements, as well as changes in the patterns of dependency, obligations, and entitlements of individuals and families relative to their communities and societies. These linkages are shown in Figure 1.1. They are listed below as a set of ideas and propositions to be developed and examined in the following chapters.

1. *Decline in Mortality.* The first stage of demographic transition is substantial long-term and permanent decline in the level of mortality. At the level of societies, the decline of mortality first sets off substantial population growth and puts pressures on the societies' resources and arrangements for provision and maintenance of sustenance for the growing numbers. At the level of individuals, the decline of mortality results in extended survival and life spans and resulting new life-course structuring, timing, and horizons.

2A. *Population Growth.* If population growth is to be sustained, rather than lost to additional mortality, societies must adopt

3A. *Strategies of Adaptation.* These have consisted mainly in societal arrangements of

4A. *Migration, New Settlement, or New Forms of Settlement,* including urbanization, metropolitanization, megalopolitization, and the like;

4B. *Invention, Development of New Technologies, or Adoption of More Productive Technological and Organizational Innovations;* and

4C. *Fertility Limitation.*

2B. *Individual Life Course-Changes.* Increased life expectancy in general (at birth) and at all specific ages has resulted in restructuring, and in greater age differentiation within, the individual life course as well as development and legitimation of new kinds of life-course activity, and social participation, whether age-graded or not.

2C. *Family-Cycle Changes.* Increased life expectancy has also been direct and indirect cause of profound changes in family size, in intrafamily patterns of joint survival, and the size, composition, longevity, and activities and interrelationships of kin dyads, triads, and networks of every type and complexity; that is, the individual life course and family-cycle changes give rise to the

3B. *Dependency Crunch.* In the early stages of demographic transitions, the changes in kinship and family cycles inevitably involved growth in numbers of family and kinship network members and extension of the length of their joint survival. Both for adults and for children in transition to adulthood the larger numbers and extended survival very frequently implied serious problems of economic support and sustenance weighing on family breadwinners and often never resolved in lifetimes of poverty and want. Large numbers of dependent children born and surviving, and surviving, but often disabled and typically economically dependent, parents or sometimes other kin confronted adult householders with unrelenting pressure on space, earnings, time, and attention; and forced recruitment of older children or youngest adults into employment or participation in family survival and sustenance activity. As levels of living improved and literacy, schooling, and especially the educational attainments of women, have increased, the dependency crunch has been resolved in very considerable measure by

4C. *Fertility Limitation* (noted above also as a major societal strategy of adaptation), by

4D. *Women's Labor Force Participation and Paid Employment,* and by various forms of nonemployment related income entitlements, which we denote here as

5. *Citizen Income Entitlements,* often described as transfer payments, transfer income, or income from nonemployment-based income maintenance schemes. The latter are also related, or perhaps indeed rendered possible, by the complex of technological and organizational developments and innovations developed or adopted as part of societal strategies of adaptation to population growth.

Fertility limitation and women's labor force participation are shown as closely interrelated and mutually supportive, and indeed extensive research has not yet unraveled the precise lines and directions of causality in these relationships.

4C. *Fertility Limitation.* Whether effected through delayed or even foregone marriage, contraception, abortion, or infanticide (even in the West it is probably appropriate historically to view a considerable part of infant mortality as, in effect, infanticide), it is fertility limitation that has been the main factor in

7A. *Stabilization of Population Growth and Aging of Populations.* The downward inflection in fertility, and its subsequent near-convergence to the level of mortality, have led to the demographic regime characterized by low balance and slow if any growth in population. The diminishing numbers of births and proportions of children and young persons in the population have led to the increased proportions of older adults and elderly persons characterizing aging populations.

4D. *Women's Labor Force Participation and Paid Employment.* Together with fertility limitation, women's labor force participation has resulted in further profound changes both in

7B. *New Individual Life-Course Changes,* and

7C. *New Family-Cycle Changes* at the more advanced states of the demographic transitions. The contraction of parenting in the life course, on the one hand, and the organization of both schooling and the early life course and adult stages of the life course around anticipated and actual employment, on the other hand, have changed the content, timing, and organization of events in the life course of both females and males. Similarly, the reduction of numbers of children and, derivatively, of cousins and kin generally, and the compression of parenting, have allowed and encouraged changes in the content, priorities, and timing of activities and relationships in the family cycle and in the behavior of family members. In particular, there is a dramatic *contraction* of

6. *Male Employment.* Delayed entrance into full-time employment, progressively earlier retirement, chronic unemployment, and reduction of numbers of weekly working hours are all expressions of the contraction of paid employment in the life course of men. The entrance of married women into paid employment and the contraction of intrafamily dependency both through fertility limitation and availability of citizen income entitlements combine with technological changes, reorganization of material production regimes, enhanced productivity, and expanded income transfer schemes to reduce both the demand for and the supply of male labor, especially at the younger and older edges of the traditional working ages.

Finally, the societal, family, and individual developments of the later stages of the demographic transition:

7A. *Population Aging,*
7B. *Individual Life-Course Changes,* and
7C. *Family-Cycle Changes,* under the conditions of contemporary
4B. *Technology and Organizational Innovations,* give rise to new age-roles, age-graded activity and social participation, and options for alternative timing and sequencing of activity. At the same time, they give rise to new needs and combinations of needs, some of which can be addressed privately by individuals and families, some of which can be addressed by market institutions and mechanisms, and some of which require publicly organized or public sector response. New practices and institutions of age grading itself, or of relaxation of the rules and practices of age grading, are called for in contemporary society to allow the flexibility of activity and social participation that can assure productive and healthy lives and fulfillment of potential at all ages.

More detailed consideration of these processes will be presented in the following chapters. In this chapter we briefly review some concepts and social meanings of age and aging.

AGE AND AGING: MEANINGS AND MOTIFS

Age and Aging of Individuals, Social Subsystems, and Populations

Age and aging are attributes of individuals, groups, social subsystems of all types, and entire populations and societies. We can distinguish among a number of aspects of age and aging, each of which has important social meaning, as follows (see Table 1.1):

> *Historical or Calendrical Identity:* This includes an individual's date or year of birth or a social unit's date, year, or calendar period of origin or formation; when the individual reached age 1, or when he or she reached any other given age or age period or stage, or when he experienced a transition from a given age or stage to

Table 1.1. Examples of Social Meanings and Motifs of Age and Aging for Individuals, Social Subsystems, and Populations

SOCIAL MEANINGS AND MOTIFS	INDIVIDUALS	GROUPS, SOCIAL SUBSYSTEMS	SOCIETIES, POPULATIONS
1. Historical identity	Depression babies, Vietnam generation	Established firms, New businesses	Ancient societies (China, India), old kingdoms (Sweden, France), Newly independent societies (Algeria, Ghana)
2. Developmental	Infant, child, adolescent, adult senior citizen	Newly-wed couple, "empty nest" "infant industry"	Developing nations, developed countries
3. Positional	Pupils, employees, spouse, parent, grandparent	Ivy League Universities, State Universities	Generally not applicable
4. Stratum-generating	Youth, students, retired persons	Old established neighborhoods, new housing,	Generally not applicable developments
5. Compositional	Not applicable	Old industries (mining, railroading), young industries (hi tech, fast foods)	Old populations (Sweden, Germany), Young populations (Mexico, Pakistan, Syria)
6. Turnover	Not applicable	Young family neighborhoods, old family neighborhoods, stable areas	Low longevity nations (Kenya, Bangladesh), high longevity nations (Norway, Argentina, U.S.)

the following one; and, correspondingly, when a social unit reached a given age or stage, and when it experienced age- or stage-transitions.

Developmental: These include the accumulation, or the loss, of physiological characteristics, psychological traits or capacities, social statuses or rewards or resources, or social relationships associated with age, with time alive or with seniority or time duration elapsed in a social or ecological system or organization.

Positional: These include the hierarchical, power or prestige, superordination or subordination, or control of resources or behavior associated with age, seniority, or time in the system.

Group- or Stratum-generating: These comprise the tendencies to form or institutionalize groups or strata, or to create and enhance social solidarity, based on similarity of age or of time in the system.

Compositional: These refer to the relative numbers of young, or new-in-the-system, and of old, or long-in-the-system, individuals or units respectively that carry out the activities and interaction, and which have age- or time-in-the-system-related differential claims on positions and rewards.

Turnover: These refer to the pattern or mode of replacement of participants or members in the social unit by new participants, or to the positive or negative growth in the numbers. In the course of its existence, membership of a family or a group or a population turns over: Individuals die or depart from the unit, or are born or enter into the unit.

As noted below, some of these refer to individuals, groups, and entire populations alike, while others refer to individuals only, to groups or populations only, or to some combination of two.

AGE AND AGING OF INDIVIDUALS

Individual Historical or Calendrical Identity

The obvious historical or calendar identity for the individual is date of birth. Date of birth is generally not an historically neutral piece of information about a person. Rather, it indicates or hints at the possible bearing of historical features of that date or period upon that individual's characteristics or attributes; for example, if he was born during a period of prosperity or recession, peace or war, favorable or unfavorable climate or circumstances for himself, his family, or his community. Similarly, age or date of birth may indicate the possible bearing of historical features of the dates or periods of childhood, youth, or adolescence, or the dates or periods of important life transitions, such as school graduation, marriage, or first employment.

Thus a person aged 40 in 1989 was born in 1949, became an adolescent in the mid-1960s at the height of the Vietnam conflict, perhaps married in 1972 or 1973. A person 65 years old in 1989 was born in 1924, reached adolescence in the late 1930s, the period of the Great Depression, reached young adulthood in the mid-1940s, during World War II, perhaps married and began family-building in the post-World War II boom periods. Effects of such historical identities upon activities, behavior, or attitudes and values of groups studied in the United States (Modell, Furstenberg, and Hershberg, 1976; Elder, 1974), Norway (Featherman and

Sorensen, 1983), and Germany (Carroll and Mayer, 1986; Mayer, et al., 1987) have been shown to continue throughout the life experience of birth cohorts—those born in the same year or the same period and affected by common historical circumstances during their childhood and socialization, schooling, transitions to adulthood, employment and career beginnings, and so forth.

Individual Age and Development

Perhaps the most familiar meaning of age is that associated with level of individual physiological, psychological, and social development. Individuals undergo physiological development throughout life. Growth in size and weight, muscular and organic development characterize human and animal organisms and are especially dramatic early in life. Midlife is typically associated with some stabilization or leveling off of physiological development; later life is characterized by senescence, or deterioration, of certain physiological functions and organs (Riley and Foner, 1968). We typically associate age—being young or old, being five months old or five years old or thirty-five years old— with physical stature and capacities, differential frequencies or risks of illness or mortality, appearance, skin texture, hair fullness or color appropriate to the physiological development stage implied by a five-month-, five-year-, or thirty-five-year-long life history and development.

Along with physiological development throughout life, individuals undergo psychological development. This includes development of motor, cognitive, and emotional capacities that are also very dramatic in early life, level off at some midlife point or points, and deteriorate in later life (Riley and Foner, 1968). Reaction time, the various sensations of visual, hearing, taste, smell acuity and so forth, memory, and the components of intelligence are examples of age-related psychological traits. The development of sexual drives, instincts, or interest and the question of their stability or deterioration is an example merging the physiological and psychological development themes.

Social development associated with age occurs both in consequence of accumulation of life and social experience in conjunction with physiological and psychological development, and from socially defined roles and behavior expectations. The concept of age represents amount of time lived by an individual, so that being any given age, say 35 years old, implies a past: having been 0 years old (an infant), 1 year old, 2 years old, ... 33 years old, 34 years old at some time in the past. The 35 years of life comprises also the cumulative knowledge, experience, practices, and social relationships of earlier ages and the experiences of earlier transitions: from age 0 to age 1; from age 1 to age 2; ... from age 33 to age 34; from age 34 to age 35.

Individual Age and Social Position

In all societies there are socially determined age roles: patterns of behavior expected of individuals of a given chronological age. Infant, child, adolescent, young adult are examples of age roles implying certain kinds of expected or prescribed behavior. For the most part age roles related to the normal or presumed-normal physiological and psychological development of the individual are generally consistent with capacities and experience associated with children, adults, or the elderly.

The concepts of age and age roles incorporate dimensions of position and relationships among persons of equal or different ages. Often the age-related positions are hierarchically ordered, that is, there are positions of superiority or inferiority, with respect to a variety of activities, rewards claimed, or resources controlled. In general the authority, rank, and rewards associated with age positions are higher the higher the age, up to some peak in middle adulthood, and then they are lower the higher the age. There may be a hierarchy of honor, deference, or prestige; a hierarchy of responsibility and control of persons and resources; and a hierarchy of reward entitlements associated with age-based roles. Thus, the young are supposed to defer to the more mature. Adults control the behavior and material goods allocated to children and are presumed to be responsible for their safety and welfare. Young or middle-aged persons may also be responsible for the health and welfare of elderly persons, many of whom are deemed dependent. Many age-graded roles are not obviously ordered hierarchically: Age-graded family roles such as spouse, parent, grandparent, or widow, are examples with no implicit hierarchical order.

There are very practical consequences of age grading for personal and social life. At certain ages persons work and earn; at other ages they are dependent and only consume. At certain ages persons are allowed or encouraged to marry, set up households, have children, and carry on legitimate sexual relationships; at other ages all or some of these activities are proscribed. At certain ages one qualifies for elementary school, secondary school, military service, certain kinds of employment, retirement, benefits and entitlements, and civic privileges or obligations.

Thus, for the most part older children enjoy more freedom and have more privileges than younger children. Indeed they exercise authority over younger children not only by virtue of superior strength and experience but by virtue of their institutionalized age positions. Adults claim respect and esteem from children and typically exercise authority over children, control more resources than children, and claim greater social rewards than children. Superior strength is often cited as the explanation of this relationship, but superior knowledge or experience are often invoked as well.

Middle-aged adults typically claim respect and esteem from young adults and typically exercise authority over young adults, control more resources than young adults, and claim greater social rewards than young adults. These positional relations occur despite the typically superior strength and stamina of the younger adults compared to those of middle-aged adults leaving the superior knowledge, experience, and perhaps organizational capacities of the middle-aged adults as the main explanations for their favored rank or position. But middle-aged adults typically enjoy superior rank and rewards and authority compared to the elderly as well, the presumed extended experience and knowledge of the elderly not withstanding. The diminished strength and stamina of the elderly, on the one hand, and the obsolescence of their knowledge and experience, on the other hand, are often invoked as explanations of their reduced status. In many circumstances young adults may enjoy higher rank and rewards than the middle-aged adults in their families or communities, for example, educated young adults relative to their unschooled parents, or highly mobile young adults relative to their immobile or downwardly mobile elders.

A very important meaning of aging is the sequence of *transitions* among age-related social roles and positions; for example, the transition from childhood to adolescence in societies where these are both recognized kinds of social positions, from adolescence to adulthood, from singlehood to marriage, from middle age to old age, and so forth. We will discuss in detail in later chapters issues of the order and timing of important transitions in the individual life course and family life cycle.

Individual Age and Social Strata

A theory of age stratification developed primarily by M.W. Riley and her associates (Riley, Johnson, and Foner, 1972; Riley, 1976) highlights the simultaneous age-based and age-graded differentiation of human activity, groupings, and social relationships on the one hand, and the processes of cohort flows through society and its age divisions, and of individual aging within these cohorts, on the other hand. (Cohorts are groups of individuals born, married, beginning or completing school, or otherwise beginning some major activity at about the same point in calendar time; for example, a birth cohort, or those born in the year 1950; a marriage cohort, or those married in 1975; the graduating class of 1980 or the cohort entering college 1985.) Age affects roles in the social system and the people who act in these roles. People form age strata—composed of persons of similar age—in a population and these vary in size and composition at any moment in time.

Age strata, such as the young, middle-aged, and elderly, are related to other social groupings, and the relationships may be more or less well defined and more or less rigid. For example, adolescent peer groups are comprised entirely of a single age stratum, whereas kinship groupings cut across several age strata. Armies, kindergartens, and nursing homes for the aged tend to be age-stratum-specific; large places of employment, residential neighborhoods, and voluntary organizations may be more or less age-stratum-specific. The relationships between age strata and other social groupings may imply age segregation or age integration. For example, friendship, interaction, solidarity, joint activities, and time budgets are often age-group-bounded and conform to the norms attached to the respective age strata. But sometimes they cut across age groups and conform to the norms attached to inter-age-stratum relations, for example, peer group solidarity as compared to extended family solidarity.

Age strata are characterized by inequalities especially with respect to available or accessible roles, the expectations one has of them, facilities accorded for role performance, and rewards. The very roles and positions an individual may occupy—especially occupational roles as well as work standards, expected behavior in family and household, political rights and obligations, military service, and career-performance expectations—all are typically age-graded. The young and the elderly are excluded from many occupational positions. Those of normal working age are typically subject to age grading and age criteria for positions of varying responsibility and authority, complexity of tasks, and autonomy.

In a variety of spheres—but, again, especially in the occupational sphere—there are age criteria for, and age grading of, facilities and rewards accorded for the performance of the various roles. Thus older, experienced employees generally command more resources, supervise subordinates, have access to specialized equipment and knowledge, and enjoy more autonomy in carrying out their work roles than younger employees, and their income and rewards are higher. Older housewives are typically more advantaged than younger ones in the household facilities at their disposal, in the networks of information and help accessible to them, and presumably in the satisfaction received and resources they control. On the other hand, the elderly or middle-aged couple in the empty nest—the household from which all the children have married or departed—may have in many respects reduced satisfactions and rewards in the household setting.

The theory of age stratification views age divisions as fundamental axes of social organization, differentiation, and solidarity, with the age-related inequalities generating solidarity, collective action, and behavioral, attitudinal, and political features specific to each such grouping. There is clearly mobility across age strata, as individuals inevitably age and experience transitions from one age stratum to the following one, that is, in this sense aging is a type of social mobility. However, such mobility is irreversible and hardly shares all the features associated with the concept of social mobility. More generally the entire theory of age stratification, and the premise of age strata conflict, is fairly controversial. As Parkin (1971) has pointed out, an age status is fundamentally a temporary status but, at the same time, it is universal in that all society passes through it at some time. Thus there is no permanent entrapment or disadvantage characterizing the nonadvantaged age strata, for the other age strata are also impermanent. Moreover, Parkin points out, the life experiences of persons in any given age group are typically more varied according to social or economic class group than they are the same by virtue of age similarity.

Age Groups and Age Sets in Social Organization

Age groups are found in varying degrees of recognition, salience, or importance in social organization. It is always possible to define an age group formally as consisting of the group of persons a given age or a given age range, say 5-year-olds, or the group aged 14 to 17, or those 65 and over. But the meaning and salience of such groupings in social life have varied historically and across societies. Thus childhood, adolescence, or old age has not had the same meaning and the same importance in all societies at all times. For example, Eisenstadt (1956) has analysed the emergence and roles of youth and adolescent groups in modern societies and hypothesizes that they have been important vehicles for preparing and socializing young persons, whose earlier social experience is dominated by particularistic features of family and household relationships, for the universalistic and achievement-oriented features of adult, and especially, occupational life and relationships.

Of course modern school systems generate much more universally recognized and meaningful age groups by differentiating among first-graders, second-graders, and so forth. Similarly, legislation ordering obligations and benefits, for example, military service, retirement compensation, similarly generate and sustain age groupings that inevitably have assumed economic, social, and political importance (Mayer and Muller, 1986).

The concept of age sets is employed generally with reference to preliterate societies and refers to named groupings—usually of males—based on age or generation. Membership in such age groupings is publicly recognized and is generally retained for the bulk of the life course. Membership in age sets usually circumscribes the allocation of significant social roles in the society; there is joint movement of age-set members from one age grade to the next (for example, joint transitions from childhood to youth status, or from adolescence to adult status); at any moment in time there are differential social rewards accorded to the various age sets. Age-set societies vary in the number of age sets recognized, and there may be varying degrees of corporateness or other organizational features of the age sets (Foner and Kertzer, 1978). In age set societies, then, one meaning of aging is the turnover or movement of birth cohorts across age sets.

AGE AND AGING OF SOCIAL GROUPS AND SUBSYSTEMS

Group or Subsystem Age and Social Strata

These are in general the analogues or near analogues of individual historical or calendrical identity, age and development, age and social position, or age and social strata. We may understand the age of a family, school, business organization, community, or other social unit as locating it historically; this indicates the circumstances or features accompanying its formation or organization, or accompanying given stages of the unit's growth or development.

Alternatively, the age of a social unit or subsystem may be taken as indicating aspects of its development, its cumulative experience or acquisition of resources; for example, the stage of the family cycle is indicative of household composition, types of family possessions or consumption, or typical time budgets of family members; or the age of a town or other community is indicative of the levels, mix, quantity, or quality of community services provided or community participation. Age of a social subsystem or unit may indicate, instead, position in a system of such units; for example, young versus old industries, new schools as distinct from, but related to, old or traditional schools, a 5-year old section or department in a large bureaucratic organization as compared to 10- or 15-year old sections in the same organization.

Finally, we may think also of age of social units, say, schools or neighborhoods, as stratifying them in the sense of ordering them hierarchically by prestige or by resources which they command or with which they are associated. In this sense the youngest, next-youngest, … "middle-aged," … next-to-oldest, and oldest subgroups of schools, neighborhoods, churches, businesses, or whatever social units are being considered may be said to comprise age strata of such units.

Group or Subsystem Age, Aging, and Composition

As indicated earlier, this has reference to relative numbers of younger and older individuals participating in the family, business firm, or other social unit or subsystem. An old industry would be one in which a substantial proportion of those employed are, say, middle-aged or older employees, with relatively few young employees. Thus, railroading, meat packing, and mining are relatively old industries or economic branches, while the computer and data processing industries are young ones. In the 1950s and 1960s the television and the airline industries were quite young, but they have since aged, in the same sense; that is, the proportion middle-aged among their employees has grown and the proportion of young employees has diminished. In a similar vein, an old church may be one with many elderly parishioners, while a young church would refer to one with many young persons, couples, or families among the membership. An old university would be one overloaded with senior faculty members, presumably middle-aged or older, while a young institution would have relatively few.

Group or Subsystem Aging and Turnover

In general we tend to find rapid turnover of families, neighborhoods, organizations, or other social subsystems associated with relatively high proportions of young individuals among the participants. Conversely, we find slower turnover of membership and participants in older organizations and social units. This relationship between age composition and turnover in subsystems is not a logically necessary or inevitable one (as we shall note below, it is in the case of population age composition and turnover). But it does follow from the fact of much higher probabilities of mobility among younger persons: Residential mobility, occupational mobility, marriage and divorce, school entrances, completions, and dropouts, and many other types of changes and transitions occur much more frequently among the young.

AGE AND AGING OF POPULATIONS

Population Age, Aging, and Age Composition

In principle it is possible and perhaps meaningful to identify an entire population's birth or time of origin, to discuss the population's development over time in terms of its growth and evolving features and attributes, and even a given population's position or rank relative to other populations as related to the time elapsed since its birth or time of origin, that is, in terms of its age. More likely, we reckon a population's age in the sense of historical or calendrical identity with reference to some important event. Such an event might be achievement of national unification, nation-state identity, or political independence. Or it could be some natural event such as a flood, earthquake, or drought, or some economic period or event, such as an economic crisis or depression, a boom, or adoption of some organizational or technological innovation. There is considerable interest in comparison of populations along the axis of time elapsed—that is, age, since the beginnings of their respective historical declines in mortality or since the beginnings of their declines in fertility.

However, the usual sense of population age and population aging has reference to the *age composition* of the population, that is, to the absolute and relative numbers in the population at each age or in each age group. Populations are considered young or old, depending upon whether they have high proportions of young or old persons. The population of Sweden with 17 percent aged 65 or over and only 18 percent under 15 years of age in 1987 is an old population. The population of Kenya with only 2 percent aged 65 or over and 51 percent under 15 in 1987 is a young population. Populations with large proportions of adults, and relatively small proportions in both the younger and older ages of dependency, are generally believed to be in a favorable position with regard to levels of living, investment, and development. Age divides a population into groups of potential producers and consumers: The independent adults in the middle range of the population are both producers and consumers, while the dependent children and the retired or infirm are consumers only.

A population's age composition has a wide-ranging influence on social and economic arrangements and institutions, from maternity wards, kindergartens, and schools to entertainment, transportation, religion, and homes for the aged. Moreover, central social and economic processes such as family formation and home-purchasing, job-seeking, retirement, savings, migration, and mobility are closely related to the age composition of a population.

A population's age composition depends first and foremost upon its level of fertility and only secondarily upon its level of mortality. However, migratory movements are important factors determining age composition, especially in relatively small or localized populations. Aging of a population describes a gradual process where the proportions of adults and elderly persons increase and the proportions of children and adolescents decrease over time. Aging is always a consequence of low or declining fertility, but it is very important to bear in mind that fertility decline is for the most part contingent upon prior declines in mortality.

Population Aging and Turnover

As we shall see in more detail in Chapters 2 and 3, aging populations experience turnover and replacement relatively slowly, while young populations turn over more rapidly. The discussion earlier concerning the mobility of younger, compared to older, persons in groups or subsystems applies to entire populations as well. However, fertility and mortality also bear on the rate of turnover. Since aging populations are characterized by low fertility, and by definition have relatively small proportions of young persons, the younger cohorts are not sufficiently large to replace any existing population until a sufficient number of successive new cohorts are born. Moreover, it will generally be found that populations with low fertility are also characterized by low mortality and relatively high longevity. Thus the demise and replacement of any given or existing population due to its own mortality are slower in older populations as well. The pace of replacement and turnover affects the character of all the spheres of social organization, whether work and production, education and training, government and power, family life, and so forth.

Young populations typically have relatively short time and longevity horizons. They must organize for relatively frequent and rapid replacement of incumbents in social roles generally and in key social roles in particular. Older populations typically can organize with longer time and longevity horizons. They can anticipate longer individual survival in any given social role and longer joint survival in families, work spheres, and social subsystems generally. Even in young populations characterized by low mortality and high longevity, survival, and joint survival, at any moment in time a substantial number of roles and social subsystems are performed by young persons, relatively new to their incumbencies and recent increments to the social organization, if not necessarily replacing departed incumbents.

PLAN OF THE BOOK

In Part II we examine first the demographic factors and trends affecting (1) population size, composition, growth, and turnover, and (2) individual and social unit survival, life span, and kinship configurations, and explore the dimensions of population aging worldwide and in industrial societies especially (Chapters 2 and 3). We then turn to two types of macrosocietal issues and responses to population aging: economic (Chapter 4) and public and social services (Chapter 5).

In Part III we study individual and family life course. We identify and explore the variations in age grading of social roles, dimensions of the life course, and characteristic life-course transitions (Chapter 6). We consider changes in the duration and timing of major life-course activities, in particular employment and parenting (Chapter 7). We explore the implications of demographic changes and individual life-course changes for the family structure (Chapter 8).

In Part IV we study the group created, enlarged, and affected most dramatically by recent trends in the United States and world population—the elderly. We address first the question of the social status of the elderly from an historical and comparative perspective (Chapter 9) and review sociological theories of aging and the aging process (Chapter 10). We then examine processes of disengagement and contraction of social networks among the elderly, including retirement and widowhood (Chapter 11) and consider the traditional and emerging societal responses and support networks and systems (Chapter 12).

The book concludes, in Part V, with remarks on prospects, scope, and directions for socioeconomic and demographic developments, and for public intervention, and their likely bearing upon the aging process for individuals and for societies (Chapter 13).

2

THE SOCIAL DEMOGRAPHY
OF AGING I

populations, demographic transitions,
and age structure

INTRODUCTION

Population aging is already plainly evident in the developed industrial countries
of the world, and it is under way in the less developed countries (LDCs) as well.
This chapter reviews the sociodemographic background of population aging. In
particular, we examine the way in which population aging is reflected in the
shifting of the age composition of populations toward increased numbers and
percentages of middle-aged and elderly persons and decreased proportions of
children and young persons. Such developments bear importantly upon the
volume and composition of capacities, social relationships and interdependencies,
and activities and behavior in each society, as well as upon needs, resources, and
social and economic participation of virtually every type.

World population has grown dramatically in the last 350 years, and
explosively in the period since 1950. Population growth has been viewed both
favorably—as offering opportunities for labor force development and exploitation
of resources, economic and productivity growth, social division of labor, and so
forth—and unfavorably—as exhausting resources, threatening sociopolitical im-
balances, and frustrating development. The debate over prospects and possibilities
for policy and intervention continues.

Some facts concerning the long-term population trends seem quite clear.
Great population growth has taken place in the course of transitions from a
demographic regime of high mortality and high fertility (with very little population growth resulting from these offsetting vital phenomena—the so-called high-
balance demographic regime) to a demographic regime of low mortality and low

fertility (again, with little population growth occurring—the so-called low-balance demographic regime). The subsequent low levels of fertility have caused declines in the proportions of young persons and increases in the proportions of older persons in the populations—that is, aging of populations.

In the course of such demographic transitions, downward inflections in mortality have almost always preceded the downward inflections in fertility, thus giving rise to very high population growth over some period of time—sometimes fairly short, but often fairly long, periods of high growth due to low mortality but continued high fertility. Different populations have varied, and indeed contemporary populations vary today, with respect to their historical locations vis-à-vis their demographic transitions: whether they have completed them long ago, have recently completed them, are in the midst of such a transition, or are barely beginning their transitions.

National populations also vary with respect to the homogeneity or heterogeneity of the positions of their subpopulations vis-à-vis *their* demographic transitions. For example, the population of the United States is basically past the major stages of the demographic transition and in a low-balance demographic regime and in a process of aging of the population. However, various immigrant population groups in the United States, for example, certain Hispanic groups, and some Southeast and Western Asia immigrant groups, are only at the beginnings or in the midst of such transitions.

The demographic transitions have affected much more than the growth of national populations or world population. Changing mortality and changing fertility have also entailed changes in the life span of individuals and its internal organization, in family sizes and in joint survival of family members, in the time spent in each stage of the family life cycle, and in the nature of dependency and mutual obligations at each stage of the individual and family life cycles. Address-

Figure 2 .1   The Population Explosion.

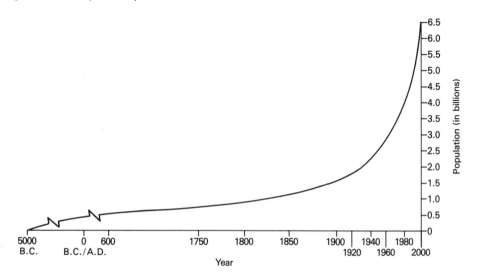

ing the individual opportunities and social exigencies following from these profound changes has, in turn, transformed both individual life course and social organization in the aging populations.

The Population Explosion

The world population has exploded in the twentieth century. World population has grown from about 1.5 billion at the turn of the century to about 5 billion in 1987. It seems likely to exceed 6 billion by the year 2000—in other words, a growth of 4.5 billion, or roughly a quadrupling of world population in the twentieth century (Figure 2.1). In the nineteenth century the world's population also grew at a previously unprecedented rate—by about 78 percent, from 0.9 billion in 1800 to about 1.6 billion in 1900. But neither the absolute growth nor the rate of growth then was even remotely comparable to the current population growth.

Not only is the current rate of world population growth unprecedented in human history, but it is easy to show by simple calculations of person-space relationships that such growth cannot go on indefinitely. The population growth of the recent past has already had profound effects on mankind. How long it continues will affect all of mankind's future welfare, culture and social forms, and probably its very existence. One of the most remarkable aspects of the recent population explosion is that it has been so widely noted and discussed, even if it hasn't always been well understood. In large measure this is so because the population explosion has coincided with the development and extension of literacy and education and of the mass media—newspapers, motion pictures, radio, and, especially, television. People everywhere understand that the populations to which they belong, or the numbers of persons around them, have increased very rapidly in the recent past and in many societies are continuing to grow at unprecedented rates.

Although the fact of the world population explosion is beyond dispute, its meanings and interpretations have been topics of lively controversy (Matras, 1977). One school of thought views the world population growth as a crisis for mankind, human sustenance, and living space (Ehrlich, 1968). A second school views the current population growth as presenting an unprecedented opportunity for social and economic development (Simon, 1977, 1981). Finally, a third point of view asserts that the population explosion is the basic ingredient of most, if not all, the nation's and the world's current social, political, and welfare problems (Berelson, 1974).

WORLD POPULATION GROWTH

World population growth, and growth of specific populations, have come about primarily as the consequence of declining mortality and enhanced longevity. In Europe, areas of European settlement, and certain areas of Asia, the historical downward inflection of mortality was followed eventually by a downward inflection in fertility, resulting in much diminished rates of population growth. An historical shift in mortality and fertility rates and in the rate of natural increase (the difference between birth and death rates) from (a) very low rates of natural increase in consequence of quite high, but nearly equal, birth and death rates (often denoted the high-balance demographic regime), through (b) very high rates of natural increase in consequence of continuing high birth rates together with declining or low death rates (denoted transitional-growth regime), to (c) low rates of natural increase again, but now in consequence of quite low, but nearly equal, birth and death rates (often denoted the low-balance demographic regime) is generally referred to as a *demographic transition.*

Demographic transitions have taken place first in Northwestern Europe, later in North America, in Southern and Eastern Europe, and more recently in Japan and in certain other Asian countries. These have varied not only in their historical timing and beginnings, but also in their durations, slopes of—and lags between—mortality and fertility inflections, the levels at which mortality and fertility have leveled off, and other features.

World Population Since 1650

As already noted, there has been tremendous population growth in recent times. World population increased more than eightfold between 1600 and 1985, from

Table 2.1.   Estimates of World Population by Regions, A.D.14 to 1987 (in millions) and Projections to 2020

DATE A.D.	WORLD TOTAL	AFRICA	NORTHERN AMERICA	LATIN AMERICA	ASIA	EUROPE	OCEANIA
14	256	23	—	3	184	44	1
350	254	30	—	5	185	33	1
600	237	37	—	7	168	24	1
800	261	43	—	10	173	34	1
1000	280	50	—	13	172	44	1
1200	384	61	—	23	242	57	1
1340	378	70	—	29	186	90	2
1500	427	85	1	40	225	74	2
1600	498	95	1	14	305	95	2
1750	791	106	2	16	498	167	2
1800	978	107	7	24	630	208	2
1850	1262	111	26	38	801	284	2
1900	1650	133	82	74	925	430	6
1950	2516	224	166	165	1376	572	13
1965	3335	317	214	249	1861	676	18
1975	4076	413	239	321	2354	727	21
1987	5026	601	270	421	2930	789	25
Projected							
2000	6158	880	296	537	3598	819	29
2020	7992	1479	326	712	4584	857	35

Sources: To 1986: United Nations Annual *Demographic Yearbook* (New York: United Nations). 1987 and projection: Population Reference Bureau, "World Population Data Sheet," Washington, D.C.: 1987.

under 500 million to more than 4 billion. It took all of human history before 1650 to reach a world population of one-half billion. But the second half billion was achieved in less than 200 years, the third in 50 years, the fourth in 30 years, the fifth in just over 20 years, the sixth in a little more than a decade, and the seventh in only 8 or 9 years. The growth rate of the world's population has increased from about 0.3 percent per annum in the period from 1600 to 1750 to 2 percent per annum in 1971.

Population growth has not taken place uniformly throughout the world. Between 1750 and 1850, for example, the population of the area of European settlement—including Europe, Asiatic Russia, North and South America, and Oceania—virtually doubled. But at the same time, the population of Asia (excluding Asiatic Russia) increased by about 60 percent, and the population of Africa hardly increased at all. The growth pattern looks much different later on. Between 1900 and 1975, Europe's population increased by only 69 percent, but Africa's population grew by 202 percent, Asia's by 144 percent, North America's by 189 percent, and Latin America's population by 338 percent! As of 1985, the total population of the world is growing at an annual rate of about 1.8 percent, but the rate for Europe is only about 0.6 percent, while Asia's is 2.1 percent, Africa's is 2.6 percent, and Latin America's is about 2.6 percent.

Both the phenomenal growth of the world's population in modern times and the different patterns of growth in the different parts of the world can be explained mainly by changing patterns of births and deaths. Population growth has two components: *natural increase,* which is the numerical difference between births and deaths, and *net migration,* which is the difference between the number of in-migrants and out-migrants. In the case of the total population of the world, of course, only natural increase need be considered. And in the case of the separate continents, only during certain periods in North and South America and Oceania has net migration accounted for a substantial part of population growth.

Data on population size, numbers of births and deaths, and migratory movements are nonexistent for most countries for most years. However, there are long statistical series available for a number of countries, notably those of Scandinavia. With these we can reconstruct Europe's fertility and mortality profile at about the time of the Industrial Revolution. In addition, the census and statistical activities now conducted throughout the world give us data about most recent trends, although this is hardly a complete body of information.

On the basis of historical data from European countries and data collected more recently throughout the world, we can tentatively say that preindustrialized populations are characterized by both very high mortality and very high fertility rates. A crude birth rate[1] of between 30 and 40 per thousand of population may have characterized the European countries in preindustrial periods, and even higher rates

---

[1]The crude birth rate, the simplest and most familiar measure of fertility in a population, is conventionally calculated as the total number of births in a population in a given calendar year divided by the total midyear (or average) number in the population in that year, and this fraction is multiplied by 1000, with the rate conventionally expressed as "the number of births per thousand population," that is,

CBR = [(Total Births)/(Total Midyear Population)] × 1000

Table 2.2.   Crude Rates of Birth, Death, and Natural Increase (per 1,000): World Total and Selected Countries, 1987

AREA OR COUNTRY	CRUDE BIRTH RATE	CRUDE DEATH RATE	CRUDE RATE OF NATURAL INCREASE
World Total	28	10	18
More Developed Countries	15	10	5
Less Developed Countries	36	12	24
United States	16	9	7
Canada	15	7	8
Mexico	31	7	24
Costa Rica	31	4	27
Venezuela	32	6	26
Austria	12	12	0
West Germany	10	12	-2
USSR	19	11	8
Poland	18	10	8
Hungary	12	14	-2
Sri Lanka	25	7	18
Singapore	17	5	12
Japan	12	6	6
Turkey	30	9	21
Israel	23	7	16
India	33	12	21
Pakistan	44	15	29
Iran	45	13	32
Iraq	46	13	33
Egypt	37	11	26
Algeria	42	10	32
Ethiopia	46	23	23
Gambia	49	28	21
Sierra Leone	47	29	18
Zaire	45	15	30

Source: Population Reference Bureau, "1987 World Population Data Sheet," Washington, D.C.: 1987.

(between 40 and 50 per thousand) characterize less developed countries (LDCs) today. The crude death rate[2] in preindustrial Europe fluctuated widely from year to year in accordance with climate, wars, famines, and pestilence, but it averaged about 30 to 35 deaths per thousand. Even higher crude death rates may have characterized non-European preindustrial countries until fairly recently. But conditions have improved so much that, today, it can be said that nowhere do national crude death rates exceed 30 per thousand. Under past high fertility–high mortality conditions preindustrial populations could grow only very slowly. Indeed, in many periods they actually

[2]The crude death rate is, analogously, taken as the total number of deaths in a population in a given calendar year divided by the total midyear (or average) number in the population in that year, and this fraction is multiplied by 1000, with the rate conventionally expressed as "the number of deaths per thousand population," that is,

$$CDR = [(\text{Total Deaths})/(\text{Total Midyear Population})] \times 1000$$

declined in size. Recent improvements in conditions are one factor that has contributed to the modern population boom.

Demographic Transitions

Death rates began to decline in northern and western Europe during the second half of the eighteenth century; this pattern continued until the early twentieth century. Because birth rates remained high through most of this time, the gap between birth and death rates became wider and wider, generating unprecedented rates of population growth. But by the second half of the nineteenth century, birth rates also began to decline in northern and western Europe. This narrowed the gap between births and deaths and diminished the rate of population growth somewhat.

This process, represented in data for Sweden from 1751 to 1979 in Figure 2.1, was repeated in other European countries, although not exactly at the same time. In general, mortality rates began to decline with the beginning of several social and technological movements: these included industrialization, the agricultural revolution, the consolidation of nation–states, and the improvement of transportation and communication and food storage and marketing. The entire

Figure 2.2 Demographic Transition, Sweden, 1751-1979.

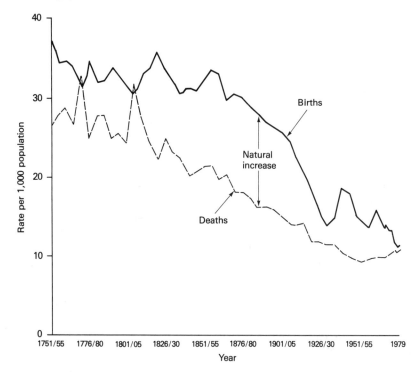

process as described above has been outlined in the *theory of demographic transition.* The general model of the process is generally viewed as having three stages:

1. A period of high fertility and high mortality (high balance) characterized by low growth or by no growth at all and generally young population composition.
2. A stage of declining mortality and high or medium fertility (transitional growth) characterized by high growth, very large families, and very young population composition.
3. A final stage of low fertility and low mortality (low balance) characterized by low growth or by no growth at all, and old or aging population composition.

In its general outlines, this model does describe the course of population trends in many European countries, even if some modifications are required in a few cases. The three stages are thought to be related to, and in part caused by, industrialization, urbanization, and the spread of literacy and education. These are trends with which demographic transitions have certainly been associated in Europe. But a major issue confronting demographers, scientists, and administrators is whether or not the model of the demographic transition can be applied to newly developing countries. Will declining birth rates and subsequent aging of the population follow the already spectacularly declining mortality rates and phenomenal population growth of the underdeveloped world? There are examples of developing countries that have recently experienced dramatic declines in mortality with, so far, very little indication of impending downward inflection in the birth rates, for example, Mexico, Nicaragua, Kenya, Uganda, and Jordan. But a number of developing countries, such as Singapore, Taiwan, Chile, and Sri Lanka, have recently experienced dramatic declines in fertility as well.

AGE STRUCTURE AND POPULATION AGING

Declining fertility has caused the aging of populations, that is, the decline in the relative—and sometimes the absolute—numbers of children and young persons in a population, and the increase in the relative—and generally in the absolute—numbers of elderly persons in the population. The sex and age composition of a population is often represented graphically as a pyramid. The aging of a population due to contraction of the proportion of young persons is called "aging at the base" (of the pyramid), while the aging of a population due to expansion of the proportion of elderly persons is called "aging at the apex" (of the pyramid).

Age Structure

Populations are frequently distinguished and classified in terms of their age structures and growth characteristics (primarily fertility). However, it is not always recognized that age structure and growth characteristics are very intimately related. A young population is one with a relatively high proportion of children, adolescents, and young adults, and a relatively low proportion of

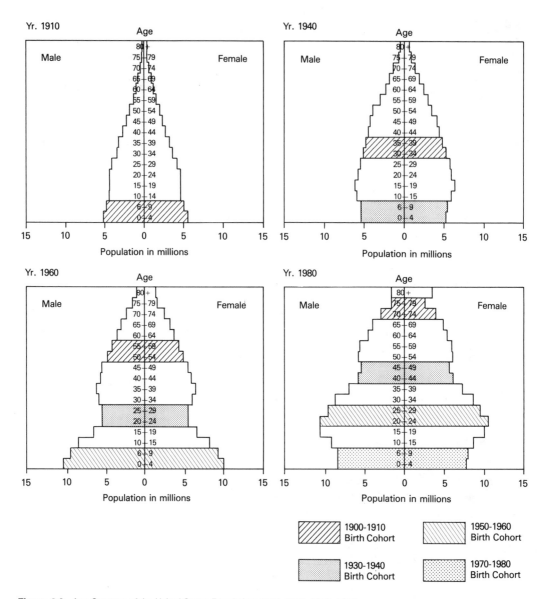

Figure 2.3 Age Structure of the United States Population: 1910, 1940, 1960, 1980.

middle-aged and elderly persons; such a population has a high potential for growth. An old population has a relatively high proportion of middle-aged and elderly people, and it usually has lower growth potential. Figure 2.3 shows young and old populations for the United States in 1910, 1940, 1960, and 1980.

Populations that have both high mortality and high fertility tend to be quite young populations; at the turn of the century the United States had medium mortality and high fertility and a young population. Populations characterized by both low mortality and low fertility—such as the United States in 1940—tend to be old populations. The pyramid for 1960 reflects the low fertility prior to World War II and the high fertility of the extended postwar baby boom, and, again, a relatively young population. The pyramid for 1980 reflects the tapering off of fertility in the second half of the 1960s and low fertility throughout the 1970s, leading to an old population (although not yet as old as the Western European populations that did not experience the extended postwar baby boom of North America).

Modern demographic analysis has shown conclusively that the central factor in the age distribution of a population is the schedule of fertility rates. High fertility implies a young age distribution (high proportions in preadult ages), and low fertility implies an older age distribution (high proportions at adult and older ages). Moreover, changes in mortality have only minor effects on the age distribution of a population, whereas changes in fertility have a significant and rapid effect on age distribution (Coale, 1956).

Thus the population pyramid shown for 1910 is broadest at the base and narrower at each higher and older age group. This reflects continued high fertility, with each aggregate of new babies larger than that of the previous year for some time before 1910. After the mid-1920s the number of births in the United States declined, and it did not begin to recover until 1940. This trend is reflected in the population pyramid for 1940, in which the base is narrower than the middle. After World War II, the number of births increased annually, reaching a peak in 1959 to 1961 and then declining sharply. This is reflected in the 1980 population pyramid in the small base, which becomes sharply broader in the 15 to 19 and 20 to 24 year age groups. The population pyramid for 1980 shows the effects of continuing low fertility over the 1970s, a trend that has continued through the 1980s decade as well.

Age Composition and Macrodependency Ratios

We have already noted that countries and continents have different patterns of population growth. Table 2.3 indicates some of the variations among selected populations in 1984. For instance, the proportion under 15 years of age ranged from about 15 percent in West Germany to about 51 percent in Kenya. For the percent 65 and over the range was from 2 percent in Kenya, Libya, and Nigeria to 17 percent in Sweden.

In the United States the population aged 65 and over, conventionally viewed as the elderly population, included almost one out of eight, about 12 percent, of the total population in 1987. In Sweden this ratio reached more than one out of six, about 17 percent, in the same year. Among the modern industrialized urban countries, those of Western Europe and Scandinavia began to experience the aging of their populations earlier than the United States; and they currently have higher percentages of middle-aged and elderly population and lower percentages of children, adolescents, and young adults. In other countries such as Canada,

Table 2.3. Age Composition and Dependency Ratio, Selected Countries, 1987

COUNTRY	AGE (IN PERCENTAGES)			DEPENDENCY RATIO		
	15	15–64	65+	Total	Youth	Elderly
World Total	33	61	6	.64	.54	.10
United States	22	66	12	.51	.33	.18
Canada	22	68	10	.47	.32	.15
Sweden	18	65	17	.54	.28	.26
West Germany	15	70	15	.43	.21	.21
USSR	26	65	9	.54	.40	.14
Japan	22	68	10	.47	.32	.15
China	28	67	5	.49	.42	.07
Egypt	40	56	4	.78	.71	.07
Brazil	36	60	4	67	.60	.07
Mexico	42	54	4	.85	.78	.07
Nicaragua	47	50	3	1.00	.94	.06
Kenya	51	47	2	1.13	1.09	.04
India	38	58	4	.72	.65	.07
Pakistan	45	51	4	.96	.88	.08
Sri Lanka	35	61	4	.64	.57	.07
Singapore	24	71	5	.41	.34	.07
Iran	44	53	3	.89	.83	.06
Iraq	49	47	4	1.13	1.04	.09
Lebanon	38	57	5	.75	.66	.09

Source: Population Reference Bureau, "1987 World Population Data Sheet," Washington, D.C.: 1987.

Japan, Israel, and the USSR, the onset of the population aging processes either began later or have progressed more slowly or both; the percentages of population 65 or over in those countries are somewhat lower than in the United States.

Conversely, the developing countries of Asia, Africa, and Latin America have not yet begun to experience population aging in the sense indicated here. As their populations have grown rapidly, the absolute numbers of elderly persons have been increasing very rapidly as well, but the percentages in the elderly age groups remain quite low due to the continuing high fertility in those countries. Examination of the percentages under 15 years of age and 65 years old and over in Table 2.3 in relation to the crude birth rates shown in Table 2.2 shows the close correspondence between low fertility and aging of the population: The countries with high percentages aged 65+ are without exception countries with low birth rates, while all the countries with high birth rates also have high percentages in the "under 15" age group and low percentages in the "65 or over" group.

The fourth column of Table 2.3 shows ratios of the population total of the "under 15" and the "65 and over" to the middle population group between ages 15 and 64. This is called the *dependency ratio*. It is so named because it measures the ratio of the population in ages too young or too old to work (but consumers, just the same) to the population of working age. It measures a kind of macrodependency in the population in question; later we will have occasion to distinguish this from microdependency, the specific dependency of individuals upon the material resources, or upon the instrumental or emotional assistance of other individuals or agencies.

The fifth and sixth columns of the table partition the "dependency ratio" into parts due to "youth dependency" and "elderly dependency" respectively. The table shows that Nicaragua, Kenya, and Iraq had very high dependency ratios because of the large percentages under 15 years of age. The dependency ratios of Singapore and West Germany are lowest. West Germany's is lower than the United States' despite a larger percentage of the elderly because of substantially lower youth dependency. Variations like those shown in Table 2.3 could be sketched for the fifty American states, the country's major racial and religious population groupings, or each of the community areas in any major city, or more generally for any population groups.

There are very important consequences of the variations and change in age structure. A population's age composition has a wide-ranging influence on social and economic arrangements and institutions from maternity wards, kindergartens, and schools to entertainment, transportation, religion, and homes for the aged. Moreover, central social and economic processes such as family formation and home-purchasing, job-seeking, retirement, savings, migration, and mobility are closely related to the age composition of a population. Although some of the alarm and the panic expressed so frequently concerning the recent and future trends toward the aging of the population is exaggerated and not very well grounded in actual facts and analysis, there are very good reasons to be concerned about these trends, to monitor and study their social, economic, and political implications, and to explore and develop appropriate public and private policies and programs for addressing them.

SEX, AGE, AND SOCIOECONOMIC STATUS VARIATIONS IN DEMOGRAPHIC RATES

Mortality, migration, marriage and divorce, and fertility have characteristic patterns of variation by sex, by age, and by socioeconomic characteristics. These patterns, in turn, have changed over time in consequence of social, economic, and demographic factors, for example, urbanization and industrialization, literacy and education.

Age, Sex, and Mortality

The most common measure of mortality is the crude death rate, taken as the number of deaths per thousand population. More detailed measures are age-specific mortality rates and measures of life expectancy at birth or at subsequent specific ages. There is a universal age variation in mortality rates: a fairly high rate immediately following birth (around 10 to 20 deaths per 1,000 births in Western Europe, North America, and Oceania, but as high as 200 to 300 deaths per thousand births in underdeveloped countries); a diminishing rate throughout the ages of childhood, reaching a minimum between ages 10 and 14 (about 0.5 to 1.0 death per 1,000 in Western populations); and, finally, an increasing rate at

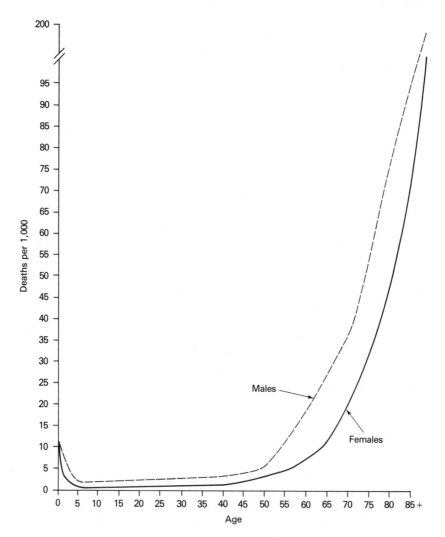

Figure 2.4 Deaths per 1,000 Population, by Sex and Age, United States, 1986. *Source:*
U.S. Bureau of the Census, 1987. *Statistical Abstract of the United States,* 1988
(108th ed.). Washington,D.C.: Government Printing Office, Table 111.

subsequent ages (about 30 to 50 deaths per 1,000 at age 65) in Western populations, then rising very sharply). Figure 2.4 depicts this age variation in mortality
rates with regard to both male and female populations in 1986.

Male mortality is usually higher than female mortality at all ages. For
example, infant mortality in the United States in 1986 was 12 per 1,000 births for
males, but only 9 per 1,000 for females; the death rate at ages 75 to 84 in the same
year was 83 per 1,000 for males but only 51 per 1,000 for females (see Figure 2.4).
Thus the overall pattern of mortality for any population is described by a set of

Table 2.4   1986 Death Rates Per 1,000 Population

AGE	MALES	FEMALES
<1	11.57	9.12
1–4	0.56	0.45
5–14	0.32	0.21
15–24	1.52	0.53
25–34	1.90	0.70
35–44	2.87	1.40
45–54	6.67	3.52
55–64	16.48	9.14
65–74	36.60	20.98
75–84	82.97	51.33
85+	181.68	141.54

Source: U.S. Bureau of the Census, *Statistical Abstract of the United States, 1988* (Washington, D.C.: Government Printing Office, 1987), Table 111, p. 73.

mortality rates by age and sex. Such a set of age-sex-specific mortality rates is conventionally called the *mortality schedule of a population.* Dramatic changes and declines in the mortality schedule were the initial processes of the modern demographic transitions and their accompanying population growth.

Trends in Mortality

In Europe crude death rates declined from levels of 30 per 1,000 or higher at the beginning of the eighteenth century to levels around or below 15 per 1,000 in the early decades of the twentieth century, and infant mortality has continued to decline throughout the present century. Outside of Europe and European-settled countries, mortality remained high until about World War II; then it declined spectacularly in the postwar decades, although some areas of Africa and Asia still have very high death rates. The causes of the European historical declines in mortality include social and education improvements, political stability, economic development, enhanced incomes and levels of living, social reforms, and sanitary and medical improvements. The more recent declines in mortality outside of Europe are accounted for largely by introduction of public health and preventive medicine measures rather than social, economic, or political development.

Socioeconomic Variations in Mortality

The study of differential mortality both among and within nations has served both to describe health and living conditions and to point to some causes of disease and death. The measurement of differential mortality has presented special difficulties, but a number of approaches have documented quite consistent inverse relationships between socioeconomic status and its components—education, occupational status, income, favorable residence—and risks of death. Two separate processes operate in this relationship. First, persons of lower socioeconomic status are more exposed to risks of illness and injury than people of higher socioeconomic status; second, people in the lower socioeconomic groups have generally limited access to medical knowledge, care, and treatment.

Age and Migration

Theories about the causes of migration have centered on two concepts: the pursuit of economic opportunity or enhanced levels of living, and people's age or life-cycle propensities to move. Persons in their late teens, twenties, and early thirties are much more mobile than younger or older persons. Migration is highly associated with first commitment and acts of adjustment of adulthood that are made by adolescents as they mature; for example, entrance into the labor force, marriage, family formation. Those with the highest propensities to migrate are young single adults and young adult couples with small children (see, also, the data bearing on this point in Table 4.1 of Chapter 4). Populations with high proportions in these categories tend to have high rates of out-migration.

Depressed communities and prosperous communities both experience out-migration in relation to their age composition. However, while prosperous communities attract in-migrants from the national pool of persons on the move, and especially from nearby places, depressed communities do not attract enough in-migrants to replace their out-migrants. Hence, depressed communities are frequently characterized by both net out-migration and a shift in the age composition toward higher proportions in the less mobile ages. By contrast, prosperous communities attracting an excess of in-migrants over out-migrants may also experience a shift in their age composition over time toward higher proportions in the younger, mobile ages.

Age and Universality of Marriage

The frequency of marriage, the frequency and acceptability of nonmarriage, and patterns of age at marriage have been traditional concerns of marriage research in population studies. In most societies and in most periods of history, marriage has been virtually universal as the normal, desirable mode of existence for adults.

Modern Europe has deviated markedly from the universal marriage patterns for some three centuries, with significant numbers of men and women remaining single. While the historical common pattern has been one of quite early marriage, especially for girls, in modern Europe marriage has tended to occur relatively late in life. Age at marriage usually varies directly with educational achievement or socioeconomic status for both males and females.

In the United States, Canada, and Australia, remaining single has always been less common than in Europe, although marriage has not generally been as universal as in non-European societies. In North America and Oceania marriage has been, on the average, much earlier than in Europe. Both Europe and the countries of European settlement experienced marriage booms, a return to more nearly universal marriage, and to earlier marriage, beginning in the 1940s and continuing through the 1960s. A return to delayed marriage, as well as greatly increased divorce and remarriage, has taken place in the 1970s and 1980s, but it remains to be seen if the frequencies of eventual marriage and nonmarriage will shift.

The major attempt to explain the European pattern of late marriage and frequent nonmarriage finds the central cause in the desire to avoid marriage and family formation in the absence of sufficient economic security. Thus, young persons with no property, occupation, or assured employment have traditionally delayed marriage or avoided it entirely. In the middle of the twentieth century, a similar explanation holds: Birth control was sufficiently well known and extensively adopted to enable more young persons to marry, and to marry younger, without the immediate entailment of childbearing and its responsibilities.

Responsibility for determining a young person's eligibility for marriage, his choice of a spouse, the various conditions of the betrothal, and indeed the residential, employment, and life style of the newlywed couple have traditionally been in the hands of parents or relatives, instead of being left to the young persons involved. Even in modern marriage, parents are typically able to manipulate the settings in which young persons of opposite sex are likely to meet and court. Conventions governing choice of marriage partner have varied over different societies and in different social groups and strata within a society. But a principle of homogamy, where the choice of a partner is informally limited by similarities in social and cultural characteristics, is found very frequently.

Choice of marriage partners may depend not only on social conventions, but also on availability of socially acceptable eligible unmarrieds of appropriate age. Fertility trends or social changes may generate a "marriage squeeze" where there is an imbalance between the number of eligible males and the number of eligible females from the point of view of both age and social acceptability. Resolution of a marriage squeeze can take place by delaying marriage—either for a short period, until new eligibles enter the marriage market, or indefinitely—or by changing the rules of mutual acceptability (Matras, 1977). The ways in which marriage squeezes are resolved, or fail to be resolved, may themselves have very important social consequences (Guttentag and Secord, 1983).

Age and Fertility

Human fertility, the direct antecedent of population growth and composition, has been the primary focus of population studies and speculations since the time of Malthus. Today, particularly with the recent worldwide trend toward lower mortality and the widespread concern over rapid population growth in most parts of the world, and with aging of the population in the developed countries, the analysis of fertility, childbearing, and family building has come to dominate population studies more than ever before.

Although the most familiar measure of fertility is the crude birth rate (the number of births per thousand in the total population), birth rates vary markedly

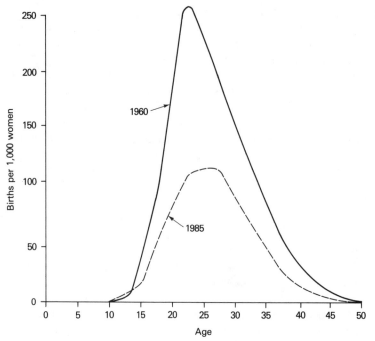

Figure 2.5 Births per 1,000 Women, by Age. United States, 1960 and 1985. *Source:* U.S. Bureau of the Census, 1987. *Statistical Abstract of the United States, 1988* (108th ed.). Washington: Government Printing Office, Table 83.

by age of women. These variations are usually portrayed in age-specific fertility rates. These rates are very high at ages 15 to 19 where females marry early, but in the United States they are intermediate, with peak fertility between the ages of 20 and 24 instead. Fertility remains high through the ages 25 to 29 in the United States; then it declines (see Figure 2.5). In the twenty-five-year period from 1960 to 1985, age specific fertility rates declined by almost 60 percent at ages 20 to 24 and by about 44 percent at ages 25 to 29.

Table 2.5. Birth Rates per 1,000 U.S. Women, 1960 and 1985

AGE	1960	1985
10–14	0.8	1.2
15–19	89.1	51.3
20–24	258.1	108.9
25–29	197.4	110.5
30–34	112.7	68.5
35–39	56.2	23.9
40–44	15.5	4.0
45–49	0.9	0.2

Source: U.S. Bureau of the Census, *Statistical Abstract of the United States. 1988* (Washington, D.C.: Government Printing Office, 1987), Table 83, p. 60.

Trends in Fertility

Among the more developed countries (MDCs) some had already reached very low levels of fertility by the onset of World War II (that is, Western Europe, Hungary, Northern America, and Oceania had crude birth rates not exceeding 20 per 1,000). With the exceptions of Germany and Hungary, all of these low-fertility nations experienced a baby boom following World War II. There were two kinds of baby booms. Short booms mostly reflected fertility that had been postponed. They brought about no change in patterns of completed family size for the most part, and they were followed by even lower birth rates. In contrast, extended baby booms reflected both catching up on previously postponed fertility and some increase in average numbers of children born per woman or per couple. These occurred in the United States, Canada, Australia, and New Zealand, and they were followed in the late 1960s and 1970s by sharp fertility declines.

A third pattern was evident for MDCs. In this pattern, the trend toward lower fertility only began around or after World War I, and it had achieved only moderately low fertility by World War II (crude birth rates were over 20, as in some countries of Eastern and Southern Europe and Argentina). Countries with this pattern continued their steady fertility declines and, except for Romania, all had crude birth rates under 20 per 1,000 by 1970.

The lower fertility MDCs that experienced baby booms after World War II have histories of regional, religious, ethnic, and socioeconomic differentials in fertility rates. Although some of these differentials remain pronounced, the overall recent trend is of convergence of marriage, family building, and fertility patterns among the various subgroupings. In the MDCs that only recently attained low fertility on a national level, there are substantial regional, ethnic, and socioeconomic differences.

Virtually all the less developed countries (LDCs) had crude birth rates exceeding 35 per 1,000 on the eve of World War II. Two groupings of LDCs may now be identified as those in which there have been notable declines in birth rates since World War II, and those with continued high fertility. The LDCs were in the past characterized by uniformly higher fertility, with few signs of place-of-residence or socioeconomic differentials. However, there is some evidence now of differential fertility in the LDCs exhibiting recent declines in birth rates, especially among literate or educated as compared to illiterate women.

Population Policy and Fertility

Remarkably, the MDCs with fertility approaching replacement or zero population growth levels exhibit very little in the way of articulated national population policies. With few exceptions, they have also had relatively few publicly sponsored efforts to introduce or promote the use of contraception. In some non-Catholic capitalist countries of the West there have been commercial and sometimes medical-profession promotions of contraception, but even this has been absent in most of the low fertility MDCs. Thus, the origins of the small families and low birth rates in these countries seem not to be connected with public population policy or measures of intervention.

The extent to which national population policies or organized efforts to introduce family planning and birth control practices have been influential in those LDCs where birth rates have declined is a topic of lively debate. Currently efforts are under way to develop systematic means of evaluation. The previously separate views—that these LDC fertility declines are a direct consequence of the introduction and promotion of birth control, or that they are a consequence of social and economic development—have drawn closer together. Most students of population today view modern social and economic development as including the introduction of new family values and means to achieve them, and they see the successful introduction and acceptance of family planning as depending upon some threshold of social and economic development sufficient to institutionalize new levels of living demands and expectations (but see Caldwell, 1982, for an important alternative view).

These views are incorporated into a number of competing theories of fertility variation and trends. They include microanalytical theories stressing the role of individual or household preferences and fertility decisions and inquiring about the factors which influence them. Alongside these are macroanalytical theories stressing the role of social conditions in the very fact and acceptability of abstraction, evaluation, and decision making about marriage, family formation, and numbers of births.

AGE VARIATION IN INTENSITY AND FREQUENCIES OF TRAITS, BEHAVIOR, AND ACTIVITIES

In the discussion of meanings of age and aging in the previous chapter, we have already alluded to the age-related differences in social roles, activities, and behavior associated with and extending beyond the age-based physiological and psychological capacities and constraints. In this chapter we have already discussed the age-related variations in mortality, migration, marriage, and fertility. Young adults experience lower rates of mortality than older adults. Adult women in their late twenties typically have higher rates of fertility than those in their thirties or forties; women older than their late forties have practically no fertility at all. Given the same age-specific mortality and fertility rates, a young population would have more babies and fewer deaths than an old population of the same size.

It should be clear from these discussions, everyday observation and experience, and more formal extensive systematic investigation that there is age-related variation in virtually every sphere and dimension of human characteristics and activity. The behavior and needs of infants are different from those of children; and children's are different from those of adults. Those of young adults are different from those of the elderly. Nonetheless, it will be useful to list a number of specific types of age variation in personal characteristics, needs, and social activity and participation (see, also, Table 4.1 of Chapter 4) because much of the discussion of the broader implications of population aging—the increase in the proportions of

older persons and decrease in the proportions of younger persons in a population—is based upon such age differences and variation.

Family roles and related activities are probably the most obvious among
those varying with age. Marriage, household formation, childbearing and
parenting, home and family consumption, family and nonfamily leisure and
recreational activity, residential shifts, family- and child-related participation in
church, school, and community activity, and the like are all based on age as well
as on family status in their nature and intensity. Family offspring remaining in,
and departing from, the parental home are age-related activities. So, too, are school
enrollment, continuation, or termination and entry into employment.

More generally school enrollment, employment and unemployment, earnings and other income, consumption, saving, and investment are all age-related.
Travel, whether by private automobile or public transportation, varies in frequency and distance by age. Leisure, entertainment, and recreation preferences
and participation vary by age, as does use of public and commercial facilities and
offerings. So, too, are there differences by age in degree of interest and involvement
in community and political activity.

Finally, and not least important, there are steep age differences in frequency, nature, and intensity of deviance of all types. The most familiar and most
important example is illness and health impairment and disability. This is generally very low in childhood but climbs steeply thereafter with increasing age. Other
kinds of deviance including delinquency and crime, sexual deviance, religious, or
political deviance also have characteristic age variation.

Thus, a wide range of traits and behavior, reflecting the participation and
contribution or the needs or predicaments of individuals and social units, vary in
frequency and intensity by age. It is for this reason that the age composition of a
population—whether an entire society or a group, subsystem, or organization—is
correctly viewed as a representation of the resources and the needs of that population. It is for this reason that the *change* in age composition—for the most part
aging of populations—is viewed as change in resources and needs, and the balance
between them.

3

THE SOCIAL DEMOGRAPHY
OF AGING II

life years, the life course, and the family cycle

MORTALITY, LONGEVITY, AND LIFE YEARS

It is a truism that declining mortality implies enhanced and extended survival. Yet the implications of enhanced and extended survival are not always clear. In this chapter we examine the survival patterns of birth cohorts. We begin to explore some of the meanings and implications of improved survival in terms of the volume and composition of life years lived by cohorts, and we see what these imply for longevity and life expectation of individuals and families. In addition we consider briefly some implications of declining mortality and lower fertility for family and kinship structure and for patterns of family dependency and obligations at successive ages and life stages.

Declining mortality has caused the increase in longevity, or in the average length of life, volume of life years or life span, of individuals. In a similar vein, the declining mortality has caused the increase in the joint longevity; that is, people live longer together in couples, families, or in pairs or other groups of individuals joined or related to each other.

It will be useful here and in subsequent chapters to introduce the concepts and basic measurement of

(1) Survival function, or pattern of survival rates, of a cohort;
(2) Life years lived by a cohort;
(3) Average future life, or life expectancy, of a cohort.

By "cohort" we mean those born at the same time, or beginning life (or sometimes, beginning marriage, beginning school, or beginning employment, or beginning some other important activity) at the same date or calendrical period.

Table 3.1.   Survivors, Cohort Life Years Remaining, and Average Life Expectancy, by Sex and Age, Canada, 1978

AGE	SURVIVORS		LIFE YEARS		LIFE EXPECTANCY	
	Males	*Females*	*Males*	*Females*	*Males*	*Females*
0	100,000	100,000	7,080,000	7,830,000	70.8	78.3
1	98,700	99,000	6,978,100	7,741,800	70.7	78.2
5	98,400	98,700	6,583,000	7,333,400	66.9	74.3
10	98,200	98,600	6,098,200	6,842,800	62.1	69.4
15	98,000	98,500	5,605,600	6,353,200	57.2	64.5
20	97,300	98,200	5,118,000	5,862,500	52.6	59.7
25	96,400	98,000	4,636,800	5,370,400	48.1	54.8
30	95,700	97,700	4,153,400	4,885,000	43.4	50.0
35	95,000	97,300	3,676,500	4,388,200	38.7	45.1
40	94,000	96,800	3,205,400	3,910,700	34.1	40.4
45	93,000	96,000	2,752,800	3,427,200	29.6	35.7
50	90,100	94,600	2,297,500	2,951,500	25.3	31.2
55	86,200	92,500	1,836,100	2,479,000	21.3	26.8
60	80,500	89,500	1,416,800	2,022,700	17.6	22.6
65	72,300	85,100	1,041,100	1,591,400	14.4	18.7
70	61,400	78,600	700,000	1,179,000	11.4	15.0
75	47,900	69,200	426,300	809,600	8.9	11.7
80	33,000	56,200	227,700	494,600	6.9	8.8
85	18,600	39,000	98,600	257,400	5.3	6.6
90	7,900	21,000	34,000	107,600	4.3	5.1

Source: R. Wilkins and O. Adams, *Healthfulness of Life* (Montreal: Institute for Research on Public Policy, 1983), Table 1.1.

Table 3.1 and Figure 3.1 show the survival rates at each age for males and females in Canada based on mortality conditions and rates in Canada in 1978.

Among a cohort of, say, 100,000 males born at the same time and subject to the death rates observed in 1978, a total of 98,700 would survive to reach age 1 (to their first birthday); 98,400 would survive to reach age 5; and 33,000 would survive to the eightieth birthday; 18,600 would survive to age 85; and only 7,900 would survive to reach 90. By assumption in the table and figure, all would die before or at age 100.

The lower mortality of females is reflected in the higher survival rates (greater numbers of an initial cohort of 100,000 surviving) at each age: 99,000 compared to 98,700 at age 1; 94,600 compared to 90,100 at age 50; and 69,200 females compared to only 47,900 males surviving to age 75. In the figure, the higher survival rates of the females are reflected in the fact that the entire curve of the females lies to the right and above that of the males.

The calculation of survival rates or probabilities, or of proportions of a cohort surviving to each given age, on the basis of death data or vital statistics rates using life tables, is explained in texts dealing with techniques of demographic analysis. The middle columns in Table 3.1 show the numbers of life years

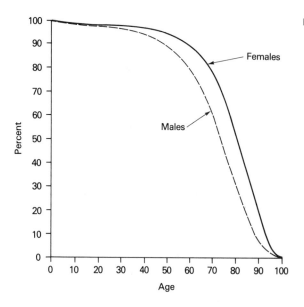

Figure 3.1 Survivors by Age and Sex, Canada, 1978.
Source: Wilkens and Adams, 1983a.

remaining to a cohort at each age and subsequently until all in the cohort have died. Thus at birth (age 0) the male cohort as a whole (comprising 100,000 at birth, by assumption) have 7,080,000 remaining life years; and upon reaching age 65 the cohort is left with 1,041,100 life years. Both the total volume of life years for the female cohort (at birth, or age 0) and the volume of life years remaining at each subsequent age exceed the corresponding numbers of life years for the males, reflecting the females' lower mortality, higher survival rates, and greater longevity.

Calculation of total life years and numbers of life years remaining at each age is also explained in demography texts. However, careful examination of the graphs of the survival rates in Figure 3.1 will show that the total volume of life years lived by each cohort is represented by the area under the survival curve; the number of life years remaining to the cohort subsequent to each respective age is represented by the area under the survival curve *to the right of the ordinate* representing the age in question.* (See note at end of chapter.)

Thus, in Figure 3.1 the area under the curve representing the total life years for a female cohort implied by the 1978 mortality rates used in deriving the survival rates and curve is notably greater than the area for the males, reflecting again the lower mortality and greater volume of life years enjoyed by the female cohort compared to the male cohort. We may note, also, that the additional life years enjoyed by the female cohort are primarily life years at older (over 65) ages. Similarly, Figure 3.2 shows the survival curves for U.S. males at the turn of the century, in 1950, and in 1983.

Comparison of the curves for 1900 and 1950 shows not only the higher survival rates at all ages, but that (a) the major change in the pattern of survival occurred at infancy and childhood ages; and also (b) the major increase in number of

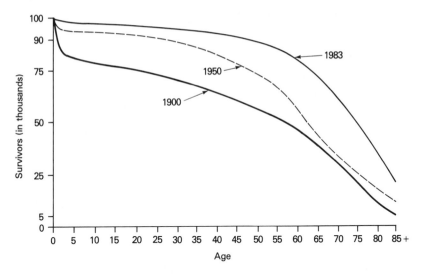

Figure 3.2 Survivors by Age, United States Males, 1900, 1950, and 1983.
Source: 1900, 1950: *United Nations Demographic Yearbook*, 1953,
New York: 1954. 1983: *United Nations Demographic Yearbook*, 1985.

life years occurred at adult or working years primarily, and only secondarily at ages over 65. In the later period, there was dramatic improvement in survival at ages 60 and over. The percentage of total life years of a cohort lived at ages 50 and over was 24.5 percent in 1900, increased slightly to 25.4 percent in 1950, but rose to 32.2 percent in 1983. In 1983 just under 15 percent of total male life years lived comprised life years at ages 65 or over, compared to about 10 percent in 1950 and just over 9 percent in 1900. We shall have several occasions to compare survival curves, and to examine and compare the age composition as well as the activity composition (what people do in the various categories of life years) of the areas under such curves that represent volume of life years lived altogether and at the respective ages.

Returning to the last, right-hand, columns of Table 3.1 labeled "life expectancy," we now have a direct interpretation and, indeed, the principle for calculation, of the term: The average number of life years remaining to survivors at any given age (in the life years column of Table 3.1) divided by the number in the cohort surviving to that age is what is conventionally taken as the "expectation of life" or "life expectancy" at that age. In particular, the total number of life years lived by the cohort divided by the total number born (for males shown in Table 3.1: 7,080,000 divided by 100,000) is the life expectancy at birth, a number taken as an overall index of longevity and of mortality at all ages.

In Canada, the 1978 life expectancy at birth for males was 70.8 years and for females it was 78.3 years. In other words, the cohort subject at each age to the age-specific mortality recorded in Canada in 1978 would live and die in accordance with the pattern, and rates depicted in the survival rates of Table 3.1 and Figure 3.1, would have the volume and age composition of life years indicated in the middle column of the table and by the area under the survival curve in the figure, and would have an average of 70.3 years of life if male and an average of 78.3 years of life if female.

INCREASING LONGEVITY

In the present century mortality rates have continued to decline while life expectancy has increased substantially. Life expectancy in Western Europe and the United States increased by twenty years in the first half of the twentieth century. Judging from life tables for France (1817 to 1831) and Sweden (1816 to 1840), the average life expectancy at birth in Western Europe at the end of the first quarter of the nineteenth century was around 40 years. At the turn of the century, average Swedish life expectancy was just over 50 years and French life expectancy was about 47 years. Thus, expectation of life increased by only about seven to ten years from the first quarter of the nineteenth century until the close of that century—but this increase doubled in the following fifty years. Improvements in mortality conditions have been far from uniform for all age groups. The decrease in mortality rates has been most spectacular for ages 1 to 4 and for the one-year period following birth. Improvements have been substantial in adult ages and, in the last two decades, even impressive at elderly, after 65, ages.

Cross-Societal Variations in Life Expectancy

The onset of the decline of mortality took place at different times in different countries and populations, and indeed most often it began earlier or later among different subgroups of the same population. Nor has the risk of death declined at the same pace in the various cultures and in the various areas of the world. For the most part mortality rates have declined even in the less developed countries and even in contemporary preliterate societies, but there remain very sharp differences in levels of mortality, and correspondingly in life expectancy, among the various nations and populations. Table 3.2 shows 1987 estimates of life expectancy at birth in the world (63 years) and in selected areas and countries.

Life expectancy reached 73 years in the more developed countries, compared to only 59 years in the less developed countries. Among the MDCs, life expectancy at birth reached 74 years in the United States, 75 years in Israel, 76 years in Norway, Switzerland and Canada, and 77 years in Iceland and Sweden. But it reached only 71 years in Eastern Europe, and 69 years in the USSR. Among the LDCs, life expectancy was 48 years in East Africa where it ranged from 41 years in Ethiopia to 54 years in Kenya; in Southern Asia it averaged 54 years, ranging from 39 years in Afghanistan to 55 years in India, 50 years in Pakistan, 57 years in Iran, and 70 years in Sri Lanka.

Extended Longevity and the Composition of Life Years

Some important features of the patterns of declining mortality in Canada and their implications for the life course of individuals and life cycle of families are

Table 3.2.   Life Expectancy at Birth: World Total and Selected Countries, 1987

AREA OR COUNTRY	LIFE EXPECTANCY AT BIRTH (YEARS)	AREA OF COUNTRY	LIFE EXPECTANCY AT BIRTH (YEARS)
World Total	63		
More Developed Countries	72	Egypt	59
Less Developed Countries	57	Algeria	60
		Nigeria	49
United States	75	Sierra Leone	35
Canada	76	Gambia	36
Mexico	67	Ethiopia	41
Brazil	65	Kenya	54
Argentina	70	South Africa	56
Peru	60	Turkey	62
		Israel	75
Sweden	77	Afghanistan	39
Norway	76	Iran	57
Iceland	77	Iraq	62
United Kingdom	74	Lebanon	65
Switzerland	76	South Yemen	48
Greece	74	India	55
Spain	76	Pakistan	50
		Sri Lanka	70
USSR	69	China	66
Hungary	70	Taiwan	73
East Germany	73	Japan	77
Poland	71	Australia	76

Source: Population Reference Bureau, "World Population Data Sheet, 1987," Washington, D.C.1987.

represented in Table 3.3 and in Figure 3.3 that show life years lived in successive age intervals of male and female life tables for Canada in 1921, 1951, and 1981.

Thus there was an increase of 22 percent in the number of life years lived by the male cohort subject to 1981 mortality levels compared to that for males subject to 1921 mortality levels. Even more dramatic was the finding that female cohorts subject to 1981 mortality rates would enjoy more than 30 percent more life years than those subject to 1921 mortality.

As we may note in Table 3.3, beyond the differences between improvements in male and female longevity and life years, the increments to the volume of life years did not take place uniformly over the period examined, 1921 to 1981, nor were they uniform among the age levels. For males and females alike the increments to the volume of life years lived were much more pronounced and dramatic in the first half of the period, 1921 to 1951 (column 2), than in the second half, 1951 to 1981 (column 3). For males the number of life years lived by the hypothetical cohort increased by almost 13 percent in the early part, compared to an 8 percent increase in total life years achieved in the later part of the 1921 to 1981 period; and for females the increase was 17 percent in 1921 to 1951, compared to an 11 percent increment in 1951 to 1981.

Table 3.3. Life Table Life Years, L(x), in Selected Age Intervals, by Sex. Canada: 1920–22, 1950–52, and 1980–82

Age	LIFE YEARS LIVED			% CHANGE, 1920–22 TO 1980–82		
	1920–22	1950–52	1980–82	1921–81	1921–51	1951–81
Males						
Total	5884297	6640474	7187867	22.2	12.8	8.2
<20	1745343	1892677	1969819	12.8	8.4	4.1
20–60	3081732	3518959	3734835	21.2	14.2	6.3
60–75	782971	898875	1029115	31.4	14.8	14.5
75+	274251	329963	454098	65.6	20.3	37.6
% Dist						
Total	100.0	100.0	100.0	100.0	100.0	100.0
<20	29.7	28.5	27.4	17.2	19.5	14.1
20–60	52.4	53.0	52.0	50.1	57.8	39.4
60–75	13.3	13.5	14.3	18.9	15.3	23.8
75+	4.7	5.0	6.3	13.6	7.4	22.7
Females						
Total	6,060,369	7,090,403	7,905,888	30.4	17.0	11.5
<20	1789008	1915157	1977637	10.5	7.0	3.3
20–60	3148375	3647144	3855584	22.5	15.8	5.7
60–75	814112	1054911	1234864	51.7	29.6	17.1
75+	308874	473191	837803	171.2	53.2	77.0
% Dist						
Total	100.0	100.0	100.0	100.0	100.0	100.0
<20	29.5	27.0	25.0	10.2	12.2	7.7
20–60	52.0	51.4	48.8	38.3	48.4	25.6
60–75	13.4	14.9	15.6	22.8	23.4	22.1
75+	5.1	6.7	10.6	28.7	16.0	44.7

Source: J. Matras, "Demographic Trends, Life Course, and Family Cycle—The Canadian Example: Part I. Changing Longevity, Parenting, and Kin Availability. *Canadian Studies in Population,* forthcoming a., Table 1.

In summary, there were large gains in longevity in the 1921 to 1951 period and somewhat more modest gains in the 1951 to 1981 period. In the earlier part of the period the gains were concentrated in the adult ages, 20 to 60, and may be said to have yielded additional life years at ages traditionally characterized by employment, parenting, and adult and middle-age activity for cohorts experiencing those mortality patterns. In the latter part of the period the gains were more concentrated in the later ages, 60 to 75 and 75 and over—and especially dramatically for females at ages 75 and over. These later gains in longevity may be said to have yielded additional life years at ages characterized by postemployment and postparenting activity for the cohorts.

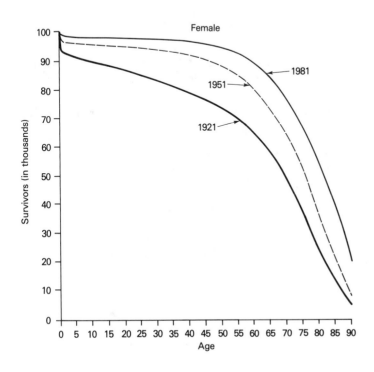

Figure 3.3 Survivors Out of 100,000 Born Alive at Selected Ages by Sex, Canada, 1921, 1951, and 1981.

FERTILITY AND THE CONTRACTION OF PARENTING

The Compression of Parenting

The historical long-term decline of fertility in the West was indicated in the previous chapter; the association of smaller families and employment of women in the organized labor market with declining fertility is widely recognized. An important link between the recent trends in mortality and fertility and the entire range of personal and socioeconomic activities and relationships is that which derives from the compression and compacting of parenting in the life course of adults, and of adult women especially; that is, the diminishing intensity and reduced durations of parenting even as the numbers of life years have expanded.

Age-specific fertility rates for Canadian women in 1871, 1891, 1921, 1951, 1961, and 1981 are shown in Table 3.4. These data reflect clearly the decline of fertility in the first part of this century, some recovery (the baby boom) in the years following World War II, and the steep decline in the most recent decades. They reflect also the near disappearance of fertility at the later ages of fecundability, say at ages over 35, a trend that continued even during the years of the baby boom. Although earlier marriage in the 1940s and 1950s contributed to the decline in the mean age at fertility, the most important and most consistent element in the decline in age at fertility has been the reduction of fertility at the older ages.

A measure of life years of parenting is presented in Table 3.5. For each age group this measure, Lp(x), is calculated as the product of the total life years, L(x), and an estimate, Par(x), of the probability of being a parent at that age. Measures of the life years in parenting at each age level in Table 3.5 are based on the female life years lived and on the fertility schedules for each of the years 1921, 1951, and 1981. The left panel shows life years in parenting while the right panel shows the percent in parenting of the total life years lived at each age. A cohort of 1,000

Table 3.4.   Age Specific Fertility Rates (per 1,000), and Total Fertility Rate (per woman) in Canada, 1871–1981

AGE	1871	1891	1921	1941	1951	1961	1981
15–19	37	23	38.0	30.7	48.1	58.2	25.9
20–24	174	165	165.4	138.4	188.7	233.6	94.7
25–29	310	274	186.0	159.8	198.8	219.2	124.2
30–34	353	249	154.6	122.3	144.5	144.9	66.6
35–39	320	179	110.0	80.0	86.5	81.1	19.0
40–44	152	83	46.7	31.6	30.9	28.5	3.1
45–49	20	11	6.6	3.7	3.1	2.4	0.2
Total Fertility Rate	6.83	4.92	3.53	2.83	3.50	3.84	1.67

Source: 1941–1981, CANSIM-Statistics Canada; 1871–1921, J. Henripin, *Trends and Factors of Fertility in Canada* (Ottawa: Queen's Printer, 1968), Table 6.2.

Table 3.5.   Estimates of Female Life Years in Parenting by Age. Canada: 1921, 1951, and 1981

	LIFE YEARS IN PARENTING			PERCENT PARENTING OF TOTAL LIFE YEARS		
Age	1921	1951	1981	1921	1951	1981
15–19	40460	55187	31323	9.2	11.6	6.4
20–24	205231	254392	155566	47.6	53.7	31.6
25–29	338535	397208	302997	80.1	84.2	61.7
30–34	378069	436150	368603	91.4	93.1	75.3
35–39	373855	431425	355234	92.7	92.8	72.9
40–44	341914	387834	262319	87.2	84.5	54.2
45–49	271560	285875	118676	71.6	63.4	24.8
50–54	156480	144032	29436	43.1	32.9	6.2
55–59	48404	37738	4000	14.1	9.0	0.9
60–64	5166	3039	221	1.6	0.8	0.1
Total				45.9	43.0	25.4

Total Life Years
at all ages 15+:

				Average no. remaining life years per female surviving to age 15:		
4709719	5651409		6421534	53.4	59.2	65.0

Total parenting life years
at all ages 15+:

| 2159674 | 2432880 | | 1628375 | 24.5 | 25.5 | 16.5 |

Total nonparenting life years
at all ages 15+:

| 2550045 | 3218529 | | 4793159 | 28.9 | 33.7 | 48.5 |

Source: J. Matras, "Demographic Trends, Life Course, and Family Cycle—The Canadian Example: Part I. Changing Longevity, Parenting, and Kin Availability, *Canadian Studies in Population*, forthcoming a., Table 3.

females subject to the mortality conditions and fertility rates observed in Canada in 1921 would live a total of 4,709,700 life years at ages 15 or over, of which 2,159,700, or 46 percent, would be years spent parenting one or more children under the age of 15. Of the 53.4 years total average remaining lifetime for females surviving to age 15 under the 1921 demographic conditions, a little under half (24.5 years) would be spent in parenthood, and an average of 28.9 years would be life years not in parenthood. About 9 percent of life years at ages 20 to 24 would be taken up with parenting for such a cohort, but by ages 35 to 39 this would rise to almost 93 percent of life years at ages 35 to 39. At ages 40 to 44 about 87 percent, and at ages 45 to 49 just under three-fourths, of life years for such a cohort would be taken up with parenting (Figure 3.4a).

Under mortality and fertility conditions observed in 1981, a cohort would live a total of 6,421,500 years at ages 15 or over, but only 1,628,400 life years, or just 25 percent, would be devoted to parenting. This represents an average of just 16.5 years in parenting per woman reaching age 15, compared to an average of 48.5 years, on the average, not in parenting. In such a cohort about three-fourths of the total life years lived at ages 30 to 34, and just less than 73 percent at ages 35 to 39 (normally the peak parenting ages) would be devoted to parenting (see Figure 3.4c). Thus younger cohorts

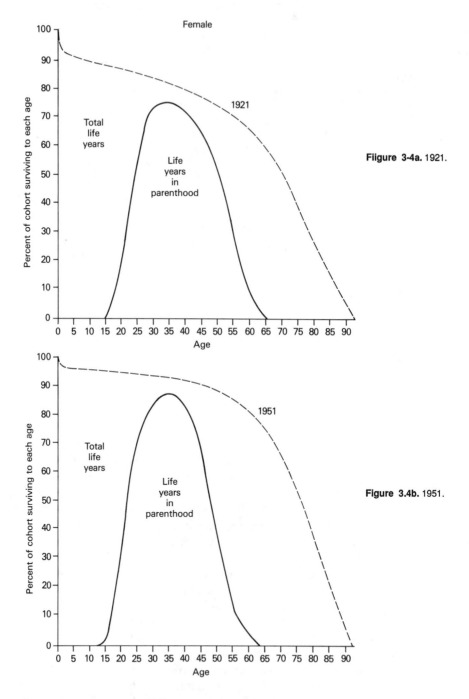

Fiigure 3-4a. 1921.

Figure 3.4b. 1951.

Figure 3.4 Survival Rates, Total Life Years, and Life Years in Parenthood.
Canada Females, 1921, 1951, and 1981.

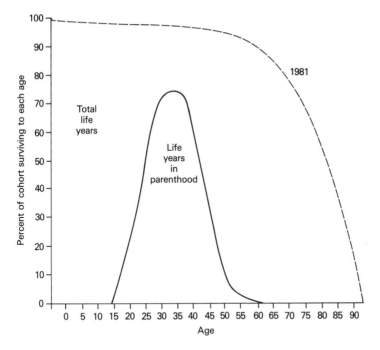

Figure 3.4c 1981.

have experienced substantially reduced mortality and considerably larger numbers of total life years, but both the absolute numbers of life years and the percentages of life years lived at each age that are taken up with parenting are very much smaller.

THE CONTRACTION AND COMPACTING OF PARENTING

Declining fertility has meant not only fewer births and smaller families, but also compression of parenting into fewer years and shorter parts of the total life span of both mothers and fathers. The downward inflections in fertility, where they have occurred, have generally resulted first in lower numbers of higher order births, that is, in women completing their lifetime fertility relatively earlier and after fewer total births. However, delays in the initiation of childbearing have frequently occurred, whether because of delayed marriage or due to extended time intervals between marriage and first births. In some periods and population groups there have been high rates of voluntary childlessness. Regardless of the specific patterns of timing, the meaning of reduced numbers of births per couple has inevitably implied reduced time in the individual life course and in the family cycle devoted to parenting.

The consequences of the contraction of parenting are evidently quite different for women and for men. For women, absence of obligations to care for dependent children has been translated into freedom *to expand* social participation and, in particular, into freedom to seek and hold employment outside the home. For men, absence or early termination of obligations to support dependent children has been translated into freedom *to contract* and withdraw from employment, or to refrain from seeking full or new employment if previous employment is curtailed. Thus the trend toward lower fertility in the MDCs has been closely associated with the massive entrance of women into the labor force as well as some demand and movement in the direction of expansion, if not necessarily full equalization, of the economic opportunities open to women. The same trend toward lower fertility and compact parenting has resulted in diminishing male lifetime preoccupation with and commitment to employment, making it much easier for men to withdraw from employment or to lessen their employment both because of the entrance of wives, alternative family breadwinners, into employment *and* because of diminished obligations and needs for extended support to dependent children. We return to this topic in Chapter 7.

Kinship and Kin Availability Across the Life Course

Intuitively it is easy to see that mortality and fertility affect family patterns and the numbers and age differences among kin. An important contribution to relating explicitly the demographic variables such as the mortality and fertility schedules to family structure is developing in the work of Keyfitz and his collaborators and followers on the demography of kinship (Keyfitz, 1986; Goodman, Keyfitz, and Pullum, 1974). They have developed procedures for estimating the probabilities of survival of kin—for example, parent, sibling, child, or of the number of kin born and surviving—at each age of an individual. Thus, for example, under the mortality and fertility conditions of Canada in 1971 for a woman reaching age 20 the probability of having a mother still alive is 0.967; for a woman reaching age 60, the probability of having a mother still alive is 0.322. But under the 1981 Canadian mortality and fertility conditions, the corresponding probabilities are 0.983 and 0.396 respectively. Under the lower mortality conditions of 1981 an individual woman herself reaching age 60 years of age is considerably more likely to have her mother still surviving and alive than would be the case under the 1971 mortality regime (Keyfitz, 1986, Table 2).

Taking as an example the numbers of daughters born and the numbers surviving under the 1971 and the 1981 demographic regimes respectively, Keyfitz calculated that, under 1971 conditions, for women themselves surviving and reaching age 60 the average number of daughters ever born would be 1.036 and the expected number still alive (when the mothers reach 60) is 1.001. But, under the 1981 conditions the average number born would be only 0.813 while the average number surviving and still alive when the women reach 60 years of age is 0.797. In this instance, the main factor in the change from the 1971 to 1981 demographic conditions is the decline in fertility, which overrides by far the effect of the mortality decline in the same period.

More dramatic examples of the rapid shifts in life-course kinship networks implied by steep mortality and fertility inflections have been derived by A. Shmueli (1985) for subpopulations in Israel, such as Jews of Asian or African birth or origins and Moslems, both with recent histories of greatly diminishing mortality and even more recent beginnings of fertility decline. For example, the expected number of daughters of non-Jewish women in Israel subject to the 1960 demographic regime born and still alive at age 45 was estimated by Shmueli as 3.51 daughters per woman (the Moslem total fertility rate in 1960 was 9.31); for those subject to the 1980 demographic regime (total fertility rate for Moslem women was 5.98 in 1980), the expected number of daughters born and still alive at age 45 was down to 2.75. The expected number of living sisters a non-Jewish woman aged 65 would have had under the demographic regime of 1960 was 2.47, while the corresponding figure under the 1980 demographic regime was 1.94. Finally, the probability that a non-Jewish woman reaching age 60 still had a living mother was 0.209 under the 1960 demographic regime, while under the fertility and mortality conditions of 1980 the corresponding probability reach 0.302, an increase close to 50 percent (Shmueli, 1985, Table 18).

More generally Keyfitz and his associates have shown that while Western populations have experienced both declining mortality and declining fertility, the outcomes with respect to the availability of kin at each age differ for parents and for other kin. With respect to the survival of parents, each person in a population has only one pair of natural parents, and declining mortality enhances the chance of having a surviving parent at each age although these are not entirely indifferent to fertility variations. The earlier in his parent's lifetime that an individual is born, the greater the chance of the parent's survival to any given age of the individual.

However, with respect to the numbers and survival of siblings, children, and second- or higher-order kin, declining fertility tends to override declines in mortality and reduces the numbers of all kin, even as each one born is likely to survive longer. Thus, the present generation of adult parents has, to be sure, fewer children making claims on time and attention and resources than earlier generations. However, as elderly couples or individuals they will also have fewer surviving children and grandchildren, improved mortality not withstanding, to entertain or care for them in old age.

Joint Survival of Couples

Unfortunately these models and calculations have not yet dealt in detail with a most important kin relationship—that between husbands and wives. However, it is possible to make some calculations of probabilities of joint survival of couples using the data on life years of Canadian cohorts subject to the mortality conditions of 1921, 1951, and 1981 (Matras, forthcoming a., Appendix Table A). Such calculations are shown in Table 3.6 for couples with three separate combinations of age at marriage and age differences between groom and bride. Joint survival means simply that both members of the couple are

Table 3.6.   Estimated Probabilities of Joint Survival of Husbands and Wives Marrying at Selected Ages in Canada, 1921, 1951, and 1981

YEAR AND AGES AT MARRIAGE	SURVIVAL PROBABILITIES			
	20 years	*30 years*	*40 years*	*50 years*
1921				
Groom aged 25	.9073	.8164	.6464	.3548
Bride aged 20	.9089	.8421	.7303	.5167
Joint Survival	.8247	.6875	.4720	.1833
Groom aged 25	.9073	.8164	.6464	.3548
Bride aged 25	.8971	.8096	.6533	.3750
Joint Survival	8139	.6609	.4223	.1331
Groom aged 30	.8863	.7578	.5234	.2057
Bride aged 25	.8971	.8096	.6533	.3750
Joint Survival	.7951	.6135	.3419	.0771
1951				
Groom aged 25	.9397	.8444	.6578	.3740
Bride aged 20	.9679	.9243	.8324	.6398
Joint Survival	.9096	.8173	.5476	.2392
Groom aged 25	.9397	.8444	.6578	.3740
Bride aged 25	.9549	.8920	.7568	.4885
Joint Survival	.8973	.7532	.4978	.1827
Groom aged 30	.9101	.7703	.5328	.2190
Bride aged 25	.9549	.8920	.7568	.4885
Joint Survival	.8690	.6872	.4032	.1070
1981				
Groom aged 25	.9576	.8839	.7203	.4426
Bride aged 20	.9843	.9585	.8982	.7663
Joint Survival	.9426	.8472	.6470	.3392
Groom aged 25	.9576	.8839	.7203	.4426
Bride aged 25	.9767	.9366	.8468	.6559
Joint Survival	.9354	.8278	.6100	.2903
Groom aged 30	.9353	.8217	.5980	.2847
Bride aged 25	.9767	.9366	.8468	.6559
Joint Survival	.9135	.7696	.5064	.1867

Source: J. Matras, "Demographic Trends, Life Course, and Family Cycle—The Canadian Example: Part I. Changing Longevity, Parenting, and Kin Availability, *Canadian Studies in Population*, forthcoming a., Table 4.

alive. (This can occur with the marriage intact or otherwise; at this point no information is used on stability or dissolution—other than by death of one spouse.)

For each such combination, probabilities of joint survival for 20 years, 30 years, 40 years, and 50 years are estimated for grooms and brides of the respective ages. For each type of couple (where each type reflects some combination of ages at marriage and age differences between groom and bride) the probabilities of joint survival for twenty years after marriage are notably higher for couples subject to 1951 mortality than for those subject to 1921 mortality; they are even higher for those subject to 1981 mortality. Indeed the changes are fairly substantial, especially in the earlier part of the period, 1921 to 1951.

The probabilities of joint survival for longer periods—30 years, 40 years, and 50 years—vary even more sharply and dramatically, and are very substantially higher for those subject to the 1951 and 1981 death rates. It is the survival rates of the women that underwent the greatest increase between 1921 and 1951, with the rates for the men improving only modestly. Survival rates for both men and women improved notably in the interval from 1951 to 1981, except at the young adult ages, where they improved to a much lesser extent.

Thus, for a bride and groom both 25 years old and marrying in 1921 and subject thereafter to the mortality conditions of 1921, the probability that both would survive another 30 years and reach age 55 was 0.6609; for the couple both aged 25 and marrying in 1981 and subject thereafter to the mortality conditions of the year 1981, the probability that both would survive 30 years and reach age 55 was 0.8278. The latter represents an improvement in this joint survival probability amounting to about 25 percent. For the same type of couple, the probability of surviving 40 years after marriage improved by 44 percent (from 0.4223 under 1921 mortality rates to 0.6100 under 1981 mortality conditions); the probability of surviving 50 years after marriage improved by 118 percent (from 0.1331 to 0.2903).

These analyses and estimates are important for alerting us to, and measuring the relative weights of, changes of various types and magnitudes in the mortality and fertility regimes upon size and composition of kinship networks. Moreover they can be combined to study the changes in kinship networks at successive ages through the life course: The size and the composition of an individual's network of kin changes as he himself ages and passes through life. For example, as Keyfitz has shown for Canadian fertility and mortality conditions of 1971 and 1981, while probabilities of having living parents and living grandparents decline through the life course, average numbers of live siblings rise to a peak at about age 25 and decline thereafter; average numbers of live children rise to a peak at about age 45 and decline thereafter; and average numbers of cousins also peak at about age 25 (Keyfitz, 1986), all in consequence of the regime of mortality and fertility.

It is hard to overstate the importance of the kinship network and its changes in the life course of the individual. It is a "convoy of social support" (Kahn, 1979), on the one hand, and a collection of obligations and claims on one's own energies and resources, on the other. But the availability of kin as directly determined by the demographic regime is only one dimension of the relationship between kin networks and life-course activity and transitions of individuals. It is the nature of the relations of mutual support, dependency, obligations, and entitlements in the kinship network that bears most heavily on individual life-course activity and transitions. These support and obligation relationships are conditioned, on the one hand, by the size and composition of the kin network at any stage or point in time, as well as by longevity and joint survival horizons and parenting norms and horizons. On the other hand, they are conditioned by existing alternative—extra-kin-network—support, dependency, obligations, or entitlements.

LIFE YEARS, PARENTING, KINSHIP CONSTELLATION, AND THE LIFE COURSE

We have already characterized the life course as the physiological, psychological, and social process and sequence of capacities and age-graded events, activities, and relationships characterizing the individual from birth through death. As Elder has written:

> The life course refers to pathways through the age-differentiated life span and social patterns in the timing, duration, spacing, and order of events. The timing of an event may be as consequential for life experience as the event itself and the degree or type of change it brings. Age differentiation is manifested in expectations and options that impinge on decision processes and the course of events that give shape to life stages, transitions, and turning points such as leaving home, marriage, or retirement. Such differentiation is based in part on the social meanings of age and the biological facts of birth, sexual maturity, and death. These meanings have varied through social history and across cultures at points in time, as documented by evidence on socially recognized age categories, grades, and classes. (Elder, 1978, pp. 21–22.)

A central concept in the description and analysis of the life course is the *age role,* a social role associated with a given chronological age. The concept of age grading in society refers to the association of social roles with chronological age, for example, association of school entrance, marriage, citizenship obligations or entitlements with given chronological ages. Age grading tends to impose social norms about the expected behavior, activity, and relationships at the ages in question and, for the succession of age-graded roles, for the life course generally. One of the central hypotheses of the research on the life course is the historical trend toward increasing age grading in complex societies both with regard to the numbers of activities and activity domains that are age-graded and the detail with which they are differentiated by age.

Life expectancy of individuals at birth and at each age, the volume and composition of cohort life years, and parts of the cohort and individual life years earmarked for the central sociodemographic, vital, and economic processes—marriage, parenting and child-raising, and work—bind and constrain the life course in all societies even if individual deviations may occur. As we have seen in this and the previous chapters, fundamental changes in the volume and age composition of life years, on the one hand, and in the volume and age composition of the years allocated to parenting (and, as we shall note later, to work and employment as well) have taken place in the wake of the historical demographic transitions.

The shift in demographic regimes from the young-population, short life-span high-balance regimes to the aging population, long life-span low-balance, demographic regimes has increased longevity, increased life years generally and most dramatically in old age; it has compacted parenting drastically. It has also brought overall decline in the numbers of available kin, implying diminished dependency and obligations at certain ages, and dramatically diminished potential support networks. The hypothesized increase in the extent of age grading noted above is consistent with the need for ordering and regulation of the longer life span that is also less regulated by parenting and work requirements. We explore some of the implications of these changes in the chapters to follow.

LIFE YEARS, PARENTING, KINSHIP CONSTELLATIONS, AND LIFE CYCLE OF THE FAMILY

The sequence of events and changes over time that a family undergoes include marriage, the birth of first and subsequent children, the growth and eventual departure of the children from the household, and the dissolution of the couple by death of one of the members. This sequence is called the *family cycle*. The family cycle includes changing numbers of persons in the family unit, changing age, and changing marital status. In some instances there is turnover by virtue of death of a child and subsequent birth of another child. For larger or extended families there is routinely turnover by virtue of deaths and births as well as by marriage, divorce, and widowhood.

In the course of the family cycle there are several changing constellations of role relations—husband-wife, father-child, mother-child, brother-sister, elder-brother-younger-brother, and so forth—with many triads and coalitions forming and reforming. In addition, the content of role behavior varies over time, and so do the allocation of time, attention, interest, and authority. Thus the time of the wife may be initially taken up with work, then later with childbearing, and still later with work again. The couple may spend some part of the family cycle alone prior to birth of children and again after the children's marriages and departures—but this does not mean that the couple returns to its original relationship. The ages, as well as the accumulated experience and time in the system of the married couple, as well as their interests, abilities, tastes, and aptitudes change as part of the aging process.

Large families have different patterns of allocation of time and resources than small families. But for all families, the addition of new members forces shifts in the allocation of time and resources and, sometimes, in the very mode in which sustenance and resources are assured. The growing family may send additional members to work, or the major earner or some other family member may seek new employment, perhaps in a different place of residence. Patterns of intrafamily authority, dominance, and dependency also shift as the family grows, and new patterns develop as the family and its members age.

Intrafamily relations, dependence, and mutual support and, indeed, the very composition of nuclear and extended families, are very closely linked not only to the patterns of marriage and fertility generating the families in the first place, but also to mortality and patterns of survival and joint survival. Increased life expectancy, then, means not only that on the average individuals survive longer, can expect to survive longer compared to their forebears, and think, plan, and behave in accordance with their images and expectations of enhanced survival (Fourastie, 1959). It means also that *joint survival* of couples, brothers and sisters, parents and children, and kin of all types is also extended and enhanced. Recognition of enhanced joint survival, in turn, with its implications for changing patterns of dependence and mutual support, has led to important changes in family organization and behavior and newly institutionalized and legitimated life-course patterns for all—especially for women. As mortality, marriage, fertility, and migration patterns change over time, so too do the life-span family and dependency configurations undergo change. We return to these in more detail in Part III (Chapters 6, 7, and 8).

Concluding Remarks: Toward a Social Demography of Dependency

Issues of dependency have been discussed in social demography in a number of contexts. Probably the most familiar treatment of dependency in demographic theory and analysis is the imputation of dependency to persons younger or older than normal working age, say 15 to 64 or, sometimes, 20 to 64, the calculation and analysis of dependency ratios—of youth dependency or aged dependency—and analysis of the demographic and socioeconomic causes, correlates, and implications of such dependency. This approach has been associated especially with the discussion of economic implications of fertility and fertility limitation in general and in developing countries in particular, at least since demographic theory has demonstrated so clearly the relationship between fertility and age distribution in populations (Coale, 1956; Coale and Hoover, 1958; United Nations, 1973). A related and more recently developed theme is that of age stratification, age-related entitlements, and competing claims or institutionalized entitlements of the respective young and elderly dependent subpopulations on societal resources [not least of which are love, attention, and commitment (cf. Preston, 1984)].

A second context for the discussion of dependency in social demography has been the analysis of changing household and family implied by shifting fertility and mortality regimes and, in particular, by the demographic transition from the high-balance constellation of high birth and death rates through transitional-growth stage leading to the low-balance constellation of low birth and death rates (Ryder, 1975; Bongaarts, 1983; Shmueli, 1985).

An important derivative of this analysis of dependency change in the context of demographic transitions is the theory imputing a central role in demographic behavior of individuals and in longer-term demographic trends and inflections to changing dependency itself, and to the responses to dependency (Friedlander, 1969, 1983; Caldwell, 1976, 1982). A central idea of this analysis is that the "strains" or "new" dependency accompanying diminished mortality and enhanced survival—the dependency crunch described in the opening chapter—are addressed by demographic behavior introduced, adopted, or legitimated in response to the new exigencies. The latter is related *inter alia* to alternative socioeconomic or political arrangements or strategies for dealing with dependency.

A third sociodemographic context for the discussion of dependency is one dealing with the effects of changing population composition upon dependency related to sociometric, market, or mutual choice regimes. The most prominent example is probably the analysis of marriage markets, mate selection, and marital status and their accompanying rhetorics and ideologies (see especially Guttentag and Secord, 1983; also Becker, 1976; Carter and Glick, 1976; Matras, 1973, 1977). A central idea of this discussion is that a mutual choice regime; for example, the rules and practices of a marriage market, operating at any moment or period of time, are inherently unstable in that population changes tend to upset the balance or constellation of eligibles of the respective sexes, ages, characteristics, and qualities (the marriage squeeze). Adjustments of the choice regime or mutual selection rules (and of the ideologies and rhetorics), or else in the frequency or timing of selection and choice arrangements, or both, necessarily derive from the population shifts. The markets or choice regimes themselves, as well as their demographically induced changes, generate sexual, socioeconomic, and emotional dependencies. These in turn are variously dealt with at both individual and collective levels with major societal consequences (Guttentag and Secord, 1983).

A final sociodemographic context of dependency has appeared increasingly in analyses of the life course or life cycles of individuals or families and concerns the age-related or duration-of-marriage-related emergence and variations in dependency, relative deprivation, economic stress, and the individual or family responses they evoke. The concept of the life cycle of the family (Glick, 1977) incorporates the idea that there are characteristic stages of family life, role relations, economic activity, and so forth associated with the ages of the parent couple, the duration of the marriage, and the number, timing, and ages of the children, and, implicitly varying types and degrees of dependency characteristic of the different stages of the family life cycle.

These concepts have more recently been extended to the study of individual life course and the associated sequences of life events, participation in the respective social and economic domains, age-related roles and role relationships, patterns of care-giving and care-seeking, and life-course transitions (cf. Modell, Furstenberg, and Hershberg, 1976). The study of dependency variations and changes in the life course and in the family life cycle has been made explicit by Oppenheimer (1982) in her use of the concept of life-cycle squeezes in which individuals, couples, or families experience relative deprivation and economic stress because of age-occupational earnings patterns in relation to the actual or anticipated burdens and costs of marriage and setting up a household or in relation to child dependency. The latter especially varies and changes during the life cycle and in accordance with the number and ages of children. The responses to life-cycle squeezes and dependency that Oppenheimer analyzes include postponement of marriage, the timing of childbearing and family limitation, and, especially, the labor force participation of wives.

SUMMARY

The concept of the aging of populations has a very clear meaning: It is a change in the age composition of populations in the direction of increasing proportions in older age groupings, or the middle and older age groupings, and decreasing proportions in the younger ages. It is very important to understand that such changes do not occur independently of other profound demographic and social changes: The immediate and most important factor in the aging of populations is the decline in fertility and sustained low fertility.

Low fertility is itself associated with both different status and life-course patterns and options of women, different patterns of family structure and family life cycle, and different family relations and dependency over the course of the family life cycle, compared to those characterizing the high fertility regime. In turn, low fertility itself is an outcome of previous fundamental sociodemographic changes, the most important being the decrease in mortality and the dependency crunch, and the social and demographic redundancy of extended parenthood and consequent practice and institutionalization of family limitation in its many and various forms. It is very important to recognize that the aging population is also a small family and short-term parenting population, and a working-women population.

Note:

*Another way to see this is as follows: Consider a cohort of 100,000 newborns on a given date, and suppose that the entire cohort lives to be exactly 100 years old, and that all die on the one-hundredth birthday. Under those circumstances, the survival function is described by the following curve, which is actually a horizontal straight line forming a rectangle.

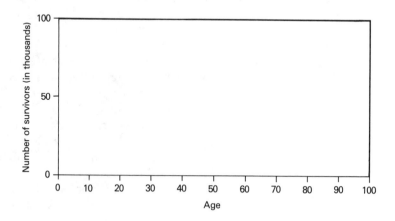

Clearly the number of years lived by the cohort between birth and age 1 year is 1 year × 100,000 = 100,000 years. The area under the curve between Ordinate 0 and Ordinate 1 represents 100,000 life years. Correspondingly, the number of years lived by the cohort between age 5 and age 20 is 15 years × 100,000 = 1,500,000 years; and the area under the curve between ordinates x = 5 and x = 15 represents 1,500,000 life years. Finally, the number of life years lived by the cohort between birth (age 0) and the moment that all die (age 100, under the hypothetical conditions) is 100 years × 100,000 = 10,000,000 years. Thus the entire area under the curve (a horizontal straight line, in this case) represents 10,000,000 life years lived by the cohort from birth until all in the cohort have died. The area between, say, age 0 and 10 represents life years (1,000,000 of them) in childhood. The area between, say, age 65 and 100 represents life years (3,500,000 life years, in this hypothetical case) in old age.

Consider, now, a cohort among whom only half those born survive the entire 100 years, while the other half dies early, say, exactly at age 50. The survival curve is, in this case, a step curve, as follows:

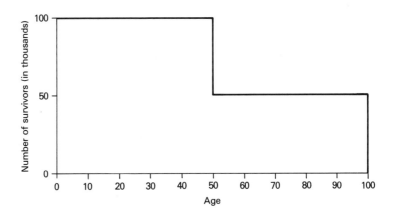

The number of life years lived by this cohort from birth to age 50 is 50 × 100,000 = 5,000,000 years. The area under the curve between x = 0 and x = 50 represents the 5,000,000 life years lived by the cohort at those ages. The number of life years lived from age 50 to age 100 is, for this cohort, only 50 × 50,000 = 2,500,000 since only 50,000 survive past age 50 and live to be 100 years old. Thus, for the entire cohort, the total number of life years lived from birth and until all in the cohort die is 5,000,000 + 2,500,000 = 7,500,000. This figure is represented by the total area under Curve 2. The number of life years lived after age 65 in this cohort is 35 years × 50,000 = 1,750,000 life years in old age. For the first cohort (described by Curve 1) the number of life years lived in middle age, say, between ages 45 and 65, is 20 years × 100,000 or 2,000,000 life years. For the second cohort (described by Curve 2) the number of life years in middle age would be (5 years × 100,000) + (15 years × 50,000) = 500,000 + 750,000 = 1,250,000 life years.

4

POPULATION AGING
AND THE ECONOMY

INTRODUCTION

Population aging bears on a nation's or a community's economy in several distinct ways. First, the changing age composition affects the aggregate of economic characteristics, behavior, activity, or decision making. Thus, other things equal, a smaller proportion of young children in a population has the effect of raising the overall proportion of the population in working ages and, presumably, the potential and actual fraction of workers in a population. Conversely, a larger proportion of elderly persons in a population has the offsetting effect of lowering the overall proportion in working ages and, presumably, lowering also the potential and actual fraction of workers.

Measurement of this type of effects of population composition is the point of the dependency ratios presented and discussed in Chapter 2. The aging of the working force itself is often conjectured to affect aggregate productivity. The aging of the consumer population works to shift the composition of aggregate demand, increasing the demand for products and services associated with older populations, for example, health care, and diminishing demand for those associated with young populations, for example, schooling.

Second, the major factors of population aging—diminished mortality and extended life span and diminished fertility, parenting, and family dependency—lead to changing individual patterns of economic behavior, activity, and decision making. The most dramatic examples are probably the massive entrance of married women into the working force and the increasing and earlier retirement of middle-aged and elderly men. Substitution of market-bought or publicly provided goods and services for some previously produced and supplied by families and the growth of single-person and other nonfamily households are other important examples.

Finally, there are important macroeconomic responses by governments, private industrial and economic sectors, or trade unions to the aging of populations and to changing economic behavior of individuals and families. Examples of government responses include, of course, the entire range of public income maintenance and health programs for the elderly, and the support of public education primarily for the young. The industrial and economic sectors have adjusted both their mixes of goods and services, their employment and wage policies, and in some cases their production processes and capital, labor, and skill input mixes in response to changing age composition of workers, consumers, and the population generally. Trade unions have had to examine carefully their priorities and means to protect the jobs, wages, and welfare of members of the various age groups as well as fight for their membership and bargaining status in the face of both changing age composition and changing sources of new entrants into the working force. More generally, the societal mix of institutions governing production and allocation of goods, services, and income undergoes critique and adjustment to address the new combinations of needs and resources evolving as populations age.

These trends and responses of the economy to population aging have not always been distinguished analytically, nor have they received equal treatment in the literature. It is the effects of population aging on government programs and expenditures, and their effects on labor input and production, that have received by far the most attention.

Effects of Changing Age Composition on Aggregate Economic Activity

In Chapter 1 we mentioned the variations in physiological and psychological characteristics and capacities, and the variations in socially approved and expected behaviors and relationships, associated with age differences. In Chapter 2 we illustrated the classical dimension of demographic analysis—age variation in demographic rates—and we noted again the more general phenomenon of age variation in behavior, activity, and social roles and status or virtually every type. Sociologists, economists, and many in the helping professions have long been alert to the age variations in a wide variety of human behavior, whether marriage or mental illness, taking jobs or committing crimes, consumption of ice cream cones or home ownership.

In a human population the *aggregate* number of deaths is comprised of the total of deaths to persons of all ages in the population, and the aggregate number of births—or marriages or migratory moves—is comprised of the total of such events occurring among persons of all ages. Thus the overall death rate, or marriage or birth rate, or migration rate of the population is affected by the relative numbers of persons of different ages in the population. In the same way, the *aggregate* number of workers, consumers, investors, and so forth, in a population is affected by the age composition.

Table 4.1 Age Variations in Selected Personal and Socioeconomic Characteristics and Activities, United States, 1985 and 1986

AGE	MALES PERCENT			FEMALES PERCENT			PERCENT MOVING 1985–86	
	Marr'd.	Wid'd.	Live Alone	Marr'd	Wid'd.	Live Alone	Same County	Different County
Total	65.5	2.6	9.4	60.5	12.4	13.4	17.8	9.1
15–19			0.5			0.6	10.1	6.5
15								
16–17								
18–19	3.7	—		11.0	—			
20–24	23.1	0.2	7.0	38.9	0.2	5.9	22.2	13.1
20–21								
22–24								
25–29	53.3	0.1 }		63.8	0.5 }		20.4	12.5
30–34	68.9	0.1 }		73.5	0.8 }		14.4	8.1
			} 10.7			} 6.8		
35–39	78.0	0.4 }		76.1	1.4 }		} 9.7	} 6.0
40–44	79.5	0.3 }		76.1	2.6 }		}	}
45–49 }	83.8	1.4 }		} 76.1	6.1 }		} 6.1	} 4.0
50–54 }		}		}	}		}	}
			} 9.0			} 13.0		
55–59 }	83.7	3.6 }		} 70.3	16.8 }		} 3.9	} 3.5
60–64 }		}		}	}		}	}
65–69 }	81.0	9.1 }	12.7	} 51.2	38.8 }	34.6	} 2.5	} 2.0
70–74 }		}		}	}		}	}
75+	69.8	22.5	19.2	23.9	67.0	51.0	3.2	2.3

AGE	MALES				% VOTED	
	Enrolled in School	% in Lab. Force	% Unemployed	% Work Disabled	1984	1986
Total	n.a	76.3	6.9	9.1	59.9	46.0
15–19		56.4	19.0			
15	97.6			}		
16–17	92.3	45.3		}		
18–19	54.6	68.3		}	36.7	18.6
				} 3.8		
20–24		85.8	11.0	}	43.5	24.2
20–21	33.0			}		
22–24	17.9			}		
25–29	8.9	} 94.6	6.7	} 5.9	54.5	35.1
30–34	6.0	}		}		
35–39	}	} 94.8	5.1	8.2	63.5	49.3
40–44	}	}				

Table 4.1 Age Variations in Selected Personal and Socioeconomic Characteristics and Activities, United States, 1985 and 1986 (*cont.*)

AGE		MALES			% VOTED	
	Enrolled in School	% in Lab. Force	% Unemployed	% Work Disabled	1984	1986
45–49	}	} 91.0	4.4	11.3	}	
50–54	}	}			}	
	} 1.8				} 69.5	58.7
55–59	}	} 67.3	4.3	23.3	}	
60–64	}	}			}	
	}					
65–69	}	}				
70–74	}	} 16.0	3.2	n.a.	67.7	60.9
75+	}	}				

AGE	MALE MEAN	1985 EXPENDITURES		CHARITABLE CONTRIBUTIONS	
	Earnings 1985	Health Care	Entertainment	Religious Orgztns.	Others
Total	$27,430	$1,037	$1,085	$470	$180
15–19		}			
15		}			
16–17		}			
18–19	}	} 396	680	}	
20–24	} 14,300	}		}	
20–21	}	}		} 290	80
22–24	}	}		}	
				}	
25–29	} 24,067	711	1,201	}	
30–34	}			350	150
35–39	} 31,565	910	1,518	}	
40–44	}			}	
				} 660	260
45–49	}			}	
	} 32,379	1,177	1,409		
50–54	}			}	
				} 570	300
55–59	} 30,247	1,289	1,025	}	
60–64	}			}	
65–69	}	} 1,539	661	}	
70–74	} 25,369	}		} 340	70
	}			}	
75+	}	1,509	317	}	

Source: U.S. Bureau of the Census, *Statistical Abstract of the United States, 1988,* 108th ed. (Washington, D.C.: Government Printing Office, 1987), Tables: 24, 48, 63, 196, 364, 418, 586, 601, 608, 611, 688.

Table 4.1 illustrates the age variation in rates or intensities of some important social and economic characteristics and activities of American males in the 1980s. In each instance, the rate, frequency, or intensity shown for the *total* of American males is in fact simply a weighted average of the separate and different rates for each age group. Thus, a shift in the age composition implies change in the age group weights or proportions, and hence in the overall rate or intensity of the activity even if the age-specific rates remain unchanged. It is the consideration of such changes that has been at the center of the analysis of economic implications of population aging.

Thus it is small wonder that the conventional inquiry concerning the economic effects of population aging—that is, a *change* in the age composition of populations leading to higher proportions of middle-aged and elderly and lower proportions of young persons in the population—has focused primarily upon analysis of such compositional effects and their implications for aggregate size of the working force, aggregate and per capita output, aggregate consumption and its composition, and aggregate savings and investment.

In this chapter we shall review this conventional discussion briefly. We shall also suggest that this discussion, which deals primarily with the impact of changing age composition—population aging—upon *production* and *productivity*, should be expanded to address much more adequately than it has heretofore the impact of population aging on *household formation* and *consumption* as well. We shall try, also, to introduce the new discussion of economic implications of some of the changes in the individual life course, the family life cycle, and the social and political organizational dimensions of changing patterns of economic activity and dependency. As we noted in the previous chapter, these accompany and, indeed, are integral parts of the sociodemographic processes of the aging of populations.

The effects of changing age composition of the population on the economy are conventionally viewed in terms of

1. The size and age composition of the labor force
2. Production and productivity
3. Savings and investment
4. Consumption and demand for services
5. Patterns of youth and elderly dependency

We will consider each of these briefly and then examine some relationships between age structure and household formation and their related economic implications.

SIZE AND AGE COMPOSITION OF THE LABOR FORCE

The labor force refers to the part of the population employed for pay or profit, or else wishing or available for employment. In contemporary working force analysis, the labor force is conventionally identified, described, and measured in population censuses or surveys using behavioral criteria. An individual is considered to belong to the labor force if just prior to being queried in the census or sample survey he was actually employed or actively seeking employment.

The overall labor force participation rate, and the size of the labor force, in any given population is a weighted average of the age- and category-specific rates of participation. Labor force participation rates by age and sex, or by age and educational attainment, or by age and race or ethnic origin are examples. While the weighted average obviously varies with the varying weights or relative sizes of the age group and category components, the age-category-specific rates of labor force participation have themselves been changing as population composition has changed. Thus the literature on the relation between aging of the population and labor force participation rate seems inconclusive.

Overall Labor Force Participation Rate

Aggregate rates of labor force participation are subject to two contrasting influences as populations age. Initially aging at the base (of the population pyramid, induced by declining fertility) operates to increase the percentage in the population in the prime working age range, that is, declining numbers of children imply a larger proportion in the population aged 15 to 64. However, at the same time, the increased proportions in the highest age groups, say 50 and over, among those in the prime working age categories, operate to reduce the participation rate of the prime working age population because of high rates of early retirement or disability in this group (50 and over). As the age of entry into the labor force has risen, and as the age of retirement has declined, the sensitivity of the aggregate labor force participation rate to age composition tends to decline (Clark and Spengler, 1980; Habib, 1985).

The size of the working force depends on the extent or rates of participation at each age and for each population group (young persons, old persons, single females, married females) and propensities to seek and accept employment. Population factors may also affect *rates* of participation: High fertility implies reduced working force participation of women, and the opposite holds true as well. Rural-to-urban migrants may have lower participation rates than the nonmigrant population, while urban migrants are likely to have higher rates of participation. The long-term trends in industrialized countries have involved declining rates of participation among young males and elderly males, and increasing rates of participation among married women. The very fertility declines that are associated with aging at the base and the declining numbers of children have, in turn, rendered it possible and progressively more likely that married women will be free to seek and accept employment, that is, to enhance labor force participation at ages of motherhood and, hence, in the population generally.

Readiness to work must be matched by availability of employment if the productive potential of the working force is to be realized. The great increases in production and social welfare notwithstanding, the fear of unemployment and the fact of unemployment remain a major challenge to the fabric of Western society. At least since the 1930s, an important tradition of economic analysis has held that the rate of investment required to sustain full employment cannot be maintained under conditions of stationary or declining population. According to the

Keynesian analysis, at least some minimal population growth is necessary to avoid excessive unemployment; in the absence of population growth, governments must increase expenditures to offset the investment shortage occasioned by declining population growth and causing unemployment.

However, more recent analyses have viewed diminished rates of population growth as favorable to high levels of employment. A number of arguments have been marshalled by J.J. Spengler (1972). First, the employment of young people, who are new entrants into the working force, is more difficult when the population is growing at a rapid rate than when it is growing at a low rate or not at all. Under conditions of growth, large numbers of additional jobs are required each year; under conditions of nongrowth the number of jobs made available by death or retirement of incumbents is close to the number needed for new entrants. Second, the rate of capital formation tends to be inversely related to the rate of population growth. In rapidly growing populations, the capital shortage will probably especially affect the employment-oriented investment, with the result that inputs complementary to labor will grow less rapidly than the working force, or not fast enough to maintain full employment. This means that under rapid population growth unemployment, underemployment, and "disguised unemployment" are likely to be high—a condition that is conspicuous in high fertility LDCs. Spengler's third point is that employment is facilitated by a low and nonfluctuating rate of natural increase. This is because these conditions (where the relative number of new entrants into the working force does not fluctuate) allow the physical and personal capital essential to the maintenance of health and employment to be formed at a relatively high and constant rate.

In developing countries, important dimensions of the economy are the very absence of capital, the shortage of land, and a general imbalance between the supply of labor and the supply of other factors of production, which means that labor is typically underemployed to start with. In the LDCs, high population and working force growth may be conducive to higher unemployment and underemployment through factors such as the decrease in land per worker, recourse to land of inferior quality, or fragmented or overcrowded holdings. In the absence of employment opportunities outside agriculture, the migration of unemployed rural working force may simply imply the transfer of underemployment or unemployment to the cities.

Unequal economic and population growth in various parts of the world or within any given country are the rule rather than the exception. A basic hypothesis in population studies has been that migration is the major factor in bringing about an adjustment between different countries or regions. In MDCs, minimum degrees of migration and mobility are necessary for maintaining high levels of employment. But in the LDCs, employment problems may be created rather than resolved by rural-to-urban movements; such movements often reflect not so much differential development and adjustments as much as chronic deficiency in the demand for labor. Low incomes and low levels of employment in agriculture, together with high density or high population growth rates, are among the main causes of out-migration from rural areas.

It is worth remarking that the discussion of relations between population change and employment rests largely on theoretical rather than on empirical analyses. Thus the role of population factors in determining levels of employment is still difficult to evaluate precisely, and even the directions in which population changes influence employment remain a controversial matter. For, as we noted at the close of the previous chapter, the population changes themselves occur in sociohistorical contexts and imply changes in the life-course patterns and dependency contingencies of individuals and families.

PRODUCTION AND PRODUCTIVITY

One of France's outstanding mid-twentieth century social scientists and pioneer demographers, Alfred Sauvy, devoted much of his work to exploration of the implications of France's and Europe's declining fertility, and in particular to population aging. In a major treatise (Sauvy, 1954), he paints a picture of crisis and demoralization in the economies of aging populations due to (a) the diminished overall productivity of their working force comprising increased proportions of older employees with impaired capabilities and obsolete skills and training, and (b) "gerontocratization" of management, and its accompanying demise of initiative, innovation, and creative entrepreneurship. These concerns have been shared by fellow scholars and publicists and by a larger public as well.

In fact the average age of men in the working force in the United States and in other Western countries is higher in the 1980s than it was in the 1950s and 1960s, despite trends toward early retirement. How has this affected production and productivity? Similarly, the average age of business executives, managers and administrators, and proprietors and self-employed persons has also risen. Have these trends resulted in the anticipated or feared stagnation?

Aside from its effects on labor force participation and employment rates, aging of the population has been asserted to affect production and productivity in two ways: 1.) Changing aggregate levels of per worker productivity associated with the aging labor force, and 2.) Changing volume and efficiency of labor mobility associated with the aging of the labor force (Spengler, 1978, Chapter 7).

Direct studies of productivity have generally concluded that productivity does not decline with age on the average, although it may be the case that knowledge and experience may sometimes be substituted for physiological or mental components of individual productivity. Where there is rapid increase in technology and new knowledge, the importance of the older worker's experience is diminished, and retraining capacity becomes a key factor in the preservation or enhancement of productivity. According to Habib (1985, p. 486) the existing evidence regarding the retraining capacities of the older workers is sparse and inconclusive.

Comparative international studies of production and productivity have occasionally been carried out or cited to examine the relationship between population aging and productivity. Productivity or trends in productivity of some other country—for example, Japan, Taiwan, Korea—are compared to those of the United States to fortify the hypothesis relating diminishing productivity to population aging. First, there are very high-productivity countries, for example, Sweden and West Germany, with populations even older, than the U.S. population. Second, there is very little meaning to global productivity comparisons. The meaning of measures and indexes of productivity in any given economy and culture is problematic in itself, based generally as they are on economy-specific or culture-specific concepts of amounts or value of output in the respective sectors and branches. Moreover, each country has its specific mix of economic branches and sectors, rendering global comparisons of measures and trends in productivity and, especially, imputing them to differences in age composition of the working force, more difficult and problematic.

There is fairly extensive and consistent evidence of diminishing job mobility with increasing age. To the extent that high mobility levels are in fact associated with high productivity, aging of populations would have a negative effect on productivity. Whatever the logic of the premise linking high mobility with productivity in an economy or in a sector, there does not seem to be much empirical evidence to support it yet. There is, however, some evidence of declining job mobility as the labor force ages (*Business Week*, Oct. 28, 1985), and there is evidence of declining returns to higher education for younger workers (R.B. Freeman, 1976, 1979; Perlman, 1981).

AGING, SAVINGS, AND INVESTMENT

Considerable attention has been paid to the implications of population aging for the volume of savings and investment. In the case of private or household savings, the major relationship considered has been that between the age distribution and savings. In general, when age distribution favors high levels of labor force participation (the case when there is a low dependency rate with relatively large proportions aged 15 to 64 and lower proportions aged 0 to 14 or over 65), the savings potential is believed to be relatively great. Thus, age distribution affects savings most directly through the relative consumption needs of those not in the labor force. It also bears indirectly on saving through its influence on household size and composition, income, and income distribution.

Discussion of relationships between age composition and savings has pointed to diminishing savings or, indeed, to dissavings among the elderly, while at the same time, there are peak savings among the middle-aged still in the labor force. A so-called life-cycle theory of savings implies reduction of aggregate savings as the population ages, but offsetting enhanced saving rising over the working years with diminishing fertility and lower average numbers of children per worker (Clark and Spengler, 1980). The empirical evidence, however, points to continued saving, rather than dissaving, among the elderly. Moreover, reviewing the literature on the effect of alternative ways of financing retirement income upon aggregate savings, Habib (1985, pp. 489–490) concludes that the evidence runs against the claim that pay-as-you go financing of retirement income, as in the American national Social Security system, contributes to or implies a decline in the rate of savings.

THE STRUCTURE OF DEMAND AND CONSUMPTION

Aging of populations generates important changes in the structure of demand for and consumption of goods and services. The most obvious and perhaps most dramatic shifts are those from child- and youth-oriented goods and services, such as educational services and child- and youth-related housing goods and services, to those of elderly and retired-oriented goods and services. The latter include health, impairment, and disability care and services and housing goods and services for the elderly. Shifts in the composition of given types of services, for example, leisure and recreational services, transportation, or entertainment, to address the growing market of elderly consumers and participants have likewise occurred (*Business Week*, Nov. 25, 1985).

A detailed and systematic study of the demographic effects on composition of demand (Musgrove, 1980) finds that the effects of population composition on the composition of demand are small. Rather, the principal factor in the changes in composition of spending has been growth of per capita income, and this has taken place largely independently of the variations or changes in age composition or other characteristics of the population.

Population Aging, Marriage and Nonmarriage, and Household Formation

The very important trend toward formation of single-person and other nonfamily households, however, reflects *both* the rising per capita income and changes in individual life-course and family-life cycles. This trend has accompanied a trend toward increasing numbers of childless-couple households. The latter include both young couples delaying or forgoing childbearing and older couples in empty-nest households, after the departure of their children from the parental home.

Studies by Kobrin (1976), Pampel (1983), Sweet and Bumpass (1984), and others have suggested that the great increase in single-person household formation and maintenance among, say, elderly widows, rests upon their liberation from financial dependence upon their children. The very few studies of the timing of departure of youths or young adults from parental homes suggest the importance of either employment and self-support or sufficient parental support for establishment of separate dwelling arrangements as factors in the early (premarriage) departure from parental homes (Goldscheider and DaVanzo, 1985; LeBourdais and Goldscheider, 1986; Young, 1974, 1975).

The underlying factors in these trends are clearly the changes in age structure, life course, and family cycle accompanying the transition to low levels of mortality and fertility (Kobrin, 1976; Burch, 1980, 1982). As we shall indicate below in more detail, aside from and far beyond the importance of new household patterns for the volume and composition of demand and consumption of goods and services, these trends are fundamental factors in economic and social participation of family and household members within as well as outside the household at each juncture of the life course and the family cycle.

YOUTH AND ELDERLY: SHIFTS IN THE COMPOSITION OF DEPENDENCY

Aging of the population leads, in general, to lower dependency ratios, although the more extremely aged populations (with, say 13 to 14 percent or more aged 65+) have higher dependency ratios than the more moderately aged populations. But very young populations tend to have much higher dependency ratios than old populations. While the overall rate of dependency may decline in some patterns of population aging, within the dependent population there is a shift to a larger share of elderly dependency compared to child dependency (Table 4.2).

In the United States the overall dependency ratio fell dramatically between 1900 and 1940 as birth rated declined, and the youth dependency ratio declined. But in the same period the elderly dependency ratio increased by one-half, from .066 to .100. The next two decades, which witnessed the turnaround in U.S. birth rates and the onset and zenith of the post-World War II baby boom, also brought sharply increasing dependency ratios, both for the youth and elderly components. Since 1960, the sharp drops in birth rates and subsequently in absolute numbers of births in the United States brought declining youth dependency and declining total dependency ratios, while elderly dependency ratios have continued to rise.

The economic significance of this shift is typically viewed as resting on the relative needs of elderly compared to those of children in the society. Habib (1985)

Table 4.2. Dependency Ratios: Total, Youth Dependency, and Elderly Dependency. United States, 1900–1987

YEAR	TOTAL	YOUTH : AGES 0–14	ELDERLY: AGES 65+
1900	.626	.560	.066
1940	.468	.368	.100
1960	.676	.521	.155
1970	.622	.462	.160
1987	.515	.333	.182

Source: 1900–1970: Executive Office of the President, Office of Management and Budget, *Social Indicators, 1973* (Washington, D.C.: U.S. Government Printing Office, 1973), Table 8.8, p. 255. 1987: Population Reference Bureau, *World Population Data Sheet, 1987*, Washington, D.C., 1987

has demonstrated the complexity and, ultimately, the inconclusiveness of this discussion and analysis. He cites findings indicating that public expenditure on the elderly is much higher than expenditures on children, but that, when public and private expenditures on children and on the elderly are both reckoned, those on children exceed resources expended on the elderly. Additional discussion on this issue addresses private consumption expenditures on children at various ages, with varying numbers of siblings or in varying family settings, and so forth. There is also discussion on the meaning and costs of pension adequacy with reference to the needs of retired, compared to those of nonretired, adults (see, also, Crown, 1985, 1987).

Reviewing these findings and considering, also, the issues of welfare equivalence and equivalence scales, Habib (1985) has concluded that there would not seem to be any conceptual basis for arriving at a single relative needs measure that encompasses public and private expenditure. In this sense there is no one simple answer to the question of whether a decline in the proportion of children might offset the impact of a rise in the share of the elderly. Instead, Habib formulates two alternative questions: (1) What is the relationship between the number and age composition of children to real family income? and (2) What is the relationship between a population's age structure and the share of national income required to maintain a given level of public services? To what extent does a decline in number of children or a change in their age composition increase real family income? To what extent does a change in age composition increase the rate of tax required to finance public services? In Habib's view, comparison of increase in real disposable income arising from reduced needs of children to the rise in the tax rate arising from population aging can be indicative of the bearing of population aging on per capita consumption standards (Habib, 1985, p. 483).

There are further complications pointed out by Habib. Discussion of expenditures on the elderly has typically not taken into account the age composition of the elderly themselves; that is, they have not separated the old from the old-old. Expenditures on the old-old tend to be much higher than those on the younger old, and over time the old-old are a rapidly increasing proportion of the total elderly population (see, for example, Rosenwaike, 1985). Nor have these analyses taken sufficient account of consumption and expenditures of time and attention, in addition to money, to the contributions of time and attention to the welfare of children, grandparents, or adults, and intrafamily time inputs and tradeoffs against both private and public money expenditures in the total welfare packages of young children, older children, working adults, or the elderly.

CHANGING LIFE-COURSE PATTERNS
IN THE LOW MORTALITY–LOW FERTILITY REGIME
CONTEXT OF POPULATION AGING

Individual economic activity and behavior have changed and responded to the aging of population and its component factors and elements in certain characteristic directions. Recognition of enhanced longevity and extended personal life span, durations of joint survival of couples, children and parents, and the multi-generational households, duration of survival in retirement, and widowhood, durations of joint survival in empty-nest households, and so forth, have affected labor force, consumption, savings, and investment behavior of individuals, whether in response to new situations that have occurred or in anticipation of them.

Reduction in numbers of births and the span of childbearing and childrearing associated with the fertility reductions that cause aging of the population have, in turn, been related to alternative activities and new life-course trajectories for women. The changing age composition, increased numbers of elderly and reduced numbers of youth and young adults, changing systems of competition for jobs, resources, deference, prestigious social positions, and so forth, have probably attached some scarcity value to the work of young persons. However, the massive entry of women into the labor force has taken up some of that opportunity.

The fundamental change in life-course organization and trajectories of women, and their massive entrance into the labor force and into extra-home social participation generally, and more or less concomitantly the great increase in the volume and proportion of the life years of men spent in reduced employment or outside of employment entirely, are the most important direct economic consequences of declining fertility, increased longevity, and the aging of populations. The same trends engendering the aging of populations, occurring with basic technological and communications trends and improvements, have given rise to changing patterns of life-course organization generally and to changes in life-course economic behavior, participation, and activity in particular.

Beyond the nature of dependency, population trends have other impacts on behavior and social relationships in the life course of individuals. Actual and anticipated longevity bears upon behavior, time-related investments and tradeoffs, interpersonal relationships and sociometric choice regimes, and the partitioning of total life years into years single or married; years at school, in housekeeping or childrearing, at work, or in retirement; or years in one kind of household, residence, community, or in another.

Organization of the individual life course has undergone dramatic changes under the impact of the demographic transformations, of technological changes and shifts in the regime of material production, and of the revolution in knowledge, communication, information, and mutual visibility. Length of schooling has been extended for both males and females, working life is shorter for men but longer for women—and childbearing years are fewer for women—than in the past. The empty-nest years of couples are extended, widowhood is contracting for women as age gaps between brides and grooms decline, household formation or continuation among not-married persons and single parenthood are more frequent or extended in duration. Numbers of siblings, children, and kin are smaller throughout the life course, but joint survival and durations of the relationships are longer (Kobrin, 1976; Burch, 1980, 1982; Fuchs, 1983).

The legitimate and acceptable activity- and relationship-sequences, especially for women, have changed: Increasingly, education, career activity, and extra-household participation are legitimated throughout the life course, and women are allowed to transfer care activities—child care, parent care, and infirm-husband care—to agencies outside the family. There has been, of course, correspondingly increased demand for private and public sector organized care activities and facilities. The great rise of two-earner families has had massive implications both for income and consumption generally and for the structure of within-family economic, social, and power and dependency relationships (Davis, 1984). It has led also to industrialization of housework, replacement of household-produced by market-produced goods and services, and the professionalization of childcare and personal services (Eichler, 1983). These, in turn, have given impetus to entire new sectors of the economy.

What I have referred to earlier as the dependency crunch occurring because of enhanced joint survival of family members and close kin occurred in fairly close chronological proximity to the creeping redundance of employment through large parts of the adult males' life courses. These two problems have sought—and in the view of many, have found—some resolution in the political intervention and takeover of what have traditionally been considered liberal or free market economies in order to assure acceptable allocation of employment and income, and to support and sustain demand and consumption of the economies' output. Such intervention and direction of income maintenance schemes are almost surely the most important indirect economic consequence of the aging of population.

Larger-scale organizations and employers—governments, trade union federations, large firms and employers—have introduced new organizational features, production processes, training services, health services, income maintenance schemes, technological changes, and reorganization of production and marketing processes in response to population aging. For the most part these measures reflect the political intervention, as noted above, in the labor market, production, and income and resource allocation, by either legislation or collective bargaining. These are likely to include both legitimized alternatives to employment such as extended schooling, military or other national service, and subsidized motherhood as well as more extensive work-sharing and subsidized employment measures and schemes in the future.

THE EMPLOYMENT CRISIS AND THE COLLAPSE OF WORK

Aside from issues of war and peace and nuclear holocaust, the most important and dramatic social, economic, and political issues and developments facing the societies with aging populations are those associated with the reduction of employment in the life span while the life span itself is extended and the life years devoted to parenting are compressed and diminished as well. This contraction of employment, variously discussed under the more dramatic rubrics—the employment crisis, the collapse of work, and the like—is typically imputed to increased productivity due to dramatic technological advance or to increasingly widespread adoption of technological innovations, to the rise of the multinational economy and the failure of national economic policies and measures to protect national markets and employment, or the competition of the third world labor markets with their disciplined and low-paid work forces (for comparative perspectives, see Bruno and Sachs, 1984).

It seems clear that a necessary, if not sufficient, cause of the redundance of employment is embedded also in the changing patterns of life spans, family life cycles, and the compression and contraction of parenting and child dependency. Addressing the problems of diminishing employment demand and finding acceptable resolution of the two central problems it generates—allocation of income, material and social rewards, and status, and use of time—require analysis and understanding of population aging and its concomitant individual life-course and family life-cycle correlates.

Useful consideration and attention to these problems is possible only to the extent that skeptical and critical attitudes to the traditional work values themselves are adopted or, at least tolerated or entertained. The association of gainful employment with Virtue, and of its absence or avoidance with Evil, is distinctly counterproductive for any attempt to address the real problems of changing relationships between production and distribution of goods and services, on the one hand, and employment for pay or profit in the organized labor force, on the other hand. However, recognition of the depth with which such values are held throughout virtually all strata in Western societies and indeed their historical centrality in economic and social organization in the modern era is very important for analysis of the efforts to address problems of employment and unemployment and for an understanding of their shortcomings and failures.

The Struggle for Employment

The increasing redundance and scarcity of employment and the absence of alternative legitimate access to income and other social rewards associated with employment and occupations have combined to continue, and in some sense to render even more dramatic, the historical struggle for access to and control of employment. Radical analysts throughout modern history have always cast this struggle as one initiated and promoted by the dominant political and economic groups. The capitalists and bourgeoisie are said to be pitted against the workers in capitalist societies (more generally, the rulers and oppressors against the ruled and oppressed) in order to enjoy the benefits of the reserve army of unemployed, keep the wages of the employed at minimum levels, and appropriate and accumulate the product of the labor of the propertyless and powerless.

The struggle for employment has in fact taken place independently of property rights and the economic and political power of employers and workers. The maintenance of high levels of production and output with decreasing manpower needs and marginalization of jobs and employees is a fact in industries and organizational settings of all types. This has been true as well in countries in which workers and their organizations and political parties have been able to gain leverage and power or even monopolize political power, for example, under Social Democratic party governments in Western Europe (Myles, 1987). For the most part, the expression of the leverage and power of workers has been in the form of sharing control over remaining employment with employers rather than in retaining or creating new employment opportunity.

The weapons in the struggle for employment have increasingly been weapons of privileged access and exclusion; alongside outright discrimination have been the weapons of credentialism and age grading. Many axes of discrimination are familiar, and these may be applied both grossly and in more genteel forms: Sex, marital status, racial, and ethnic characteristics are familiar ascriptive bases for either privileged access to jobs or for exclusion from jobs and remain such however discredited these may be in public rhetoric. Kinship and cronyism are probably not less familiar, although these have been subject to much less attack and are for the most part acceptable or, at least, not publicly discredited, in many of the less elaborately organized economic sectors. Other factors could include handicaps and disabilities, membership in political or other organizations, residential origins and current residential characteristics, and features of personal histories.

Credentialism is the principle of basing access to, or exclusion from, employment and specific jobs on some recognized prior educational attainment, training process, or prior employment experience other than in the same or similar job. High school diplomas and college degrees are familiar examples of credentials invoked or demanded. All manner of licensing, state or professional grading, and the like are also examples of credentialism. Obviously there have always been great opportunities for somewhat less gross discrimination in access to employment by the indirect means of discrimination in access to the credentials demanded for employment.

These weapons in the struggle for employment are extensively identified and discussed in a massive literature on equality and inequality, discrimination and social opportunity, and sex, race, and ethnic relations and inequalities. Our own concern in this volume will be primarily with age grading, age discrimination, and ageism as weapons in the struggle for employment, and with age grading in social interaction and organization generally.

Age Grading in Employment

Employers, politicians, and trade unions have made common cause in favoring young adult and early-middle-aged men, say aged 30 to 55, for employment and in excluding or discriminating against younger or older persons. A variety of reasons and justifications are invoked, beginning with the needs of men at these ages for employment and the concentration of family dependency, obligations, and responsibilities upon men at these ages through the imputations of job stability, productivity, or efficiency of men at these ages. The merit of these reasons and justifications is not at issue at this point but, rather, only some of the consequences of this process and the success of this weapon in the struggle for employment.

Table 4.3. Male Labor Force Participation Rates by Age: United States, 1920, 1950, and 1986

AGE	1920	1950	1986
Total	85.9	82.4	76.3
14–19	55.9	47.5	n.a.
16–19			56.4
20–24	90.7	86.9	85.8
25–34	96.2	94.4	94.6
35–44	96.6	96.5	94.8
45–54	94.5	94.6	91.0
55–64	87.4	85.1	67.3
65+	57.1	45.0	16.0

Sources: 1920, 1950: G. Bancroft, "Trends in Labor Force," in W. Haber et al., eds., *Manpower in the United States: Problems and Policies* (New York: Harper &. Bros., 1954). 1986: U.S. Bureau of the Census, *Statistical Abstract of the United States, 1988,* 108th ed. (Washington, D.C.: Government Printing Office, 1987), Table 608, p. 366

A first and perhaps most obvious consequence of this process is the curve of labor force participation rates of men by age, and the recent changes in this curve. Table 4.3 shows labor force participation rates of men by age in 1920, 1950, and 1986. Peak rates in all periods are, of course, at ages 30 to 55, but the rates of labor force participation at younger ages and, especially, at older ages are dramatically lower in 1986. In 1986, labor force participation rates for 14- and 15-year olds are no longer reported, reflecting the virtual complete demise of full-time or regular (as distinct from casual or sporadic) employment at these ages and the near universal extension of compulsory school attendance to these ages.

We conventionally account for the decline in labor force participation among adolescent and young adult men by reference to increasing school attendance: Completion of secondary school and studies in postsecondary and higher education are very much more frequent currently than they were in even the recent past. We generally view the extension of schooling, education, and training as a great social and cultural achievement. But, as we shall indicate below, we must also view extended schooling as a mechanism for excluding young persons from employment, or delaying their entrance to employment, and for legitimating their nonemployment and continued dependency upon parental and family support or, often, on public support. This has been possible only because of diminished fertility, smaller sibships, and generally more circumscribed intrafamily dependency. In short, the extension of schooling has been a powerful age-based weapon in the struggle for employment. A wide variety of behavior, attributes, and social relationships and position of the young persons are related to their exclusion from employment or relegation to less desirable employment.

Trends in retirement are the conventional explanation of the decline in labor force participation among middle-aged and elderly men. The income maintenance measures and the retirement itself are also hailed as significant social achievements offering change and relief from the lifetimes of labor, drudgery, and routine. They offer dignity and economic independence despite diminished health and capacities, also rendered possible by declining fertility and shorter parenting and child-dependency in the life course. These, too, must be understood as a mechanism for excluding middle-aged and elderly persons from employment, and for legitimating their nonemployment and dependency, for the most part on public transfer and income maintenance arrangements. Even more than schooling for young persons, it is clear that the history of the institution of retirement for older persons is the history of an important age-based weapon in the struggle for employment (Graebner, 1980). Much of the position, status, behavior, and social relationships and participation of the middle-aged and elderly follows from their exclusion from employment or relegation to the least desirable employment.

Institutionalizing, Legitimating, and Financing Nonemployment

A central social and economic imperative for societies with aging populations has been the institutionalizing, legitimating, and financing of nonemployment. So far this has been addressed primarily to adolescents and young adults, and to middle-aged and elderly persons, and around continuation of schooling or retirement from paid employment. Occasionally, however, there are initiatives to promote or to revive more extended, intensive, or serious parenting and very occasionally some attempts to endow other care giving with new or additional legitimacy. These directions have been consistent with the long-standing patterns of sex- and age-grading of exclusion from employment.

However, as it appears increasingly to analysts of the employment crisis and the collapse of work, these directions either do not suffice to resolve the problems of redundance of employment or they are unsatisfactory, and the discrimination that they entail is no longer acceptable, or both. Accordingly there is a new search for schemes for promoting, organizing, fortifying, or legitimating nonemployment, or leisure, as economists often connote it, including schemes that are much less obviously age-graded.

Some of these schemes include more flexible schooling and retirement arrangements, that is, additional possibilities for delay of entrance into paid employment or for hastening withdrawal from paid employment with provision of some income independent both of current employment and of claims upon close kin. Others consist of a variety of mid-career temporary withdrawals from employment for shorter or longer periods for a wide range of purposes—from schooling and training to parenting or other family care activity, and from rest and recreation to participation and incumbency in community organization roles and positions. Such schemes do in fact address the major problems of redundance of employment in that they would provide (1) legitimate extra-employment entitlements to income and (2) organize and legitimate nonemployment time and activity. Opposition to such schemes generally rests upon the traditional connection of income entitlements to employment, the persistence of the view of gainful employment as virtuous and nonemployment, or idleness, as evil, and the failure to understand the nature of employment crises.

There is another type of shortcoming to the schemes advanced to legitimate and finance nonemployment. Unfortunately they do not typically address or
correct the pattern of age-graded exclusion from employment already in place in
most Western societies: the exclusion of the young and of the middle-aged and
elderly from employment, or their relegation to the least satisfactory or least
rewarding employment, and the personal and social costs of this pattern on the
measurement and analysis of trends in joblessness (see Hirschman, 1988). We
return to this issue in Chapter 7.

5

PUBLIC AND SOCIAL SERVICES FOR THE AGING POPULATION

INTRODUCTION

Public and social services have grown—or as some would have it, exploded—in Western countries in the twentieth century, especially in the second half, after World War II. This growth has taken place notwithstanding the unrelenting rhetorical, ideological, economic, and political attack on such services as unjustified public expenditures and a menace to individual freedom, family solidarity, and responsibility. In this chapter we shall view as "public services" those organized and provided by governmental or private not-for-profit organizations. Following Beattie (1978), we shall view "social services" in this chapter as those services that reflect organized societal approaches and use of knowledge, skills, or resources for amelioration of deprivations or conditions considered as unacceptable at any historical point in time.

Conventional analysis of implications of population aging for social and public services focuses first and foremost upon the health care and support service needs of the growing elderly population. We examine the persons and agencies providing such services and the ways in which they are organized, financed, and delivered. We study the allocation of the burdens and costs of such care to various groups and individuals other than the elderly themselves. But in addition, other types of services to the elderly, for example, housing, employment, recreational services, will be considered; shifts in the scope and levels of services to the nonelderly—especially educational services—are considered as well, whether in relationship to the former or independently.

In this chapter we follow these conventions at least to the extent of the changing balance among health care and educational services associated with population aging. We also examine briefly the need for services in the areas of housing and living environments, recreation, family service, and gerontological service, as well as legal, licensing, regulatory, and police services associated with relative growth of the numbers and proportions of the elderly and younger persons in the population.

We also continue the theme of population aging as the outcome of profound demographic and social changes bearing not only on the numbers of old and of young in the population, but also on the life course, family structure, and dependency and obligations throughout the various stages of the family cycle, and on the social, economic, and political organizational responses and arrangements addressing them. We review some of the discussion of the shift from family- and household-provided services to market- or public-sector services. Also we try to direct attention to the needs for what have been called preventive and developmental social services, as distinct from the more familiar remedial social services, as they evolve in a social order characterized by changing kinship constellations and by diminishing time and commitment of males in employment and diminishing time and commitment of females in childrearing in the aging population.

Target Populations

Public and social programs and services always address needs, preferences, demands, or entitlements of persons identified either implicitly or explicitly in some population or population group. These are denoted variously as consumer, client, beneficiary, or eligible or entitled populations in the social welfare policy and planning literature (see, for example, Lauffer, 1978; Rein, 1977; Offe, 1984; Gilbert and Specht, 1974); as populations at risk in the epidemiological and health services literature (for example, Susser, 1973; Lilienfeld and Lilienfeld, 1980); or as vulnerable age, school age, working age, military service age, or retirement age populations or as home-buying age or car-buying age populations in the literature dealing with socialization and education, employment, or marketing fields respectively (for example, Pressat, 1972; Kleinberger, 1969; Jaffe and Stewart, 1951; Inbar, 1976). We shall call them simply target populations. Thus programs and services address the needs, preferences, demands, or entitlements of the population as a whole or else of some particular subpopulation or target population.

Target populations may be determined by legislation, decision of elites or bureaucratic hierarchy controlling service agencies, market elements and constellations, or other factors and processes. At any moment in time a target population, as the population generally, has a given size, sex and age composition, spatial distribution, and other characteristics, attributes, and internal relationships; these bear on the nature of needs, resources available to address needs, and the demand for services. Like population generally, target populations grow and change over time in sex and age composition, spatial distribution, and in composition by a variety of other characteristics.

Life-Course and Family-Cycle Contingencies

One concept of the public and social services has them providing services that by their nature cannot be effectively provided on a private market basis except to a small part of the population, for example, educational services, physical living environment services, licensing, regulatory, and police services. A second concept has public and social services providing services to the part of the population which cannot, or would not, purchase them in the private market. However, the need for services in the first place, and the ability or inability to purchase them privately, are very often closely connected to life-cycle stages, or in the terminology of Oppenheimer (1982), life-cycle "squeezes." Economic life-cycle squeezes occur when there is some imbalance between

(1) the family's (or individual's) life-style aspirations;
(2) the cost of these aspirations; and
(3) the income currently available to achieve the aspirations, given their costs.

Economic life-cycle squeezes, according to Oppenheimer (1982, p. 47), may produce behavioral responses such as marriage and/or birth postponement, reduced fertility, wives' going to work, and so on. They may also herald situations of inability to buy and pay for services on the private market and the turn to public services to address certain needs. Economic life-cycle squeezes or other life-cycle squeezes (for example, extended dependency of children, accession of parents or relatives to a household, own or relative's widowhood or marriage breakup, employment or termination of employment, separation from kin) can themselves generate the need for services in the first place (Hareven, 1982; Walker, 1982). Not only do changes in the numbers of the population in each age group generate changing volume and composition of needs and demand for services, but the changing timing and nature of life-course events and squeezes also generate new or changing needs for services or changing resources for private addressing of such needs.

THE IMPACT OF CHANGING AGE COMPOSITION

Schooling and Educational Services in Aging Populations

Projections of the needs and demands for educational services on the basis of present age-specific rates of school-enrollment are probably misguided and misleading. The declining numbers of children and, increasingly, of secondary and postsecondary-school-aged young persons would, on the face of it, imply sharply declining demand for educational services. In fact, at the elementary school level there have been serious declines and teacher employment dislocation, budget cutting, school closures, and the like. At the secondary and postsecondary levels the declines have not yet materialized. This has been partly due to changing enrollment and continuation rates for young persons and, also, to expansion of continuing education schemes for adults and elderly adults.

School enrollment at the secondary and postsecondary levels is sensitive to employment opportunities as well as to actual and perceived returns to further studies, training, or credentials. Manski and Wise (1983) have shown that virtually all high school graduates in 1972 could have been admitted to some college of average or better quality. Thus the fact that almost half did not attend postsecondary school was a matter of individual choice.

Enrollment trends of the late 1970s and the 1980s suggest that (1) the educational institutions themselves, through their curricula, opportunities, and admissions packages, (2) the weak and unattractive employment situation and prospects for young persons, and (3) the possibility and legitimacy of being supported by parents or by public sources of funds, may converge to encourage higher rates of continuation and enrollment in postsecondary education and training. Moreover, the explosion of programs and schemes for enrollment of retired persons in part-time and full-time higher education as well the great expansion of less formal continuing education programs have shown that educators are alert to opportunities for redesigning the missions, messages, and clientele of the education industry, and for obtaining the necessary private and public financial support for them, in the face of contraction of their traditional child and youth client populations.

Measuring Health and Projecting Health Care Needs

There is a characteristic age-related curve of morbidity and mortality, and hence age-related needs for care. Clearly changing composition of the population implies changing composition of health care needs. In particular, the growth of the aged population and especially of the old-old among them has skyrocketed demand for medical care, nursing and long-term care, and various impairment- and disability-connected services. The elderly have many more visits to physicians, greater drug use, more frequent hospital admissions, and longer stays in hospitals than the rest of the population (Table 5.1). Moreover, there now seem to be improving prospects for enhanced longevity and "rectangularization" of the survival curve. An important question is whether or not rectangularization of survival will be accompanied by parallel rectangularization of health or whether, conversely, the gain in life years implied by rectangularization of survival will imply increments of life years of impairment, disability, and astronomic rises in health care needs. (Davies, 1984; Wilkins and Adams, 1983, 1983a, 1983b, especially Tables 1.1 and 4.1 and Figure 4.3).

Table 5.1. Short-Stay Hospital Usage per 1,000 Population, by Sex and Age, United States 1985

AGE	PATIENTS DISCHARGED			DAYS OF CARE			AVERAGE STAY (DAYS)			BEDS OCCUPIED*
	Total	Males	Females	Total	Males	Females	Total	Males	Females	
Total	148	124	171	959	849	1053	6.5	6.9	6.2	261
<1	210	234	185	1391	1477	1300	6.6	6.3	7.0	381
1–4	64	74	54	226	246	205	3.5	3.3	3.8	62
5–14	37	41	34	151	174	127	4.1	4.3	3.8	41
15–24	117	60	173	488	344	631	4.2	5.7	3.7	134
25–34	141	75	205	664	468	855	4.7	6.3	4.2	182
35–44	115	96	133	667	591	738	5.8	6.2	5.5	183
45–64	170	176	163	1193	1220	1168	7.0	6.9	7.1	327
65–74	295	320	275	2418	2577	2293	8.2	8.1	8.3	662
75+	277	528	449	4389	4672	4236	9.2	8.8	9.4	1203

*Average Daily Number of Beds Occupied per 100,000 civilian population
Source: U.S. Bureau of the Census, *Statistical Abstract of the United States, 1988* (Washington, D.C.: Government Printing Office, 1987), Table 154, p. 97.

Whereas in the past the improvements in mortality led to increased life years at childhood, youth, and early adult ages and only to a lesser extent to increased life years in middle and old age, there is some anticipation now that future improvements in mortality will result in rectangularization of the curve of survival probability by age and increase of the volume of life years in middle and old age. In North America and in Western Europe there have already been declines in mortality of males at advanced ages indicative of such a trend. The critical question concerns the kinds of life years that will be added—whether years of health and effective personal and social functioning, creative work or leisure and social participation, or years of illness and infirmity and extended dependency. In other words, will the rectangularization of the survival curve be accompanied by a corresponding rectangularization of the health curve as well? The research, discussion, and even the speculation on this issue are, for the time being, bogged down by problems of convincing and acceptable empirical representation and measurement of the health curve (Davies, 1984).

The views about the likelihood of rectangularization of middle- and old-age morbidity are distinctly mixed (see, for example, Fries, 1983, whose view is affirmative, compared to Verbrugge, 1984, whose view is negative on this point). But, as Fuchs (1984, pp. 151–54) points out, changing age composition and aging of the population, to the extent that there is an element of increasing longevity associated with it, does not inevitably imply increasing utilization of health services: The highest use of health services is in the year prior to mortality, followed by the year before that one. As longevity increases, the peak-utilization ages are pushed ahead, with rates of utilization at other ages slightly lowered. On the other hand, there have been studies showing increased morbidity among middle-aged and elderly persons since the late 1950s simultaneously with, and despite, the decline in mortality from the same diseases, that is, the pattern of "longer life but worsening health" (Verbrugge, 1984).

Another correlate of changing population age composition and declining fertility has been declines in maternity care services, though rise in numbers of abortions and abortion-connected demand for care. Infant mortality has declined to an all time low in the industrialized countries not only because of improvements in medical knowledge, technology, and access but, apparently, because a substantially greater proportion of children born are *wanted* children (cf. Fuchs, 1974), enjoying better prenatal and postnatal care. Presumably this improvement in care carries over into early childhood as well. Improved levels of educational attainment may be associated with improved health and less utilization of services. On the other hand, expansion of insurance schemes and coverage seems to be associated with increased utilization of services (Fuchs, 1984, pp. 149–50; 1974). Younger persons should enjoy better health, perhaps need less—or, less expensive or less complex—health care than in the past because of these considerations.

A policy and trend toward deinstitutionalization of the mentally ill has been adopted and in place for some two decades, with its results a matter of considerable debate (see *Milbank Memorial Fund Quarterly*, Fall 1979). A substantial part of the future demand for health care will depend upon public policy and measures concerning institutionalization in general and institutionalization of the mentally ill in particular. On the other hand, we can probably depend upon the medical profession and the health care industry to sell itself effectively regardless of health needs (see Fuchs, 1974 and 1983, on the disconnection between health and health care. See also Verbrugge, 1984).

Housing

Despite the traditional view that one's home is his privately acquired castle, a considerable proportion of private residential housing in the United States, and much more in many other countries, is at least partially subsidized or else planned and constructed as part of public housing or planning schemes. Virtually all urban housing is subject to urban planning or zoning and to planning, regulation, and control of much of the living environment: roads, lighting, sanitation facilities, parks, and so forth. Housing needs are determined by characteristics of newly formed households and by those of households changing, improving, expanding, upgrading, or in many instances downgrading, their actual physical residential arrangements.

An obvious housing need under conditions of population aging is for housing for increasing numbers of elderly persons, couples, and households in the population. Perhaps the greatest growth in households in the past two decades has been among widows and elderly couples. At the same time, as income has increased while marriage and fertility have been delayed, the number of single never-married individuals establishing their own households, separate from their parents, has grown dramatically in recent years.

Finally, trends toward increased divorce rates have been accompanied by increased household formation on the part of divorced men and women, generally single-person households among the men, but with both single-person and single-parent-with-children households among the divorced women. These household types have been associated with demand for characteristic types of housing and housing environments, generally different in at least some respects from the housing used by couple-and-children families. Not only have the numbers of such persons (for example, widows, single parents) increased dramatically, but the extent to which they form separate households rather than live with families or others, has also risen sharply. Thus the growth in senior citizens' and singles' housing has exceeded the growth in the numbers of elderly or single adults.

Other Services

Use of recreational services, family service, legal service, police protection, and, of course, gerontological services varies sharply by age, as do the types of services used. A first approximation of the changes and adjustments in the service packages entailed by aging of populations is obtained by projection. In many instances, the age-specific rates of utilization are changing under aging of populations because the changing family settings, life-cycle squeeze factors, employment, or dependency patterns effect certain changes in service needs.

A large part of social services comprise those addressing problems or deprivations associated with insufficient income or with illness, impairment, or disability. Yet there are many individual and community problems and deprivations not originating in income or health deficiencies but, rather, in unsatisfactory employment, environmental or social stress, strangeness or alienation, or unmet individual or group needs. The large number of nonwork activities that have recently proliferated, such as do-it-yourself activities, volunteer activities, continuing education, may be said to represent counterpart outlets that reflect the needs of their participants.

For the most part, these activities have developed through traditional market mechanisms and address the concerns or interests only of those able to pay and in response to relatively narrowly conceived initiatives. An increasing range of developmental-approach services, such as self-help and community education programs, advocacy services, peer-group support activities, and opportunity programs of various sorts, have as their objective not only the remedial and preventive concerns for individual and family welfare but community-building, integration, and solidarity themes as well. That their major expansion is probably of most immediate interest and benefit to the elderly reflects perhaps the more obvious demand for integrative programs and activities—as distinct from the large array of activities, situations, and predicaments that have the effect of segregating the elderly from the community at large. But the needs, far from being restricted to the elderly in society, are probably both more acute and more profound among the nonelderly in aging populations.

Population Aging and Social Services in the Developed Countries

An outstanding example of a comparative analysis of the implications of population aging for social services and expenditure in the developed countries is a comparative study carried out by the International Monetary Fund (IMF) of trends and projections in seven major industrial countries: the United States, Canada, the United Kingdom, West Germany, France, Italy, and Japan (Heller et al., 1985). The study examines social expenditure in the seven countries in relation to general economic activity and output. For each country social expenditures for 1980 are taken as baseline and expenditures for the years 2000, 2010, and 2025 are projected under three alternative economic and demographic scenarios.

Table 5.2. Social Expenditure under Alternative Economic and Demographic Scenarios, 1980–2025 (As a percentage of GDP)

		BASELINE ECONOMIC AND DEMOGRAPHIC SCENARIO			BASELINE ECONOMIC AND "GREATER AGING" SCENARIO			PESSIMISTIC ECONOMIC AND "GREATER AGING" SCENARIO		
	1980	*2000*	*2010*	*2025*	*2000*	*2010*	*2025*	*2000*	*2010*	*2025*
Canada										
Medical care	5.55	5.93	6.45	8.44	5.84	6.33	8.39	5.99	6.50	8.63
Pensions	3.50	3.10	3.10	4.30	3.10	3.20	4.50	3.40	3.60	5.30
Education	7.47	5.56	5.32	5.60	5.30	4.84	4.84	5.48	5.00	5.00
Subtotal	*16.52*	*14.59*	*14.87*	*18.34*	*14.24*	*14.37*	*17.73*	*14.87*	*15.10*	*18.93*
Unemployment	1.33	1.06	1.06	1.06	1.06	1.06	1.06	1.64	1.64	1.64
Family benefits	0.62	0.37	0.30	0.26	0.38	0.30	0.26	0.39	0.31	0.27
Other	1.82	1.33	1.17	1.03	1.36	1.22	1.12	1.40	1.26	1.16
Total	**20.29**	**17.35**	**17.40**	**20.69**	**17.03**	**16.95**	**20.18**	**18.30**	**18.31**	**22.00**
France										
Medical care	6.70	7.70	8.25	9.38	7.44	8.10	10.21	7.60	8.40	10.70
Pensions	10.00	11.00	11.50	13.00	10.80	12.20	15.60	11.00	12.60	16.30
Education	4.90	4.44	4.36	4.39	4.21	3.95	3.76	4.30	4.10	3.94
Subtotal	*21.60*	*23.14*	*24.11*	*26.77*	*22.45*	*24.25*	*29.56*	*22.90*	*25.10*	*30.94*
Unemployment	1.70	1.70	1.10	0.80	1.65	1.10	0.80	2.48	2.28	2.35
Family benefits	3.80	3.50	3.30	3.30	3.10	2.90	3.00	3.20	3.06	3.18
Other	3.90	4.10	4.10	4.20	3.90	4.00	4.40	4.03	4.22	4.66
Total	**31.00**	**32.44**	**32.61**	**35.07**	**31.10**	**32.25**	**37.76**	**32.61**	**34.66**	**41.13**
Germany, Fed. Rep. of										
Medical care	6.10	7.10	8.10	9.70	7.03	8.02	9.90	7.10	8.10	10.00
Pensions	13.30	17.10	18.60	20.50	17.10	18.80	21.20	17.10	18.80	21.10
Education	4.38	3.75	3.50	3.57	3.44	3.00	2.98	3.47	3.03	3.01
Subtotal	*23.78*	*27.95*	*30.20*	*33.77*	*27.57*	*29.82*	*34.08*	*27.67*	*29.93*	*34.11*
Unemployment	1.50	0.80	0.80	0.80	0.80	0.80	0.80	1.10	1.10	1.10
Family benefits	1.20	1.00	0.90	0.80	0.90	0.80	0.70	0.90	0.80	0.80
Other	4.60	3.40	3.40	3.40	3.40	3.40	3.40	3.40	3.40	3.40
Total	**31.08**	**33.15**	**35.30**	**38.77**	**32.67**	**34.82**	**38.98**	**33.07**	**35.23**	**39.41**

Table 5.2. Social Expenditure under Alternative Economic and Demographic Scenarios, 1980–2025 (As a percentage of GDP) *(cont.)*

	1980	BASELINE ECONOMIC AND DEMOGRAPHIC SCENARIO			BASELINE ECONOMIC AND "GREATER AGING" SCENARIO			PESSIMISTIC ECONOMIC AND "GREATER AGING" SCENARIO		
	1980	2000	2010	2025	2000	2010	2025	2000	2010	2025
Italy										
Medical care	5.96	6.47	7.01	7.76	6.48	7.09	8.14	6.54	7.13	8.16
Pensions	12.10	14.60	16.70	20.70	14.90	17.60	23.00	15.10	17.70	23.10
Education	4.00	3.20	3.10	3.00	2.97	2.88	2.59	3.00	2.90	2.60
Subtotal	*22.06*	*24.27*	*26.81*	*31.46*	*24.35*	*27.57*	*33.73*	*24.64*	*27.73*	*33.86*
Unemployment	0.50	0.90	0.90	0.70	0.90	0.90	0.80	1.00	0.97	0.83
Family benefits	—	—	—	—	—	—	—	—	—	—
Other	2.50	2.50	2.50	2.50	2.50	2.50	2.50	2.50	2.50	2.50
Total	**25.06**	**27.67**	**30.21**	**34.66**	**27.75**	**30.97**	**37.03**	**28.14**	**31.20**	**37.19**
Japan										
Medical care	4.80	6.05	7.08	8.06	6.21	7.24	8.35	6.27	7.31	8.43
Pensions	4.20	9.61	12.89	13.40	10.38	14.28	15.30	10.49	14.40	15.50
Education	5.10	4.10	4.60	4.40	3.97	4.26	3.77	4.00	4.30	3.80
Subtotal	*14.10*	*19.76*	*24.56*	*25.86*	*20.56*	*25.78*	*27.42*	*20.76*	*26.00*	*27.73*
Unemployment	0.30	0.30	0.30	0.30	0.30	0.30	0.30	0.45	0.45	0.45
Family benefits	—	—	—	—	—	—	—	—	—	—
Other	1.00	1.00	1.00	1.00	1.00	1.00	1.00	1.00	1.00	1.00
Total	**15.40**	**21.06**	**25.86**	**27.16**	**21.86**	**27.08**	**28.72**	**22.21**	**27.45**	**29.18**
United Kingdom										
Medical care	5.80	6.59	6.84	8.35	6.59	7.04	8.85	6.59	7.04	8.85
Pensions	5.80	6.65	7.22	8.36	6.85	7.66	9.34	6.85	7.66	9.34
Education	5.60	4.60	4.60	4.50	4.50	4.20	4.10	4.50	4.20	4.10
Subtotal	*17.20*	*17.84*	*18.66*	*21.22*	*17.93*	*18.90*	*22.29*	*17.93*	*18.90*	*22.29*
Unemployment	0.50	0.40	0.40	0.40	0.40	0.40	0.50	0.40	0.40	0.50
Family benefits	1.30	1.10	1.10	1.10	1.30	1.30	1.20	1.30	1.30	1.20
Other	3.90	3.60	3.80	3.80	3.60	3.90	4.00	3.60	3.90	4.00
Total	**22.90**	**22.94**	**23.96**	**26.52**	**23.23**	**24.50**	**27.99**	**23.23**	**24.50**	**27.99**
United States										
Medical care	4.50	5.39	5.84	7.76	5.54	6.24	8.75	5.57	6.27	8.80
Pensions	6.30	5.80	5.70	6.90	6.00	6.10	7.90	6.40	6.60	8.50
Education	4.87	3.95	3.73	3.58	3.77	3.36	2.95	3.80	3.38	2.97
Subtotal	*15.67*	*15.14*	*15.27*	*18.24*	*15.31*	*15.70*	*19.60*	*15.77*	*16.25*	*20.27*
Unemployment	0.60	0.40	0.40	0.40	0.40	0.40	0.40	0.50	0.40	0.40
Family benefits	—	—	—	—	—	—	—	—	—	—
Other	1.40	0.90	0.90	0.80	0.90	0.80	0.70	1.00	1.00	0.90
Total	**17.67**	**16.44**	**16.57**	**19.44**	**16.61**	**16.90**	**20.70**	**17.27**	**17.65**	**21.57**

Source : P.S. Heller, et al., *Aging and Social Expenditures in the Major Industrial Countries, 1980-2025.* (Washington, D.C.: International Monetary Fund, 1985), Table 14.

1. *Baseline (1980) economic and demographic scenario:* This scenario projects continuation of levels of economic activity, rate of growth in productivity, and employment levels, and a slight increase in levels of fertility and in life expectancy, observed in and around 1980.

2. *Baseline economic and "greater aging" scenario:* This scenario projects continuation of 1980 economic activity, continuation of the low fertility levels observed in 1980, and slightly greater increase in life expectancy.

3. *Pessimistic economic and "greater aging" scenario:* This scenario projects slightly lower rates of growth in productivity and higher unemployment, along with the continued low fertility and increased life expectancy.

There will be a substantial increase over the next forty years in the proportion of the elderly, and a decrease in the proportion of the young, in the populations of all seven countries studied. In Germany, Italy, and the United Kingdom these have already begun and will be accentuated over the coming decades. Because the North American baby boom extended to the mid-1960s these changes will occur in the United States and Canada only after the year 2010. In Japan the changes will come especially quickly and dramatically.

The relationship of social expenditures to economic activity and output is formulated and calculated as the percentage of each country's gross domestic product (GDP) allocated to such expenditures. The IMF study's summary of percentages of GDP allocated to social expenditures in six major categories, and projections for the years 2000, 2010, and 2025 are shown in Table 5.2. The major social expenditure categories are

1. Medical care
2. Pensions
3. Education
4. Unemployment Compensation
5. Family Benefits
6. Other, which includes the various social services

Direct expenditures on nousing were not included because of difficulties in measuring and comparing the off-budget credit and tax subsidies accorded to housing sectors in the various countries.

Under the projected patterns of population aging, that is, under the changing age composition of the populations projected through the year 2025, maintaining the 1980 per capita real levels of social benefits for the various age groups in the respective populations would lead to very significantly greater social expenditures in all the countries. These range from a 70 percent increase in Canada to a 361 percent increase in Japan. But, the IMF team points out, when viewed relative to the growth in GDP that would be implied by projections of the labor force and historically reasonable productivity assumptions, these increased expenditures appear financially manageable. In the United States, as in Canada, France, and the United Kingdom, the ratio of social expenditure to GDP would actually decrease.

But real benefits are not likely to remain at 1980 levels. Rather, both real pension levels and medical expenditures have risen, and can be expected to continue to rise, in relation to aggregate productivity and real wage rates in each country. Accordingly, the projections incorporate assumptions about the relationship between the growth in real benefit levels and productivity in the economy.

Projections to the year 2025 indicate a significant *increase* in the ratio of govern-ment social expenditure to GDP in most of the countries, except Canada. These will be especially marked in Japan, in Germany, and Italy (Table 5.2).

There are differences among the seven countries in the *timing* of the aging trends that give rise to the pressures toward increased social expenditures. In the North American countries the ratios will actually *decrease* until 2010 and rise only thereafter, substantially for the United States, but only very mildly for Canada. For the United Kingdom and France there are mild increases through the year 2010, and sharper increases thereafter. For Japan, Germany, and Italy dramatic increases are indicated even prior to the end of the century.

There are differences in the benchmark (1980) components of social expen-ditures in the respective countries. And there are some differences in the compo-nents of the changes projected through the year 2025. In all seven countries there are dramatic increases projected in the ratio of government expenditures on medical care to GDP. In all countries except France, there are projected *declines* in the ratio for education. For the four countries with government family benefit expenditures in 1980 (Canada, France, Germany, and the United Kingdom), some decline is projected in these ratios. Finally, the countries differ substantially in the timing and the steepness of the increases in the ratios to GDP of expenditures on pensions. These differences are related primarily to the differences in timing and pace of the aging of their populations.

LIFE COURSE AND FAMILY CYCLE:
THE CHANGING CALCULUS OF CARE

Individuals and families need, in addition to shelter and basic material needs and the income to assure these, a mix of care and services. Care and services are needed by those unable to care fully for themselves *and* for those entitled to care and services by virtue of their involvement in, or time commitment to, other activities. Traditionally women have provided such care and services in the household to husbands and dependents alike. Women have routinely mobilized the aid of daughters old enough to participate. Only rarely have they been helped signifi-cantly by husbands and sons, whose time and attention have been devoted to the more important concerns of production and gainful employment, sometimes ceremonial and political activity, or plain leisure.

As we have repeatedly noted, a fundamental facet of the aging of popula-tions caused by the low mortality and low fertility demographic regime is the change in organization of individual life course and family cycle characterized now by longer individual and joint survival and by compression of parenting and of child dependency. The greatly increased frequency and commitment of women in paid employment have been two of the most dramatic outcomes.

Even as the life course of women in contemporary complex societies and aging populations has been so dramatically reorganized, women in their various roles at the various ages—as daughters, sisters, wives, mothers, sisters-in-law, daughters-in-law, aunts, nieces, grandmothers, neighbors, or friends—remain the central agents and sources of care and services to household and extended family members and friends and neighbors. Their emergence from the household and the emergence of specialized and professionalized care and services have drastically altered the considerations and perceptions of possibilities, benefits, and costs of extrahousehold-produced services.

From the point of view of the potentially employable woman, it is very clear that a substantial part of the range of care and service activities tradition-ally performed were so massive that they precluded extrahousehold employ-ment for pay or profit. Thus, activities such as care of her own small children, her own or spouse's elderly parents, or older children and other family mem-bers with impairments, disabilities, or other special needs clearly entail fore-gone-income costs for the otherwise employable woman. Organization of other household activities, whether food preparation, housecleaning, recreation, or transportation of family members, also entails such costs, although perhaps not so massively or obviously. For middle-class or upper-class women, there may be some awareness and assessment of costs of foregone extrahousehold activi-ties other than employment for pay or profit. But, in all events, there has been increasing understanding of potential and actual payoffs to women purchasing or otherwise obtaining outside the household some of the kinds of care and services previously produced (primarily by women or their daughters) within the household.

In addition to the consideration of economic and preferred activity payoffs to the women choosing the extrahousehold services, the development and profes-sionalization of such services has been accompanied by, if not necessarily the cause of, assertions of absolute or relative incompetence, or even the dangers or menace of household provision of services. Education and medical care are, of course, the obvious examples of services now perceived utterly beyond the competence of households to provide, although obviously provided except in exceptional circum-stances, by households and families in the past (see, for example, Forder, 1983). Both have custodial as well as professional preventive or remedial dimensions mixed in varying proportions.

Arguments in favor of public provision of services at the fringes of pres-ently available educational and medical services typically stress the incompetence of many contemporary families and households to provide the minimum levels of care or services. Failure to provide such services in effect denies the available care to dependent or needy children or elderly, and either immediately or ultimately implies individual hardship and direct or indirect social costs elsewhere in the system of social services to address these deficiencies. Arguments against public provision of services point to their releasing family members, primarily women, from the commitments and obligations to provide the care and services in question. We can illustrate these by reference to the discussion surrounding issues of provision of day care for preschool children and provision of home care and services for noninstitutionalized frail elderly.

The alleged incompetence of various types of parents and their inability to care for or educate their children properly have long been an assertion made in support of public education generally and of special categories of education in particular. Foreign-born parents, teenaged, single, and unwed parents, working parents, physically or mentally impaired parents, poor (income-wise) parents, parents of large numbers of children, parents convicted of crimes, and others have all sometimes or often been asserted to be incapable of protecting, caring for, nurturing, or educating their children in the manner of the mainstream or dominant culture. The principle of equal opportunities for all children demands provision of alternative socialization settings, including schools and, for some, live-in arrangements, away from home and parents.

Even parents without stigmatized attributes are perceived, and often acknowledge themselves, less competent than professional educators for teaching and socialization. Thus, parents often believe that by denying their children professional care, socialization, and education, they shortchange their children and exclude them from the educational opportunities offered by the more competent professionals in their respective state-of-the-art learning and socialization settings. Thus, entering and keeping children in organized schooling from the earliest possible age until near-adulthood and beyond not only frees mothers for other, usually employment, activity, but it is perceived generally to be in the best interests of the children as well. This reasoning and sentiment is invoked in the case of ordinary normal children and for children with special needs or impairments.

Day Care for Preschool Children

The most recent movement for expansion of extra-home child care from as-early-as-possible to as-late-as-possible is now more explicitly cast as addressing the needs and convenience of employed mothers. But it also incorporates some of the good-for-the-child themes. This is, of course, the campaign for preschool child-care arrangements organized by employers, voluntary organizations, public bodies, or government.

There is already a broad range of private for-profit child-care institutions and small-scale baby-sitting and child-minding arrangements in place or arranged on an ad hoc basis; there are many not-for-profit child-care organizations and institutions as well. But those committed to collective action to promote women's status, rights, and opportunities have increasingly viewed the availability of publicly financed or subsidized preschool child care as the key to the movement from the peripheral labor market and the marginal, dead-end-job employment, which has been the lot of many or perhaps most women employees, to core labor market and stable career employment opportunities. Opposition to this movement and to such schemes invokes, as always, considerations of cost. But it invokes, also explicitly, the alleged threat-to-the-family measures and care options that transfer traditional family responsibilities and commitments to extrafamily bodies (OECD Centre for Educational Research and Innovation, 1982; Gilbert, 1983; Ontario Economic Council, 1981).

Expansion of Postsecondary Schooling:
Day Care for Postschool Children?

There has been much evidence pointing to a decline beginning in the early 1970s in the benefits and relative economic advantage of college and university education for young adults (Freeman, 1976). Various explanations have been advanced, including especially the end to expansion of public welfare programs and of publicly financed research and development programs. Yet more than half (57 percent in 1980) of young Americans aged 20 to 24 now attend some type of postsecondary schooling—universities, colleges and community colleges, or vocational training institutions—compared to just under one-third (32 percent) as late as 1960. The United States has long led the world in enrollment rates at both the secondary and the postsecondary levels of school. But extension of schooling beyond the secondary level has been, if anything, even more dramatic in other advanced industrial countries. In Germany the corresponding postsecondary education enrollment percentage (among persons 20 to 24 years old) rose from 6 percent in 1960 to 28 percent in 1980; in Japan from 9 percent in 1960 to 30 percent in 1980; and in Italy from 7 percent in 1960 to 27 percent in 1980 (Heller et al., 1985, Table 31).

What are all these young persons doing in postsecondary education? Most are presumably adding to their knowledge, skills, and human capital, perhaps, and preparing themselves more adequately for more satisfying, productive, and remunerative employment. It remains to be seen how many will in fact convert their postsecondary schooling to more productive and remunerative employment. For many, however, continuation into postsecondary schooling represents a legitimate, acceptable, and, hopefully, profitable alternative to stable and attractive employment and family-building commitments at this stage in their life courses. Studying in higher or other postsecondary education may also represent a partial transition to adulthood, even though employment, self-support, and own family-formation may be delayed.

In the past young persons from working-class families left home to marry, serve in the military forces, or take employment away from home, all these generally precluding postsecondary schooling other than relatively brief vocational courses. While they remained in the parental home, they would seek employment at least to support themselves, very often even prior to completing secondary school. And often, they would be expected to contribute to support of the household. Care and support of other children, the struggle to make ends meet under unstable employment and income conditions, and the absence of schooling-directed rhetoric and tradition all worked to make the families prescribe early employment of young unmarried adults, however unpromising or marginal it might be. Support and encouragement of continued schooling were the exception.

In the United States completion of secondary school is now nearly universal, and in the seven major industrial nations it has been greatly expanded as well. That alone enlarges the rate of enrollment in postsecondary studies. But it is the declining family size and diminished burden of family dependency and obligations, coinciding with further marginalization of employment opportunities, the end of universal military service, and delayed marriage and childbearing for young persons that have led to the great increase in postsecondary school enrollment (cf. Featherman, 1986, and references cited therein).

Home Care and Services for Noninstitutionalized Frail Elderly

Health care systems throughout the Western world have generally emphasized curative medicine, disease control, and attention to acute health disorders with much less attention to chronic disorders, preventive medicine, or to health care outside of the realm of medical intervention. The greater part of health care costs are those connected with hospital care, and the larger part of recent increases in health care costs are associated with steep increases in the range and costs of curative technologies available mostly in hospital settings.

The increased numbers of elderly persons in the population, and the increased proportions and numbers of old-old, those aged 75 or over, among the elderly, have also expanded very much the numbers receiving long-term care in institutional settings: nursing homes, for the most part, but in hospitals as well. A substantial part of the recent increases in health care costs derive from the absolute growth of the institutionalized elderly population.

At the same time, it is widely recognized that the great majority of the elderly at all ages, including those with impairments or chronic health disorders, live in their own homes or family households. Most of the elderly with impairments or chronic health disorders receive help and care from their spouses, children, or other family members; some receive help from neighbors, organized community services, or they may *buy* care and assistance from commercially available services. This recognition and simple bookkeeping have led politicians, community leaders, and health care planners to turn to schemes for encouraging and supporting continued residence of the elderly in their own or family's homes, rather than institutionalization, through publicly supported or subsidized provision of home care and assistance.

There has been quite lively discussion and debate concerning the scope and types of care and assistance that should be supported. As in the case of day care for preschool children, the programs combine custodial dimensions with various types of professional services, and also with elementary kinds of unskilled chores. Some elderly must simply be looked after; others need high-tech attention, therapy, and treatments requiring highly qualified personnel; some require only assistance with shopping, transportation, or housecleaning.

Again, both traditionally and currently the major providers of such services to the elderly are wives, daughters, or daughters-in-law. But under the demographic conditions leading to population aging, there is both diminished availability of kin *and* the available kin are much more likely to live long distances away or to be engaged in extrahousehold and extrafamily career and employment commitments (Eversley, 1982; Parker, 1980, 1981).

Already there has been enormous growth in the number of private for-profit organizations and agencies offering home care and assistance to frail or impaired elderly, enabling them to continue residing in their own homes (Gilbert, 1983). There are great problems in regulating these agencies, measuring and assessing quality of care provided, and assuring minimum standards (problems which, indeed, are probably no less complex and difficult in the case of nursing homes). Yet there is clearly great need for additional and more affordable or free services of this type.

Here, too, opposition to such programs of support for home care and assistance programs is expressed not only on grounds of their cost. There are also strong reservations expressed about rendering support to the detachment of the elderly and their care from the participation and responsibility of their families. But a key counterargument made has been that such programs in fact have the effect of preserving and fortifying the family and enhancing the quality and solidarity of family life.

PUBLIC AND SOCIAL SERVICES: DESTRUCTION OR SALVATION OF THE FAMILY?

The history of public and social services is the development of services for people unable to meet all or some of their needs within the confines of their own family and intimate social circles. That history has been haphazard, veering between anxiety about the consequences to society of aiding its dependent members, and thereby encouraging dependency on others, and the compassion aroused by contact with people who lead wretched and impoverished lives. Protection of the weak has had to reconcile fears about the consequences of interfering with individual liberty, family rights, and integrity with the need to help the helpless. The growth of personal and social services has centered on certain groups that have been identified as having special needs, such as orphans, the frail elderly, the physically handicapped, immigrants, the homeless, juvenile delinquents, addicts, as well as on the emergence of social work as a profession.

Both statutory and voluntary agencies have made contributions to the development of social work services. In the statutory services emphasis initially and inevitably lay in administering the law and fulfilling the duties and obligations laid on the local bodies, as in the English Poor Laws, the emerging health services, and the compulsory education acts. It was in the voluntary agencies that the processes of casework and group work were identified and training for social work developed. A wide range of voluntary agencies grew up alongside the statutory services, frequently prompting critique, review, and sometimes reform or extension of the statutory provisions.

In the mid-twentieth century, important inflections in the nature and scope of public social services took place in most of the highly industrialized capitalist countries. The systems expanded to include income maintenance provisions to replace employment income for the unemployed and for those retired from employment because of old age. They came to include health care provisions. Entitlements became universalistic rather than needs-tested or income-tested.

The public social services and welfare provisions were transformed from organizations and measures addressing the needs of the unfortunate, impoverished, and disabled lacking in other support or resources for seeing to their needs privately. They became comprehensive income maintenance, welfare, and service systems playing a major role in fashioning and maintaining the quality of life for the stable working and the growing middle classes as well. The capitalist countries were transformed into welfare states with substantial proportions of national product and income redistributed and allocated to such social programs and benefits through the public sector, with the political support driven by the self-interest of broad working and middle-class beneficiaries rather than by altruistic concern for the well-being of the unfortunates in society.

These transformations of capitalist societies into welfare states have been accompanied by ongoing struggles among the various social, economic, and political groupings in the population over (1) the acceptable size, extent, and pervasiveness of the state, government, and government activity in general, and the proportion of national product and resources that may be controlled and allocated by government and the public sector; and (2) the purposes, ways, and directions to which the state and governments may allocate and distribute the product and resources in their control.

Generally, the more conservative groups have favored less state, government, and public sector activity and minimal state appropriation and allocation of national product. They have favored restriction of social welfare measures to needs-tested programs to ameliorate the conditions of the unfortunate. The more liberal groups have favored more state activity in general, as well as expansion and universalization of welfare measures and benefits in particular.

This history and its accompanying political and ideological struggles have been extensively documented and discussed. It continues to occupy the attention of analysts, proponents, and opponents of one or another of the facets and dimensions of public policy concerning welfare measures and social services (see, for example, the reviews in Myles, 1984, 1987; Flora and Heidensheimer, 1981; Friedman and Friedman, 1980; Piven and Cloward, 1971; and Gilbert, 1983).

Of particular interest to us here is the issue of the relationship of public services in the welfare state to the viability of the family as a social institution in modern society. It is an issue that has been raised and reraised in this public policy discussion and struggle. Our mention in the earlier chapters of the life course, the family cycle, and availability of kin against the background of recent demographic trends has prepared us in a special way to review some of the arguments surrounding this issue.

There are basically three positions or points of view concerning the relationship between broadly available and frequently universalistic public services and the viability of the conventionally favored nuclear family—parents and own children—unit in modern societies:

1. The first position holds that the conventional nuclear family is subverted and under attack by conditions of modern society: Availability of public services erodes the family and its internal functions, interdependence, and solidarity even further, exacerbating its weaknesses and threatening its total demise.
2. The second position holds that while the nuclear family is indeed under pressure in modern society, the availability of public services fortifies the family and its functions and solidarity and contributes to its continuing viability.
3. The third position holds that, whether or not the nuclear family is threatened in modern society, its continuing viability is independent of and largely indifferent to the provision or availability of public social services. Some proponents of this position agree with the premise that the family is subverted and fragile in modern societies, while others hold that the family is alive, well, and thriving.

A Fading Role for the Conjugal Family?

In the view of Fuchs (1983), the evidence for the "fading role of the conjugal family as a major institution in U.S. society" includes the growing proportion of unwed mothers, the growth of one-person households, and the growing importance of nursery schools, on the one hand, and of nursing homes, on the other.

There are three major ways in which public social services subvert families. In the first place, according to Fuchs, governments are assuming care and social service functions traditionally carried out by families. These include educational, health care, custodial, housing, material support, protective, transportation, food preparation, and recreational services. Sometimes, Fuchs acknowledges, government insurance is more efficient than private insurance because it overcomes the problem of adverse selection. But, Fuchs asserts, the main reason for the spread of government programs is the pressure for income redistribution: Most government social insurance-type programs, such as Aid to Families with Dependent Children (AFDC) or Social Security retirement or health benefits, have important redistribution components, and the wish for more egalitarian societies has been the driving force behind most social legislation in the United States and elsewhere in the developed capitalist world.

When families were the dominant social and economic institution they did indeed redistribute resources among their own members, Fuchs observes, but there was also great inequality among families. Fuchs seems not to have noticed that, prior to the public and redistributive social insurance-type provisions, many of the families left to their own devices to fulfill their family functions were simply unable to organize their priorities or to afford the education, care, health, and welfare of their members.

Second, Fuchs points out, government frequently provides assistance for individuals contingent on the use of nonfamily services. He acknowledges that provision of assistance in extrafamily organizations and institutions can be planned and controlled more effectively, but ways should be found or developed to subsidize and support assistance that could be provided by family members in the home. As it is, the support and provision of care and services by public or by private extrafamily agencies renders family members receiving such assistance independent of their families and family members, and it frees the other family members of obligations.

Finally, in Fuchs's view, just as appears to be the case in other institutions and in society generally, the movements and pressures for equality that have led to redistributive public social programs, have also led to the weakening of hierarchical relationships within the family. Authority of husbands over wives, and parents over children has been weakened, just as the authority of priests over parishioners, employers over employees, and teachers over students, has been notably diminished (Fuchs, 1983, p. 225).

Although other discussion in his work draws extensively upon supportive research and data, Fuchs, a distinguished economist, does not present any evidence in support of this remarkable analysis. But neither does he advocate abandoning either public social programs or egalitarian values and movements in order to fortify or revive the nuclear family. Rather, his prescription is for promoting "adequate investment in children" on the part of both public and private sectors by trying to "reconstitute it [the nuclear family] on a more democratic, egalitarian basis while enhancing its role as a vital, viable institution for socialization" (p. 226). The details of this prescription are not elaborated.

A Negative Impact of Welfare State Social Markets on Family Life?

In an analysis of the evolvement of coexisting "economic" and "social" markets, Gilbert (1983) points out that "while economic activity in the United States is heavily invested in the private sector, a system of welfare capitalism has developed in which social and economic markets coexist. Ideally, ...the economic market is impelled by individual initiative, ability, productivity, and the desire for profit. In contrast, the social market of the welfare state allocates benefits in response to need, dependency, charitable impulses, and the wish for communal security." The relationship between social and economic markets is ambivalent, in part complementary by joining individual ambitions and collective responsibilities and in part antagonistic by reflecting competing ideologies, groups, and interests. In particular, it is the evolvement of universalistic social service entitlements that have brought public sector or welfare state activity into areas in which it potentially or actually competes with private enterprise, rendering the conflict and struggle over such programs the more intense. In Gilbert's view, the inroads of universal entitlement programs enacted in the United States between 1960 and 1980 led to the erosion of distinctions between the social and economic markets. It also led to reassertion of public preference for private enterprise, to the detriment and enforced retrenchment of the welfare state's universal programs, and to a resurgence of selectivity in public social programs. It is under the cloud of this retrenchment that Gilbert examines the potential of addressing care and welfare needs by increasing mutual aid through family supports and other voluntary alternatives.

The welfare state's disposition toward family life is, in Gilbert's view, a "confused mix of humanitarian sentiments and the egalitarian aspirations of collectivism." Although preservation of the family is important, the egalitarian thrust brings the welfare state into conflict with the family as the main institutional vehicle through which privilege is transmitted across generations. When obligations and affections of kinship take precedence over loyalty to the community, the investment of family energies and resources is inconsistent with what Gilbert calls the "collectivist objectives" of the welfare state.

The welfare state, according to Gilbert, faces two basic dilemmas in its positions with respect to the family as an institution. First, the various ostensibly family-oriented social insurance schemes, for example, financial benefits and health care to the elderly, reduce the pressures on children to discharge their traditional obligations to parents. They cause the state to replace the family as major provider for the elderly. Although under American Social Security arrangements it is the children's generation which is in fact paying for the support to the retired elderly, the intergenerational transfer takes place with the state as mediator rather than directly. But the well-intentioned humanitarian arrangement has the effect of reducing the family's traditional responsibility to provide for its members. Similarly, family-oriented programs such as day care and guaranteed minimum income schemes have a destabilizing influence on married life by eroding mutual social obligations and economic interdependence.

Second, there is what Gilbert calls the "egalitarian dilemma" of family programs. He cites in particular the set of recommendations emanating from a White House Conference on Families in 1980. He notes that the egalitarian zeal of welfare state advocates dictates even treatment to all forms of human relationships, with traditional stable family arrangements not preferable and not favored in public policy over newer, more fluid and unstable, or unconventional life styles and relationships (see, also, Steiner, 1981; Eichler, 1983). The dilemma, according to Gilbert, is that if the definition of family becomes a vessel into which any human arrangement can be poured there is little basis to distinguish family policy from any other policy that might promote social welfare. Conversely, identification of preferable family arrangements targeted for greater public support and encouragement is possible. But it carries the accompanying danger of stigmatizing and discriminating against families not conforming to the preferred mold.

Finally, Gilbert notes, the expansion of social services in work settings under the auspices of private business and dealing with a variety of employee problems are not likely to be supportive of the traditional form of nuclear family life and relationships. Businesses have been called upon to develop family-oriented work policies such as maternal leave, child-care arrangements, and job sharing. But these have typically been directed toward the needs of two-career couples or single working parents, and they have tended to facilitate the shift of women's labor from the home to the market economy. Although there may be economic benefits and the stimulation of independent careers, these programs tend to reduce the interdependence of family life by providing each spouse with his own income and social assistance in areas such as child-care services, work place benefits, legal services, and the like.

As evidence of these relationships, Gilbert cites findings of the Denver and Seattle Income Maintenance experiments showing that the rates of marital dissolution among families receiving income support were overall approximately twice those of the control group (those not receiving income support) families (Gilbert, 1983, p. 99).

However, elsewhere in the same work he cites evidence that families continue to provide the major portion of social care and support for the elderly and disabled (p. 121). Gilbert's prescription for public policy is direct and indirect "support for domesticity," advocating a scheme to compensate families for the foregone income and career loss of full-time homemakers. He advocates a system of social credit awarded by the federal government for each year a full-time housekeeper remains at home with children under 17 years of age. The social credits could be exchangeable later for either advanced education and training or for preference points in federal civil service examinations, in a spirit akin to veterans' benefits granted in recognition of people who sacrificed career opportunities while serving the nation.

Welfare Provisions and Liberation
from Oppressive Family Situations

Gilbert himself cites some complications and anomalies in the income maintenance studies' findings cited. In particular, the marital dissolution rates for each group at higher levels of support were less that those at lower levels. If degree of financial independence contributes to the risk of divorce, the opposite relationship would have been expected. The confusion and difficulties in interpretation of such findings underscores the failure or refusal (by Gilbert, Fuchs, and others) to address except in a most superficial and essentially derogating way the negative or oppressive features of family life to which women frequently, and men occasionally, are subjected. This failure leads to the view of conventional nuclear family life as virtuous under all or most circumstances, and to the view of its alternatives as generally evil.

In fact there is and has always been much brutality, abuse, and exploitation in family relations (Straus and Hotaling, 1980; Albrecht and Kunz, 1980; Eichler, 1983). Wife beating, child abuse, and exploitation and abuse of aged parents are increasingly recognized as part of the panorama of family life. There would seem to be no limit to the variations and possibilities for other types of abuse and distress within families, even if less frequent or not yet discovered by the mass media. It is very frequently the lack of alternative, extrafamily financial or other support that entraps individuals and prevents them from extricating themselves from impossible or even disastrous family circumstances.

If public social support schemes sometimes enable such individuals to terminate marriages or depart from oppressive or tragic family circumstances, this is probably best viewed as an achievement of the programs rather than as another loss to the traditional nuclear family camp. The point to be made is that a program that may sometimes, or even frequently, provide opportunities for dissolution of misguided, oppressive, or unhappy marriages, or one that frees either the young or elderly from the terrors and insecurities of oppressive dependency, cannot reasonably be faulted for eroding, or exacerbating the weakness, of the family,

family life, or family solidarity in contemporary society. Conversely, conventions and circumstances that deny individuals in oppressive family situations any opportunity to free themselves or change their situations can hardly be applauded as fortifying and enhancing the family and family solidarity.

Conclusion: Some Direct Evidence and Analysis

A direct study and frontal examination of the extent to which contemporary families are giving up the caregiving function and transferring responsibilities to the state and how such transfers of functions and responsibilities are related to the expanding welfare state has been attempted by Moroney in the United Kingdom (Moroney, 1976) and in the United States (Moroney, 1986). Using a variety of original, secondary, and published data sources and reviewing a wide range of earlier research, Moroney focused on two types of families: those caring for frail elderly parents and those caring for severely mentally retarded children. He concluded that (1) there is no evidence that health and welfare services are misused or undermining family responsibility; (2) the major beneficiaries of the public programs and services are dependent persons who had no family or none within reach; (3) families providing care for elderly or handicapped persons experience hardship and severe stress, and there are few supportive services available to them.

Social services, in Moroney's view, have two primary functions: social development/nurturance and social control. The first function is concerned with improving social skills of individuals (who may or may not be living in a family setting). Services must enlarge the resource base of each individual's social network and enhance the prosocial orientation of the network by linking the individual and family to mainstream community values and institutions. The second function is concerned with positive control when necessary. When a family's capacity to meet the needs of individual family members becomes impaired, the social development/nurturance function begins to overlap or blur with the social control function as social services are introduced to restore the family to some level of adequate functioning. Indeed, in some cases, these provide services that in part or wholly take over family functions.

From the point of view of public policy, the family is usefully understood and defined, in Moroney's view, as a social service. As such they, as well as community, society, and state social services, must help individual family members meet their basic needs, enhance their social functioning, develop their potential, and promote their general well-being. The discussion, measure, and evaluation of the quality and viability of the family should, in this context, rest on its effectiveness as a social service alongside the extrafamily services; the critical question is whether or not the existence or expansion of community or state services and intervention impairs or constitutes a disincentive to families in performance of the social service function.

Reviewing evidence bearing upon the past performance of families of the social service functions, Moroney concludes that the image of past widespread effectiveness and self-sufficiency of families and local communities in providing care and services for all members throughout the family cycle is largely myth with some mix of nostalgia for agrarian small-community life. Deteriorating or weakened families existed long before the introduction of the modern welfare state, even during the Poor Law era of the eighteenth and nineteenth centuries when there was an attempt to coerce family responsibility through repressive social policies. The charge that the welfare state brought about changes in family responsibility and willingness to care for dependent members is without foundation.

Just the same, contemporary families differ significantly from those of the nineteenth century. In Moroney's view, a number of these differences bear importantly upon a family's capability and willingness to provide effective social care for their dependent members, that is, to function as a viable social service. Examples are smaller family size and the increasing proportions of two-person families, earlier completion of childbearing, increased employment of women, the declining ratio of potential caregivers (women aged 45 to 54) to the elderly (total aged 65+), increasing divorce, increased numbers and proportions of female-headed families and single-parent families and, finally, changes in expectations that people have toward family life and marriage. In Moroney's view, these change have all, in some measure, operated to impair the social service functioning of families, and families are neither in a position to be caregivers nor are they expected to be. Those assuming the responsibilities of massive care for handicapped children or elderly parents are in many respects deviant in contemporary society, indeed more deviant than single-parent or dual-career families.

But it is not social welfare measures that create dependency, nor do they prevent families from taking responsibility for dependents. State income maintenance measures may prevent individual dependency, say, of elderly retired or of unemployed workers. In this sense they may be viewed as essential if families are to continue to function as major social institutions in modern society. State welfare measures may foster continued dependency by some families when eligibility for assistance is means-tested, but it does not create dependent families.

Following a formulation by Kamerman and Kahn (1976), and based on the particular problems and stress of those families carrying out support functions for handicapped children and frail elderly, Moroney's prescription would have public social services seeking to support informal support systems for family well-being. This should include intervention to stimulate by financial support, professional expertise, and so forth the growth of support networks and provide them with support when necessary. This would result in more self-sufficient families, to be sure, but not in the shrinking of the welfare state.

For the foreseeable future there will be dependent families, whether the dependency is financial, physical, or psychological, requiring state intervention. Social welfare measures that prevent economic dependency must continue so that the elderly need not become negatively dependent upon children and grandchildren. Thus, in Moroney's view, if families are to be strengthened, the state must not consider retrenchment of the social welfare system but rather it should enter into partnership with families and develop relationships characterized by reciprocity.

6

AGE GRADING, STAGES AND DOMAINS OF THE LIFE COURSE, AND LIFE-COURSE TRANSITIONS

INTRODUCTION

Long or short, fragile or resilient, human lives are finite. This is an observation that has received not only the attention of philosophers, priests, and poets. Rather, every culture and every subculture, every language and every normative system, every body of popular or folk knowledge embodies some understandings, analyses, and generally some prescriptions and proscriptions concerning the passage of time and the use of time in human lives. Thus human biographies are generally *ordered;* that is, they exhibit characteristic timing and sequences of events, activities, and relationships. And it is only exceptionally or pathologically that human biographies are chaotic, that is, without order.

Some part of the order in human lives is biological or physiological in origin. Infants and children, adolescents and adults, differ in their physiological attributes and capacities. And the physiological attributes and capacities develop and change in recurring and familiar directions over the lifetime of individuals: growth, sexual development, strength, stamina, speed, and coordination, first enhanced and later diminished. At any moment in time, and over entire biographies of individuals, such capacities constrain the individual's behavior, activity, and relationships. At the same time, they introduce and enforce certain dimensions of order into the lives and biographies of individuals.

But much, perhaps most, of the order in human lives and biographies is cultural and social in origin. Following Hareven (1975), Modell, Furstenberg, and Hershberg (1976), Neugarten and Datan, (1973), Featherman and Petersen

(1986), and others, we shall refer to culturally or socially induced order, norms, and standards for use of time and for timing and sequences of events, activities, and relationships in human lives and biographies as *social time*. We conventionally distinguish social time from biological time or life time, referring to order induced by biological or physiological attributes and development. We also distinguish these from historical time, the order or directions in human lives and biographies induced by historical events such as wars, unusual economic booms or depressions, natural catastrophes or major accidents, or special political social, or economic events or circumstances (Neugarten and Datan, 1973; Clausen, 1986).

Throughout Parts I and II of this book we have alluded to the life course and the family cycle. We have noted that, on the one hand, they have been dramatically affected by changing mortality and fertility as well as by historical and technological changes; and, on the other hand, that the changes in life course and family cycle have very important consequences for individual well-being, the economy, and social and political organization generally. Historically and under the changing demographic and socioeconomic conditions, the life course and the family cycle have become both of much longer duration *and* less circumscribed by the exigencies of work and parenting. These trends raise questions about the changing forms and bases of social pattern, order, and control of the life course. This chapter and the following two chapters that comprise Part III examine directly the features and changing structure of the individual life course and the family cycle.

We have earlier defined the life course as physiological, psychological, and social process and sequence of capacities and age-graded events, activities, and relationships characterizing the individual from birth through death, or the trajectory of sociodemographic states or roles through which members of a birth cohort pass over their lifetimes. From the point of view of the individual, the life course is his or her biography viewed in terms of socially prescribed activity, events, processes, and durations. From the point of view of a cohort, the life course is the cohort's distribution across time over the domains of activity and characteristic events, event sequences, and processes experienced by the cohort. In this chapter we review the central concepts of the life course and some of the important hypotheses and findings concerning historical and contemporary trends in life-course structure and transition patterns.

AGE GRADING

The mechanism by which biological time, historical time, and social time induce order in human lives and biographies is *age grading*. Age grading is the assignment of social roles to given chronological ages. The age may be exactly prescribed: At age six children are expected to enter grade one; at age 65 employees are expected to retire. Or it may be only approximately prescribed: At about ages 20 to 25 single girls are expected to marry and become wives; at about ages 18 to 22 young men are expected to become economically self-supporting. Thus age grading in society associates a substantial proportion of social roles—ranging from family member-ship, school, community and citizenship, to economic and political roles—with given chronological ages. And age grading tends to impose social norms about the expected behavior, activity, and relationships at the ages in question and, for the succession of age-graded roles, for the life course generally.

The *number* of differentiated age grades varies broadly among societies. But none is without at least two age classes: uninitiated and initiated, in anthro-pological terms, or simply children and adults in everyday language. Indeed, most societies have at least three age-grade distinctions: children, adults, and elderly. But, of course, in complex modern societies age grades are more numerous and tend to be highly differentiated. We shall see a little later that age-grade distinctions and age classes are often very closely associated with types and levels of depen-dency, obligations, and entitlements within the family, community, or society. Although some economic and social contributions are typically expected from children, children are generally dependents in that they are too young for full participation. Elderly are generally dependents in that they are too old for full participation.

In a relatively simple and undifferentiated society a single age-grade system becomes formalized and applied to all the major institutions of that society. As the individual moves from one age grade to the next, he takes on a new set of family, economic, political, and religious roles at the same time. The social age grades and the periods of the life course are closely matched and relatively well-defined. But in more complex societies multiple systems of age grading arise, differentiated and defined with respect to particular social institutions or, as we shall indicate, to the different social, economic, and political domains of the life course. These institutions and domains vary in the extent to which age grades are explicit and formal. An individual's transitions into, out of, or within one domain are not necessarily or inevitably related to those in another domain (Neugarten and Hagestead, 1976).

Historical Changes in Recognized Age Grades

It is instructive to take note of the historical changes in recognized age grades. Even elementary age classes that we recognize today—infancy, childhood, adolescence, adulthood, middle age, and old age—were either not identified at all in the past or were identified and characterized in different ways and in different relationships to chronological age and to one another than today (cf. Rosenmayr, 1981).

Childhood   In his now classic study *Centuries of Childhood*, Philippe Aries points out that each of the ages of life has evolved historically as a concept and a set of behavioral, attitudinal, and social relations norms and prescriptions. Child-hood, which was clearly recognized and distinguished from adulthood from prehistorical through ancient times, went "out of currency," so to speak, in

Medieval civilization. It was rediscovered only in the seventeenth century among the nobility, the middle class, and the richer artisans and laborers and only well into the nineteenth century among the poorest classes (Aries, 1962).

Using paintings, diaries, characterizations of schools and their curricula and practices, and accounts of games and skills, Aries describes the development of the concept of childhood in France and elsewhere in Europe during the last four centuries. He contrasts this with the treatment of children as small adults who, until the end of the Middle Ages and even longer among the poor, mingled, played, worked, and competed with mature adults almost as soon as they were weaned. Only in the nineteenth century did childhood become a privileged age, in the sense that enormous energy and resources were devoted to isolating, protecting, socializing, and developing children both as objects of coddling and love and as future adults and household participants.

Aries points out (1962, pp. 25–29) that until the seventeenth century the word for child (French *enfant*) covered persons of all ages in a state of dependency. In the course of that century a change took place in the more affluent classes (in Aries' words, "in families of gentle birth") where the vocabulary of childhood began to refer to the first age, with the idea of child eventually restricted to its modern meaning. But for the masses, the idea of child as dependent or subordinate was retained with virtually no differentiation of age grade or biological state. Nor was closeness to or distance from puberty implied or widely recognized.

Only later did childhood emerge in distinctive games, dress, behavioral prescriptions, education, and discipline. Most important in Aries' analysis, it is only with the emergence and differentiation of childhood that the modern sense of the *family* takes hold and that the nuclear family achieves its modern institutionalization and prominence.

Adolescence Ancient texts recognize and depict adolescence as the "third age," following infancy and childhood, beginning after age fourteen, and characterized by growth and ability to beget children. It lasts until the late twenties or early thirties, when it is followed by youth, the age of greatest strength and ability. Youth, in turn, was said to last until about age 45 or 50 and followed by "senectitude," a half-way period between youth and old age (Aries, 1962, p. 21). But in the Middle Ages adolescence, too, was dropped from the European vocabulary and virtually unrecognized until quite recently.

The origins of the modern concept of adolescence have been traced to Rousseau's novel *Emile*, published in 1762 (Neugarten and Hagestad, 1976) or even later, in Wagner's operatic characterization of *Siegfried* (Aries, 1962). But it is generally agreed that it took on its modern meaning only late in the nineteenth century and achieved widespread acknowledgment and popularity only in the twentieth century (Demos and Demos, 1969; Gillis, 1974). The idea of adolescence as a time of turmoil and search for identity dates back to the discovery less than 100 years ago of this period between childhood and adulthood.

In the view of Clausen (1986), it is largely the extension of schooling beyond the primary grades that has given rise to adolescence as a social category. Until the late nineteenth century the concept of adolescence hardly existed. On farms and in towns children over seven tended to move into the world of adult work, assisting parents or serving as apprentices. In the nineteenth century, as elementary education became more widespread, many children went as far as the sixth, seventh, or even eighth grade, but very few remained in school beyond age fourteen.

The demands of increasing urbanization and technological development for more highly trained employees and the expansion of educational opportunities were accompanied by widespread exclusion from employment and deferral of entry into the labor force until well after the onset of puberty. The years of the transition from childhood to adult status were increasingly occupied with continued schooling and delay of employment, marriage, parenthood, and adult relationships and commitments. They came to be characterized as a period of moratorium and identity-seeking connoted adolescence (Clausen, 1986, pp. 86–87).

That the character of behavior and relationships at these postpuberty adolescent ages is strongly influenced by cultural patterns is dramatically illustrated in the cross-cultural comparisons of adolescents in Western and nonliterate societies pioneered by the famous anthropologist Margaret Mead (1961) and others. There is also mounting evidence of what Gove (1985) has connoted "biopsychosocial" factors, such as physical strength, staying power, and ability to rebound (comprising, together, physical energy), and the need for stimulation related to increases in the hormone plasma testosterone. Finally, as cited earlier in Chapter 1, the emergence of formal organized youth and adolescent groups in modern societies has been viewed by Eisenstadt (1956) as mechanisms in the transition of young persons from particularistic family and household social experience, settings, and relationships to the universalistic occupational and organizational relationships and expectations of adulthood.

The New Old Age   While old age has probably always been recognized as an age category, the greatly increased numbers of persons *surviving* to old age, and the increased length of time, or, as indicated earlier, the increased volume of cohort and individual *life years* lived in old age, have changed its features and range of characteristics very dramatically. Old age now includes young-old (generally taken as those in ages 65 to 74) and old-old (those aged 75 or older). It includes persons employed or otherwise economically active, and it includes retired persons. It includes married and widowed; very healthy and less healthy persons; persons heading their own households, living with children or families, or living in institutional settings. There are persons with independent incomes or property or both and persons economically dependent upon welfare or children's support or assistance; and persons with many alternative types of roles and role profiles (Habib and Matras, 1987).

Much of this variety in the roles and characteristics of the elderly is of recent history. Improvements in survival and longevity have been dramatic within the past century but, nevertheless, have occurred over an extended period of time. New patterns of income maintenance, household arrangements, and consumption are recent and rather more dramatic. Thus the activities, social participation, and general situations of the elderly have indeed undergone quite dramatic shifts in a fairly short period of time. We shall return to these issues in much more detail in Part IV.

As we shall note below, one of the central hypotheses of the research on the life course is the historical trend toward *increasing* age grading in complex societies. This occurs in both the numbers of activities and activity domains that are age graded and the detail with which they are differentiated by age. There is also keen attention in modern life-course research to the patterns of simultaneity or sequencing of changes, movements, and transitions in the distinct life-course domains.

STAGES OF LIFE AND STAGE THEORIES OF AGE GRADING

The universal recognition of the ordering of human lives and biographies has given rise to the concepts of the "ages of man," as cited by Aries and others. These have been expanded and elaborated with the introduction of psychological dimensions to the broadly recognized physiological stages, giving rise to a number of "stage theories" of age grading (Clausen, 1986, Chapter 2).

Much of the impetus for the formulation of such theories derives from the works of Freud, who traced the origins of adult psychopathologies to factors in infant and childhood psychosexual development and adaptation. Probably the best known of the stage theories is the set of Eight Stages of Man posited by the psychoanalyst E.H. Erikson. In formulating and describing these stages, Erikson focused upon the sequence of dilemmas or psychosexual crises and task resolution that each individual, in his view, must confront and resolve at the respective successive age levels or stages (Table 6.1).

Table 6.1.   Stages of Life, Psychosexual Crises, and Radius of Significant Relations

AGE LEVEL	PSYCHOSEXUAL CRISIS	RADIUS OF SIGNIFICANT RELATIONS
Infancy	Basic trust vs. mistrust	Maternal person
Early childhood	Autonomy vs. shame, doubt	Parental person
Play age	Initiative vs. guilt	Basic family
School age	Industry vs. inferiority	Neighborhood, school
Adolescence	Identity vs. confusion	Peer groups and outgroups, models of leadership
Young adulthood	Intimacy vs. isolation	Partners in friendship, sex, competition, cooperation
Adulthood	Generativity vs. stagnation	Divided labor and shared household
Old age	Integrity vs. despair	"Mankind," "my kind"

Source: Adapted from E. H. Erikson, *The Life Cycle Completed: A Review* (New York: Norton, 1982), Chart I, pp. 32,33. Reprinted by permission of W.W. Norton & Company, Inc. Copyright ©1982 by Rikan Enterprises Ltd.

Erikson's model and other so-called "normative crises" models of human psychosocial changes thus involve tasks that must be accomplished or resolved in sequence if the individual is to continue to grow psychologically and socially. These formulations and models remain controversial in both their content and their universality.

Stage theories are interesting, illuminating, and provocative. In social scientific literature, and in the literature of associated professions and disciplines such as education, social work, and social gerontology, they evoke the images and problematics of *adaptation* or *adjustment* to the new human situation implied by movement or transition from one stage to the next. Adaptation or adjustment to adolescence, marriage, marital dissolution, middle age, retirement, and to old age are familiar motifs in the literature. Varying levels of psychological well-being are frequently associated with the different stages and with the transitions among them (Campbell, 1981). We return to this topic in Chapter 8 in connection with stages of the family cycle.

Even more important from our point of view is that stage theories and formulations evoke some of the imagery of dependency and obligations. The theme of the individual's mutual involvement with significant persons, which Erikson has also connoted "an ecology of mutual activation within a communal unit such as the family" is prominent in this discussion. The normative crises and tasks that must be resolved at each stage are closely connected with the patterns of dependency and obligations characterizing them. Psychosocial development over the life cycle, Erikson asserts,

> depends at every moment on three processes of organization that much complement each other. There is, in whatever order, i) the biological process of the hierarchic organization of organ systems constituting a body (*soma*); ii) the psychic process organizing individual experience by ego synthesis (*psyche*); and iii) the communal process of the cultural organization of the interdependence of persons (*ethos*). (Erikson, 1982, pp. 25–26)

Thus, in Table 6.1, each stage is associated with a "radius of significant relations." The success of adaptation, that is, the normality, or absence of pathology, in adaptation at each stage and following each transition, is thus associated with acceptable management of the significant relations.

But the structure and changes in the radius of significant relationships itself are not typically addressed or studied in this tradition. Moreover the stage theories are empirically ambiguous in that individuals cannot generally be uniquely identified in, or assigned, or associated with, a stage, and their entry into or departure from that stage cannot be determined unambiguously. Thus not only is it difficult to study the antecedents, correlates, and outcomes of movement through the stages of life for individuals, but it is difficult to explore the social structural antecedents and ramifications of such movements. Moreover, stage theories cannot account for historical change in the age categories and age classes differentiated, identified, and loaded and reloaded with meaning: childhood, adolescence, old age, retirement, young-old, old-old, and so forth.

Recent social-historical and social scientific attention to the life course has, instead, inquired about the *social construction* of age grades and life stages. For example, they have asked: Given (1) the life span and the patterns of variation in life span in a population or in a society, and (2) the physiological (or, if they hold, the physiological *and* psychological) universals how, if at all, does *society* arrange a life path or life paths?

1. Does society make any arrangement at all? Is there a normative life course at all?
2. Is it incumbent on all to follow such arrangements? How many, or how universal, are the socially designed life paths, or how idiosyncratic can they be?
3. What are the features of society's arrangement? How detailed is the arrangement? How rigid or flexible is the arrangement? How institutionalized is the normative life course?

In contrast to the stages-of-life formulations and theories, a life-course domains framework offers unambiguous identification of participation in a domain, the start and end of such participation, and so forth. As we shall see, a very substantial part of modern empirically grounded research on the life course has increasingly drawn upon such a framework.

LIFE-COURSE DOMAINS

Life-course domains are simply social role spheres or spheres of activity, attachment, participation, or membership in which individuals can be observed, or can report themselves, at any moment in time. At any moment in time an individual either is or is not a student, is or is not married, is or is not employed. So that at such a moment the individual is or is not in the schooling domain, is or is not in the married persons domain, is or is not in the employment domain.

When the individual *enters* a domain by making some change—becoming a student, getting married, finding a job—he or she undergoes a transition in the life course. This may be a very important transition or a very minor one. It may be very closely related to factors such as one's status with respect to other life-course domains, other previous or simultaneous life-course transitions, or other factors, or to none at all. It may be very individual or highly patterned with the respect to its timing or other circumstances.

The person may *remain* in this domain, that is, continue his or her role, membership, or activity in this domain, for a long time or a short time. If the person completes his or her studies, is widowed or divorced, or leaves a job or retires, he or she *leaves* one or all of the respective domains. Thus involvement, membership, role-incumbency, or participation in the various life-course domains may be of varying durations. Here too, the durations may be very individual or idiosyncratic, or they may be highly patterned. We conventionally call movements into or out of life-course domains that are highly patterned with respect to timing and durations and that appear to entail some sanctions for deviance *normative* life-course movements or transitions.

Examples of life-course domains include household and residence, school, employment, military service, marriage and parenting, retirement, economic dependence or self-sufficiency, widowhood, and kinship. Thus life-course domains can include membership in social units, activities, or characteristics associated with social statuses and roles. There may be movement into and out of domains. And these would typically represent types of life-course transitions, for example, leaving school, entering full-time employment, marriage, child-launching, retirement from employment, disability, or widowhood. But there may also be movement *within* domains, for example, career movement, successive births, changes in income, residential mobility. Some of these, too, might also be viewed as life-course transitions.

Changing Allocation of Women's Life Years among Schooling, Employment, and Parenthood

An early example of the study of life-course domains is the analysis of the allocation of early adult females' (between ages 18 and 29) life years among schooling, employment, and parenthood carried out for synthetic cohorts in the United States for the 1960 to 1976 period by J. Sweet (1979a, 1979b). Using national census and survey data, Sweet calculated estimated life years spent by American women in these three domains and in their intersections (that is, in one, two, or all three of the domains simultaneously). For example, under 1960 conditions white women would spend an average of 5.14 years childless in the twelve-year span from ages 18 to 29, but for 1976 the average number of childless years reach 7.10.

Childlessness in all years varied very sharply by educational attainment, and so did the changes. In 1960, women with less than 12 years of schooling had only 3.57 life years childless (among the 12 in the age span), compared to no less than 7.12 years childless among women with more than 12 years of schooling. In 1976, the average number of childless years was essentially unchanged among those with less than 12 years of schooling, 3.46 years; among those with more than 12 years of schooling, the average number of childless years under the 1976 conditions was up to 9.00 years (Sweet, 1979a, Table 3).

Numbers of life years unmarried (that is, in the spinster domain) and life years employed increased sharply among white American women in the period in question, and numbers of life years enrolled in school increased as well. Moreover, the number of life years married *and* childless increased sharply, from 1.96 years for 1960 to 2.71 years for 1976. This was due primarily to the increase in life years married and childless among women with more than twelve years of schooling—from 2.17 years in 1960 to 3.05 years in 1976—and somewhat less dramatic increase among those with exactly twelve years of schooling (from 2.08 years in 1960 to 2.54 years in 1976). The number of life years in these two domains, marriage and childlessness, actually declined slightly among those with less than twelve years of schooling (Sweet, 1979a, Table 6).

Time Spent by Young Men in Seven Life-Course
Domains: Cohort, Race, and Social Origin Differences

While Sweet's estimates of time allocated to each of the respective life-course domains were estimated for synthetic cohorts applying rates of school enrollment, labor force participation, and marital status to computed numbers of life years (similar in logic to the estimates of years in parenthood presented in Chapter 3), *direct* measures of person-months spent at each age from 14 through 29 in seven life-course domains—school, work, military service, with parents, with family of origin, married, and parenting—were derived by Featherman, Hogan, and Sorensen (1984) from the detailed life histories collected retrospectively among a national sample of young American men. These researchers were able to compare mean numbers of person-months spent in each of the separate domains and in each intersection or combination of domains, altogether and at each age or age span separately, among younger and older cohorts, among white and black men, among sons of manual worker and nonmanual worker fathers respectively (Table 6.2).

Thus between ages 14 and 29, respondents spent an average of 56.5 months (of a total of 192 months) in school, 21.9 months in military service, 116.5 months in full-time employment, 75.4 months in marriage, and 54.7 months in parenting. In these ages, the respondents spent an average of 63.9 months in the parental household or, alternatively by another household classification scheme, an average of 71.3 months in the family of origin household. Examination of the mean person-months in the respective domains at each single year of age in Table 6.2 reveals the pattern of diminishing and completion of school enrollment in late adolescence, entry into full-time employment, marriage, and parenthood in the early twenties, concentration of months of military service in the late teens and early twenties, departure from parental or family of origin households beginning in the late teens.

Comparison of these measures among the older (born 1929 to 1933) and younger (born 1934 to 1939) cohorts suggests that they were generally similar in the total durations in the school, work, and household domains in the ages in question, 14 to 29. But the older cohort spent substantially more time, on the average, in military service and substantially less time in marriage and parenting than the younger cohort. Probably a substantially larger proportion of the 1929 to 1933 cohort served in the armed forces during the Korean conflict than the younger cohort, which, in turn, reached and largely passed the ages of compulsory military service prior to massive American involvement in the Vietnam conflict.

Race and social class comparisons indicate very sharp differences both between black and white men and between manual and nonmanual origin men with respect to schooling. These are in the expected direction, and there are corresponding, although less sharp, differences in durations of full-time employment. Black men reported fewer months married, but more months parenting than white men. Blue-collar origin men reported both more months married and more months parenting than did white-collar origin men.

Table 6.2. Mean Person-Months Spent in Selected Combinations of Life Domains by Age

LIFE DOMAINS	AGE															
	14	15	16	17	18	19	20	21	22	23	24	25	26	27	28	29
	Mean Person-Months															
Unmarried, Childless																
Enrolled, not employed, not in military	9.5	8.8	7.5	5.6	2.9	1.8	1.3	1.0	0.7	0.5	0.4	0.3	0.2	0.1	0.0	0.0
Enrolled, employed, not in military	0.6	1.0	1.1	1.0	0.7	0.5	0.5	0.3	0.2	0.2	0.2	0.2	0.1	0.1	0.1	0.1
Not enrolled, not employed, not in military	1.0	0.7	0.6	0.9	0.9	0.6	0.5	0.5	0.4	0.4	0.2	0.2	0.2	0.2	0.1	0.1
Not enrolled, not employed, in military	0.0	0.1	0.2	0.7	1.5	2.1	2.4	2.3	1.7	1.1	0.6	0.3	0.1	0.1	0.1	0.0
Not enrolled, employed, not in military	0.7	1.2	2.1	3.2	4.9	4.9	4.1	3.4	3.2	3.0	2.8	2.5	2.1	1.8	1.6	1.4
Married, Childless																
Not enrolled, not employed, in military	0.0	0.0	0.0	0.0	0.1	0.2	0.5	0.7	0.7	0.6	0.5	0.3	0.2	0.1	0.1	0.1
Not enrolled, employed, not in military	0.0	0.0	0.1	0.1	0.3	0.6	0.9	1.2	1.4	1.5	1.6	1.7	1.6	1.6	1.5	1.2
Married, with Child																
Not enrolled, employed, not in military	0.0	0.0	0.0	0.0	0.1	0.4	0.9	1.6	2.4	3.5	4.4	5.4	6.2	6.8	7.5	8.0
All Other Combinations	0.2	0.2	0.4	0.5	0.6	0.9	0.9	1.0	1.3	1.2	1.3	1.1	1.3	1.2	1.0	1.1

Source: Adapted from D. L. Featherman, D. P. Hogan, and A. Sorensen, "Entry into Adulthood; Profiles of Young Men in the 1950's," *Life Span Development and Behavior* 6(1984):159–202, Tables 1, 2.

LIFE-SPAN DEVELOPMENT ACCOUNTS
AND THEORIES OF AGE GRADING

An interdisciplinary approach to the study of human development and behavior, age grading, and the life course encompassing especially psychologists and sociologists and emphasizing empirical research and empirically grounded and tested theory has emerged in recent years and addresses description and analysis of the human life span and life-span development. The underlying themes of life-span development research and theory are indicated cryptically by Baltes and Brim in their Preface to a recent collection of research papers titled *Life-Span Development and Behavior* (Baltes and Brim, 1978):

> ... research and theory in life-span development have given increased attention to the issue of constancy and change in human development. The assumption that the experiences of infancy and early childhood have a lasting effect on adulthood and personality is under increasing challenge by careful studies of the effects of early experiences, the results of which have not been entirely supportive of the traditional view. Second, life-span scholars are more sensitive to the restrictive consequences of studying only specific age periods such as old age, infancy, or adolescence. A life-span development view encourages every scholar to relate the facts about one age group to similar facts in other age groups, and to move toward the study of transformation of characteristics over the life span. A third issue of high salience in current life-span research is the effect on human development of growing up in different historical eras. The course of history influences the life patterns of different birth cohorts, and we see that each birth cohort has features of uniqueness because it shares the experience of certain events and conditions of the same age as it moves through its lifetime. (Baltes and Brim, 1978, xiii–xiv)

In an important review paper, Featherman (1985) has traced the themes, motifs, and interdisciplinary convergences in social scientific research informed by life-span perspectives. These include, for example, six central propositions:

1. Developmental change, synonymous with aging, occurs over the entire course of life. Neither aging nor development is limited to or even centered upon any particular time of life.
2. Developmental changes reflect biological, social, psychological, and historical events.
3. There are multiple determinants of constancy and change in behavior and personality. Their influences are expressed interactively and cumulatively and define sequences or trajectories of life events.
4. Individuals are active participants in their own development. Life histories result from interactions among multiple determinants of development and motivated responses of individuals. For this reason there can be few generalizations about constancies in adult human development.
5. Successive birth cohorts age through different possible trajectories of events reflecting sociohistorical change and individual responses to it.
6. Intervention to affect the course of development among adults and the aged may be as effective as that among the young, since behavior and personality are malleable throughout the life course.

Beyond the elucidation of these and other themes and motifs, Featherman is very careful to eschew claims of any special "life-span theory" informing research in this perspective, or of any theoretical breakthroughs imputed to the life-span perspective or its interdisciplinary convergences. Yet, he poses the inquiries into the sociology of life chances, psychometric intelligence, and the social history of family relations and human development as areas of inquiry in which this perspective with its special outlook on constancy and change, and on the relationships between individual or family development and societal change, offers promise of special value or progress in academic understandings as well as in age-related public policy.

The Central Hypotheses of Age Grading and the Life Course

It is from the research conducted in the life-span perspectives of the several disciplines that the central hypotheses of trends, variations, and change in the life course and age grading have been emerging in recent years:

Compared to the past,
1. Age grading is more encompassing, affects more spheres of life, activity, relationships.

Thus, for example, schooling, driving instruction and licensing, dating and courtship, eligibility for marriage, conscription to military service, voting privileges and candidacy for public office, retirement and income entitlements upon retirement are all affected by norms and even legislation linking these activities and relationships to approximate or exact ages.

2. Age grading is more detailed, more complex; year-by-year, rather than category-by-category; many more age-grades per decade and per lifetime.

School grades are generally reckoned in specific years or even half-years rather than by age category. Job seniority, or time in grade in large bureaucracies, are similarly reckoned in specific years rather than in periods. Eligibility for adult activities, such as drinking and recreation, driving, marriage, adoption of children, and the like is determined in terms of specific ages rather than by general adulthood status.

3. Age grading is more differentiated, with different patterns, clocks, timing, durations for the separate social spheres or domains the more highly differentiated social and economic life and relationships.

Thus departure from parental home, marriage, military service, eligibility for public office, professional licensing, employment histories, and householding are all related to adulthood. But they are entered at different times and described by separate standards and clocks.

4. Social time overwhelms biological time, for the most part. Age-indifferent policy intervention is feasible.

Age-related activity and fundamental transitions such as those relating to employment and career patterns, or marriage, household formation, parenthood, and empty nest are not driven only, nor even primarily, by chronological or biological age. Rather, they are initiated and carried out under the impetus of social contingencies and norms.

5. Social time was traditionally dominated by (a) family and family considerations, subsequently by (b) workplace and employment contingencies, and most recently, increasingly by (c) the state.

Thus the state compulsory school attendance rules and late adolescent or early adulthood schooling and training options, rather than consideration of family or labor market contingencies, govern the timing of departure from parental home and entrance into employment or marriage. Similarly, state pension and income maintenance arrangements as well as, or perhaps more importantly than, family and labor market contingencies, govern retirement. In between schooling and retirement, a variety of other state provisions and activities—from wars and obligatory military service to family allowances, community and housing development, tax policy, and economic and social development activities—impinge upon the age-graded activities and relationships of family life, residence, work histories, and community participation.

To these we may add a hypothesis emerging from the discussion in Part I concerning the bearing of demographic trends, patterns of joint survival, and the availability of kin, on life-course transitions:

6. The pattern of dependency, obligations, and entitlements inside and outside the kinship network is a major determinant of the timing and directions of major life-course transitions.

The numbers, ages, physical locations, personal situations, and relationships and mutual dependencies and obligations of parents, children, siblings, and spouse at any given point in the life course bear strongly upon the needs, wishes, abilities, ease, and directions of transitions into, out of, or within virtually all of the life-course domains. Moreover, *change* in the pattern of dependency, obligations, or entitlements is often itself a life-course transition. Thus the departure or death of a close relative, the changing employment or health status of a spouse, the marriage of a child, are all themselves life-course transitions for the individual. We return specifically to this hypothesis in the next section on life-course transitions.

LIFE-COURSE TRANSITIONS

Both the concepts of psychosocial or developmental life stages and life-course domains implicitly imply the idea of life-course transitions. We noted earlier that the life stages discussions almost invariably embody the question of adjustment or adaptation to that stage, implying the problematic dimensions of transition from the previous stage. Also, movements into and out of life-course domains are frequently viewed as examples of life-course transitions. Thus, differences in levels of psychological well-being characterizing responses of different ages or different life stages were *imputed* by Campbell (1981) to life-course or family-cycle transitions—for example, improvements in well-being associated with marriage or declines associated with marital dissolution. However, he has qualified these analyses somewhat and recognized the need for inferences based on longitudinal studies rather than the cross-sectional comparisons actually made. The more recent research on the life course has increasingly sought ways to study life-course events and transitions directly rather than synthetically by comparisons of age groups or by models incorporating data from distinct age groups.

Cohort Changes in the Transition to Adulthood

Early analyses of transitions of a cohort into adulthood were carried out by Winsborough (1978, 1979), who examined the length of time required for successive cohorts to complete transitions in four domains: completing school, taking a first full-time job, entrance to and exit from the armed forces, and entrance into first marriage. The basic data used for this analysis are survey respondents' reports of dates or ages at which relevant life-course events took place (for example, completion of school, first job, marriage), even if the respondents did not report subsequent changes, events, or histories. The length of each transition for a cohort was measured as the difference in age at which 25 percent and age at which 75 percent of the cohort had accomplished the passage. Winsborough found that for the earliest cohorts the entire progression—movement through all four transitions—took about eighteen years, but for recent cohorts it took slightly less than ten years. Thus the length of time a cohort spends in the transition from schoolboy to adult has almost halved.

Normative Order of Transitions in Different
Life-Course Domains

Hogan (1978) showed that there is a characteristic, or normative, *order* in which men move through the three transitions: school completion, entrance into the labor force, and marriage, in that order, and that deviation from the normative order on transitions carries sanctions or costs in terms of subsequent socioeconomic attainments (Hogan, 1978, 1981). In contrast to Winsborough, who studied mainly the successive cohort distributions by ages at which relevant events or transitions took place, Hogan studied the individual life-course transitions reported in the same or similar survey materials, the correlates of their variations, and effects of early and late, or on-time and off-time transitions.

For example, Hogan found, not so surprisingly, that American men of high social origins have on the average completed school later, entered first postschooling full-time jobs later, and married later than those of lower social origins (Table 6.3). But

Table 6.3.   Median Age at School Completion, First Job, and First Marriage, and Measures of Normative Ordering and Duration of Transitions to Adulthood: U.S. Males Born 1907–1952, by Social Class Background

TRANSITION TO ADULTHOOD	SOCIAL CLASS BACKGROUND				
	High White Collar	Low White Collar	Skilled Blue Collar	Unskilled Blue Collar	Farm
Median age at:					
School completion	22.16	20.97	18.61	18.20	17.46
First full-time job	22.12	21.29	19.47	18.90	18.72
First marriage	24.41	24.33	23.62	23.53	23.65
*Percent distribution by degree of normative ordering**	100.0	100.0	100.0	100.0	100.0
Normative	51.4	55.9	62.4	66.2	66.4
Intermediate nonnormative	18.5	19.2	18.5	18.9	20.7
Extreme nonnormative	30.1	24.1	19.1	14.9	12.9
Duration of transition to adulthood (years)	9.44	9.87	9.92	10.76	12.54

*Normative ordering of events occurs when a man first completes school, next begins to work, and lastly marries. The intermediate nonnormative pattern occurs when a man begins a job prior to finishing school or marries prior to beginning work, but after the completion of schooling. Extreme nonnormative ordering occurs whenever a man marries prior to the completion of his education. *Source:* Adapted from D. P. Hogan, *Transitions and Social Change: The Early Lives of American Men.* (New York: Academic Press, 1981), Tables 5.1–5.5. Reprinted by permission of the publisher.

he found, also, that men of higher social origins were much more likely to experience extreme nonnormative (marrying prior to completion of education) ordering of these life-course events than the rest of the men. On the other hand, the durations of the transition to adulthood, reckoned as the number of years between the ages at which one-quarter of the men in each social class group complete their schooling and three-quarters of the men marry, are substantially longer among the men of farm and of unskilled blue-collar origins compared to the durations of transitions to adulthood among those of higher social origins.

Retrospective Life History Studies in Analysis of Life-Course Events and Transitions

In the most recent studies of life-course transitions using survey materials, researchers have attempted to obtain and analyze data on transitions in the context of full life histories reported as sets or sequences of events in each domain. These have included, for example, schooling histories, including details of all the schools attended, courses or curricula, dates begun and completed, attainments at each grade, reasons for termination or change (Shavit, 1984); or, for example, employment histories, including details of all jobs held, dates begun and completed, reasons for terminations or change (Coleman, 1984; Blossfield, 1986; Carroll and Mayer, 1986; Mayer and Carroll, 1987). Many investigations have included marriage and family formation histories, including dates of entry and termination of marriages (Marini, 1979; Michael and Tuma, 1983; Sorensen and Sorensen, 1983); births of children, and in at least one study (the Family History Survey carried out in Canada in 1984) the dates of departures of children from the parental home (Burch, 1985b).

Increasingly the studies based on such materials are illuminating the characteristic patterns of movements of individuals into, within, and out of the major life-course domains, singly and in combination (Featherman and Sorensen, 1983; Sorensen, 1983a, 1983b; Tolke, 1987); the bearing of background characteristics, historical factors, socioeconomic settings and contexts, and prior life-course experiences and transitions on such events and movements (Shavit, Matras, and Featherman, 1987); and the outcomes and effects of life-course events and movements on individual well-being (McLanahan and Sorensen, 1985) and social structure (Featherman, 1985; Featherman and Selbee, in press; Mayer et al., 1987).

Transitions among Life-Course Stages

Life-course transitions are at the same time both very familiar and quite elusive individual and social phenomena. We have already alluded to the concepts of life course and life-course transitions of cohorts as distinct from life course and life-course transitions of individuals. The ideas of stages of the life course and of life-course domains are both helpful, as is the concept of status passage in role theory (Rosow, 1976, 1985) in giving meaning to concepts of life-course transitions. Hogan (1985) views life-span transitions as "changes in discrete demographic statuses," meaning for the most part demographic events such as marriage, parenting, divorce, widowhood, and so forth occasioned by some single "vital event," although presumably it could refer to other types of status, say employment, also engendered by some single event such as taking a first job. These are surely role transitions, but they do not capture the idea of life-course transitions such as the transition to adolescence or transition to adulthood, to old age, to retirement, and so forth.

Guillemard (1982) has cast the transition from mature adulthood to old age as one involving transformations in the role and status system. In her view, there is unanimity in holding that "in our society the transition from late adulthood to old age is matched by a decline in social standing and by a shrinking of the role system, even though the loss of certain roles may be 'partially compensated' by the assumption of other new roles" (Guillemard, 1982, p. 234). Thus some change is implied in the *set* of roles performed in late adulthood to some partly different set of roles performed in old age, but there is no attempt to specify which roles are involved. This approach is strongly suggestive of the developmental stages of the life course mentioned earlier (see Table 6.1; also Clausen, 1986).

An Example: Life-Histories-Based Study of the Transition to Adulthood

An important step was taken by Featherman, Hogan, and Sorensen in the study cited earlier entitled "Entry into Adulthood" (1984). This study explicitly addresses and seeks to describe a life-course transition into a stage rather than a single role transition; at the same time, the analysis is based upon analysis of events in clearly identified life-course domains. Featherman, Hogan, and Sorensen in fact are able to describe and study the transition into adulthood using life-course domain data by defining specific combinations of values, or of events, in the several domains as stages. Thus, they argue that a social definition of adulthood can be taken as (1) having completed schooling, (2) employed at a full-time job, *and* living with his own family of procreation (that is, with a wife and, sometimes, children). This definition translates into a specific set of combinations of events or values in the schooling, employment, and marriage domains, not being in school, employed, and married. They view the specific combination—enrolled in school, not employed, not in military service, unmarried, and childless—as the translation of a definition of schoolboy state or stage.

Between adolescence and adulthood there are intermediate stages as well: Young men can leave school and remain unmarried or without obtaining full-time employment; or they can become employed without leaving school; or they may have other combinations different from the combination defined as adulthood. Featherman, Hogan, and Sorensen measured the total and mean person-months spent by their male respondents in "schoolboy," "intermediate," and "adult" stages at each single year of age from 14 to 29 (Table 6.4) and thus describe very rigorously the transition of the cohort into adulthood. At age 14, the cohort spent an average of 9.5 person-months in the "schoolboy" state, that is, more than three-fourths of the life years lived at this age. But by age 21, less than 10 percent of the life years are spent in the "schoolboy" state; by age 25 more than half, and by age 29 more than three-fourths, of the life years are spent in the "adult" state.

The manner of description of the cohort transition to adulthood used by Featherman, Hogan, and Sorensen is similar to that employed in the early studies by Winsborough. The later studies, however, provide much more detailed studies of both the events in each life-course domain and the combinations of events representing the "transitions to adulthood" of the individual respondents, so that the latter can be studied in detail with respect to the factors and correlates of variations in timing, the specific role (or specific life-course domain) transitions encompassed in the transitions to adulthood, and the outcomes in subsequent lives of the respondents. Indeed these researchers are able to draw interesting comparisons of numerous facets of entry into adulthood between cohorts, between white and black respondents, and between manual and nonmanual occupational origin men in the sample they studied as well as drawing some cross-cultural and historical comparisons (Featherman, Hogan, and Sorensen, 1984, pp. 192–95 and Table VI).

Table 6.4. Mean Person-Months Spent in Each Life-Course Domain by Age, Birth Cohort, Race, and Father's Occupation

LIFE-COURSE DOMAIN	AGE																
	14	15	16	17	18	19	20	21	22	23	24	25	26	27	28	29	Total
	Mean Person-Months																
School	10.3	10.0	9.0	7.0	4.0	2.9	2.5	2.2	1.8	1.5	1.3	1.1	1.0	0.9	0.6	0.5	56.5
Work	1.4	2.2	3.4	4.4	6.2	6.7	6.5	6.6	7.4	8.5	9.4	10.2	10.6	10.8	11.1	11.2	116.5
Military service	0.0	0.1	0.2	0.8	1.8	2.8	3.5	3.7	3.1	2.1	1.4	0.8	0.6	0.4	0.4	0.3	21.9
With parents	10.4	9.1	8.5	7.6	6.1	4.9	3.9	3.0	2.4	2.0	1.7	1.4	1.0	0.8	0.7	0.5	63.9
With family of origin	11.7	11.5	11.2	10.2	8.2	6.1	4.3	2.7	1.8	1.2	0.9	0.6	0.4	0.3	0.2	0.1	71.3
Married	0.0	0.0	0.0	0.1	0.6	1.5	2.6	4.0	5.3	6.5	7.6	8.4	9.1	9.6	10.0	10.2	75.4
Parenting	0.1	0.2	0.2	0.2	0.2	0.6	1.0	1.8	2.9	4.1	5.2	6.2	7.1	7.8	8.3	8.9	54.7

POPULATION GROUP	LIFE-COURSE DOMAIN						
	School	Work	Military Service	With Parents	With Family of Origin	Married	Parenting
Total	56.5	116.5	21.9	63.9	71.3	75.4	54.7
Birth cohort							
1929–33	56.5	115.2	24.9	63.8	71.4	73.0	52.3
1934–39	56.5	117.8	18.7	64.1	71.3	77.9	57.3
Race							
Black	45.0	121.3	19.2	60.4	76.2	72.2	56.4
White	58.0	115.9	22.2	63.1	71.3	74.1	53.9
Father's occupation							
Blue collar, farm	51.7	119.5	22.6	66.0	71.8	77.0	56.5
White collar	71.3	107.6	19.3	60.6	70.8	69.2	48.8

Source: D. L. Featherman, D. P. Hogan, and A. Sorensen, "Entry into Adulthood: Profiles of Young Men in the 1950's," *Life Span Development and Behavior*, 6(1984):159–202, Table 5.

Dependency, Obligations, Entitlements, and Life-Course Transitions

An important theme in historical studies of the family is the substitution of market, public, or state loci of support, dependency, obligations, and entitlements for those traditionally located in the family and in kin networks, and that such substitution bears importantly upon the structure and timetables of the individual life course (Modell et al., 1976; Katz, 1982; Hareven, 1982). These in turn are viewed partially as outcomes of the demographic transitions themselves and partially as outcomes of the industrialization, modernization, migration and urbanization, and differentiation of family from employment and productive activity over time.

Unfortunately broadly based (distinct from case study) information even on the availability of kin, much less on the characteristics of kin network members and on the ways in which kin are supportive and provide resources to—or, conversely, in which kin place demands upon and drain resources from—the individual is very meager. Yet a central hypothesis of this work is that the pattern of dependency, obligations, and entitlements inside and outside the kinship network is a major determinant of the timing and directions of major life-course transitions—whether schooling, household formation, marriage or other sexual union formation or dissolution, seeking employment or withdrawing from employment, and possibly health and morbidity transitions. Exploration and testing of this hypothesis is the major challenge posed here; an important part of this challenge is the development of useful and credible measures of dependency, obligations, and entitlements of individuals in the various life-course domains and stages.

The hypothesis is by no means a novel one, although perhaps it is formulated here rather more generally than usually found. Sibship size, and also birth order, have been found to have statistically significant effects on various facets of status attainment and socioeconomic achievement (Boyd, 1985; Boyd, Featherman, and Matras, 1980; Featherman and Hauser, 1978; Hauser and Featherman, 1977; Duncan, Featherman, and Duncan, 1972; Blau and Duncan, 1967), although no exact mechanism or dependency conditions beyond the presumption of availability of parental time and resources have been established. There is a prominent hypothesis and some suggestive findings relating earning capabilities of women to the propensities to divorce and separation; indeed at least one study has suggested that income maintenance or provision schemes have the effect of allowing women otherwise entirely dependent on husbands to separate or divorce (Groeneveld, Tuma, and Hannon, 1980; Tuma and Hannon, 1984, secs. 6.2 and 7.2).

Studies in the American negative income tax experiment have suggested that availability of extraemployment income entitlements bears on the propensity of youths and adult men and women to remain in employment or to seek new employment after job terminations (McDonald and Stephenson, 1979; West, 1980; Robins, Tuma, and Yaeger, 1980). The very few studies of the timing of departure of youths or young adults from parental homes suggest the importance of either employment and self-support or sufficient parental support for establishment of separate dwelling arrangements as factors in the early (premarriage) departure from parental homes (Goldscheider and DaVanzo, 1985; LeBourdais and Gold-scheider, 1986; Young, 1974, 1975). Kobrin (1976), Pampel (1983), Sweet and Bumpass (1984), and others have suggested that the great increase in single-person household formation and maintenance among elderly widows rests upon their liberation from financial dependency upon their children. Residential patterns of elderly are frequently found to be related to their independence or dependency in activities of daily life (ADL).

Finally, and perhaps most important, is the analysis of Oppenheimer relating the entrance of women into the labor force to family life cycle-based income squeezes coincident with the possibility, from the point of view of age composition of family members, for women to seek extrahousehold employment (Oppenheimer, 1982). According to this analysis, individuals, couples, and families experience relative deprivation and economic stress in relation to the actual or anticipated burdens and costs of marriage and setting up a household, or in relation to child dependency. The latter, especially, varies and changes during the life cycle and in accordance with the number and ages of children. The responses to life-cycle squeezes and dependency that Oppenheimer analyzes include postponement of marriage, the timing of childbearing and family limitation, and, especially, the labor force participation of wives.

Concluding Remarks: Life-Course Transitions and Public Policy

The most familiar—and probably the most important—of the life-course and family-cycle transitions are leaving school, leaving the parental home, entering employment, marriage, childbearing, household formation, migration, job mobility, large gain (or loss) of income, departure (or death) of children, withdrawal from employment, own or family member's serious illness, death of parents, death of spouse, other marital or union dissolution, and death of friends or intimates. Other important transitions could include those involving second- or higher-degree kin (for example, grandparents, aunts, uncles, or cousins) or friends, and personal life-course transitions tied to the developments, changes, or transitions of extrafamilial social units: business organizations, political parties, and so forth. For systematic study and analysis, each of these requires translation into combinations of life-course domain events.

The more familiar transitions listed almost always carry some direct or indirect implication of increment or decrement or change in demand for a public or social service (Davis and van den Oeven, 1981). These include most obviously health care, educational, and income maintenance services, but also planning, regulatory, protective, legal, and administrative services as well.

We know in a general way that the frequency, timing, and directions of these transitions vary in the population, and that their distributions have changed over time. Yet we have surprisingly little knowledge of the actual baseline frequency and timing distributions of the major transitions. For example, How many women have never worked outside the home? What are the ages at which young persons leave school? At what ages do men enter their first full-time jobs? What is the distribution of durations of employment in first full-time jobs? How many young persons leave their parental homes before marriage, and when? At what ages are women widowed? How many men experience widowhood, at what ages, and for how long? How long do couples live in the houses into which they move after marriage? How many additional residences do they have until widowhood or marital dissolution? What is the distribution of durations of widowhood ended by remarriage, or widowhood ended by death?

Clearly the answers to these kinds of questions are of considerable importance in the planning and evaluation of a wide range of public and social services. So, too, are answers to questions concerning the individual, family and kin network, and socioeconomic factors that bear on variations and change in the distributions of frequencies, timing, and directions of life-course transitions. Client and target populations of the public and social service agencies and organizations are, of course, not only persons of given ages and sexes, but persons in various states and statuses, engaged in activities in the various life-course domains, and characterized by given configurations of resources as well as needs. These, in turn, are direct and indirect outcomes of the present and past structure of the life course, with individuals moving across the life-course stages and transitions in accordance with rules and regularities so far primarily conjectured and hypothesized, but hopefully to be investigated and ascertained systematically.

7

WORK, PARENTING, AND THEIR ALTERNATIVES IN THE LIFE COURSE

INTRODUCTION

Throughout history adult men and women in Western societies have been taken up with work and with parenting, and children have been taken up with preparing for work and parenting. People have not only been physically *engaged* in work and parenting, but—at least since the Protestant Reformation and perhaps even earlier—societies have been taken up culturally, normatively, and ideologically with work and parenting. This has been so regardless of the actual instances or tolerance of exceptions and deviations. Moreover, we are tied to rhetoric, ideology, and norms of work and parenting despite the dramatic reductions in manpower input requirements to sustain acceptable levels of material welfare and despite the dramatic reductions in fertility and childrearing required to sustain population levels. For the most part we have been unable to legitimate and institutionalize alternative life-course activities other than prechildrearing and postchildrearing housekeeping, schooling, sometimes military service, and most recently retirement.

Each of these alternatives is, for its part, conditional upon arrangements for the material support and basic welfare of the individuals not employed, and not able to claim income from employment in the paid labor force. In other words, in the absence of imperatives for employment or for parenting, there are only a few legitimate and acceptable activities—other than schooling, soldiering, housekeeping, and retirement—with which to fill our lives.

The Struggle for Scarce Employment in the Absence of Alternatives

The search—or as many would have it, the struggle—for jobs results in politicization of the labor market and segmentation on ascriptive and primordial bases. Exclusion from desirable employment is typically arranged with reference to sex, race, religion, or ethnic origins. That is, employers—and often trade unions and professional or licensing agencies and organizations—may prefer or may exclude persons of some particular sex, race, religion, or ethnic origin. But more than anything else, recruitment to and exclusion from employment are rigged in terms of age criteria; basically, the young and the old are excluded from the best employment, as are the women of all ages.

In this chapter we describe the continuing centrality of work and parenting in the life course of men and women in contemporary societies. We also explore some of the variations and changes in life-course patterns of work and parenting. And, in particular, we return to the theme of the historical contraction and compacting of work and parenting in the lives of individuals and families and consider some of the emerging alternatives and their implications and problems for individual, family, and social well-being.

EMPLOYMENT AND CAREERS

How much of life is devoted to work? By some accounts, all of it. Yet the answer to this question surely varies in accordance with the historical time to which we refer and to whom we are referring. And not least, it probably depends further on the ages or life-course stages of those about whom we are inquiring. Moreover, for many periods and socioeconomic settings, and for many types of individuals, the very definition of work is problematic; it is probably correct to assert the measurement of work is problematic virtually always.

For purposes of this discussion we shall initially ignore problems of definition and measurement and adopt the gainful worker, labor force participation, and employment and unemployment concepts in the international population censuses and labor force and employment surveys usages, recognizing that these do not always capture activities or statuses that we might wish to view as work. Thus, for example, all who have engaged in child care, housekeeping, care of a family member, or volunteer activity know that these demand effort, commitment, and often skills that are not less than those accorded paid employment. Yet in conventional census and survey usage these are not identified as work unless performed for pay or profit.

On the basis of data for the various countries and populations, and beginning with nineteenth-century European census indicators, it is probably correct to say that most men, at most ages, have reported being at work or in gainful employment. There has been an historical decrease in the frequencies or rates at which boys, adolescent males, young adult or postadolescent men, and late-middle-aged and elderly men have been at work, gainfully employed, or seeking employment. In the past women and girls were only infrequently at work or in gainful employment—and those who were were mostly nonmarried women—but the numbers and proportions of women at all ages and in all marital statuses, employed or in the labor force has increased dramatically in this century.

Calculations and inferences employing such data and constructing hypothetical cohorts, their total life years and life years at each age, and their life years in employment at each age and altogether (Smith, 1982) show that

1. For both males and females total volume of life years has increased with declining mortality and increasing longevity.
2. Total volume of life years in the labor force (employed, or seeking employment) has increased; but
3. For males the proportion of total life years spent in employment or in the labor force has decreased markedly while
4. For females the proportion of total life years in employment or in the labor force has increased (Figure 7.1).

However, such calculations and models of hypothetical cohorts do not yield satisfactory, much less definitive, answers to the question, "How much of life is devoted to work?" for actual people or groups, nor do they give us *distributions* of a population or cohort by work-life time, volume, or pattern. We generally do not have data that can describe lifetime or life-course patterns of work—the actual numbers working through entire lifetimes, the numbers working only through part of their lifetimes, and perhaps those never, or almost never, working at all.

It is important to distinguish between current work and lifetime work. At any moment or period of time, some persons are working or have worked very intensively, say many hours of the day, or many days of the week or month, or many days or weeks of the year, while others work less intensively, say fewer hours or even less than full time, fewer days weekly or monthly, or with more frequent holidays, and still others may not be working at all in the period in question. Thus *current* work or employment varies in intensity, and it is of interest and importance to study and understand the reasons for this variation and the trends over time in intensity of current employment or work.

Over the lifetimes of any group of persons, some will have worked very intensively, perhaps for virtually all the years of their lives or even, hypothetically, from early childhood until death. Others may have worked somewhat less intensively, starting later though continuing to work to quite advanced ages or to death, or starting early but withdrawing from work or employment relatively early or, at least, a number of years before death. Still others may have worked even less intensively over their lifetimes, starting employment quite late, withdrawing or retiring early, or perhaps even withdrawing temporarily once or even more times. Finally, some may not have worked or been employed at all during their lifetimes, either in the absence of any need or wish for employment or because they were engaged in other activities, for example, housekeeping, childrearing, or care of others. Thus *lifetime* work or employment varies in

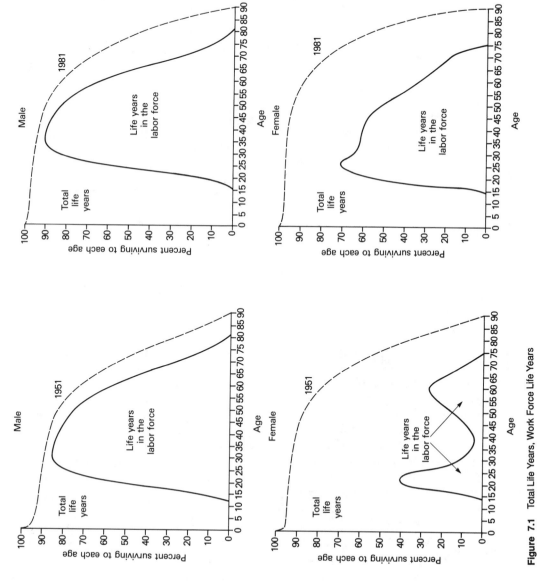

Figure 7.1 Total Life Years, Work Force Life Years

intensity. As in the case of current work, it is interesting and important to study and understand the reasons for this variation and the trends over time in intensity of lifetime employment or work.

The questions we wish to pose in this chapter include:

1. What, if any, are the modal patterns and main variants of current work behavior at each age and what, if any, are the modal patterns and main variants of lifetime work behavior? How have they been changing over time?
2. To the extent that the intensity of current work *and* the intensity of lifetime work have been declining or contracting, what are the main reasons, factors, or correlates of the contracting and compacting of work and worklife? What are the weights of the alleged preference for leisure, evolvement of alternative sources of income, factors of health and disability, or labor market and employment factors?
3. To the extent that the intensity of current work and/or the intensity of lifetime work have been increasing or expanding, what are the reasons, factors, and correlates?
4. How many and who *never* work? What do they do?
5. Among those who work, what are the main features of their lifetime work patterns, histories, careers, or employment trajectories? What do they do when they don't work? What income sources, entitlements, or support do they have when they don't work? How, if at all, is what they do when they don't work related to what they do when they do work?

We turn first to a very brief examination and review of patterns of current work behavior by sex and age.

Current Labor Force Status

For all countries for which data are available, and for all the years or time periods for which they exist, virtually all men aged 25 to 50 years are reported in census or survey data to be working or in the labor force. For men in these ages, working has clearly been the usual situation for all but a very small percentage, say 4 or 5 percent. The latter probably include persons disabled, physically or mentally ill, or other deviant cases. For men at other ages—that is, for children, adolescents, or even young adult men under 25 years of age, and for men aged 55 and over, and for women at all ages—no such pattern of universal working attachment is observed across the various countries or over time, and no such generalization is possible (see, for example, Table 7.1). Rather, there are variations among the various countries in the percentages working or participating in the labor force among those of the various age groups. There have been some dramatic changes over time.

Women in industrial societies are much more frequently reported working (in the sense of the participation in the labor market, for pay or profit, and outside their households generally) than women in agrarian or in semi-industrial societies. Moreover in industrial societies there has been very dramatic growth in the numbers of women of all ages, especially married women, in the labor force. In agrarian societies and in semi-industrial societies, the percentages of women, especially women in the traditional childbearing ages, 15 through 45 or 49,

Table 7.1.   Labor Force Participation Rates by Sex and Age: United States, 1920–1986

	MALE				FEMALE			
Age	1920	1950	1970	1986	1920	1950	1970	1986
Total	85.9	82.4	79.7	76.3	24.1	31.9	43.3	76.3
14–19	55.9	47.5	n.a.	n.a.	29.6	26.4	n.a.	n.a.
16–19			56.1	56.4			44.0	53.0
20–24	90.7	86.9	83.3	85.8	39.3	44.4	57.7	72.4
25–34	96.2	94.4	96.4	94.6	25.0	33.5	45.0	71.6
35–44	96.6	96.5	96.9	94.8	20.6	38.0	51.1	73.1
45–54	94.5	94.6	94.3	91.0	19.4	36.9	54.4	65.9
55–64	87.4	85.1	83.0	67.3	15.3	27.3	43.0	42.3
65+	57.1	45.0	26.8	16.0	8.2	9.5	9.7	7.4

Source: 1920, 1950: G. Bancroft, "Trends in Labor Force," in W. Haber et al., eds., *Manpower in the United States, Problems and Policies* (New York: Harper & Bros., 1954); 1970, 1986: U.S. Bureau of the Census, *Statistical Abstract of the United States, 1988,* 108th ed. (Washington, D.C.: Government Printing Office), Table 608, p. 366.

reported as working or in the labor force have been and remain low, generally under 20 percent. Indeed in many industrial societies the percentage of women in the labor force, other than adolescents, did not exceed that figure by much until recently (Table 7.1).

After World War II and especially since the 1960s there has been a steep increase in numbers and percentages of women working outside their households. The trend toward increasing female labor force activity has accompanied declining fertility in the industrialized countries as well as profound changes in the occupational structure of the labor force. These have involved, on the one hand, great expansion of professional, service, and clerical and administrative activities and occupations and, on the other hand, introduction of production and assembly processes in manufacturing, both of which have tended to increase employment opportunities for women.

Participation of adolescent, and even young adult, men in the labor force has undergone more or less continuous decline throughout the twentieth century in industrialized and semiindustrialized societies and even to a certain extent in agrarian societies. This trend has been accompanied by extension of schooling and vocational training, in part due to compulsory school attendance legislation, but in more recent years largely extending well beyond compulsory schooling. Successive cohorts of men have enjoyed progressively higher median years of schooling, reaching 12.0 years among those born in the United States in 1921 to 1924 and 12.3 years among those born in 1931 to 1934. In the United States in 1980 no fewer than 58 percent of young persons in the 20 to 24 age group were still attending school, whether in higher education or vocational training, reflecting substantially higher rates in median school attainment than in other industrialized countries but, nevertheless, illustrating the trend (see Table 7.2).

At the other end of the age scale, there has been a trend toward diminishing participation in the labor force among men aged 50 and over, especially since the late 1960s. A trend toward diminishing labor force participation among men aged 65 and over in industrial societies is discernible even earlier and is presumably associated with the growth of retirement whether enforced by mandatory job separation rules or encouraged by pension plans and benefits, or both. However, after 1965 to 1970 there have been dramatic reductions in numbers and percentages of employed men in the 50- or 55–64 age groups as well as in the 65 and over groups, a trend generally connoted early retirement (Table 7.1).

In summarizing changes in the twentieth century in worklife relative to total life years, S. J. Smith (1982) notes that in 1900 the total life and the worklife expectancies of young men were very similar: Men at age 20 could anticipate spending an average of only 4.4 years outside the labor force. By 1977 men's total life expectancy increased by 23 years. The bulk of this increase—about 17 years—has been allocated to non-labor force activities. The growth in worklife expectancy in this period was less than six years. At the turn of the century about 69 percent of life years were devoted to labor force participation or activity. But by 1977, this percentage dropped substantially to about 55 percent.

The labor market worklife, or what Smith calls the "formal worklife," of women has, by contrast, increased dramatically during this century. In 1900, life years of women in the labor force amounted only to an average of six years. But by 1977 life expectancy for women increased by 29 years, of which no less than 21 years, on the average, are devoted to labor force participation and activity. Indeed most recently, length of expected worklife has increased much faster than length of total life. Between 1970 and 1977 worklife durations rose by five years, while life expectancy increased by only 2.3 years. Thus there has been a reallocation of time—represented by the average of three life years per woman—from home to labor force activities, in this short period. Women in 1900 spent, on the average, 13 percent of their life years in labor force participation. But by 1977 this percentage increased to almost 36 percent.

Thus worklife durations of men and of women have been converging in this century. In 1940 the total work years of women amounted to no more than about 30 percent of men's total work years. But this percentage had increased to 57 percent by 1970. By 1977 women's total work years reached to about 71 percent of men's (Smith, 1982).

In general it is difficult to determine *cause* of working or not working. Although there are a number of studies in which respondents have been asked to give reasons, there are many difficulties both in assessing the reliability of responses to such questions and in interpreting them. An important avenue of inquiry concerning factors in the variation in propensity or rates of labor force participation at the different ages and their changes over time has been through comparison of rates of participation among various subgroups in the population.

Thus, for example, in the past the rates of labor force participation were relatively high among women with most education, with few or no small children, in large cities, or with husbands with middle to upper-middle incomes and educational attainment and with middle to high occupational status. However, recent trends in labor force participation of women suggest that women in the categories previously characterized by low labor force participation (including those with small children and those with lower-education- or lower-status-husbands) are increasingly in the labor force, that is, working or seeking paid employment.

Among adolescents or young men, rates of labor force participation have been inversely related with factors associated with extended schooling or vocational training, to be sure. However, recent studies have developed the hypothesis that extended schooling has often occurred in the absence of employment opportunities for adolescent or young adult men. The relationships between schooling, labor force participation, employment, and unemployment now appear to be different for black and Hispanic minorities than for white majority young men (Coleman, 1984; Hirschman, 1988).

Among middle-aged or young elderly men, it appears to be those in blue-collar or manual occupations with highest propensity to withdraw from employment relatively early; for example, prior to age 65, while self-employed men and men in professional or managerial occupations tend to continue in the labor force to more advanced ages. But, as we shall note below, actual detailed studies of entrance into or withdrawal from employment and labor force participation are few.

Careers or Job Histories?

The concept of career has reference to the sequence or succession of employment episodes or jobs that an individual has during his working lifetime. In general, the idea of career, as distinct from job, denotes some sort of progression among successive jobs; usually the expectation is that career progressions involve successively more complex or more responsible tasks, more autonomy or job authority, higher intrinsic or extrinsic rewards, or higher social status related to the jobs; that is, that the episodes of an individual's career are stages, are ordered, and have some hierarchical relationships. However, it is also possible—and indeed empirically very frequent—that successions of jobs are characterized by no particular order, hierarchical relationships, or increments to rewards, authority, or prestige. S. Spilerman, a pioneer researcher of occupations, jobs, and careers, has labeled the two contrasting types of job sequences *ordered careers* and *chaotic careers* respectively (Spilerman, 1977; see also Wilensky, 1961).

The actual study of careers is not yet very well developed. First, the distinction between a career and a job or a sequence of jobs remains ambiguous. Second, the many ways of characterizing careers are not yet sorted out in any definitive way. Intuitively it would seem that initial job and one or more subsequent jobs, or sometimes the last job, should be included in such characterizations. But the possibilities for choice of jobs to include, and for ways to characterize them, seem very, very numerous. Finally, once a procedure for delineating careers is adopted, it often turns out that the number and variety of distinct careers are so vast as to defy classification other than in most elementary ways and, hence, render description of relationships between careers and personal or social factors very open and allowing virtually limitless and sometimes confusing directions.

Thus, careers can be characterized in terms of their length in time; the numbers of jobs involved; characteristics of first, final, and intervening jobs; patterns of job authority; and intrinsic and extrinsic job rewards. Careers may be viewed as social trajectories that exist independently of those having them; for example, the political career, medical career, professional sports career. Careers can be viewed in terms of their impact upon those moving through them, in terms of the family and community implications of their structure, or in terms of the social strata which clusters of careers generate.

In a paper reviewing the issues and findings of studies on work histories of women and men, Treiman (1985) notes the great complexity of studying sequences of jobs, career lines, or job trajectories. Indeed he is skeptical about the very possibility of classifying or aggregating individual job histories into coherent sequences or careers that can be systematically studied. Nonetheless his review of work histories is very illuminating and an important milestone for further investigation. He examines first the patterns of labor force participation over the life course and confirms that male labor force participation patterns have not changed much in recent years. The exception is that participation rates of young men have declined because they are remaining in school longer than they used to. Participation becomes nearly universal among young men in their thirties and forties. It subsequently declines as men begin to retire in their fifties, whether voluntarily or because of injuries or impairments preventing them from continuing.

Among women, labor force participation has increased steadily in the twentieth century. This has been accompanied by a notable change in age-specific patterns of participation. Among female cohorts entering the labor force after the turn of the century and until the mid-1950s, there was a double-peak pattern of labor force participation, in which women worked before marriage or childbearing, left the labor force to raise children, and then returned after their children were partially grown, albeit, Treiman notes, at younger and younger ages. But among cohorts completing school and entering the labor force since the 1960s, the women characteristically have *not* left the labor force for extended child*rearing*, but only briefly for child*bearing*. This pattern is evident in the data presented in the right-hand columns of Table 7.1.

Canadian data on work histories in relation to family histories have shown that, whereas marriage was previously not only the major reason for women's employment interruption, such interruptions were previously permanent. Only among later cohorts did women return to employment after years of childrearing. More recently marriage is only a minor reason for work interruptions, and they are brief. The major reason for work interruptions now is pregnancy and childbearing, and their length has diminished dramatically over successive cohorts of Canadian women (Robinson, 1987).

Job histories of both men and women in the United States are characterized by very extensive occupational mobility. According to Treiman (1985), Americans apparently change both jobs and occupations much more frequently than workers in other industrialized countries. The propensity to change occupations is highest at youngest ages, or earliest in the work histories. It declines with age or work experience, and then rises slightly near the end of careers or work histories. But even in mid-career ages there is extensive occupational mobility. Of men and women aged 30 to 39 when enumerated in the 1970 census and who had been in the labor force both in 1965 and 1970, about two-fifths had changed occupations in the 1965 to 1970 interval. Among those over 40 about one-third changed occupations.

A large fraction of the men begin their work histories as semiskilled or unskilled workers, and many experience substantial upward mobility in the course of their careers, often moving into skilled manual or managerial positions. Women tend to begin their work histories in higher status occupations than men, because a large fraction of them begin as clerical workers. In contrast to the men, women on the average experience slight *downward* mobility in the course of their work histories. Treiman (1985) offers a very interesting and provocative analysis of these differences.

Job Sequences or Careers of Women

Do women have careers or only jobs? How many women have careers? What are the special features of women's careers? What are the relationships between jobs and family roles and between "careers" and family roles? What are the measures of satisfaction, attainment, and other features of career paths of women? What is the meaning of sexual equality in the employment spheres? What are the interesting or useful comparisons between men and women with respect to job histories and to careers? Are there sex-typed careers? Do careers free women and render them independent of their fathers, brothers, husbands, and so forth, in their personal lives and their social participation?

These are questions that fall far short of the heart of the emerging debate on gender and stratification. (See, for example, Huber and Spitze, 1983; Crompton and Mann, 1986; Mason, 1986; England and Farkas, 1986 for statements and background discussions on gender and stratification.) They are probably central enough to the prospects and outlook for women's employment in a future characterized by continuing reduction of total labor market employment and diminishing proportions of total lifetime in such employment. They are also central to the present and future quality of the lives of women and their families. But, our knowledge of work histories and careers of women, as of men, is quite restricted. Again, we turn to Treiman's (1985) review.

As noted above, women's labor force participation has in the past been characterized by the double-peak pattern: initial entrance into the employment, followed by withdrawal associated with marriage and childrearing, or, more recently, with childbearing only. A new pattern of continuous labor force participation without interruptions for childrearing has been emerging only recently. The large fraction of women leaving and returning to work after a period of time outside the labor force are believed to be at a great disadvantage in the competition for jobs, compared to men or compared to women with continuous work patterns. Presumably, the changing pattern in the direction of employment continuity should result in similarity and convergence of women's and men's career opportunities.

However, comparison of the careers of women who *have* had continuous work experience—a small minority in the total—with those of men does not seem to suggest that such a convergence of opportunities is present. The women have typically worked at different kinds of jobs, have had less upward mobility over the course of their working lives, and have earned much less than men. Treiman speculates that as continuous labor force participation comes to be the norm for women, which is what seems to be happening currently, there may possibly be a reduction in occupational and career segregation of men and women and some convergence in their earnings. At the same time, he notes that in Eastern Europe, where women have long had continuous labor force participation, there has been as much occupational segregation and nearly as great an earnings gap between men and women.

The employment discontinuities are very frequently held to affect women's chances for promotion or upward mobility. At least one study has documented the inverse relationships between women's marital and maternal status and their occupational mobility patterns (Sewell, Hauser, and Wolf, 1980). But, as Treiman has pointed out, even never married women with continuous work histories have less upward mobility than men. Despite being better qualified, on the average, than men, the women are less likely to move into managerial or nonretail sales jobs, and more likely to get smaller returns or payoff to their employment experience in terms of income, than men.

For the majority of women experiencing interruption and discontinuities in their work histories, there has been a so-called depreciation of human capital. This refers to the erosion of the value of their skills, training, and experience, during absence from employment. Moreover there are disadvantageous bargaining positions for those returning to employment after an absence. Both factors have been advanced as explanations for the inferior career and mobility opportunities of women of equal or superior training compared to men.

Despite the paucity of systematic materials on work histories and careers, Treiman offers a tentative summary of gender differences in career patterns:

> On the average, the occupational status of men, especially white men, increases substantially over the course of the career; and attainment patterns of men depend upon the position of jobs within labor-market structures. Women, by contrast, show little gain in occupational status over the course of the career, although there is a small return to work experience for women—much less than for men. But the careers of women, like those of men, are substantially affected by women's personal characteristics and job moves within internal labor markets [within-firm recruitment pools] heavily dependent on age and job duration.
>
> These results suggest the importance, but do not directly address, gender differences in the functioning of internal labor markets. It has been claimed that a major

reason for the lack of career advancement of women is that women's jobs, in contrast to men's jobs, are often dead-end positions with no promotion opportunities within the internal labor market. This is clearly a crucial issue but one that has not been much studied in a systematic way. (Treiman, 1985, p. 228)

Sex Segregation, Job Satisfaction, Dependency, and Women's Careers

In a study of more than 400 work organizations in California between 1959 and 1979, Baron and Bielby (1985) measured the extent of organizational sex segregation and found that 59 percent of the organizations were perfectly segregated by sex; that is, that workers of one sex were either entirely excluded from employment or else concentrated in job titles filled exclusively by the same sex. There was a high degree of sex segregation even in the firms not perfectly segregated, so that fewer than 10 percent of the entire work force were in jobs that included both sexes. Baron and Bielby found, moreover, that this segregation drastically restricts women's career opportunities by blocking access to internal labor markets and their benefits. They also cite a list of additional firm and organizational barriers to gender equality which, in addition to familial norms and patterns, and household division of labor and obligations, all converge to limit severely the career opportunities of women.

Yet data on work satisfaction and on levels of well-being associated with employment seem to indicate remarkably little difference by gender. Referring to national sample studies carried out in 1971 and again in 1978, Campbell (1981) noted that

It is curious that women workers as a whole describe their jobs in much the same terms as male workers do. Considering the fact that most women go into low-status occupations and are paid on the average about 60 percent as much as men, it would not be surprising to find them describing their work rather negatively. The fact that they do not must mean that women do not have the same expectations from their jobs as men do and evaluate them on a different basis ....

Women, despite their occupational disadvantages, are on the average as satisfied with their jobs as men, although when workers of different educational levels are compared, women with some college but not a diploma fall short of all other educational groups, men or women, in their satisfactions with their jobs. None of these differences is very impressive, however, and it is clearly difficult to predict from a knowledge of the kind of job a person has how satisfied that person will be with it ....

Objectively their jobs would appear to be less rewarding than those of men, but women do not describe them as such. It is an interesting and perhaps related fact that relatively few women feel they suffer from discrimination in the job market; one working woman in six does, and this proportion did not change in the 1970s. Most women appear to enter the work force with a basically undemanding attitude, accepting the wage and other differentials that exist between them and male employees, and expressing satisfaction with the conditions of the job as they find it. And despite the federal affirmative-action programs and much aggressive advocacy of women's rights, this pattern changed very little between 1971 and 1978. (Campbell, 1981, pp. 139, 141, 142)

The question of the ways and extent to which employment "frees" women of dependency upon fathers and husbands seems quite complex and does not appear yet to have been unraveled in any systematic or convincing fashion. And the extent to which such freedom from dependency is actually salient to women would seem, on the one hand, ambiguous and controversial judging from the antipathy and public opposition to the various organized women's liberation efforts and movements by other women. On the other hand, its salience would seem beyond question judging from the masses of women availing themselves of opportunities for extrahousehold activities, initiatives, and options ranging from part-time employment to divorce and serial monogamy or to single-parenthood (cf. Preston, 1985). In any event, the question of the salience of economic and other independence of women also awaits more extensive and systematic research.

Unemployment and Its Meanings

For society as a whole, unemployment is the weak underside of industrial capitalism. However, in the analysis of the radical tradition, the maintenance of a reserve army of unemployed is the fundamental mechanism by which capitalist employers are able to maintain downward pressure on wages. Modern measurement of unemployment assumes a wage labor market and the active search for employment among those wishing to work. Thus unemployment is generally measured either as (a) the number without employment but actually actively searching for employment, or else (b) persons recently losing previous employment with current claims on unemployment benefits whether or not actually seeking other employment.

Thus there is a certain variety of nonemployed persons who are reckoned in the description and measurement of unemployment, and there is also a variety of nonemployed persons who are *not* reckoned in the conventional measurement of unemployment. For example, persons never before employed and seeking their first jobs are, in national censuses and surveys, considered to be both "in the labor force" and "unemployed." But persons not employed who believe there are no jobs available or who have given up looking for work are considered "not in the labor force" and therefore neither "employed" nor "unemployed." Persons who have been "retired" from previous employment and receive pensions are "unemployed" if they seek new employment. Students seeking summer or part-time jobs are "unemployed." Women keeping house who would take jobs if they were offered or if they thought that they were available, but not actively seeking employment during the time of inquiry or measurement, are not "unemployed." Persons who have jobs but are actively seeking different employment are not, of course, considered "unemployed."

Unless they have been offered or handed the only job or *all* of the jobs they have ever had, the work histories of individuals typically include some spells of unemployment. The search for first employment is one such spell. The spells between jobs, termed frictional unemployment by economists and frequently believed to reflect efficiency of the labor market in adjusting employees to new patterns of employment opportunity, is another example. Temporary layoffs from ongoing jobs are another example. The most difficult type of unemployment is outright dismissal from a job without prospects for alternative employment at hand.

While there has been some effort to measure the various types of unemployment in the literature dealing with the labor force, the study of unemployment in the life and job histories of individuals is relatively new. It is getting under way only as studies of job histories and careers are increasingly undertaken and becoming both more numerous and sophisticated. A number of classical studies of individuals and families affected by unemployment (Bakke, 1940; Elder, 1974; Jahoda, Lazarsfeld, and Zeisel, 1971) have documented the poverty, economic distress, and social and psychological stress associated with loss of income and loss of status. Elder (1974, 1982) has documented long-term effects of unemployment experiences both upon subjects' own and upon their spouses' and children's later attitudes, behavior, and social and economic relationships.

Several developments, however, may be changing the meaning of unemployment for younger cohorts. First, there are now widespread programs of income support for unemployed individuals and their families in place in many industrialized countries. This has diminished the economic hardship associated with unemployment spells. For some groups and individuals the income support programs may also have altered the calculus of job seeking. Indeed, an intended consequence of some of the income support programs is surely the removal of some nonemployed persons from the market of job seekers, from the labor force, and from the ranks of the unemployed (*New York Times*, 1987).

Second, the large number of couples and families with two or more earners has rendered each such couple or family much less vulnerable to the economic hardship entailed by the loss of employment of *one* of them. The other side of this is, of course, the concentration of poverty and hardship among divorced, separated, or widowed women and their dependent family members. Income support programs that may be adequate for family units in which one person is unemployed but some other family member remains employed are often sadly inadequate for families with no member employed.

Finally, the recent trends in employment and unemployment in the industrialized countries of the world, reduction of previously considered stable or career employment in certain economic sectors, and marginalization, or increase of low-skill, part-time, and temporary employment as a proportion of total employment in many important economic sectors, may have the effect of destigmatizing unemployment, legitimating delayed entry into employment trajectories and commitments, encouraging frequent withdrawal from and later reentry into employment, and promoting early retirement. The patterns of employment and unemployment spells in the careers or work histories of individuals may, under these trends, be changing significantly, and their meaning for attitudes, behavior, social relationships, and the life course generally may be undergoing changes. For the time being, however, the recent evidence seems to point to involuntary unemployment still entailing high levels of stress, strain, dissatisfaction, and perceived ill-being among both men and women not only with respect to work and income but with respect to other life domains, for example, neighborhood, housing, health, and education as well (Campbell, 1981).

For the most part we know very little about what individuals who are unemployed or who are not employed actually *do* at any moment in time or in the life-course spells in question. The stereotyped and stigmatized images of the unemployed portray economic hardship and destitution, on the one hand, and social deviance, on the other hand. There is some portrayal of shame and humiliation, withdrawal from social life, and identity crisis. But some of the findings concerning the situations of retired elderly persons may suffice to give us some pause in this respect. Retirement among the elderly is also frequently described in terms of disengagement from conventional social roles, identity crises, hardship, and humiliation. Yet findings concerning adjustment to retirement and general life satisfaction have suggested that the central problems for the retired are health and income maintenance, and that, given reasonably good health and adequate income, the adjustment and satisfaction levels of the retired are not lower than those of persons employed (Atchley, 1980; National Council on Aging, 1981; Campbell, 1981). Moreover, there are many acceptable, indeed preferable, alternative roles and activity spheres for elderly persons withdrawing from employment.

Ending Employment: Retirement from Jobs and Careers

Retirement has become a widely anticipated and accepted alternative to employment at older ages. It can be entirely voluntary, imposed by employers unilaterally, or enacted through collective agreements. Retirement can be a final or permanent state of unemployment due to physical impairment, labor market conditions, or disinclination to seek new employment. In modern industrial societies retirement is typically, though not inevitably, associated with some postemployment income entitlement, although in the past those unable to work in old age may have been entirely dependent upon personal savings, the support of children or relatives, public assistance, or charity.

Historically, retirement schemes have been introduced and received support as means of protecting prime-age male employment, as humane attention to income needs of impaired or disabled workers instead of welfare, as mechanisms for employers to overcome seniority commitments and expense, and as mechanisms for employers to manage employee turnover and replacement of obsolete skills and knowledge. Both large employers and politicians have viewed retirement schemes as means of dampening potential political and economic unrest. It is probably not unfair to assert that only secondarily have retirement proposals and arrangements been intended to benefit or entitle elderly persons (cf. Graebner, 1980; Myles, 1984). Be that as it may, retirement has become very widely institutionalized to the point that only a relatively small minority continues to be employed beyond the conventionally recognized ages of retirement (Table 7.1), and those are mostly part-time employees.

Retirement, however vaguely defined and understood, is a broadly legit-imated alternative to work in late-middle and old age; we examine this in more detail in Chapter 11. At this point it suffices to note that its great popularity and attractiveness are quite clearly associated with institutionalization and expansion of public retirement income entitlements, sufficiently replacing employment in-come to enable the large numbers to retire in preference to continued employment in late-middle or old age. We have already examined the diminishing labor force participation rates at the older ages. Yet, considerations of the needs or wishes and the civil rights of the elderly, combined with concern over the scale and cost of the public pension and income maintenance schemes, have led also to movements, campaigns, and schemes to allow and encourage continued employment in the paid labor force at later ages.

Back from Retirement? Extension of Worklife in Middle and Old Age

While in traditional societies men have been employed throughout their adult lives until disability or death, in modern urban industrial, wage-and-sal-ary-employment societies, continuation of the surviving elderly in employment for pay or profit has become the exception rather than the rule. The idea of extending or continuing employment of the elderly is perceived as a deviation from norms and practice. It is not at all self-evident, and calls for some explana-tions and justifications. In general, the explanations and justifications have been cast in terms of (1) the needs and well-being of the elderly, (2) the needs or opportunities of employing firms or organizations, and (3) the needs of society and the constraints of the economy—with priority not at all necessarily assigned in this order.

Intrinsic Interest of the Elderly in Continued or Renewed Employment The view that paid employment per se constitutes a moral commitment or that it has intrinsic interest for men in Western society generally, and for middle-aged and elderly men as well as—or even more than—for younger men is frequently expressed by social scientists, writers, and persons in the helping professions. Hendricks and Hendricks (1981) assert that some, but not all, workers have thoroughly internalized the positive cultural attitudes toward work. Ginzberg (1983) also asserts that for some minority of workers intrinsic satisfactions from work are critical. Parker (1982) cites survey data about the main reasons for continuing to work after normal retirement ages. He found that 17 percent of the men reported that they "like the work" and another 21 percent reported that they "would be bored otherwise" (the corresponding percentages among women con-tinuing to work at postretirement ages were 21 percent and 13 percent respectively).

Additional findings that may be taken to confirm the concept of intrinsic interest in work are the differential retirement rates by occupation group or by educational levels and the differential rates of labor force participation at older ages by educational levels. Whether these may be taken as a demonstration of the intrinsic interest of the elderly in extended or renewed employment after normal retirement age remains unclear. As Parnes (1983) remarks, only a minority of retirees (investigated in the U.S. longitudinal studies of work and retirement at midlife and beyond, and aged 59 to 73 in 1980) manifest interest in labor market activity: Only 16 percent were in the labor force. Of the rest only 15 percent said that they would (3 percent) or might (12 percent) take a job if one were offered. We shall return later to the question of expressed desire for employment among the elderly or the retired.

Needs of the Elderly for Job-related Social Relations and Social Status
In the Harris and Associates' studies of the elderly, almost three-fourths of retired respondents (73 percent in 1974 and 70 percent in 1981) reported that after stopping work they missed the people at work. About half (50 percent in 1974 and 48 percent in 1981) said they missed the respect of others. This is a type of finding invoked in support of the concept of the needs of the elderly for employment-connected social relations and work-based social status. Ginzberg (1983) points to the importance of the social satisfactions and companionship that work provides as one of its central dimensions.

The view that extension or renewal of employment among the elderly addresses needs for social relationships and social status would thus seem to follow from the assertions and analyses of the aftermaths and consequences of termination of employment. Yet there do not seem to be any broadly based empirical materials that bear directly upon this issue. Studies of life satisfaction following retirement generally point to high levels of adjustment, adaptation, and satisfaction (Parnes, 1983), but with very little in-depth attention to the minorities expressing dissatisfaction. Even more to the point, there are only a few bodies of data bearing directly upon the comparison of levels or nature of social relations or social status of employed and of nonemployed middle-aged or elderly persons respectively (see Chapter 11 for further discussion on this point).

Income Needs of the Elderly
Historically many of the elderly in Western societies have been poor, and many of the poor have been elderly. But in most countries of the West the economic status of the elderly has improved dramatically in recent years, primarily as a result of public Social Security and income maintenance schemes. In the United States poverty among the aged, as measured by the U.S. government's poverty index, has practically disappeared, although large numbers of the elderly still suffer a large drop in living standard when they retire (Schulz, 1985). Yet Harris and Associates reported that in their 1981 survey 93 percent of the public nationwide, and 86 percent of the elderly themselves, believe that "not having enough money to live on" is a very serious or somewhat serious problem for most people over 65. More than 40 percent of older Americans *personally* experience lack of money either as a very serious (17 percent) or as a somewhat serious (24 percent) problem (National Council on Aging, 1981).

Proposals, programs, and policies for extending employment in middle and later life include basically two types of approaches and schemes: (1) Those intended to effect delay in retirement or withdrawal from employment and (2) those intended to promote reemployment of persons who have in effect once retired or withdrawn from paid employment. We review these in Part IV.

PARENTING

How much of our lives is devoted to parenting? Perhaps from the birth (or even from the adoption) of a first child and as long as the first or any subsequent child survives, we are parents and we are engaged in *some* measure of parenting. But clearly the intensity of parenting, and certainly the intensity of parenting to the exclusion of other activity, varies even as children survive and remain in the household.

In Chapter 3, we presented estimates of life years in parenting dependent children implied by fertility and mortality conditions early in the century, at mid-century, and currently. It is clear that parenting time has become very much more compact in the lives of the more recent cohorts. This has been due not only to the decline in family size but also to the compression of fertility to a much narrower age range of motherhood, largely the early twenties among contemporary women. In addition, there is somewhat more voluntary childlessness among married women. There have been somewhat larger proportions of women not only delaying marriage but remaining single altogether. Thus, a larger proportion of young adults forgo parenthood altogether. Among those who are ultimately parents, parenting is briefer and more compact.

Motherhood as an Intrafamily Entitlement

Sociological discussion of the family in the late 1940s and early 1950s revolved about the features of the emerging nuclear family of urban industrial society, and around its characteristic male-female role differentiation and specialization. The nuclear family, according to sociological wisdom of the time, was isolated and mobile with respect to its extended family origins and relatives. Its dominant feature was said to be the allocation of instrumental roles, tasks, and functions—making a living, occupational activity—to the husband and the expressive, or social-emotional roles, tasks, and functions to the wife.

There were at the time, as there have been since, challenges to this formulation of the nuclear family and its structure. But there are, as well, very recent descriptions of family life in the 1950s that portray the actual family structure at the time as corresponding to such analyses. Thus England and Farkas (1986) have written:

> In the 1950's, the marital division of labor was perfectly clear; men earned almost all the money and women did all the housework and nurturing of children. (p. 12)

England and Farkas go on to contrast the characteristic family situations of the 1980s with many more women employed, wives viewing their jobs as careers, and wives earning substantial shares of family income.

Thus, whether we depend upon descriptions formulated in the 1950s about that decade's family structure or upon currently formulated retrospective descriptions about families in that period, we have the strong assertions that until very recently, even in modern urban industrial societies, the intrafamily status and economic entitlements of wives were based essentially on their performance of parenting and housekeeping roles. Indeed, it is England and Farkas' purpose to show that marriages were in the past, and albeit with different patterns and rules are today, properly viewed as contractual arrangements in the context of given social structural rules and constraints. Households, like factories, involve production, a division of labor, distinct jobs, exchange, differentials in power, and contracts. For our purposes it is important to understand that for women it is *motherhood* that has been the traditional basis of entitlement to a share in the allocation of family goods and services despite non-participation directly in the production regime or in the organized labor force, that is, despite not being employed or seeking employment for pay or profit.

The Entitlement Crises Implicit in the Demise of Motherhood

The reason it is important to formulate traditional female household and family roles in this way is that such a formulation helps us recognize the entitlement problems implicit in the contraction of parenthood. It is true that declining fertility and diminished motherhood have taken place in close historical relationship to the expansion of women's labor force participation. Fertility has long been negatively correlated both with women's employment and with correlates of women's employment. But it is not only an oversimplification to view expanding employment as a cause of declining fertility, but probably just plain wrong to make such an inference. Rather, it is the dependency crunch, and the associated social support for fertility control and family limitation that should be viewed as proximate causes of declining fertility in the course of historical demographic transitions.

The delay, limitation, and early completion of childbearing, and the resultant contraction and compacting of parenthood—that is, the partial demise of motherhood—have for their part engendered intrafamily role, status, and material entitlement crises for modern women (Davis and van den Oever, 1982). What, in the absence of motherhood and parenting, is to entitle wives to a share in the family's allotment of goods and services and social status? For many families the answer is probably: housekeeping and care of family members, even with diminished fertility and fewer children. But for most the answer has been: entry into the formal and paid labor force and wage employment in the labor market in jobs or careers.

Thus paid employment for at least part of the life course resolves the intrafamily entitlement crisis implicit in the contraction of motherhood. But motherhood and fatherhood as well as housekeeping and care of family members remain intrafamily entitlements, even if diminished in strength and in the obligations children or other family members incur. Parents of both sexes typically are entitled to the support and care of one another throughout the life course and of their adult children as they age. Obviously all are more comfortable when invoking such entitlements is unnecessary.

But increasingly all family members have careers or, at least, paid labor market employment histories of *some* length. Each carries both some earnings history and some subsequent income maintenance entitlements of his or her own. So it is just as obvious that the intracouple economic dependencies and intrafamily economic and care entitlements do diminish in weight and importance for each individual. We return to these points in the following chapter.

SCHOOLING

The most prominent, highly legitimated, and, in terms of life years allocated to it, quantitatively most important life-course alternative to work and parenting in Western societies has been formal schooling. The declared or latent purposes of public schooling have included developing individual knowledge and skills, preserving and enhancing the cultural heritage, integrating immigrant children, investing in human capital, promoting good and enlightened citizenship, and promoting social equality. Or as the radical analysis would have it: Free and compulsory schooling is for reproducing social inequality and reinforcing patterns of class domination and subordination. In fact, free and compulsory public schooling also developed and expanded in the United States and elsewhere with an understanding of its effect in excluding first, quite small children, then older children and young adolescents, then progressively older adolescents and ultimately even young adults, from entering full-time employment in competition with adult employees.

The image and rhetoric of social opportunity in America have long been associated with and fortified by the concept of free, publicly supported education for all children. Indeed the United States has historically been the world leader in extension of literacy, rates of school enrollment (see, for example, Table 7.2) and continuation at every age and level, and in per capita public expenditures for schooling. The ideology of public education in America has almost always included the notion that education must promote cultural, social, and economic integration of individuals and the various heterogeneous groupings in America and equalization of social and economic opportunities for all, as well as the more traditional objectives of imparting knowledge and expanding personal horizons and development.

To these have been added the beliefs that schooling contributes in crucial ways to individual productivity and, in the aggregate, to the productivity of the entire labor force. This belief is consistent with the frequent observations that (1) individuals with higher educational attainment have, on the average, higher earnings than those with lesser educational attainment, and (2) societies with high average educational attainment are much more productive—have a higher per capita product or income—than those with lower average educational attainment.

Less than full access to educational opportunity has long been attacked as dooming its victims to diminished social and economic opportunity. The public and policy-makers alike, in the United States and outside, have come to associate educational opportunity with social opportunity generally and to support expansion and equalization of educational opportunity as, among other benefits, the means to expand and equalize social opportunity.

The decades following World War II witnessed unprecedented expansion of public education in North America, Europe, and elsewhere, sharp increases in school enrollment, and the raising of average school-leaving ages and average educational attainment levels (Table 7.2). Population groups previously characterized by low access to formal schooling were in many cases incorporated into the educational-ser-vice networks. Many of these characterized previously by low levels of schooling saw marked improvements in the post-World War II decades. The public and academic monitoring of both productivity and of social opportunity over the subsequent decades, the 1970s and 1980s, the economic slowdowns in those decades, and the general attack on the welfare state and its institutions have brought skepticism and reevaluation of the links between schooling and virtually all of its imputed benefits as well as criticism of the educational institutions themselves (Jencks et al., 1972; Boudon, 1974; Bowles and Gintis, 1976; Porter, 1979; Collins, 1979; Fuchs, 1983). School enrollment rates of young persons aged 20 to 24 actually declined slightly in the United States and Canada between 1975 and 1980.

Table 7.2.   School Enrollment Rates, Selected Industrialized Countries, 1960–1980 (percent enrolled in specified age group)

	1960	1965	1970	1975	1980
Secondary Level					
United States (13–17)	100	100	100	100	100
Canada (12–17)	46	56	65	92	89
United Kingdom (11–17)	66	66	73	82	83
France (11–17)	46	56	74	82	85
West Germany (6–18)	69	71	78	82	80
Italy (11–18)	34	47	61	72	73
Japan (12–17)	74	82	86	92	93
Tertiary Level					
United States (20–24)	32	40	49	58	57
Canada (20–24)	16	26	35	39	36
United Kingdom (20–24)	9	12	14	19	20
France (20–24)	10	18	20	24	26
West Germany (20–24)	6	9	13	25	28
Italy (20–24)	7	11	17	26	27
Japan (20–24)	9	13	17	25	30

Source: P.S. Heller et al., *Aging and Social Expenditure in the Major Industrial Countries,1980–2025* (Washington, D.C.:International Monetary Fund, 1985), Table 31.

Putting aside the actual benefits of extended schooling for the individual, family, community, and societal well-being and the actual processes and mechanisms by which such benefits, if any, are effected, the promotion and rhetoric of schooling alongside the clear visibility of educational attainment-related differences in virtually all indicators of health, welfare, and well-being have combined to legitimate and to render time spent in extended schooling more attractive and worthwhile to increasingly broad population segments relative to other possible use of time and the extent that it is accessible and affordable. Of course, as we have already noted, the traditional other possible uses of time have been mainly paid employment and parenting; it is under the declines of both parenting and employment imperatives that schooling has been enjoying its great legitimation and popularity. This has taken place almost without reference to its actual returns or payoffs to individuals and society, and largely in spite of the stabilization and, indeed, decline in numbers of its main preadult-aged client population.

In the previous chapter we mentioned the historical emergence and institutionalization of childhood as a privileged age, with great resources devoted to protection, socialization, and development of these dependent nonadults. Childhood, or being in this state of protection, socialization, and development, emerged as an intrafamily entitlement, alongside work and parenting entitlements. Public and compulsory elementary schooling both fortified the intrafamily childhood entitlement *and* brought the state into partnership with families in provision of educational, socialization, and custodial services to dependent children. Thus public schooling has institutionalized a societal, or state, childhood entitlement alongside the intrafamily childhood entitlement. Transition *out* of childhood ended the entitlement, and nonchildren were expected to work and/or to parent and establish adult entitlements.

Extended compulsory schooling in effect extended the intrafamily dependency and protection, socialization, and development entitlement beyond childhood and eventually into early adolescence. At the same time, it created and extended societal or state adolescent-pupil entitlements. The latter have been also, for the most part, those associated with educational, counseling, recreational, and custodial services accorded adolescents in schools. But they have often extended beyond these to other kinds of support, including residential and income maintenance support.

Support for extension of compulsory public schooling and the state entitlement have been based upon the views, beliefs, and understandings of the benefits of schooling to individual and community, to be sure. But the wish to exclude children and adolescents from the labor market, whether couched in terms of reform and protection of the young or in terms of fears of young workers' depressing employment opportunities and wage rates of the adult workers, has always been an explicit factor in public support for schooling.

In much the same vein, the attractiveness and legitimation of schooling in late adolescence and early adulthood have rendered postsecondary education increasingly an intrafamily and societal entitlement. In many countries there are direct state income grants and subsidies to all students as well as subsidized tuition. In the United States such subsidies and grants are very extensive but not universal, although there are universal tax subsidies. Both because of higher incomes and because of diminishing family size and diminishing total dependency within them, families are better able to assist their continuing student members directly and indirectly. Of course large numbers of late adolescent and young adult students also work full time or part time. But this means actually that the intrafamily and state entitlements accorded students as an aggregate are mixed in levels and components. It does not change the fact that extension of the schooling entitlements further delays employment and parenting.

CARE AND CARING ENTITLEMENTS: A NEW LIFE-COURSE ALTERNATIVE?

We begin this concluding section with a minor amendment to the opening passage of the chapter: It is true that adult men and women in Western societies have been taken up with work and with parenting as the major legitimate and acceptable life-course activities and that work and parenting have been the central social and economic entitlements. But this has not absolutely precluded some individuals and groups from engaging in alternative life-course activities, or legitimation of some alternative entitlements. Thus, for example, warmaking has been a recognized life-course activity and entitlement for some. Indeed *past warmaking*, or past military service, has been a recognized entitlement in many modern societies. As another example, conducting religious ritual, or, sometimes simply living in piety, has been a recognized life-course activity and entitlement in some societies. While deprivation per se is not a life-course activity, *past deprivation* is very frequently a legitimate social and economic entitlement, as witness affirmative action measures, or for that matter, the entitlement for past military service as a particular case.

Thus societies *do* legitimate and entitle life-course activities and statuses other than working, parenting, school attendance, and retirement. However, these have been quantitatively minor variants. The institutionalization, legitimation, and entitlement of other or new life-course activities does not necessarily entail social revolutions or radical social change. Just as public programs in the context of occurring demographic, technological, and social changes have effected legitimation and entitlement of retirement and schooling, so they may effect legitimation and entitlement of other activities. In particular, in a climate of concern over the costs and organizational arrangements for care of increasing numbers of elderly combined with constraints on the growth, or perhaps even the decline, of private sector labor market employment opportunities, we are likely to see increasing numbers of programs and initiatives to support and legitimate societal or state entitlement of informal not-for-pay caregiving as a major life-course activity.

Such proposals were mentioned in Chapter 5. The actual promotion of and assistance to informal caregiving is frought with complexities and obstacles (Parker, 1980). Not least are its bearing on existing arrangements and programs for mobilizing and employing voluntary and paid persons in care activity as currently in place. Parker (1980, 1982) has pointed to the need for rigorous analysis of the components and dimensions of informal care, or "tending," as he prefers to connote it, including the (a) duration, (b) intensity, (c) complexity, and (d) prognosis of the care or tending required in order to explore the potential for community contribution to such activity. In addition, it is necessary to determine (1) who needs care, and how many there are in each of the different categories needing care or tending; (2) who or what agencies are available to do the work; and not least, and perhaps especially: (3) on what terms.

Social policies and initiatives based on such knowledge do, in Parker's view, have some chance for success in rewarding, enhancing, and expanding informal care activity without threatening either care givers or care receivers. But, again, it is the demographic, social, and economic panorama of need, and concern surrounding the need for care, intersected by opportunity and problems posed by the contraction of work and parenting activities addressed only partially by the retirement and schooling alternatives, and reinforced by strong religious and cultural helping and caring ideologies and traditions, which may lead to such a new major life-course alternative.

CONCLUDING REMARKS: LIFE-COURSE ALTERNATIVES, LIFE-COURSE TRANSITIONS, AND SOCIETAL SUPPORT ARRANGEMENTS AND ENTITLEMENTS

It should be clear that the changing norms, legitimacy, and frequency of life-course alternatives to the traditional patterns of employment and parenthood, alongside the changing patterns of longevity, joint survival, and availability of kin, are likely to give rise—indeed, are already giving rise—to new life-course designs, new patterns of timing and directions of life-course transitions, and new sequences of life-course transitions. A long list of phrases give expression to these new patterns: single-person household, second careers, serial monogamy, working mothers, paternity leave, shared childcare, job-sharing, early retirement, single-parent families, youth unemployment, unattached persons, displaced workers, mature and senior-citizen students. These all reflect some departure from the traditional life-course transition sequences dominated in the past by work, marriage, and parenthood.

These new life-course designs, in turn, must take shape in social, political, and economic settings and arrangements that are conducive and supportive, or at least not fundamentally antagonistic. First and foremost are arrangements to assure material support or income and those to assure health care, protection and custody of dependents, and assistance when necessary in activities of daily life throughout the life course. It is for this reason that the recent major attacks by conservative governments on the public income-maintenance and health-care schemes already in place in their welfare programs have for the most part failed or been repulsed. Even where electorates have had only weak ideological commitment to the welfare state and its ideas and commitments, there has been widespread understanding that there are new sociodemographic, technological, parenting, and employment realities, that these engender new life-course designs that will not simply disappear, and that the welfare state income-maintenance and health-care provisions that support the new life-course designs cannot be allowed to disappear.

8

DEPENDENCY, OBLIGATIONS, AND ENTITLEMENTS IN THE FAMILY CYCLE

INTRODUCTION

Everyone has a mother, and so, nearly everyone has some initial family relationship, some initial dependency on a parent or adult for shelter, nurture, stimuli, and emotional response. Family is the social institution par excellence. Every society has some form of family organization and relationships, but these have varied and changed across different societies and over historical time. The family is a major topic of social scientific inquiry.

The nuclear family—the family comprising the married couple and their own children—has a characteristic cycle beginning with the marriage of the couple and ending with its dissolution by death, or sometimes by divorce. The concept of the family cycle is somewhat analagous to the concept of the individual life course: It recognizes duration-related organizational features and activities of families, and it examines and studies variations and changes of the timing and durations of significant family events, the related variations and changes in family structure, and their implications for individual behavior in the context of the family.

Conventional study of family cycle examines primarily the changing timing and durations and events and their related variations in individual intrafamily and extrafamily behavior. We review some of the issues and findings of these studies, but we shall be concerned in this chapter primarily with the individual's changing patterns of intra- and extrafamily dependency, obligations, and entitlements in the context of family cycle, and of the family structure and family relationships in each period. It is these that inform and in many ways determine life-course transitions, their timing, and their direction.

THE FAMILY CYCLE: CONCEPT AND MEASUREMENT

The major events of the family cycle are (1) the marriage of the couple, (2) the birth of the first child, (3) the departure of the last child from the parental home, and (4) widowhood, or death of one of the couple. The intervals between these events comprise what are conventionally viewed as the major stages of the family cycle: The prechildbearing stage of the marriage; the childrearing stage, including what is sometimes differentiated and identified as child-launching (that is, preparing and helping young adult children depart from the parental home); the empty-nest stage; and the stage of widowhood. Each stage, in turn, is associated with characteristic configurations of intrafamily relationships, family behavior and activities, intra- and extrafamily relationships and activities of family members, and patterns of dependency, obligations, and entitlements.

The Timing and Duration of Family-Cycle Events and Stages

The study of the nuclear family cycle has used three distinct types of measurement. A first approach, pioneered by P.C. Glick (1977) and associates at the U.S. Bureau of the Census, measures the timing and duration of family cycle events and stages, usually from the perspective of the female of the marital couple: age of the bride at first marriage, age of the mother at first birth and at departure of the youngest child, and age of the wife at widowhood, with the durations typically understood as the intervals between the ages at the respective bounding events (for example, the difference between median age at birth of first child and median age at marriage taken as the length or duration of the prechildbearing stage of the marriage). In their studies of the life cycle of the family over a number of decades, Glick and his associates as well as other researchers have been able to document dramatic variations and changes in both timing of family-cycle events and durations of stages in the family cycle (Table 8.1). These have, of course, been a consequence of variations and changes in their underlying demographic phenomena: mortality, fertility, and marriage.

In Table 8.1 we may note, for example, that the median age at marriage and median age at first birth declined and then recovered among the successive cohorts of women born starting at the turn of the century and through the 1960s and 1970s. But the median ages at the births of last-born children have declined almost monotonically, reflecting primarily the decline of fertility. The median ages of the women at the marriage or departure of the last child have generally declined over the decades. Again, this reflects primarily the decline in fertility (though there is some small effect of declining ages of the marriages of the children). The median ages of the women at the death of their husbands has risen dramatically, reflecting primarily diminished mortality and extended survival and joint survival

Table 8.1.   Indicators of the Life Cycle of the Family, U.S. Cohorts Born 1880s–1950s.

FAMILY LIFE-CYCLE STAGE	BIRTH OF WIFE / APPROX. PERIOD OF 1ST MARRIAGE	1880s / 1900s	1890s / 1910s	1910s / 1930s	1920s / 1940s	1930s / 1950s	1940s / 1960s	1950s / 1970s
Median Age at								
First marriage		21.4	21.2	21.4	20.7	20.0	20.5	21.2
Birth of first child		23.0	22.9	23.5	22.7	21.4	21.8	22.7
Birth of last child		32.9	32.0	32.0	31.5	31.2	30.1	29.6
Marriage of last child		55.4	54.8	53.2	53.2	53.6	52.7	52.3
Death of one spouse		57.0	59.6	63.7	64.4	65.1	65.1	65.2
Difference between Age at First Marriage and								
Birth of first child		1.6	1.7	2.1	2.0	1.4	1.3	1.5
Birth of last child		11.5	10.8	10.6	10.8	11.2	9.6	8.4
Marr'g. of last child		34.0	33.6	31.8	32.5	33.6	32.2	31.1
Death of one spouse		35.6	38.4	42.3	43.7	45.1	44.6	44.0
Difference between								
Ages at birth of first and last children		9.9	9.1	8.5	8.8	9.8	8.3	6.9
Ages at birth of first and marriage of last children		22.5	22.8	21.2	21.7	22.4	22.6	22.7
Ages at marriage of last child and death of spouse (="Empty Nest")		1.6	4.8	10.5	11.2	11.5	12.4	12.9

Source: Adapted from P.C. Glick, "Updating the Life Cycle of the Family," *Journal of Marriage and the Family* 39, no.1 (1977).

(although there is some effect of the diminished age differences between husbands and their wives in the periods studied).

The dramatic outcomes of these trends are highlighted in the data shown in the bottom panel of Table 8.1, data that are simply differences between median ages shown in the top panel: The durations of marriages remaining intact until death of a spouse (that is, not dissolved by divorce or separation) increase dramatically. These are represented by the differences between median ages at marriage and median ages at the death of spouse. The length of the childbearing stage, that is, the differences between ages at first and last birth, has declined dramatically, from 9.9 years for women born in the 1880s to 6.9 years among women born in the 1950s. This duration initially declined in the first part of the century, recovered somewhat at midcentury, and declined sharply in the 1960s and 1970s. Finally, and perhaps most dramatic, the length of the empty nest stage, that is, from the departure of the youngest child from the parental home to the death of the spouse, has increased very sharply, from less than two years for those born in the 1880s to almost thirteen years for those born in the 1950s.

The Frequencies of Preferred and Incomplete Family Cycles

A second approach to measurement of the family cycle, exemplified in the research of P. Uhlenberg, examines the *frequencies* of family-cycle events, event sequences, and complete or incomplete family cycles. These studies examine variations and changes in the actual frequencies or likelihood of achieving the preferred or normative nuclear family cycles comprising the marriage, childbearing, childrearing, child-launching, and empty nest events and stages. Many sequences *other than* the preferred family cycle can happen to a girl. And in fact historically, many things other than the preferred family cycle actually *did* occur to the majority of girls and women, such that only quite small minorities actually achieved the preferred family cycle until quite recently.

Using historical statistical data for Massachussetts, Uhlenberg was able to estimate, for synthetic cohorts of women subject to age-specific rates of mortality, fertility, and marriage recorded in the decennial censuses and vital statistics from 1830 through 1920, the percentages of women experiencing both complete normative family cycles and experiencing specified deviations from the normative family cycle. Examples of Uhlenberg's estimates are shown in Table 8.2.

Of a female cohort subject to the demographic conditions of 1830 no fewer than 35.6 percent (or 35,600 of 100,000 in a hypothetical cohort) would have experienced what Uhlenberg terms the "abbreviated life cycle," and died before reaching age 20, while an additional 12.9 percent would survive to age 20 but would never marry. The latter, in turn, are divided among those who are spinsters throughout life and die single prior to reaching age 50 and spinsters throughout life who die at ages 50 or later. Just under 10 percent (9,500 among 100,000) would survive and marry, but remain childless throughout life, including 2.6 percent dying childless prior to reaching age 50 and 6.9 percent childless but surviving at least to age 50. Together, these comprise what Uhlenberg calls the "barren" women among the part of the cohort surviving to adulthood and marrying.

A fourth category of deviants (with respect to the normative family cycle) are what Uhlenberg calls the "dying mothers": women who marry and have children but themselves die before reaching age 55. The dying mothers comprise two subgroups: the "motherless-child producing" women (8.1 percent), those whose husbands survive at least to age 57 (with motherless children to care for), and the "orphan-producing" women (3.8 percent), those whose husbands die prior to reaching age 57 (leaving the children orphaned). A fifth category of women, not entirely deviant, but also not exactly attaining the preferred family cycle, comprise what Uhlenberg calls the "widowed mothers": women who survive to adulthood, marry, have children, and themselves survive at least to age 55, but whose husbands die prior to reaching age 57. These

Table 8.2.   Percentages among Female Cohorts Achieving Incomplete and Normative Family Life Cycle. Massachusetts, 1830–1920 and Total United States, 1890–1934.

MASSACHUSETTS, SYNTHETIC COHORTS	*CENSUS YEAR*				
	1830	*1850*	*1870*	*1890*	*1920*
Type of family life cycle					
Total	100.0	100.0	100.0	100.0	100.0
1. Abbreviated: dies before age 20	35.6	31.4	30.9	26.3	10.8
2. Spinster: survives to age 20,					
never marries	12.9	14.2	17.8	17.8	10.6
a. dies single, <50	6.2	6.1	5.4	3.9	1.5
b. dies single, 50+	6.7	8.1	12.4	13.9	9.0
3. Barren: marries, childless	9.5	10.0	11.4	12.2	9.0
a. dies childless, <50	2.6	2.5	2.3	1.9	0.5
b. dies childless, 50+	6.9	7.5	9.1	10.3	8.5
4. Dying mother: has children, dies <55	11.5	11.7	8.7	7.8	4.0
a. Motherless-child-producing: husband					
survives to 57+	8.1	8.4	6.3	6.0	3.5
b. Orphan-producing: husband dies <57	3.8	3.3	2.4	1.8	0.5
5. Widowed mother: has children,					
survives to 55+, husband dies < 57	9.1	9.8	8.6	8.5	8.5
6. Typical, preferred: survives to age 20,					
marries, has children, survives					
to age 55 with husband alive	20.9	23.0	22.6	27.4	57.1

TOTAL U.S., COHORTS BORN					
	1890–84	*1900–04*	*1910–14*	*1920–24*	*1930–34*
Population group and type of family life cycle					
White, surviving to age 15					
Total	100.0	100.0	100.0	100.0	100.0
1. Abbreviated	17.0	12.5	9.0	6.0	5.0
2. Spinster	8.0	7.5	6.0	5.0	4.5
3. Barren	18.5	15.5	14.5	8.5	5.5
4–5. Truncated marriage, w/chdn.	14.0	17.0	18.5	20.0	20.5
6. Typical, preferred	42.5	47.5	52.0	60.5	64.5
Of survivors to age 50:	51.0	54.0	57.5	64.5	68.5
Non-white, surviving to age 15					
Total	100.0	100.0	100.0	100.0	100.0
1. Abbreviated	39.0	33.5	25.0	17.5	10.0
2. Spinster	3.0	3.5	4.5	5.5	8.0
3. Barren	12.5	18.0	19.0	15.5	7.0
4–5. Truncated marriage, w/chdn.	27.5	26.0	26.5	32.0	40.0
6. Typical, preferred	18.0	19.0	25.0	29.5	35.0
Of survivors to age 50:	29.0	29.0	33.5	36.0	39.0

Source: Top panel adapted from P. Uhlenberg,"A Study of Cohort Life Cycles: Cohorts of Native-Born Massachusetts Women, 1830-1920." *Population Studies* 23 (1969): 284-92. Bottom panel adapted from P. Uhlenberg, "Cohort Variations in Family Life Cycle Experiences of U.S. Females," *Journal of Marriage and the Family* 36(1974):284–94.

include about 9.1 percent of the total for the cohort experience 1830 demographic conditions.

Finally, of the women experiencing 1830 mortality, fertility, and marriage conditions at each age, just under 21 percent would experience the typical or preferred family cycle: They would marry, have children, and survive at least to age 55 with husbands also surviving. Uhlenberg's study has, then, shown that the changes in the family life cycle are not only quantitative—that is, longer or shorter spans of this or that activity or stage—but include shifts across qualitatively different types of life courses and family life cycles.

The typical or preferred family cycle was unusual until recently. It became the modal form only for recent cohorts, and it is *still not* the modal form in the black population. Also, it may not be the modal form in the future, if there is extensive spinsterhood, bachelorhood, and divorce. There remain steep differences among population groups in the distribution of life courses by type of family cycle; there are different probabilities or chances of having a typical or preferred family cycle.

Finally, we must recognize that persons of a given age group—say age 65 and over in 1915—represent a *mix* of distinct types of family-cycle pasts or histories, rather than a single type of history; persons age 80—say born in 1900–1910—may represent a different mix; those who will be 65 years old, say, in 10 years, were born in 1932 and reflect a still different mix of family-cycle-type histories. Again, the estimated changing frequencies or rates of experiencing the different types of family cycles—the preferred complete family cycle and the various deviant incomplete family cycles—result entirely from the changing demographic conditions, and especially changing mortality. There were also increasing rates of marriage, declining age at marriage, and changes in the extent of childlessness (increasing from 1870 to 1910 cohorts and declining thereafter) and in proportions never marrying. In the future, Uhlenberg conjectures, there are likely to be additional deviations from the preferred family cycle due to divorce and alternative life styles, including single parenthood, cohabitation, and childlessness. Because of the tentativeness of so much of the analysis in the context of dependency, obligations, and entitlements, we shall not take up the place of alternative life styles in this chapter at all.

Historical, Panel, and Longitudinal Studies of Family-Cycle Events

A third approach to measurement of the family cycle uses data on changes occurring over time in actual families. Such data include panel studies of entire samples, analysis of changes on the basis of individual or batteries of retrospective questions in cross-sectional studies, or prospective or retrospective longitudinal studies.

Perhaps the earliest large-scale example of such a study is one by Glass and Grebenik (1954) of the fertility histories of marriage cohorts in England and Wales based on a Family Census carried out on behalf of the British Royal

Commission on Population in 1946. From the National Register of England and Wales, one-tenth of the women were selected and mailed a Family Census Form that called for dates of marriages and the births of all the woman's children, and details about her own and her husband's personal and socioeconomic character-istics. More elaborate and sophisticated studies of fertility histories of women and couples have since been carried out throughout the world.

Other studies have focused upon marital couples and their adjustment over the course of their marriages and the stages of the family cycle, family income, childrearing, patterns of intrafamily authority and division of labor, women's employment, child-launching or departure from parental households, residence patterns, support from extended families, support for parents inside and outside the family household, use of social services, and other related topics. While not necessarily incorporating and identifying explicity the concepts of the family life cycle, its characteristic events, and its stages, they almost always do so implicitly, as duration of marriage and size of families are nearly always examined as background or control variables. The availability of microdata tapes from censuses and the many large-scale surveys has permitted the use of retrospective, panel, and longitudinal data on families and the family cycle that were originally col-lected for other purposes.

COUPLES AND THEIR OFFSPRING IN THE FAMILY CYCLE

We review briefly some of the characterizations of the stages of the family cycle. One of the most important points to be made about stages of the family cycle should, however, probably be made at the very outset: Each stage is actually characterized by a broad range of situations, behaviors, relationships, and out-comes. The initial characterization of the durations of stages in terms of average or median ages of the partners is itself somewhat misleading. Or, at least, it may lead us to ignore the *distributions* of ages at marriage, birth of first child, and so forth, and the *distributions* of the durations of each of the respective family-cycle stages among the total of individuals, couples, and families.

The Prechildbearing Stage

The point of the range and variety encompassed in the family-cycle stages may be picked up immediately with respect to the very first stage, often viewed as the stage of transition to marriage. The ages of marrying couples vary broadly. So do their premarital histories alone and together, the circumstances of their meeting and courtship, and their premarital residence and household circum-stances. Their employment and earnings situations and histories, whether or not the bride is already pregnant or a mother, postmarriage relationships with families of origin, and factors such as attitudes, perceptions, opinions, and their initial similarities, compatibilities, and differences may also vary widely among couples (Clausen, 1986).

To be sure, marriages are relatively concentrated with respect to ages of brides and of grooms, and even with respect to age differences between them, and they do tend to be homogamous with respect to residence, social class background, and educational attainment. Yet the watchwords of the prechildbearing stage of the family cycle appearing in the literature are adjustment to partners and adaptation to the marital state. Much of subsequent marital instability, breakdown, or dissolution is related to factors already evident or emerging in this initial stage. It may be a period of crisis and tension for the immature, for brides marrying to escape oppressive home lives (Michael and Tuma, 1985), for those whose marriage is precipitated by pregnancy (Rubin, 1976), and for the unemployed or marginally employed (Elder, 1974).

But this is also very frequently a stage at which both members of a couple are employed full time so the couple can enjoy high levels of consumption and can make savings and investments as well. As Campbell reports, this is the life stage at which women report the highest levels of satisfaction and well-being, although this is less the case for the men at this stage:

> Young women at this stage of life [early childless marriage] are more ready than any other category of women or men to declare themselves satisfied with their life as a whole, and they are among the least likely of women to show evidence of psychological strain. Young men, married but still not parents, are not so positive. They are somewhat more satisfied with their lives than young single men but not noticeably more satisfied than men or women in general. And they perceive more strain in their lives than those young men still not married. (Campbell, 1981, pp. 185–86)

The data of Table 8.1 from the Glick study suggest that the interval between median age at marriage and median age at first birth (about 1.6 years among those born in the 1880s and marrying in the 1900s) increased among those marrying in the 1930s and 1940s, and then decreased sharply among those marrying in the 1950s and 1960s. More recent data for Canada (Gee, 1986) are generally very similar, but suggest an upturn in the length of this interval among the youngest cohorts studied, those born in the 1950s, although this may reflect differences between Canada and the United States in the rates of premarital pregnancies. Again, it is important to recognize that these averages obscure the range in length of first birth intervals (Rindfuss, Morgan, and Swicegood, 1984). Couples able to postpone first births are able to adjust to one another and to marriage, establish themselves economically, and see to some of the physical household formation. They may also enjoy and share a longer period of relatively calm and comfortable mutual company than those facing immediate or quite early pregnancy and parenthood (Cutright, 1973; Sweet, 1979a; Clausen, 1986).

The Childbearing and Childrearing Stage

By most accounts the transition to parenthood is for both women and men one of the most difficult and stressful in the life course (Rossi, 1968; Russell, 1974; but see also Aldous, 1978). The childbearing and childrearing stage of the family cycle typically gets off to a difficult start. Both men and women express more feeling of strain at this stage than at any other period of their married lives, according to Campbell (1981).

First, the marital dyad becomes a triad. This opens the family to the complexities of coalitions and subsystems (Blood and Wolfe, 1960; Caplow, 1968; Matras, 1977). Second, there is both the fact of the burden of dependency, responsibility, and restriction of mobility, and the characteristic asymmetry in their allocation among husband and wife, which introduce stress. At the same time as there are greatly increased financial burdens on the family, there is likely to be a substantial cut in income as working wives have typically withdrawn from employment, at least temporarily, upon becoming mothers. Or, barring withdrawal from employment, there are likely to be the stress, doubts, and guilt surrounding the search for childcare arrangements. Finally, there has been the deepening division of labor and attention between husbands, who have typically continued or intensified their involvement with work and careers, and wives, who characteristically have reorganized their lives, activities, social relationships, and conversation—*and* their employment arrangements if they have to retain them—around motherhood and household tasks. However, some important changes in these patterns may currently be taking place, at least among the more highly educated segments of the population, as wives increasingly retain their employment and career commitments even after childbirth (Sweet, 1979a; Shapiro and Mott, 1979; McLaughlin, 1982; Robinson, 1987; England and Farkas, 1986).

Additional preschool children impose additional pressures and financial burdens on the family and, especially, on the wives. Very often these accompany pressures and strains associated with career-building, household formation and stabilization, extended family obligations, and other competing demands for time and energy. For women with several small children, this is a low point in levels of expressed life satisfaction. It is less by far than that of both childless married women the same age and of women whose children are enrolled in school (Campbell, Converse, and Rogers, 1976; Campbell, 1981).

The entrance of children into school and the beginnings of their independent activity and mobility relieve some of the pressure on wives and allow them some measure of free time and mobility as well. For many women, this is a period in which to seek or return to paid employment. Especially as children approach adolescence, there are often serious economic pressures on nuclear families, termed the life-cycle squeeze by V.K. Oppenheimer (1982). Very often they trigger a return to paid employment, postponement or forgoing of additional pregnancies, or both. Several researchers report increasing separation of husbands' and wives' activities and interests in this part of the childrearing stage: Husbands are increasingly immersed in their jobs, personal interests, and family finances as wives are immersed in home and family, and secondarily in job (Troll, 1985). This is also a period of emerging intergenerational conflicts and tensions, as children moving toward or through adolescence seek autonomy and new experiences, at the same time as they are becoming major consumers of goods and services, including higher education.

Child-Launching

Departure of children from the parental home is a critical juncture for children, parents, and family. The literature dealing with the departure of children from the parental home is relatively new and not yet very extensive. It has appeared in at least two separate sociodemographic traditions: The first has examined living arrangements, household formation, and household structure, with recent interest focusing around the trend to separate living. This concept includes the tendency of nuclear families not to share households with other persons, the tendency of individuals to live alone, and also the tendency of individuals to choose nonfamily living arrangements. The strength of the desire for privacy or residential autonomy, the availability of kin, and the income available to afford desired household options have been the major variables introduced in this discussion (see Burch, 1985a, for a more detailed discussion of the separate living concept and its theoretical underpinnings).

The second tradition has examined departures from parental home in the context of life-course development and the sequence of transitions to adulthood. Attention has centered upon the timing of this event in relationship to both the timing of other life-course events and transitions and subsequent personal and socioeconomic trajectories and careers (see Goldscheider and DaVanzo, 1985, and Featherman, 1986, for good discussions of the theoretical and research issues of this tradition). In the past most discussion of this topic has been based on biographical or case study materials and cross-sectional census or survey data describing households and population by household status. Recent empirical materials include a small number of longitudinal studies that have permitted direct observations on this process.

A few studies carried out in the 1970s addressed the issues of age at departure from parental home and reasons—especially for those doing so prior to marriage—for departure. In a study in Australia, Young (1974, 1975) found that mean age of departure of girls from parental homes is much lower than that of boys (21.5 years for girls compared to 23.8 for boys) corresponding to lower age at marriage of the girls. All but 16 percent of the girls, and all but 25 percent of the boys, left parental homes to marry and form their own households. Both boys and girls leaving home other than to marry do so earlier (mean age 20.8 among the girls, compared to 22.4 among the boys) than those remaining at home until marriage. Parental education, parents' age at marriage, and mothers' employment during respondents' childhood were all found to be significantly related to earlier departure from parental homes.

In a study of three American cohorts, Hill and Hill (1976) found that only 10 percent formed single-person households upon departure from parental homes, with the rest marrying or moving into what Goldscheider and DaVanzo (1985) have more recently called semiautonomous households. Hill and Hill primarily proposed economic explanations for the variations in timing of departure from parental homes and, in particular, the relationship between the working hours and earnings of the young persons to those of others in the family or household: To the extent that young persons are high earners and not subsidized by the rest of the family, they tend to want to depart from the parental home. Conversely, to the extent that young persons are nonearners or low earners and subsidized by the rest of the family, they are inclined or content to remain in the parental home.

In a similar vein, a number of authors in the 1970s suggested that there is generally an inverse relationship between extended residence in parental homes and, for that matter, between all manner of extended family arrangements (for example, multigenerational residence arrangements, residence with nonnuclear-family relatives, and the like), and family or household resources. Stock (1974) has viewed the extended family in modern urban societies as a response to poverty, while Schneider and Smith (1973) and Williams and Stockton (1973) concluded that, for minorities and the poor, extended family arrangements are direct responses to shortages of resources.

The literature dealing with residential migration makes some indirect reference to age at departure from parental homes. We conventionally find that rates of residential migration by age are highest in the early twenties. For example, Nam and Gustavas (1976) reported probabilities of residential moves during a single year higher than 50 percent for persons in their early twenties in the United States, while among men 18 to 64 only about 11 percent reported change in family status as the reason for residential change.

An additional point of view on departures from parental home appears in the literature describing and analyzing the stages of the family life cycle. Duvall (1962) divided the family life cycle into eight stages, in which the sixth stage is the one that begins with the departure of the first child and is completed with the departure of the last child. There is little attention paid to the reasons for or ages at departure from the parental home other than mention of the conventionally cited factors: marriage or entrance into full-time employment, military service, or schooling away from home.

In his early discussion of the family life cycle, Glick (1947) already noted the departure of children from the parental home—largely due to their own marriage, with most marrying children leaving the parental home within a year of their own marriage—and denoted the stage subsequent to departure of the last child the empty nest period. In analyzing the demography of families thirty years later, Sweet (1977) asserted that children leave the parental household to continue studies, form separate households, or marry. These studies have been similar in their indirect attention to the departure of children from parental households and in their inattention to correlates of variations in departure from parental homes, despite the acknowledgment of the centrality of this process in the family life cycle and its component stages and transitions.

Departure from Parental Home as Normative Change in Authority Pattern

In a more recent discussion on determination of residence patterns in the context of family relations, Burch (1981) has pointed out that the economic analyses of timing of departure from parental households have tended to overlook the fact that the household, beyond being an economic unit (or indeed, *before* being an economic unit) is an authority unit:

> The parent-child relation is first and foremost a relation of authority/dependence, and that adolescence and much of early adulthood revolve around the establishment of independence, the escape from parental authority; that status, deference, and conformity are all commodities that can be used to establish household equilibria, but which are not included in the usual economic concepts of price, income, and work. (Burch, 1981, p. 454)

Thus Burch argues for incorporating social interaction and conformity factors, in addition to the individual choice factors, into the analysis of residential changes generally and those involving departure of young persons from parental homes in particular.

At the center of the more recent studies addressing the topic have been those of Goldscheider and her associates (Kobrin, 1980; LeBourdais and Goldscheider, 1986; Goldscheider and DaVanzo, 1985). These are based on a panel study conducted in Rhode Island in 1967 to 1969 and again in 1979, and on the National Longitudinal Study (NLS) of 1972 American high school graduates. These researchers show that the process of departure from the parental home is perceived as a universal and normative process. With only very rare, or even pathological, exceptions, no question arises as to its occurrence or nonoccurrence but, rather, only to the questions of the timing of this event and its various consequences.

LeBourdais and Goldscheider show the very dramatic declines over successive cohorts of American (Rhode Island) males and females in the percent at early adult ages (for example, at age 18, at age 20, at 23, 26, and 30 as well as at age 45) still residing with parents. Of males reaching age 16 in the period 1920 to 1939, more than 65 percent still resided in parental homes at age 23 and half were still in their parents' homes at age 26. But of those reaching age 16 in the 1965 to 1969 period, only 43 percent were still in parental homes at age 23. And all but 20 percent had left parental homes by age 26 (LeBourdais and Goldscheider, 1986, Table 2; but see, also, Heer, Hodge, and Felson, 1985, and Grigsby and McGowan, 1986, on the opposite phenomenon—extended residence in parental households).

In an Israeli Jewish male cohort that was born in 1954 and studied in 1980 to 1981, 82 percent reported still living in their parents' homes at age 17. However, this percentage dropped sharply with the onset of compulsory military service, so that fewer than 30 percent were living at home at ages 19 and 20. At ages 21 and 22, with their release from military service, the percentages returning and living with parents recovered to 54 percent. It dropped thereafter to less than 36 percent by age 25 (Matras, Noam, and Bar-Haim, 1984, Table 2.1).

Traditional and Modern Timing of Departure from Parental Home

Two factors in the variations in timing of departure from parental homes have been studied by the researchers:

1. The ability or the willingness of parents to support an independent residence (or other nonparental-home residence arrangement) or to subsidize studies and/or marriage of children not yet economically independent; or, conversely, the needs, demands, or expectations of parents for economic, emotional, household support, and close physical presence of their children.
2. Transitions to adulthood and to adult roles in various other life-course domains, in particular marriage, studies in other communities, military service, or entrance into full-time employment and career paths in other communities.

Kobrin (1980) has called attention to the historical shift from the traditional patterns of leaving the parental home to the modern patterns that has taken place in Western society in the current century. According to Kobrin, this is connected as well to the shift in the status of children from one of resources for their families of orientation to one of consumer items for the family.

In the traditional pattern, children remain in the family home until marriage. They use the time subsequent to their completion of schooling for employment, contributing to the welfare of the family of orientation, and saving toward formation of their own independent families.

In the modern pattern, the children depart from the parental household, and from its authority and normative constraints, even prior to completion of studies and much before achieving their own economic independence. They obtain parental economic support while outside the parental household enabling them to continue in studies by way of investment in their own economic futures rather than as economic security for the parents.

In the course of this shift there is thus a shift in the direction of intergenerational resource flows; children become independent of the family of orientation even while they are economically more dependent, and for a more extended period. Empirical support for this description and such an analysis was found in the comparative study of patterns of leaving the parental homes among the various ethnic subpopulations of Rhode Island.

Effects of Deviations from Single-Nuclear-Family-Unit Residence

The connection between marriage and departure from the parental home generates variations and changes in the timing of departure from the parental home to the extent that frequency of marriage and age at marriage vary among social groups or change over time. But within a given society or social group in which there may still be two-couple or multiple-couple residential arrangements (for example, under economic stress or housing shortages when a married son and his wife reside with the parents), the relationship between marriage and the departure from parental home has become more complex, and not necessarily unidirectional.

Moreover, there has been a clear trend toward growth in the pattern of nonfamily residence, including single-person household residence prior to marriage, subsequent to marital breakup, or following widowhood. Thus, there are factors other than marriage and its timing that may bear on the timing of departure from parental home. Goldscheider and DaVanzo (1985) found that activities such as higher education, military service, and employment have significant effects upon the disconnection from parental homes above and beyond those discernable and imputable to the effects of age at marriage. The most prominent of these is military service (the latter almost *always* associated with residence away from parental homes, while the others may or may not entail departure from parental home). The relationships are not simple ones, and there are interactions among the activities and transitions in the various respective life-course domains (for example, concomitant schooling and employment or marriage and military service) and the timing of departure from the parental home.

The Empty-Nest Stage

The empty-nest stage is probably the great frontier of speculation and research on the family cycle. It has been so dramatically extended in length in this century that questions of its nature and content cannot fail to arouse the social scientific and behavioral scientific attention and curiosity. It is probably accurate to assert that the empty-nest transition occurs today in middle age, rather than in old age as in the past. Today marital partners have unprecedented opportunities to pursue joint lives unemcumbered by the childrearing responsibilities of earlier stages and, often, in relatively comfortable economic circumstances.

Many couples do indeed avail themselves of these opportunities. The later years of married life are also the years of greatest harmony in marriage. Those still married after all these years are more likely than married people at any of the earlier stages of the family cycle to describe themselves as completely satisfied with their marriage and to feel that their relationships with their spouse are amiable, understanding, and compatible (Campbell, 1981).

Troll (1985) has pointed out that the lengthening of the period when the couple is alone again has been accompanied by a number of new relationships between husbands and wives, but that most are still unstudied. On the one hand, there are reports that empty-nest stage marriages undergo new risk, or opportunity, for breakup and dissolution. On the other hand, there are reports of revived intensity of marital relationships and second honeymoons. Reports of levels of sexuality, interpersonal interactions, and marital satisfaction in this stage of the family cycle are somewhat contradictory. Possibly they reflect only the great diversity of marriages at this as at any other stage.

Perhaps most intriguing about this stage of the family cycle is the idea that the empty nest is probably typically not so empty. In the first place, children who have departed from the parental home often use the parental home as their own even as they have other residences. This may occur especially if the other residences are in quasi-autonomous households (for example, university dormitories and military bases).

Second, children who have moved out often return, especially if they have moved out while still unmarried. But they may return even if they have been or still are married. This happens often, as Troll (1985) has suggested, together with spouse and children.

Third, the empty-nest stage of the family cycle is typically the stage of the flowering of grandparenting, which in turn has a very large range and variety of expressions. Fourth, empty nest or not, there is no transition *out of* parenthood which is in any way comparable to the transition *into* parenthood. For some families there is an erosion and clear diminution of parenthood. But for many parenthood continues, albeit in new forms, throughout the lives and joint survival of parents and their children however grown and adult. These forms may include exchange of material support in one or another or both directions. They include, also, emotional support or continued sharing of some or all the entire range of life experiences, problems, and gratifications.

Fifth, the empty-nest stage is typically also the time of life during which retirement from employment, with its dislocations, loss of work role and friendships, adjustments, and characteristically substantially reduced income takes place. Even if the couple itself survives and is intact, one or the other partner may experience loss by death of parent, friend, or intimate. Finally, the empty-nest stage is frequently a stage in which one or both members of a couple may be very heavily occupied with caregiving: to an impaired or otherwise dependent spouse, to an elderly parent, or to another person.

The Widowhood Stage

Marriages that stand fast against the strains, stresses, and pressures of prechildbearing, childbearing and childrearing, and empty-nest stages of the family cycle, and those which survive the sickness and health, the better and worse, and all the marital and normative crises of the family cycle ultimately are dissolved by the death of one spouse. Although the surviving partners are often the husbands, most frequently it is the wives who survive. Moreover, since even quite elderly widowers so frequently remarry women of younger cohorts and elderly widows remarry only infrequently (Fuchs, 1983; Troll, 1985), most of the discussion of widowhood as a stage in the family cycle addresses the problems, adjustment, and well-being of widows.

Bereavement is in fact a source of stress for both men and women. In a widely cited study in the United Kingdom, Parkes (1964) found that the risk of mortality of widows and of widowers is higher in the first five years after death of a spouse than the corresponding risk for non-recently widowed at the same ages. However, the rates for those surviving later return to about the average for persons their respective ages in the population generally. According to national studies of attitudes and perceptions of the quality of life reported by Campbell (1981), the widowed are strikingly different from older people still living with their spouse in their expressions of affect, although they seem no more pressured or worried than older people who are still married. They are less willing to call themselves "very happy" and less likely to report affectively positive episodes in their recent experience. Widowed persons are far lower on measures of "affect balance" than any of the other married groups, and widows are lower than widowers.

Campbell found that the outlook of widowed people seems to be one of resignation. Although generally satisfied with most life domains, they tend to be dissatisfied with their health. The damage to the widowed persons' sense of well-being is most prominent in the years immediately following the loss, and it lessens gradually thereafter. But, not withstanding the Parkes finding about subsequent convergence of mortality rates, Campbell reports (1981, p. 192) that the consequences of the trauma are still clearly evident in the feelings of widowed people even after five years.

In the view of Gee and Kimball (1987) widowhood is a women's issue: Women are much more likely to be widowed. They are much less likely to remarry, experience personal loss, reduced income, disrupted social networks, and often poor health. Social network and personal identity problems are viewed as more frequent and more serious for widows than for widowers (Lopata, 1979).

But, as Troll (1985) remarks, women vary in the extent to which the role of wife is central to their identities, and they vary widely in their adaptations. Improved public pension and income maintenance provisions have given widows more options for living arrangements (Kobrin, 1976; Clausen, 1986). Evidently contact with friends and, especially, with other widows, is an important factor in the adjustment and morale of widows.

INDIVIDUALS IN THE FAMILY CYCLE

In Chapter 2 we presented and explained the concept of dependency in populations reckoned in terms of the ratio between the numbers in the population too young or old to be engaged in organized activities of material production to the number in the population in the range of ages in which individuals normally are employed or do participate in material production. Dependency ratios calculated in precisely this manner—ratios of population under 15 years of age and 65 or over to the population aged 15 to 64—were presented for several countries to illustrate the implications of fertility and mortality conditions for age structure and dependency in the populations and societies so compared. We called this macrodependency. Thus, macrodependency was taken as the broad quantitative ratio or relationship between those in the population of ages rendering them potentially or actually dependent on the productive activity of others; that is, children, the elderly or infirm; persons prevented from such organized activity by childrearing or household commitments; and those of ages or statuses rendering them potential or actual participants in the regime of material production—employed, entrepreneurs, property owners, or the like. Classical and refined dependency ratios, then, are used to measure various aspects of macrodependency.

In contrast, microdependency refers to an individual's inability to carry out the ordinary activities of sustenance and daily life without assistance of some other person or agency. Assistance includes economic or income support; being dressed or having meals prepared; having arrangements made for admission to schools, transportation to visit friends, or laundry services but not one's own *purchase* of services in a private market transaction. Measurement of microdependency is not extensively developed, but there are some existing schemes for measuring, say, dependency in instrumental activities of daily life (IADL), measures of frequencies of use of certain kinds of services, and so forth. These typically relate available kin, for example, children, siblings, or parents, to rates of labor force participation, use of services, leisure activities, and income support entitlements.

In the rest of this chapter and hereafter in this book, we will denote by the term, obligations, the requirement or expectations that an individual act in response to needs or address and resolve microdependencies of other individuals in some given social relationship to them, for example, obligations to parents, children, other kin, neighbors, or sometimes community or wider society. Similarly, we shall denote by the term, entitlements, the legitimate claims that individuals have on other individuals, groups, agencies, or social units to resources or services that can address their needs or microdependencies.

Each individual has, at each juncture in his or her life course, or at each age, some constellation of dependencies, obligations, and entitlements. Many, and at some ages most, of these are defined with reference to his nuclear family. But there are dependency, obligations, and entitlements defined with reference to other social units as well: extended families, neighborhoods, workplaces, communities, and societies and their governments.

Much of the individual's behavior and many of his social relationships are organized around bringing dependencies, obligations, and entitlements into some acceptable and reasonably stable balance. The fact, frequency, timing, and directions of life-course transitions are strongly informed and influenced by the individual's constellation at that age (or life-course or family-cycle juncture) of dependency, obligations, and entitlements. This constellation is in large part determined by nuclear family factors, including age of parents, education of parents, size of family, number of siblings, age of siblings, presence in the household of extra-nuclear family persons, employment of mother, and family income.

Infant and Early Childhood Socialization

The infant is the ultimate dependent: His or her well-being and very life depend upon the protection and nurture of the mother or mother-substitute. Yet the infant learns very quickly that there is mutuality and reciprocity even in this relationship: The mother is herself dependent in certain ways and for certain important gratifications upon the infant's responses and upon the infant's very dependency. The infant very quickly learns and internalizes obligations to the mother.

Later, in subsequent early childhood socialization, these extend to both parents, to one or more siblings, and sometimes to other family members, caregivers, or other close persons. But the infant pattern of dependency and obligations undergoes some differentiation or development as well. The infant's or small child's needs expand beyond those of elementary protection and nurture to include a variety of learning and stimulation needs. Correspondingly, his responses expand to include obedience, mimicking, and so forth, and his own range of initiatives expands. The infant or young child also learns the extent and range of his entitlements to sustenance and protection resources controlled by parents or other family members.

Late Childhood Socialization and Transitions to Adolescence

Older children are accorded duties and responsibilities, even as their own needs and wishes expand and differentiate further. In modern urban societies these are mostly still dependencies and obligations within the nuclear family household, although they may extend to the neighborhood or school settings as well. In traditional or rural societies children were frequently direct and significant participants in the household or the even wider community production regime in chores or activities of direct bearing on the family or community sustenance.

Even in contemporary urban nuclear families, quite small children may have obligations of household chores, care of younger siblings, or care for other family members. Correspondingly, their needs now include much more elaborate social and educational stimuli, skills, experiences, and credentials for which they may be dependent upon extrahousehold agents: schools, teachers, or playmates. These are, of course, in addition to sustenance, protection, stimuli, and moral guidance and sense of order for which they remain largely dependent upon parents, siblings, or grandparents.

It is important to note that, already in later childhood (and perhaps sometimes even in infancy and earliest childhood), there is some mix of dependency addressed within the nuclear family household and dependency addressed outside the nuclear family household. In part the mix is determined by the kinds of factors indicated earlier: age and education of parents, size, sex and age composition of the nuclear family, presence of extranuclear family persons in the household, and employment and income characteristics of the parents. We can refer to this groups of factors by the term, kin availability, and recall from the earlier discussions some of the variations and trends in kin availability in modern societies.

It is important to recognize also that within any given constellation of kin *availability* the actual behavior and interaction, and the pattern of family dependency and obligation resulting from that behavior and interaction, may vary widely. Personality variables and interactions, health, extrafamily factors, and the like may all influence family and individual dependency and obligations separately or together. It is important even in the early life course to identify and measure the specific microdependencies, for example, for food and shelter, custody and protection, play and schooling, health care, to study their variations in the various social subgroups, and to identify and study the ways in which they are addressed and resolved.

Similarly, it is important to identify and measure the specific types of obligations that the older child has in the family setting and outside. These, too, will be related both to kin availability and to specific patterns of behavior and interaction. The timing and nature of transitions from late childhood to early adolescence, including school changes and progressions, early employment, and same or opposite sex friendships and peer group activity, are probably related to the family dependency and obligations constellation even at this juncture.

Late Adolescence and the Transition to Adulthood

We have already noted in Chapter 6 that the historical novelty of adolescence, the socioeconomic moratorium associated with adolescence in modern times, and the idea that the nature and content of adolescence are probably very culture-bound even at the present time. But whatever the norms and practices governing adolescence, it remains true that adolescents ordinarily exhibit constellations of dependency, obligations, and entitlements not only with respect to their parents and nuclear households but in various directions outside their homes beyond their nuclear families of origin. Adolescents in modern urban societies very frequently—even if not necessarily always or inevitably—need economic support: They must be provided with food, shelter, and clothing. They also need care, stimuli, training, and education, and often they need mediation to the adult world and society, and a sense of social order.

Many adolescents, of course, take a major part in their own support, their own care, their own stimuli and training. Economic self-support through wage or salary employment in a full-time or part-time job is the most familiar modern version of such autonomy and participation. Adolescents have traditionally been major participants in family and household economic activity even without wages and salaries. Indeed many are intimately involved in the support, care, and stimuli of others in their families or even outside their families. These activities are accompanied or prescribed by more or less elaborate norms and expectations, many in the form of obligations in the very sense we have defined the term above. If the obligations of young children are necessarily circumscribed by their physical strength, development, and experience, those of adolescents have no such inherent limitations. Rather, they are defined by the number, composition, and circumstances of their available kin and the normative prescriptions and expectations governing the relationships and exchanges.

In most cultures the very meaning of adulthood and the transition to adulthood is connected to some change in the mixture of dependencies and obligations carried by the individual. Typically there is some departure from, or relinquishment of, dependencies and some assumption of new obligations. School-leaving and, even more, departure from the parental home are in many respects departures from dependency. Military service, full-time employment, formation of independent households, marriage, and parenthood all reflect assumption of new obligations. Of course, the assumption of new obligations typically also entails new dependencies both within nuclear families of origin and procreation, as well as in extrafamily job and community domains. But, as suggested earlier, the nature and timing of these transitions are themselves affected by the prior constellations of dependency and obligations, primarily in the nuclear family settings.

Traditional versus Modern Adulthood

The traditional dependencies and obligations of adulthood are well recognized, even if they are not necessarily identified, described, or measured as precisely as we might like for analytical purposes. They are associated especially with marriage, parenthood, and formation of independent households. They include primarily mutual dependencies and obligations among couples and nuclear family members for economic support and sustenance, care, emotional support, services of various types, companionship and stimuli, and so forth. They also include similar dependencies and obligations among members of extended families, across generations among grandparents and parents and children and grandchildren as well as among uncles, aunts, cousins, or other extended kin. They also include dependencies and obligations in employment and work settings, and some dependencies and obligations in wider community and societal settings, such as in shopping and commercial transactions, receipt of public and welfare services, or payment of taxes, exercise of civic or public obligations, and the like.

A familiar theme in the discussion and analysis especially of the family, but in discussion of other social institutions as well, is the idea that adulthood is increasingly *devoid* of dependency and obligations. A number of trends and practices are asserted to have the effect of freeing young persons from dependency and obligations in the transition to adulthood. For example, continuing economic support by parents of young adults, or public income entitlements for students or young unemployed persons free young adults from traditional dependency and obligations.

Similarly abortion and contraception allow young adults to limit or forgo entirely the dependencies and obligations associated with childbearing and childrearing. Delayed marriage or unconventional family or living arrangements may also reduce dependencies and obligations of adulthood, at least by comparison with traditional marriage and household formation. Finally, commercial and public health, custodial, and care arrangements and facilities for young children, frail elderly, or for others of any age are asserted to excuse adults from the dependencies and obligations associated with care of their own children, parents, or other family members. Proposals that such facilities and services be available as universal entitlements are frequently viewed as guaranteeing and fortifying the demise of dependency and obligations in modern adulthood generally and in family life in particular (see, also, the discussion in Chapter 5).

Research to test such views and assertions probably awaits more effective and more extensive measurement of microdependency, obligations, and the correlates of their variations among subgroups over time. At this point, it is possible to note that modern demographic trends have had the result of compressing the part of adulthood taken up with parenthood of young children, extending the years of joint survival with spouses and parents, and diminishing the numbers of available kin at all ages. On the average the overall effect of these developments may reasonably be supposed indeed to have diminished dependency and obligations in modern early adulthood, at least. There is good reason to conjecture that the obligations and burdens of care in later adulthood for aging parents may have *increased* under the modern demographic developments (increased longevity of parents, fewer siblings with whom to share care responsibilities). We return to this topic in Chapter 12.

Dependency and Obligations in the Empty Nest and Old Age

The empty-nest stage of the family cycle is frequently conceived as characterized by diminished obligations without increased dependency. Old age is frequently viewed as characterized by greatly diminished obligations offset, as it were, by very enhanced dependency. Measured by numbers of young children per household, the levels of obligations of individuals or couples in the empty-nest stage certainly do decline, and those of elderly individuals or couples decline even more. Gauged by indicators of morbidity, impairment and infirmity, low income, or institutional residence, the levels of dependency of adults in the empty-nest stage change very little, but those of the elderly certainly do increase.

Again, the available measures of microdependency and obligations seem not yet precise enough and sensitive enough for satisfactory description and measurement of variations and changes over time and over the family cycle. Nonetheless the comparison of dependency, obligation, and entitlement constellations of individuals and couples in the empty-nest stage of the family cycle with those of the elderly illuminates the separate age, health, marital status, income, and other components of the variations, even if exact determination of their respective weights must await more detailed research.

Nuclear family *dependency* of empty-nest-stage couples is primarily upon one another for income, health care, emotional support, mutual services and the like. Only exceptionally, for example, if both are in poor health, have very low income, are immigrants to the culture, or otherwise seriously disadvantaged, would they be likely to be dependent upon their own children or grandchildren and even less upon their elderly parents. Healthy married elderly couples with comfortable incomes might differ very little from the middle-aged empty-nest couples in this respect. But the elderly in poor health, the widowed, or those with inadequate incomes are much more likely to be dependent in some respect, and their dependency is highly likely to be addressed to their children or grandchildren for resolution.

Nuclear family *obligations* of the empty-nest-stage couple very frequently extend intergenerationally in both directions. Addressing the needs or ambitions of their own children and grandchildren *and* addressing the needs of their parents for support, care, and services generate obligations. Empty-nest couples and individuals may retain, undertake, or respond to such obligations willingly. Or they may respond less willingly, but in the absence of acceptable alternatives or justifiable reasons to refrain from them, manage the tensions and contradictions as best they can. For the healthy or economically well-off elderly, nuclear family obligations may be equally compelling. But frequently they are overridden by inability of the elderly to undertake or respond to them or by the dependency of the elderly individuals or couples in question.

The idea that the availability, nature, and levels of extrafamily entitlements to income, health care, and other kinds of care and support *modifies* in some very important ways the dependency and obligation constellations and the relationships and contrasts sketched above, has already been introduced at several points in this volume. Entitlements for children and parents of the empty-nest individuals and couples reduce both the dependencies of the adult children and, especially, of the elderly parents *and* the obligations of the empty-nest individuals and couples, with corresponding contributions to the quality and stability of life these may entail for all. More detailed assessment of the costs and benefits awaits systematic research.

9

THE SOCIAL STATUS
OF THE ELDERLY

historical and comparative perspectives

INTRODUCTION

In this and the three chapters that follow we turn to issues and problems of the elderly population in modern, low-mortality and low-fertility societies. In Part I we saw that the numbers and proportions of elderly persons in Western populations and societies have grown dramatically in the present century. We saw also that the changing age composition of populations raises important economic and social issues not only for the elderly but for the societies generally. In Part IV we examine the issues and review the sociological discussion of social status and social integration of the elderly, and those concerning their income support, health care, and social networks.

It is very important to note at the outset, and to bear in mind throughout the following chapters, that the elderly population like any large population subgroup is a heterogeneous population. It includes men and women in a fairly large age range, rich and poor, healthy and ill, with a wide range of educational attainments and credentials. It comprises persons with many, few, or no close family members, living in a large variety of household relationships and arrangements, retired or employed in any of a wide range of occupations and job settings, and, perhaps most important, with very, very wide range of personal, family, and social histories and biographies. It is very important to study the elderly, characterize the elderly, and compare the elderly to the equally heterogeneous non-elderly. But such characterizations and comparisons must be carried out with the recognition of the great range and variety within the elderly population.

The individual experience and the meaning of aging in the later years of life have always been problematic and surrounded by ambiguities. As Berg and Gadow (1978) have noted, it is not clear or obvious if old age is a phase of life that is both healthy and normal, or unhealthy but still normal, or unhealthy and abnormal. It is not obvious if old age is a stage of life or simply the earliest stage of dying, if it is to be valued and revered, prevented and cured, or anticipated with hope, dread, or indifference. Exploration of individual experiences and meanings of aging and life-course transitions at the close of life is beyond the scope of this volume (but see Achenbaum, 1985; Spicker, Woodward, and van Tassel, 1978). Yet, it is important to note that there is an important social organizational analog or parallel to the ambiguities of individual aging in late life. The social status of the elderly has in virtually all societies and all times been ambiguous and problematic.

All societies comprise males and females of different ages and attach meaning to sex and age differences. They must deal with the universal processes of aging and life-course transitions and development. In general, societies are dominated and controlled by their adult male populations: Females are subordinate to males, children are subordinate to adults, and the middle-aged generally dominate both younger adults and the elderly. Probably one measure of a society's development or modernity is the extent to which it has departed from or modified the traditional pattern of adult male dominance—that is, the extent to which rights, status, and opportunities are accorded women, youth and children, and the elderly (see, for example, Simone de Beauvoir's *The Second Sex* and *The Coming of Age*).

For the most part the adult men, dominant in their societies, are ambivalent to the status of women, youth, and children. On the one hand women, youth, and children have been historically deprived of power and leverage. On the other hand, they are critically important for the present and future viability and welfare of the societies and, of course, for the adult males' own well-being. By contrast, the elderly are *not* deemed critical for the present or future welfare of either societies generally or the dominant adult males in particular. This holds *except* insofar as the elderly have been able to retain control of critical, or at least significant, social roles and resources. Thus, not only has aging been always a problematic and ambiguous experience for the individual and those surrounding him or her, but the social status of the elderly as a group and as individuals has always been clouded by contradictions and ambiguities.

Meanings of Social Status

What do we mean by social status, and why should we study historical and comparative aspects of the elderly and their status? By social status we usually have reference to the idea of an individual's or a group's place in a social rank order. So the social status of the elderly can refer to the typical, average, or familiar rank of individual elderly persons relative to the ranks of other individuals in society. Or it can refer to the ranks of groups of elderly persons relative to the ranks of other groups in society.

But, rank with respect to what? Usually the idea of social rank is reckoned with reference to one or another type of social reward and resource. For example, we can and do rank individuals or groups in terms of their income, material rewards or well-being, or control over material resources. Alternatively, we rank individuals or groups with respect to type, intensity, or importance in participation in social activity. For example persons are ranked in political influence, family authority, involvement in work, school, or community affairs. Perhaps the most familiar sense in which we conceive the social status of the elderly is with reference to deference, esteem, or reputation. This includes acceptability or desirability as a participant in social relations and interaction (Would you have lunch with him? Would you live on the same street? Would you let your daughter marry him?).

Finally, an important type of social reward and resource is the degree of control over one's own activity and situation. Thus another way of reckoning social rank is in terms of personal autonomy and control. So in our case, place in the rank order of society is connected with (1) social roles played, (2) the material and social rewards received (including deference, honor, and esteem), (3) influence and control over resources and rewards (including over selves), (4) reputation and the opinions of others, and (5) participation in social activity (including family, production activities, community, or specialized age-linked activities).

Typically writers have viewed the elderly as having high status if they are loved, venerated, worshiped, admired, or perceived as attractive persons. Holding high public office or control of public affairs, owning property and control of its use and allocation of income derived from it have also been seen as indicators of high status. Enjoyment of high income, high levels of consumption, and having high levels of care, attention, and personal services accorded are further signs of high status.

When the elderly have been able to monopolize and transmit knowledge and information, religious ritual, or knowledge about links to the supernatural, they have been said to enjoy high status. When they control their own lives, the lives of their children and grandchildren, or the health and well-being of others, the elderly are thought to possess high status. Finally, the elderly's own enjoyment of health, long life, and high levels of satisfaction and gratification are associated with high social status for the elderly as well.

The point of studying historical and comparative aspects of the social status of the elderly is not only for information about previous or different societies or about earlier or different elderly populations. Rather, it is to illuminate our own situation by seeking answers to questions such as:

1. Are there universal aspects of the status of the elderly? What are they? How do we account for them?
2. What facets of the situations and social status of the elderly are unique to specific societies? What facets recur in several or many societies? What are the circumstances under which they recur? What are the variations *within* societies? How are such variations to be explained?
3. Can we identify patterns of *change* in the status of the elderly? Are they unique? Or do they recur? Under what circumstances?

Measuring and Comparing the Social Status of the Elderly

For our own contemporary societies we can mobilize the full social scientific apparatus to measure and assess the social status of the elderly. We can measure incomes; examine living arrangements, consumption, employment, and job authority; study intergenerational relations; and study community and family participation. We can interview samples of elderly. We can do content analysis of written materials—novels, magazines, newspapers, or media items—movies, TV, and so forth—to measure the opinion or values about the elderly. Indeed, in the gerontological journals there are innumerable examples of studies of the attitudes of children, teen-agers, adults, Americans, Canadians, Protestants, and Catholics to the elderly and their beliefs and opinions about them. All of these do help us put together an assessment of the social status of the elderly in contemporary society. Moreover, for contemporary society, we can *replicate* studies and *verify* results, even if in fact we do not do so very often.

For distant societies, historical societies, societies very far from or very different from our own, things are not so simple, although sometimes they seem to be very simple and require primarily faith and imagination. We turn much more frequently to literary sources, historical materials where they exist, oral traditions where they don't. Occasionally we turn to archaeological clues, sometimes to participant observation or use of informants. Sometimes we draw on the accounts of travelers. We can rarely use the apparatus that we can mobilize and with which we would approach the inquiry for contemporary society.

If we want to know something about the United States or Canada a generation or two ago, there will be some systematic records as well as historical or social accounts. We could also ask our mothers or our grandmothers. If your mother is like my mother, she will probably say that her generation was more attentive to their parents, respected the elderly more, and looked after them more than the present generation—meaning, probably, that *you* are not caring for her or about her as much as she cared for her mother. Maybe.

But if we want to know how the ancient Greeks or the Biblical peoples thought about or treated the elderly, our mothers are ordinarily not a promising source of information. We have to read the Bible, or a poet or playwright, such as Homer or Aeschylus or Sophocles, or see what we can glean from the mythology. Often it is useful or suggestive to compare such accounts. If we want to know what preliterate societies have done, or do today, about their elderly, we can go to see and live among such societies in some cases. Or we can also search the ethnographic and anthropological accounts.

The accounts and discussions of variations and changes in the social status of the elderly typically belong to one of three types:

1. Those based on historical, literary, or artistic evidence and on comparisons among items and collections of such evidence. Examples include accounts of how elderly persons are portrayed in classical literature or painting.

2. Those based on deductive theoretical analysis incorporating concepts that may reasonably be readily operationalized and measured. Examples are analyses of the economic roles of elderly men in precapitalist and in capitalist economies, or the family roles of elderly women under high-fertility and under low-fertility demographic regimes.

3. Those based on inductive analyses of measurements and findings. Examples are measurement in censuses and surveys of living arrangements, employment, earnings, or consumption among the elderly in the variously delineated subpopulations.

We shall draw upon examples of each in the sections that follow.

SOCIETAL DEVELOPMENT AND THE SOCIAL STATUS OF THE ELDERLY

The idea of societal development is usually taken to encompass broad evolutionary transitions either of specific societies or the total of the world's existing societies that involve changes in their modes of production, collective survival, and adaptation to their environments as well as their characteristic social and political organizational features. Thus the change from hunting and gathering to settled horticulture, and the change from predominantly rural to urban settlements, are examples of societal development.

Societal development has typically entailed not only economic, social, and political changes. Rather, it has generally entailed demographic changes as well, usually in the direction of larger populations and more densely settled populations (Duncan, 1964; Matras, 1973). For the most part they have also entailed some growth in longevity, some improvements in the health and capacities of middle-aged and elderly, and some growth in the numbers and proportions of elderly persons in the populations. It is not surprising that there has been great interest in the manner in which social status of the elderly has varied or changed with societal development for both its historical evolutionary interest and its potential for revealing principles, factors, and axes of differentiation and change in the social status of the elderly.

This discussion generally revolves around comparisons among broad types or categories of societies reflecting varying levels of development. To illustrate these comparisons we may adopt here the modified Duncan-Goldschmidt taxonomy of societies (Matras, 1973), which includes the following eight societal types:

1. Nomadic food-gathering and hunting bands
2. Nomadic food-gathering and hunting tribal societies
3. Settled food-gathering and hunting tribal societies
4. Horticultural village and tribal societies
5. Nomadic herding tribal societies

6. Agricultural-state societies including both peasant villages and urban communities
7. Industrial, urban-dominated, state societies
8. Industrial or postindustrial metropolitan-megalopolitan societies

The taxonomy is based on the type of sustenance-producing technologies characterizing societies, but it is obviously closely related to variation in the size and scale of the societies, the density of population settlement, and the social and political institutional structures.

The Elderly in Preindustrial Societies

Goody (1976) has pointed out that the situation of the elderly in nonindustrial societies depends very centrally on the structure of domestic groups, or family units, which are, in turn, the main agents of production in such societies. In nonindustrial societies an individual is directly dependent upon his own senior generation for the acquisition of rights in the basic means of production. The relative scarcity of resources affects the nature of the control exercised by the senior generation over the junior. The timing (for example, whether at death or earlier) and the directions (for example, whether to the eldest son only or more diffusely) of the intergenerational transmission of rights is of critical importance in the maintenance of authority, influencing the points of family fission, and ensuring support for the elderly.

Nomadic Societies   In general the very simplest societies, say, types 1 and 2, are always on the brink of starvation. They also move a great deal, and it is difficult for the elderly to keep up. Summarizing anthropological and ethnographic materials, de Beauvoir (1972) has concluded that the usual choice of communities with inadequate resources—whether nomadic or agricultural—is to sacrifice the old, either by killing them or leaving them to die. The elderly may be cheerful about it or not. But, according to de Beauvoir, there are at least three modifying dimensions to this pattern.

A first qualifying consideration concerns the nature of parent–children relationships. In societies in which parenthood, parent–child care and protection, and parent–child affection are strongly institutionalized, individuals reciprocate with care and responsibility for elderly parents. Such societies institutionalize caring and compassionate expression and behavior toward the elderly.

A second modifying dimension concerns the nature of the society's ritual. Aside from the knowledge that the elderly may have accumulated concerning ritual practices, in systems in which ancestors are worshiped, the elderly are natural intermediaries and the most appropriate persons to conduct rituals. Goody (1976) points out that this is true of most societies that have some notion of the persistence of the human persona after death, at least of the soul or spiritual part; elders are close to ancestors and filial piety is supernaturally sanctioned.

A third modifying dimension concerns the extent to which the simple societies may recognize, draw upon, and value knowledge, information, and techniques accumulated by the elderly. Even in nomadic societies the elderly may have knowledge about topography, climate, and sustenance options, or about breeding and survival of herds, which may be recognized as critical for general survival. In the absence of such knowledge or specialized skills, the elderly are devalued as they become a burden on the precarious sustenance of the group (McPherson, 1983).

Complex Preliterate Societies and Classical Antiquity   In more complex preliterate societies, the status of the elderly has been found to vary with (a) abundance or scarcity of food, (b) presence or absence of property institutions, and (c) the perceived importance of ritual, scientific, and practical knowledge of the elderly. At the extremes, in societies that generally enjoy some surplus of food, in which the elderly members control property, and in which importance is given to the knowledge stored by the older members or their special roles in ritual, the status of the elderly is high and they are sustained and protected. In societies with severe food scarcity, in which there are no important recognized property rights and leadership and authority are based on perceived ability rather than on knowledge, the elderly are effectively abandoned or even put to death. Obviously most societies fall somewhere between these extremes. McPherson (1983) has noted that other factors favoring the status of the elderly in preliterate societies include stability of residence, nuclear family organization, and availability of low-skill functional roles.

The portrayals of the situation of the elderly in Biblical and classical antiquities have contrasted the ancient Hebrew prescriptions of reverence, respect, and veneration of the elderly with the negative images of old age gleaned from the poetry and drama of ancient Greece and Rome (de Beauvoir, 1972). The Biblical admonitions to young persons to honor and obey parents as well as the prescription of both secular and priestly power and authority in the hands of the elders of the community are familiar. But in frequent passages, longevity is cast as a reward for righteousness and good deeds. The punishment of those deviating from righteousness is affirmed regardless of age. There are various suggestions that it is not age per se that is revered as much as the righteous past lives that are rewarded by survival to old age. Yet altogether, the ancient Jews appear as one of the few peoples whose cultural traditions sought appreciation and veneration for old age.

In contrast, the ancient Greek literature expresses disgust, hatred, and dread of old age and its accompanying ugliness and infirmities. Greek gods are depicted as eternally young and beautiful, while declining physical and mental capacities are the fate of the elderly. Influence and power accrue to wealth rather than to age. To the extent that the elderly in ancient Greece were powerful and influential, it was because of their accumulated wealth rather than age itself.

Similarly, the Roman sources concentrate their admiration and esteem on youth and strength, perhaps epitomized by the young citizen-soldier. In Roman drama, death, even by suicide, is presented as preferable to suffering the deterioration and indignities of old age (de Beauvoir, 1972). Emphasis on deterioration, ugliness, and indignity of old age emerges in the literature, art, and drama of the Middle Ages as well (de Beauvoir, 1972; Achenbaum, 1985). Medieval negative themes and motifs surrounding the portrayal of old age are offset by teachings of the Church and religious orthodoxy prescribing loyalty and obedience to parents and to elders generally.

A somewhat different view and interpretation of the prescriptions and images of aging and old age in antiquity is presented by Stahmer (1978), who has held that ancient Hebrew and Homeric Greek oral cultures shared a common respect for the elderly. In both cultures, according to Stahmer, the attitudes toward the elderly were somewhat ambivalent in that old age was valued but viewed primarily as a reward for earlier accomplishments (see, also, Achenbaum, 1985). In Homer's time and among the ancient Hebrews, old age was viewed with mixed feelings. Although for some it was a "noble reward bestowed on one by a divinity," most viewed old age with fear and apprehension of declining powers and capacities. Many elderly in positions of power were actually feared as often as they were revered. Many were respected publicly but derogated privately. In both Hebraic and Homeric cultures the elderly played important political and culture-transmitting roles, to be sure, but they were deemed to have earned respect and the right to grow old and to be remembered by virtue of earlier deeds.

Old-Age versus Over-Age in Societal Development   In a series of broad-ranging and widely cited studies of aging in preindustrial societies, L.W. Simmons (1945, 1960) has identified and elaborated most of the factors mentioned above as bearing on variation in the status of the elderly in preliterate societies. They include the abundance and arrangements for sharing food, the kinds of productive and ritual roles available to the elderly, the control of economic and political resources, the use of knowledge and experience held by the elderly, and the features of kinship and family organization. It is perhaps Simmons who has most prominently presented the social scientific account of the traditional agrarian society as reaching some sort of peak in the prestige and social status of elderly males, with the transition to industrial and urban features in subsequent societal development entailing a diminution in status of the elderly. Under the rubric "respect for the elderly," Simmons has concluded:

> One may state with confidence that all primitive and agrarian societies have accorded some considerable respect to old people—often remarkable deference—at least until they have reach such "over-age" that they are obviously powerless and incompetent. Under close analysis, respect for old age has been as a rule, accorded persons on the basis of some special assets possessed by them. They may receive some consideration because of their usefulness in the performance of economic, camp, or household chores. They may be regarded highly for their skill in crafts, games, dances, songs, storytelling, and the care of small children. They may be respected and heeded because of their control of property rights and the exercise of family prerogatives. They may be accorded great homage for their extensive knowledge, seasoned experience, good judgment, gifts in magic, and functions in religious rites and practices .... In general a favorable cultural milieu

for aged men has existed within a patriarchal type of family organization, where herding and agriculture have been the chief means of subsistence; where residence has been more or less permanent, the food supply constant, and the political system well regulated; and when property rights in land, crop, herds, goods, and even women are deeply entrenched.

Among all peoples a point is reached in aging at which any further usefulness appears to be over, and the incumbent is regarded as a living liability. "Senility" may be a suitable term for this. Other terms among primitive peoples are the "over-aged," the "useless stage," the "sleeping period," the "age-grade of the dying," and the "already dead." Then, without actual death, the prospects are gloomy. *There is no question about this generalized social decision: the differences lie in the point at which it is reached.* [italics supplied]

The big point for us is that, in primitive societies and, indeed, in all societies until modern civilization, this over-age period has not been very significant. Few persons reached this stage; they did not last long in it. Some were dispatched with varying degrees of dignity and prestige.

The helpless and hopeless period takes on paramount importance, however, in our own civilized times. We are so successful in keeping very old people alive that we do not know what to do with them. Added to this is the recognized fact that the useless period is largely socially and culturally determined and that it may be moved up or put off in years. The social fates are most unfortunate, of course, when so many old people are made to feel useless relatively early in life and to find the twilight years empty, lonely, and long-lasting. More and more of life with less and less in it is not a happy prospect .... there is a pattern of participation for the aged that becomes relatively fixed in stable societies but suffers disruption with rapid social change .... in the long and steady strides of the social order, the aging get themselves fixed and favored in positions, power, and performance .... But, when social conditions become unstable and the rate of change reaches a galloping pace, the aged are riding for an early fall, and the more youthful associates take their seats in the saddles. (Simmons, 1960)

The theme of declining status of the elderly under societal development was repeated in an analysis by Cottrell (1960) in which an alternative scheme, low-energy versus high-energy societies, is employed to index societal development. Low-energy societies have a characteristic set of social, economic, and political institutions. These, in turn, are associated with high social status of the elderly. The characteristic institutions of high-energy societies are those related to market economies. These are in turn associated with greatly diminished social and economic status of the elderly.

Both the later paper by Simmons and the paper by Cottrell were published in an important and influential collection entitled *Handbook of Social Gerontology: Societal Aspects of Aging* (Tibbitts, 1960) that its editor presented, and which indeed was widely received, as a "first attempt to identify and structure a new field of research and learning—social gerontology." Elaboration of the theme of the decline of the social status of the elderly in modern society in two related directions rendered it one of the orthodoxies of the emerging discussion and research on the elderly. One direction has been the formulation and elaboration of a theory of aging and modernization, associated with Donald Cowgill and his associates. The second has been the formulation and elaboration of the concept and theory of ageism, associated with Robert Butler.

Aging and Modernization

As noted earlier, Simmons, Cottrell, and others argued that the role and status of the elderly declined subsequent to the events and trends usually subsumed under the industrial revolution rubric. They held that modernization resulted in a worldwide pattern of declining relations between generations. The elderly lost power, security, and status because they no longer had functionally essential social roles and were no longer looked to for knowledge and information. Moreover, since adult children no longer lived in the parental home, many did not view themselves as having moral, legal, or social obligation to care for or support aging parents.

Drawing on the work of Simmons (1945) on preindustrial societies and on additional accounts of aging in preindustrial, semiindustrial, and industrial societies, Cowgill and Holmes (1972) developed the hypothesis that increasing modernization accounts for the declining status of the elderly. They formulated two sets of propositions concerning aging: the elderly in relation to their own children and to the total population and the status of the elderly in societies of varying levels of modernity. One set of propositions is asserted to have universal applicability. Examples are: "In all societies the elderly constitute a minority within the total population"; and "in all societies some people are classified as 'old' and therefore treated differently than are the 'non-old.' " The second set of propositions is culture-specific, and in particular propose variations in aging, old age, and in the status of the elderly related to more modernized or less modernized societies. Examples are: "Modernized societies have higher proportions of old people," or "the status of the elderly tends to decline with the increasing literacy of the population."

In general, the theory and the findings of Cowgill and Holmes support the propositions that the status of the elderly is high in societies where they perform useful, valued functions. These tend to be the least modern societies. Conversely, since in modern societies the elderly have few useful, valued functions, their status is, with a few prominent exceptions such as Japan, Ireland, and the Soviet Union, quite low. An elaborate set of explanatory propositions has also been worked out by Cowgill and various associates. These show how increased health and longevity, migration and urbanization, expansion of literacy and formal education, diminishing family size, and new technologies and enhanced productivity and income have in modernizing societies combined to render the elderly redundant in the working force, isolated residentially and culturally, devoid of family functions, and generally dependent for material, health, and social support.

Ageism

Alongside the meanings attached to sex and age differences in all societies are stereotypes and attitudes concerning those in each group. Inevitably, these include negative and invidious ones. The theory of ageism has been developed to describe, account for, and explore implications of the extension and institutionalization of the negative attitudes and stereotypes about older adults resulting from socialization in age-stratified societies, in legal and moral codes, as well as in popular views. Ageism, then, is a form of prejudice leading to discrimination against others on the basis of actual or perceived chronological age (Butler, 1975). The negative stereotypes and attitudes have become the basis for prejudicial and discriminatory social acts such as mandatory retirement from the labor force at a particular chronological age, exclusion from certain types of social interaction, and denial of equal access to certain kinds of services in the public and private sectors (McPherson, 1983).

The elderly themselves may either voluntarily or reluctantly accept the negative stereotypes, internalize the negative external evaluations, and themselves begin to behave in accordance with them, thus further reinforcing the societal stereotypes and ageism (Kuypers and Bengtson, 1973). Ageist attitudes and ageism are primarily directed toward older persons outside the family unit. But, as McPherson (1983) has noted, they may also influence behaviors within the family unit. Consistent with the modernization hypothesis, the prevalence of ageism is frequently seen as varying and changing over successive cohorts: If there was relatively little overt ageism early in this century, its incidence has increased along with increasing industrialization and social differentiation.

Changing Attitudes Toward Aging and the Elderly

Related to the theory of ageism have been the analyses of the historical shifts in the United States, and by implication in other countries as well, in popular attitudes toward aging in old age and stereotypes of the elderly. Colonial American communities were generally religious communities. Taking cues and norms from the Bible, they accorded the elderly both positions of leadership and authority and great deference and status in their families and communities alike. However, in the late eighteenth century or early nineteenth century, there was an inflection or, indeed, a turnaround in popular attitudes toward old age and the elderly. This turnaround ended the honor and veneration in which the elderly were held and moved American society in the direction of ageism.

The Fall of Veneration and Condescension and the Cult of Youth   There are at least two separate and distinct accounts and analyses of the timing and the proximate causes of this turnaround in American popular attitudes toward the elderly. Both agree that the turnaround took place *before* the onset of large-scale industrialization and urbanization in the United States. The view of Fischer (1977) is that after the American and French revolutions, the status of the elderly deteriorated as supporters of social and political equality argued that all those who work for pay were eligible to acquire power and status.

Old age was rare in the past. Those aged 70 or 80 years had necessarily already outlived half their children and grandchildren. Thus survival itself had something of a supernatural quality and was reason for veneration, deep respect, reverence, and near-worship on the part of the young. The old condescended to the young, a pattern reinforced in colonial America by Puritan views of survival to old age as a favorable sign of God with sinners condemned to early death. Elders did not retire from their offices in church, school, or state; parents retained control over landed wealth while adult children remained dependents well into maturity.

The American and French revolutions were also revolutions in age relations and signaled the passing of veneration and condescension. The numbers and proportions surviving to old age increased markedly, rendering the elderly much more abundant in contrast to their previous scarcity. Youth acquired a moral advantage that old age lost with the revolutions, a pattern reflected in clothing styles, linguistic and rhetorical patterns. In the period 1790 through 1820 American legislatures began to require public officials to retire from their offices at age 70 or even at age 60.

As the settlement of the West began in the 1800s, increased emphasis was placed on the vitality and vigor of the young adults. The latter, in many cases, were sons of Eastern colonials migrating from their places and families of origin to seek their own fortunes. A Cult of Youth began to emerge even as the average age of the working population increased. Both the high literature and the popular culture and mass media witnessed a growing gerontophobia.

The exaltation of youth, with soldiers, cowboys, and pioneers as heroes, may have reached a peak with the administration of Theodore Roosevelt (Gruman, 1978). It has extended into contemporary times with the adoption of youth dress and symbols (for example, blue jeans, miniskirts, leather boots, and beads) by the middle-aged college professors, media personages, and opinion leaders. Thus, in this view, the declining status of the elderly in America began with the change in cultural values after the American Revolution that led to emphasis on equality based on performance and income. It continued with westward migration away from the influence and control of parents and origins. As a result, in Fischer's view, many of the elderly were left in the eastern colonies to fend for themselves and ended their lives alone, often in poverty.

Obsolescence of Old Age? Achenbaum (1974, 1978) dates the turnaround in the attitude toward aging and the elderly in American popular opinion considerably later: at the close of the Civil War and on the eve of the major industrialization and urbanization trends in the last third of the nineteenth century. The elderly were honored and perceived valuable and important in pre-Civil War United States. Longevity itself was deemed proof of wisdom and virtue. It was the task of the elderly as guardians of virtue to teach others to live virtuously, morally, and healthfully. The elderly served others with their expertise in farming, public office, as oral historians and in general patriotism. They contributed in the homes where, according to the periodical literature of the time, they taught manners and served as models of behavior.

In Achenbaum's analysis, what occurred was that old age as a life stage and the elderly as a social category became obsolescent beginning in the mid-1860s. The impact of new scientific, bureaucratic, and popular ideas converging with innovations in medical practice, economic structure, and American society itself led to a transition in the ideas about getting old. Science replaced the enlightened common sense of the elderly by increasing longevity, preventing disease, and so forth. The greater roles for physicians, biologists, sanitary engineers, and other specialists downgraded the value of the elderly as promoters of healthful and moral living—in favor of professionals and scientists. Findings that old age "corrodes the mental and physical capacities" worked to downgrade the "paragon of virtue" image of the elderly. The rise of efficiency rhetoric and considerations led to disesteem for older employees in highly mechanized or rationalized industry.

The movement to wage labor and the decline of family farms and self-employment forced elderly employees into competition with younger workers. The latter enjoyed health and physical strength advantages as well as lengthier and more recent schooling, training, or apprenticeships. Wage labor reduced the power, authority, and leverage of elderly property owners over their own children. In addition, the extension of literacy and formal schooling and the introduction of new technologies and processes at home and workplace alike rendered much of the knowledge, information, and experience of the elderly inappropriate or redundant for the tasks and life styles confronting the younger generations. Thus the obsolescence of old age in America, according to Achenbaum, ushered in a period of declining perceptions, opinion, and esteem of the elderly, although *not* to any marked decline in their actual socioeconomic situations.

This period lasted until World War I, when the increasing numbers and visibility of elderly generally, and impoverished elderly in particular, led to perception of the elderly as a social problem. It led, ultimately, to the turnaround centering on the enactment of the Social Security Act of 1935. The actual socioeconomic status of the elderly changed and declined as agriculture ceased to be a major source of jobs, as formal education became a more desirable asset than years of work experience, and as mandatory retirement and some minimal pension plans spread through industry. At the same time, these factors made it increasingly difficult for the elderly to escape poverty through gainful employment. The plight of the elderly became more and more *visible* as their numbers grew.

Summary: The Conventional Pessimism

A large number and variety of studies, emerging from different disciplines, point to an erosion of the status of the elderly associated with societal development, differentiation, and modernization. The perceived value of the elderly is said to decline as their numbers increase, as alternatives to their accumulated knowledge become accessible, as wage employment diminishes the weight of their control of property, as their skills become obsolete under rapidly changing technologies, and as the family is decreasingly a unit of production of goods and services and increasingly a consumer of extrafamily services. The portrayal of the inverse relationship between societal complexity or modernity and the social status of the elderly has been modified slightly in a number of recent studies. It points to the upgrading of the status of the elderly in the most advanced industrial democracies, with the advent of welfare-state income maintenance and health care measures, on the one hand, and with the beginnings of consciousness raising and political mobilization of the elderly, on the other hand (Cowgill, 1974). But the basic relationship and pessimistic outlook for the status of the elderly are retained in these recent studies as well.

REVISIONS OF THE COMPLEXITY/ DEVELOPMENT/MODERNIZATION THESIS

Studies of the relationship between societal development and the status of the elderly are by no means unanimous in concluding that modernization has led to diminishing value, functions, influence, esteem, or status of the elderly. Maddox and Campbell (1985) have noted that four decades ago the projected rapid increase in numbers and proportions of elderly persons in industrialized countries was viewed with great concern for their integration and general well-being. The grounds for such concern (well documented, in their view) were that the values of modern industrial urban societies do appear to favor youthfulness. Social roles in late life do appear to be ambiguously defined, inviting the inference that late life is roleless. Access to important social goods and services does appear to be restricted for many older persons.

Yet in studies of social integration of older persons in all urban industrial societies the evidence of integration outweighs, in the view of Maddox and Campbell (1985), that of isolation of the elderly. Basic legal rights have been maintained and the elderly are not singular targets of social inequity. Political participation of the elderly does not differ greatly from that of other adults. Most older persons live in private households, and there are higher levels of kinship relationships than prevailing theory would suggest.

Moreover, although problems remain for substantial minorities of the elderly, social and economic security is achieved to a tolerable degree for the majority. Age per se, according to Maddox and Wiley, is not an adequate predictor of social integration and there is no necessary connection between age and social integration on either theoretical or evidential grounds (Maddox and Wiley, 1976, p. 15).

Recent Trends in Education and Income of the Elderly

Insofar as education and income are important components of social status, their recent trends among the elderly in the United States and other Western countries tend to support and fortify the analyses of Maddox and Wiley and Maddox and Campbell. As late as 1960 less than one-fifth of the U.S. elderly (aged 65 or over: 17 percent of the males and 21 percent of the females) had completed or studied beyond high school, compared to 41 percent in the total adult (aged 25+) population and compared to 61 percent among the youngest adults (aged 25 to 29) (Table 9.1). By 1986 the percent among the elderly who had completed high school or some higher education reached almost 50 percent (while the corresponding

Table 9.1. Percent Completing Selected Levels of Education, by Age Categories, United States, 1960–1986

	1960	*1970*	*1980*	*1986*
Percent completing 4+ years high school				
Total, 25+	41.1	52.3	66.5	74.7
25–29	60.7	73.8	84.5	86.1
Males 65+	17.0	26.0	39.2	48.9
Females 65+	20.9	30.0	41.8	49.6
Percent completing 4+ years college				
Total, 25+	7.7	10.7	16.2	19.4
25–29	11.1	16.3	22.1	22.4
Males 65+	4.3	7.9	10.3	12.4
Females 65+	3.2	5.2	7.4	7.5

Source: U.S. Bureau of the Census, *Statistical Abstract of the United States, 1988* (Washington, D.C.: Government Printing Office, 1987), Table 40, p. 35; Table 201, p. 125.

percent for the total adult population reached almost 75 percent). In 1960 only 4.3 percent of American men aged 65 and over had completed four or more years of college or university studies, but by 1986 this percent increased to 12.4 percent. In 1960 the median number of school years completed by adult American males (25+) was 10.3 years, but among men aged 65 to 69 in 1960 the median school attainment was only 8.3 years. By 1982, however, these had nearly converged. For the total male adult population the 1982 median was 12.6 years, compared to 12.1 years for the men aged 65 to 69 (Zopf, 1986, Table 5.3).

Not less dramatic has been the rise in income, and in particular the decline in the percent of the elderly in poverty. In 1960 more than one-third of all elderly persons in the United States were living below the poverty levels as reckoned by the Bureau of the Census. This percent was reduced to 12.4 percent of the total elderly population in poverty in 1986 (Table 9.2).

Table 9.2. Percent 65+ below Poverty Level, by Sex and Household Status, United States, 1960–1986

	1960	*1970*	*1979*	*1986*
Total 65+	35.2*	24.6	15.2	12.4
Males:				
Family Householders	29.7	16.6	8.4	6.1
Unrelated Individuals	58.5	40.0	25.3	19.6
Females:				
Family Householders	31.5	23.5	13.0	11.8
Unrelated Individuals	69.1	49.9	30.5	26.8

Source: U.S. Bureau of the Census, *Statistical Abstract of the United States, 1988* (Washington, D.C.: Government Printing Office, 1987), Table 716, p. 435; Table 40, p. 35
*1959.

The income levels of elderly unrelated individuals, that is, those living alone or in nonfamily households, remain low. Their percent below the poverty level, although dramatically lower than in 1960, remains substantial. Average income of families and households headed by elderly persons has been and remains very substantially lower than among families of younger householders.

The households of the elderly are typically much smaller than those of younger householders, and the tax burden is less as well. In 1985 the average after-tax income per household member in households headed by elderly persons was *higher* than average after-tax income per household member in those headed by younger householders. Only in households headed by middle-aged householders, those 50 to 64 years of age, was average after-tax income per household member higher than in those in the elderly households (Table 9.3).

Thus, average before-taxes household income for those headed by persons 65 years or over reached only $18,800 in 1985—much lower than the overall average $29,066 household income and even more dramatically lower than for households headed by persons 30 to 59 years old. But the reductions in income due to taxes were very much less among the elderly households than for all the rest (column 5 of Table 9.3). Reckoned on a per household basis, average annual income in elderly household exceeds that for most other subgroups.

Table 9.3.   Money Income of Households—Mean Income and Income Per Household Member Before and After Taxes, by Age of Householder, 1985 (Households as of March 1986)

	MEAN HOUSEHOLD INCOME		INCOME PER HOUSEHOLD MEMBER		
	Before taxes	*After taxes*	*Before taxes*	*After taxes*	*Taxes as a percent of income*
All households	29,066	22,646	10,884	8,480	22.1
Age of householder:					
15–24 years	17,708	14,515	7,681	6,296	18.0
25–29 years	25,697	20,142	9,723	7,621	21.6
30–34 years	29,935	23,075	9,738	7,507	22.9
35–39 years	34,166	25,926	10,083	7,651	24.1
40–44 years	37,456	28,320	10,861	8,212	24.4
45–49 years	39,129	29,506	12,107	9,130	24.6
50–54 years	37,453	28,308	13,029	9,848	24.4
55–59 years	34,561	26,176	13,525	10,244	24.3
60–64 years	29,431	22,864	13,392	10,404	22.3
65 years and over	18,800	16,198	10,622	9,152	13.8

Source: U.S. Bureau of the Census, *Statistical Abstract of the United States, 1988* (Washington, D.C.: Government Printing Office, 1987), Table 697, p. 426.

Multidimensionality of Age Status

In a review of the outstanding issues in the field of aging and the life course, Neugarten and Hagestad (1985) have pointed to the multiplicity of both meanings and dimensions of the concept of age status. One such meaning is closely akin to our own use of the concept, that is, as rank. They note the multiplicity of discussions of the changing status of the elderly in the sense of changing social rank. But, as pointed out extensively in the sociological literature, and as noted earlier in this chapter, social rank is itself multidimensional. A problem in the studies of societal development and the status of the elderly is that their discussions may encompass one or several of the dimensions of social rank, such as deference, respect, power, and material comfort, but without distinctions made between them.

The measures on the various dimensions of social rank and their changes are not necessarily mutually consistent or reinforcing. They are able to cite only a single study in which age status was operationally defined and which was able to study change in age status unambiguously defined on the basis of census data with regard to income, employment, and education. When age status is considered expressed attitudes toward the elderly, Neugarten and Hagestad cite studies suggesting that (1) the negative attitudes and stereotypes about the elderly may not be as clear and prevalent as gerontologists have presumed; (2) there is little evidence of ageism in the attitudes expressed by the public at large; and (3) the elderly themselves describe their actual situations much more favorably than the public has presumed them to be.

A somewhat similar point is made by Keith (1985) in a review of anthropological study of age and aging. In her view, a fuller understanding of variations and change in the social status of the elderly requires an "unraveling" of the concept of social status in several directions. In the first place, it is important to distinguish between the prestige that the elderly have enjoyed in most societies and the ways in which in fact they have been treated. These have very frequently exhibited quite extreme contrasts. Second, it is useful to distinguish between what old people want and what they get. A distinction must also be made between support and care of the elderly on the part of younger adults in contrast to continuing power, leverage, and active community participation of the elderly themselves. Finally, it is important to recognize the different kinds of elderly persons, including the young-old as distinct from old-old and sex and social class differences. The inferences possible from relatively unrefined and undifferentiated assertions or depictions of the social status of the elderly are, accordingly, quite limited.

Modern Critique of Golden-Past-Based Analyses

The entire tradition of historical and social scientific studies of the relationships between societal development or modernization and the status of the elderly as been criticized by Laslett (1985) on the grounds that it has substituted dogmatic theory for formal theory, and it has drawn far too heavily and uncritically on "literary and plastic data" on aging in the past, rather than on more reliable or, at least, more verifiable, documentary sources. Until the recent growth of historical demography, literary and plastic materials were virtually the only sources consulted when questions of aging were considered. The class of evidence most favored by sociologists, psychologists, and gerontologists was what Laslett calls "high literature": novels, plays, poetry, and the like portraying the old, their attitudes, or attitudes toward them. But, Laslett holds, high literature is a small and deceptive part of materials of this kind. Moreover, however interesting and suggestive, it is unreliable unless it can be checked from evidence outside itself, especially numerical evidence.

The absence of formal theory relating societal development and aging derives from what Laslett calls "the primitive state of historical sociology" and because of the quite recent development of gerontology itself. Yet, there are some quasi-theoretical assumptions that Laslett calls informal dogmatic theory. These correspond to popular attitudes, seem often to be believed by the aging and the elderly themselves, and as they are frequently invoked, affect the outlook of gerontologists as well as of those responsible for welfare policy.

There are four sets of propositions constituting this informal dogmatic theory. The first set consists of historical propositions, the major historical dogma being that there has been a *before* and *after* in the matter of aging, and that the transition between the two has been from one uniform situation (high status of the elderly) to another (low status of the elderly). This is the transition associated with industrialization, modernization, or the rise of the bourgeoisie, capitalist production, and capitalist social forms. Some versions of this dogma equate the historical distinction between absence and presence of industrialization with the geographical distinction among contemporary industrial and nonindustrial societies. In whatever form, these before and after propositions ignore the role of demography in the two contrasted phases of social development.

A set of normative propositions comprises the second group of dogmatic propositions. These hold that there was a *before* in which aging and the elderly were part of the system of belief and that the elderly themselves were, under this system, entitled to and universally accorded respect, while in the *after*, aging and the elderly are rejected, or at least allotted no prestige. Society proceeds as if the elderly do not exist, or else, as if it would be better if they did not exist.

The third set of propositions comprises dogmas concerning the functions—economic and emotional functions—of the elderly. Under these propositions, there is asserted to have been a *before* in which the elderly had specified and valued economic and emotional roles, particularly as grandparents. The multigenerational household was believed strongly institutionalized and had important functions for the elderly; in the *after* neither elderly persons nor surviving parents, grandparents, or ancestors have any obvious function as representatives of the approved and traditional. Rather, they are indeed obstacles to adoption of modern ways of life.

The fourth set of propositions in the informal dogmatic theory centers around the assertion that in the *before* there was consensus about constitution of domestic groups that included membership, responsibility, and support for all senior kin of the head of the household. These included his and his spouse's parents and siblings. In the *after* the family consists exclusively of a man, his wife, and their children living alone and independently, with no one else having any right of any kind to belong to it. In particular, the duties of caring for members of former generations and older persons generally are fulfilled by economic assistance or by visiting and being visited. They never entail changing the shape of the (nuclear) domestic group.

Altogether, these existent informal dogmatic theory propositions are part of what Laslett calls the "world we have lost syndrome." In this syndrome the deficiencies of the present are referred to the destruction of an idealized society at some point in the past. But such a complex of portrayals not only are not supported by reliable or verifiable data, but, indeed, are frequently and importantly contradicted by them where they exist.

Rethinking and Retheorizing Societal Development and Aging

As a first principle for an alternative theory of societal development and aging, Laslett suggests that (1) in the traditional English social order (and probably more generally in Europe) membership of the "coresident social group" was never specified in such a way that any person other than the head or the spouse of the head had any *right* to belong to it. Nonetheless offspring and parents alike did frequently co-reside in the household as a matter of custom or convenience. Furthermore, (2) society, rather than the kin network, was primarily responsible for the financial support of old persons in traditional western European society. There was no golden age for the elderly as in past agrarian society when they enjoyed the love, veneration, care, and support of their children and grandchildren, monopolized information and property rights, and controlled their own and their children's lives absolutely and benevolently.

The second principle that Laslett suggests for an alternative theory of societal development and aging is that the position of the elderly in the late twentieth century social structure is historically novel. That is, if the increased expectation of life and the great numbers of the elderly present us with a problem to be solved, it is a problem that has never been solved in the past because it did not exist in what has been called the *before*. The contemporary situation is novel and calls for invention rather than imitation. Thus appropriate social forms addressing the problems of the elderly in contemporary society cannot be retrieved from social history.

CONTEMPORARY VARIATIONS IN THE SOCIAL STATUS OF THE ELDERLY

Whether we think of the social status of the elderly in carefully conceived social scientific terms, or in the more popular sense of attitudes toward them and their general well-being, it seems clear that within any given society there are variations in the status of the elderly among the different subgroups at any moment in time. In addition patterns of aging in different subpopulations may have distinctive characteristics and histories. The examination of these variables and, where possible, their measurement and analysis are of importance both for our understanding of the components of the situations and social status of the elderly, as noted in the introduction to this chapter, and, not less, for purposes of public policy formulation, discussion, and evaluation.

Race, Religion, and Ethnicity

Although there has been some discussion of geographically based variations in aging and social status of the elderly, the great majority of investigations revolve around differences among racial, religious, and ethnic subgroups. Race, religion, and ethnicity are self-evident criteria and axes of inequality in racially, religiously, or ethnically heterogeneous populations and societies. Such factors may be unknown or irrelevant to social inequality in homogeneous populations. In general, the various subpopulations in heterogeneous populations are different in size, demographic composition, and geographic distribution and density. They typically have different political, social, and economic histories. In addition, of course, there are frequently intergroup relationships and ideologies of exclusion (Parkin, 1979), dominance and subordination, or pollution and contamination (Kuper, 1974).

Factors in Inequality Unraveling the correlates and causes of racial, religious, and ethnic inequalities and differences in social organizational features has long been one of the greatest and most complex challenges of social science. Many—and especially those belonging to less advantaged groups—have pointed to exclusion, discrimination, and exploitation of minority groups by majority or dominant groups.

There are, however, other factors contributing to religious, racial, and ethnic inequality. In general they may be denoted social resource factors. These include demographic characteristics, geographic distribution and density, and historical factors such as time of arrival, socioeconomic background prior to arrival, and socioeconomic conditions in the new society upon arrival and since. Finally, there are also *subcultural trait* factors—characteristic values, beliefs, orientations, aspirations, or behavior patterns (Hirschman, 1975). All these may differ among racial, religious, and ethnic groups in ways that lead to characteristic patterns of inequality generally and to differences in aging and the social status of the elderly in particular.

Modern national societies comprise heterogeneous population groups that became part of a single geopolitical unit through conquest, displacement and resettlement, or migration waves. These processes in turn gave rise to patterns of political domination and subordination; geographic and socioeconomic segregation; privileged access to or exclusion from positions and rewards; and institutionalized entitlements or deprivations based on race, religion, or ethnic association or background. Typically the dominant group reserved for itself the positions of economic and political control, and in particular it allocated higher material rewards and comfort to its own members. Subordinate groups were restricted to less favorable social, political, and economic roles, positions, and rewards.

In heterogeneous societies each racial, religious, or ethnic subpopulation tends to have its own sociodemographic history, whether as part of the society in question or prior to its inclusion therein. In the United States these various subpopulations immigrated at different times, experienced downward mortality and fertility inflections at different times, had different preimmigration resources and experiences, settled in different regions, and were exposed to different economic opportunities and different levels of competition from prior residents. Generally they brought different resources to bear on their socioeconomic participation (Greeley, 1974; Lieberson, 1980). Historical and social resource factors have been and remain very important contributors to racial, religious, and ethnic inequality (Matras, 1984). Demonstration of effects of racial, religious, and ethnic variations in values, orientations, and motivations on inequality have been generally spotty and weak (but see Kitano, 1969; and Featherman, 1971).

The study of racial, religious, and ethnic differences in patterns of aging in later life has evolved into a subdiscipline known as ethnogerontology (Jackson, 1985). Investigations of aging in the various minority or ethnic groups (not equivalent—"minority" connotes both a numerical dimension and some perception of being subjected to exclusion or discrimination, while "ethnic" connotes a dimension of membership in and attachment to some primordially defined grouping) have tended to combine scientific and advocacy objectives. They have included studies of images of and attitudes to aging, the activities of the elderly, characteristic problems of the elderly, kin availability and support networks, and need for and use of public and private programs for the elderly all specific to the various religious, racial, or ethnic groups.

The first such studies compared blacks with whites, particularly with emphasis on the question of the adequacy or fairness to blacks of public programs benefiting the elderly. They have gone on to compare dominant white with various minority groups and to explore cultural differences among white, black, and Hispanic elderly and aging processes and settings (Gelfand and Kuzick, 1979; Manuel, 1982; Jackson, 1985; Markides and Mindel, 1987).

Double Jeopardy and Multiple Jeopardy   These studies do not seem to have added significantly to the discussion of social status of the elderly that emerges from the historical and cross-cultural studies mentioned in the previous section. Rather they have explored the ways and senses in which social inequality originating in racial, religious, and ethnic differentiation, exclusion, or discrimination is more or less evident, continues, or diminishes, among the elderly and in the processes of aging in later life.

This is reflected in the central theoretical motif or hypothesis of these studies—the hypothesis of double jeopardy to which elderly of minority groups may be subject. According to this hypothesis, the minority group elderly, already disadvantaged earlier in life because of the patterns of exclusion, discrimination, or unequal opportunities affecting their groups, are doubly disadvantaged in old age. They share the common disadvantage of ageism affecting all the elderly, and they continue to be disadvantaged because of their minority status.

In a similar vein, elderly women are hypothesized also to be subject to double jeopardy of ageism compounding the lifelong disadvantages of sexism. Elderly minority women suffer from triple jeopardy, and so forth. Far from being simply a play on words and concepts, the idea and the demonstration of multiple jeopardy has, of course, very important practical and public policy implications. Programs designed to address the needs of minority or disadvantaged groups must take into account the patterns of multiple jeopardy.

The Leveling Effect Hypothesis   A counter hypothesis in ethnogerontological studies has been that aging at later stages of the life course has a leveling effect. It diminishes religious, racial, ethnic, and socioeconomic differences. This hypothesis has sometimes been taken to mean that racial, religious, and ethnic inequalities of a given type are less severe among the elderly than among the nonelderly of the same society. More often it is taken to mean that, for a given birth cohort characterized through most of adult life by racial, religious, or ethnic inequalities of social condition or opportunities, the inequalities tend to diminish as the cohort approaches and reaches old age. Obviously the difficulties in testing and verifying such a hypothesis are similar to those governing the testing of hypotheses concerning change over time in general. Frequently they can be tested only partially using cross-sectional or age-group comparisons.

In a study reported by Bengtson (1979), an attempt was made to test the double-jeopardy hypothesis against the age-as-leveler hypothesis with respect to income, health, life satisfaction, and social action indicators for a sample of white, black, and Mexican-American elderly respondents. In the study it was found that the minority group elderly (blacks and Mexican-Americans) were indeed subject to double jeopardy with respect to both income levels and health indicators. That is, the comparisons with majority group levels of income and health indicators revealed lower levels than would have been expected on the basis of ethnic disadvantage alone.

On the other hand, there was no indication of double jeopardy operating with respect to the social interaction indicators, and no double jeopardy and some leveling effects with respect to a tranquility indicator of life satisfaction. With respect to an optimism indicator of life satisfaction, Bengtson reported a double-jeopardy effect in the comparison of white and Mexican-American respondents. There was a leveling effect in the comparison between blacks and whites (Bengtson, 1979).

Ethnic and Minority Group Jeopardy versus Modernization Stage Effects and Variations   In a very recent review of ethnogerontology studies and findings, Markides and Mindel (1987) consider the data on socioeconomic differences among the elderly and the nonelderly in the major American minority and ethnic groupings (black, Native American, Asian and Pacific Island, Spanish origin, and whites). They also reviewed findings concerning health and mortality, family structure and relationships, mental health and psychological well-being, retirement, and styles of dying and death for the respective groups. These are all, of course, examples of what we have viewed in this chapter as components of the social status of individuals generally and, in this study, of the elderly in particular. Their main conclusion concerning the ethnic and minority group variations in these components of social status of the elderly is that they are, by and large, artifactual and result from the socioeconomic status differences among the groups in question. In other words, the general socioeconomic differences among the respective racial, religious, and ethnic group underlie the ethnic diversity observed in the later years.

Another observation made by Markides and Mindel is that, in the ethnogerontological literature, there is a tendency to confound what can be understood as modernization effects with ethnic or minority group effects. Very frequently the social status component characteristics of elderly minority or ethnic group members reflect some premodernization conditions, for example, little or no schooling, agrarian society origins, early marriage and high fertility. In many instances, a double-jeopardy finding might in fact reflect the outcome of modernization processes occurring cross-generationally, and not necessarily disadvantage or deprivation among the elderly.

Concluding Remarks: Who's Running the Store?   As various researchers already cited have noted, the discussion of historical levels and trends in the social status of the elderly has suffered from a certain amount of confusion concerning (1) the dimensions of social status, (2) the validity and reliability of their data and indicators, and (3) the elements and components of the elderly population actually being referred to in any particular case, observation, or data set. Indicators of social status based upon objective characteristics or survey responses of the elderly themselves tend to show favorable levels for the elderly relative to the nonelderly (for example, measures of life satisfaction, housing arrangements, family attachments). Or, where the levels are low compared to those of the nonelderly (for example, income, health) there has been marked improvement over the period for which comparable measurements are available.

The formulation by Laslett of his "second general principle in an alternative hypothetical theory about aging" holding that the position of the elderly in the late twentieth century is historically novel, seems convincing enough, but it does not go far enough. The reasons advanced by Laslett for the historical novelty are primarily the numbers and the longevity of the elderly in this contemporary period. These in turn give rise to a consideration that has been largely overlooked in the discussion of societal development and the social status of the elderly: The elderly are increasingly the major players and participants in determining their own status.

It is probably accurate to say that the greater part of the analysis and discussion of the social status of the elderly shares the assumption that it is the nonelderly—mostly young and middle-aged adults, but also children and adolescents—who by their views, norms, attitudes, opinions, and behavior determine the social status of the elderly—whether of their own parents or the elderly generally (but see Neugarten, 1985; Marshall, 1986; Ryff, 1985). It is true that the retention of control of property by the elderly is frequently cited as a factor in their social status. But retention of property, too, is more often than not viewed as an outcome of processes in which young- and middle-aged adults are the main participants. These analyses have very often been grounded in socialization-dominated sociological theory and rhetoric. Individuals are deemed to enter or leave social statuses and roles, while the statuses and roles are "out there" and intact, and their behaviors and expectations are binding on all incumbents.

An alternative view of role behavior recognizes that individuals often create or modify their own roles. The elderly create and modify *their* roles as well, although in ways which we may not yet have investigated as fully as we must. There is no question that their improved health and longevity, as well as enhanced personal human capital factors such as education and work experience, and greatly improved access to communications media and information, have contributed to the capacities and abilities of the elderly to do so.

Finally, the new numbers and longevity characterizing the elderly population now give this group extraordinary political leverage, to the extent that it is mobilized. In fact, very few public officials or legislators can afford to ignore informed, caring, and well-supported elderly constituencies and organized pressure groups. Increasingly the elderly are able to mobilize both themselves and their younger kin in support of public measures to promote and support their welfare and well-being (Keith, 1982). In the United States, for example, the American Association of Retired Persons (AARP) is probably the largest single organized lobby in the country. Its informational activities reach millions of paid members and their families; its advocacy activities penetrate the public forums and inner sanctums of policy formulation and political decision making. This and similar organizations have been part of a contemporary trend toward a determination of social, economic, and political status of the elderly by the elderly themselves.

10

SOCIOLOGICAL THEORIES
OF AGING IN OLD AGE

INTRODUCTION

Sociological theories of aging in old age have, for the most part, shared the concerns of other disciplines in and close to the social and behavioral sciences in addressing primarily the issues of the personal and social adaptation of elderly individuals to their changing physiological and social circumstances. These theories seek to provide a *sociological* account and description, distinct from physiological and psychological theories, descriptions, and accounts, of just what is happening to individuals as they age in their later years.

Increasingly, however, theorists have also turned their attention to the features and dynamics of the larger social units in which the elderly are attached or participate, on the one hand, and to the social structural features affecting the modes of change and adaptation of the elderly. Thus more recently there is attention to the changes affecting couples and families, workplaces, and communities as some of their members enter old age. There is attention to the ways in which economic, political, and social arrangements affect both the various types of transitions into old age and the ways in which earlier life-course patterns are related to, or divorced from, subsequent life-course patterns and features.

In this chapter we review some of the main issues posed in the sociological theories of aging in mid-life and later, and we examine the central concepts suggested for their investigation and discussion. We do not examine, in this chapter or elsewhere, the biological, genetic, or psychological theories of aging or senescence except parenthetically in conjunction with issues of health status and health care.

Aging in the Normative and Interpretive
Sociological Paradigms

Sociological theories of aging in old age bear very close relationships to contemporary general sociological theory. The paradigm still dominant in North American sociological theory and shared by both conservative structural-functional and radical conflict sociological theory is frequently called the *normative* paradigm. It views societies as systems and subsystems of social rules and of social roles, highly differentiated and hierarchically ordered, with incumbents' behavior largely determined by norms and expectations associated with the respective roles. The incumbents themselves are socialized, internalizing the norms, expectations, and values appropriate to successful ongoing interaction and role-performance.

In the structural-functional sociology tradition, the entire system is driven largely by value consensus emerging historically. In some views, this evolves in an evolutionary selection process, under the exigencies of societal survival and sustenance-seeking or -enhancement under given environmental and technological circumstances. With respect to the problematics of individual adaptation in old age, the structural-functional perspective tends strongly toward a blame-the-victim stance. It addresses problems of adaptation in the context of role transitions and socialization throughout the life course.

In the conflict sociology tradition, the system is driven largely by resolution of conflicts in favor of those possessing and using, or threatening to use, most effectively economic and coercive power. With respect to the problems of individual adaptation in old age, the conflict sociology perspective tends generally toward a blame-the-system stance. It addresses problems of adaptation in the context of demands and rigidities of the social system and its conflicting strata.

A competing societal paradigm, the symbolic interaction paradigm that is currently called the *interpretive* paradigm, has coexisted for many decades with the structural-functional and conflict societal paradigm. It has had fewer adherents and historically less impact upon sociological theory. The symbolic interaction paradigm views society as analogous to a game, or to a theatre, with each player attempting to understand and attach meaning to his own behavior through the perspective of others with whom they interact.

The concept of role is a central one in describing and analyzing human interaction. Individuals are said to learn to play roles of their own and to understand, manipulate, or indeed play the roles of others. The emphasis on patterns or constellations of roles, or structures, is largely absent. Moreover, there is less emphasis on the socialization of role-incumbents and their internalization of role-related behavior patterns and expectations, and more emphasis on subjective experience, construction of meaning, and human willfulness as dimensions of the social interaction, social relations, and personality development in the symbolic interaction paradigm. In recent years, the symbolic interaction tradition in sociology has given rise to a major critique of the structural-functional and conflict sociologies and their paradigm, and indeed, of the very notion of positivist observation-based, value-free, or natural-science-like replicable and verifiable social and behavioral inquiry, under the rubrics of critical sociology, interpretive sociology, ethnomethodology, and phenomenological sociology.

In a review paper on theoretical approaches to the social psychology of aging, Victor Marshall (1986) has held that research on the social psychology of aging has largely taken place without theoretical grounding. The field, according to Marshall, has from its origins a social problems focus, to the detriment of systematic theorizing. Moreover, because of the strong social psychological cast to the fields of social gerontology generally, there has been little focus on the societal contexts of aging. Until quite recently the strong emphasis in the sociology of aging on the adjustment of the individual to the society has served to decontextualize the aging experience by taking societal arrangements as comparatively non-problematic.

In the same paper, Marshall notes that the structural-functional paradigm in sociology has, however, given rise to a number of major attempts (reviewed later in this chapter) to formulate something akin to a theoretical approach to sociology of aging. These include the modernization thesis; the age stratification theory; and a number of variants on role and role transition theory, including the social integration theory. Best known of all are the disengagement and the activity theories. They are all structural-functional in their theoretical grounding in that they presume the ongoing systems of rules, roles, role-relationships, role-behaviors and -expectations, hierarchical orderings, and division of labor in production and allocation of social rewards and resources. They presume, also, that the processes affecting the elderly or the transitions to old age take place in the context of, and in mutual consistency with, these rules, roles, and relationships.

The central critique of these emerging sociological theories of aging, as of structural-functionalism generally, is that they are overly deterministic. They impose even on concepts such as voluntary action the constraint of being circumscribed by the system of rules and roles. They represent, basically, socialization and internalization of values rather than genuine voluntarism or activism on the part of the real participants in society. Some beginnings of alternative, interpretive sociological theories of aging in old age are beginning to emerge especially in new theoretical approaches to life events and the life course.

The Central Questions

The central questions, then, addressed by sociological theories of aging in old age are:

1. *How do the elderly, individually and collectively, adapt to their physiological, psychological, and social situations that are typically changing at a rapid pace as they age in the latter part of life?*

Individual adaptation is typically treated as an issue of change in the repertoire of roles and statuses that the individuals perform and as an issue of change in the status, deference, honor, and entitlements accorded them, and in the expectations about their performance of various roles held, by those around them in families, workplaces, and the communities. Roles and statuses are taken in their conventional sociological sense. Social status refers to a socially defined position within a given social structure that is separate from but related to other positions and can be acquired by an individual through personal choice, competition, or use of abilities, and either ascribed at birth (male, female, white, black) or acquired early or late in life (child, student, spouse, parent, widow, retiree, lawyer, football team member).

Associated with each status position is a social role that represents a social definition of the behavioral patterns, rights, and responsibilities expected from those occupying a specific status position. In structural-functional renditions, the tendency is to take roles as given in the social system, with the normative expectations powerful determinants of such actual behavior. Deviations from role expectations entail sanctions of one sort or another, although they may also lead to change in the roles and their relationships. In symbolic-interactionist renditions, the tendency is to view roles as carrying a range of permissible behavior, especially with respect to informal roles found outside the normative social structure.

Collective adaptation is treated as a question of the hierarchical position of the older age groups into which the successive cohorts enter. Rank and position are reckoned with respect to the entire range of social rewards and resources, including material well-being, social participation and influence, and honor and deference. A variant of this approach is the approach inquiring about the ways in which the elderly constitute a distinctive subpopulation or subculture in society.

2. What are the ways in which social structure and social change impinge upon the individual and collective processes of adaptation in old age?

A first approach to this question involves the examination of variation in adaptation patterns by sex and by socioeconomic characteristics of individuals. The latter include current or past residence, educational, occupational, income, and property characteristics, current and past family characteristics, and socioeconomic background (for example, parental, sibling characteristics). A second approach entails examination of the bearing of subcultural differentiation, for example, various primordial identities such as race, ethnicity, religion, and place of birth or origin, upon differences in patterns of adaptation.

A third approach inquires about the degree to which generational characteristics affect the life course generally and the adaptation to old age in particular. In this approach, generational characteristics are understood as the set of sociohistorical events experienced by one or several adjacent birth cohorts in more or less the same manner and circumstances; for example, the Great Depression adolescent generations, the World War II young adulthood generations, the Vietnam War late adolescent generations, or the baby boom generations. Finally, a fourth approach considers the effects of social trends and change in social structural features on either the patterns of adaptation to old age or upon age grading in general and old age grading in particular.

3. How do the patterns of transition and adaptation in aging at advanced ages affect the social units and subsystems in which the elderly are involved, and how do they affect the social structure as a whole?

At the level of families, for example, this issue would be posed in terms of the patterns of change and adaptation characteristic of the *families* of the elderly. At the level of firms, organizations, and communities, the question would be formulated in terms of the arrangements and adaptations introduced to allow for or encourage continued participation of the elderly. At the societal level, the question of the existence and the forms of manifest and latent intergenerational conflict, alienation, or polarization and their social organizational expressions would be pertinent.

We examine these questions in more detail in the sections which follow.

SOCIOLOGICAL THEORIES OF WELL-BEING, SATISFACTION, AND ADAPTATION IN THE LATER YEARS

General: Role Change in the Life Course and in Old Age

Virtually all the sociological theories of well-being, satisfaction, and adaptation at older ages are in fact theories of roles, role-transitions, role-acquisition, role-relinquishment, and socialization and resocialization. However, sociological theory of role change, or of role-and-status change, during the life span in general as well as in later years in particular is itself rather undeveloped. Rosow (1976) has pointed to a number of conceptual problems facing such theory. They include (1) elucidation of the relationships between status and role; (2) resolution of problems of (a) presence, (b) boundary criteria, (c) interaction, and (d) levels of roles and statuses; and (3) clarification of the meanings of role change.

Institutional, Tenuous, and Informal Roles To address the problem of presence or absence of a role and, at the same time, elucidate the relationships between status and role, Rosow (1976) notes first that a role and status do not necessarily and inevitably complement or correspond to one another. Those which do so correspond and bind together what he denotes *institutional* role types. Role types that embody recognized status, but no clear role are denoted *tenuous* role types, definite social positions without roles or with only vague, insubstantial roles. For example, an elderly retired person may have some status but be roleless in employment, community, or family setting. Role types that embody roles but no clear status, that is, roles serving significant group functions but not connected with any particular status or position, are denoted *informal* role types. Examples given by Rosow include the family scapegoat, the rebel, heroes, villains, fools, playboys, blackmailers, and also advisors, helpers, listeners, kibbitzers, and others.

Types of Role Change   Also important for our present concerns, Rosow elucidates the meanings of role change and their referents and implications. He identifies five different temporal connotations:

1. Simple movement between two positions that an individual holds simultaneously. An example is being father to one's child, husband to one's wife, and son to one's own parent at the same time and moving among role behaviors and role relationships within a short time span. Innumerable other examples come to mind involving frequent and routine changes among different role relations over short time intervals.

2. Roles may be modified, redefined, or transformed in content, normative expectations, and so forth, as a function of social change or in response to historical events. Earlier we cited the emergence of childhood and the changing role of the child, the emergence of adolescence and the evolving role of the adolescent. Other recent and dramatic examples include the changing roles of women in families, in careers, as widows, and as community members.

3. There are changes *within* roles through time that are correlates of age and essentially functions of different life-course or family life-cycle stages or periods. Family roles are prominent examples. The role of son or daughter changes as the individual moves through the life course. The role of mother or father changes as the family moves through the family cycle. There are different normative standards and expectations governing the behaviors of the son or daughter in early childhood, adolescence, and young adulthood. This is the case for parents in the various childbearing, childrearing, child-launching, or empty-nest periods of the family life cycle. The son, daughter, father, or mother remain son, daughter, father, and mother throughout the passage of time, but the content and normative expectations of the roles change over time.

4. A status set, the set of roles and statuses that an individual has at any moment in time, may be enlarged by accretion of a new role or reduced by attrition of an existing role. The individual adds or loses a role by joining or leaving a formal or informal group or association, whether voluntarily or involuntarily. Examples are joining or leaving a church, a political party or organization, a professional society, or a recreational or social circle. Rosow points out that the character of such changes *may* be age-related, related to life-course stages, or to evolving life styles associated with the different life-course periods, but they are not inevitably so.

5. A change of role over time may constitute what has widely come to be connoted a *status passage*, the transition between positions that are mutually exclusive, sequentially and irreversibly ordered. These involve relinquishment of one status and acquisition of the next one. Examples of status passage include graduation, marriage, or parenthood. Other examples include movement among hierarchical stages of a professional career, ritual passage from childhood to adulthood status, and, ultimately, death. The classic formulation of status passage was first published in 1908 by the anthropologist and ethnographer Arnold van Gennep, and entitled *Rites of Passage*. In this classic study, the author posits a three-step transition process including (a) separation from the initial status, (b) transition, and (c) induction into the new status.

Thus, Rosow points out, it is the role changes of the last three types—(3) modification of specific roles between age grades or periods, (4) accretion and attrition of roles, and (5) sequential status passages—that occur as the individuals move through the various periods or stages of the life course, and in particular, in aging in the later years.

Changing Importance of Role Types in the Life Course   The centrality or prominence of roles of the three major types—institutional, tenuous, and informal—varies across the life course. Rosow formulates hypotheses about the changing importance during the life span of the three types. According to Rosow, the *importance* of institutional roles rises steadily in the life course, peaks at late middle age, and thereafter declines steeply. By contrast, the *importance* of tenuous roles declines in the first half of the life course, then begins to rise at about midlife and continues to rise steeply to the end of the life span (Figure 10.1).

The *importance* of informal roles, according to Rosow, rises gently in the early life course, but not as steeply as the importance of institutional roles. The importance of informal roles levels off at about midlife, at a level below that of institutional roles; it remains approximately at that level for the rest of the life course, even while the importance of institutional roles is declining steeply.

The conclusion that Rosow derives from this analysis and these hypotheses is of considerable theoretical and policy interest. Informal roles encompass a broader range of contexts than the roles of the institutional type. They occur in both major and lesser institutional spheres, formal and informal settings,

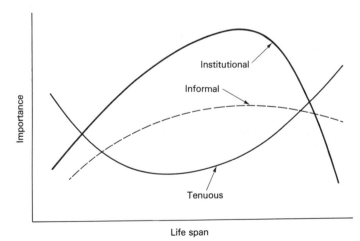

Figure **10.1** Relative Importance of Role Types in the Life Span. *Source:* Rosow, 1976.

organized and more amorphous groups. They belong to an *informal system* and operate within formal structures to supplement and modify institutional roles and adapt these to the particular local context; they remain viable spheres of participation in the later years and in the later stages of the life course, that is, in old age. They are not subject to the sharp attrition that characterizes the loss of major institutional roles. Therefore, even in retirement and widowhood, people may continue to operate in their informal groups of friends and neighbors, preserving some significant basis of their informal roles.

Informal roles are less associated with social responsibility than the institutional type of roles. This is what prevents the importance curve of the informal roles from rising as high as the importance curve of the institutional roles. By the same token, it prevents the steep drop in importance; that is, the basically flatter curve of the informal roles compared to the institutional.

The absolute numbers of persons with informal roles is smaller than the number with institutional roles. For any individual the ratio of informal to institutional roles is low prior to old age. Thus, during most of adulthood, individuals' life courses are structured primarily by their institutional roles. It is only later in life, approaching old age, that informal roles become more central for most individuals. On the other hand, there are some individuals for whom the entire life course is structured primarily by informal roles.

The informal roles are, in Rosow's words, "the major repository of people's more stable personal styles " (Rosow, 1976, p. 478). They evolve in adolescence and adulthood into attributes that confer individual tone and flavor on social identities and set a common manner in which the person fills different roles. To the extent that these inhere in relatively settled, well-developed forms, they help stabilize the curve of importance of informal roles through the individual's life course. Thus, in terms of intervention options to enhance the well-being of the elderly, attention should, in Rosow's view, be focused primarily on the *informal* social system, for example, on the networks of friendship, neighboring, and similar links that develop from spontaneous associations and voluntary activities that generate cohesive social groups. Prospective success of such intervention would increase to the extent that it mobilizes and capitalizes on status similarities among elderly people. These are not on age alone, but rather, on as many of their shared statuses as possible: sex, marital postition, race, ethnicity, social class, religion, and other aspects of common background.

Activity Theory

One of the earliest sociological theories purporting to account for successful adaptation and aging in later life has come to be known as the activity theory. It has been associated especially with later writings of the pioneer American sociologist E.W. Burgess (1960). Following on the recognition of loss of roles in later life, Burgess argued that old age should not be viewed as a "roleless role." Rather, individuals could, should, and typically do replace lost roles or social activities with new ones.

Basic assumptions of the theory are that (1) the middle-aged and aged have identical psychosocial needs; (2) individuals will resist giving up roles in favor of staying active; (3) successful aging consists of substitution of lost roles (for example, marital, friendship, or employment roles of spouse, friend, worker) or lost activities (marriage, friendship, job) with new roles or activities in order to maintain the self-identity; and (4) suitable roles are available and individuals have the capacities and capabilities to enter the new domains. Thus, a high level of activity is asserted to result in favorable self-concept and high satisfaction in later life.

The theory enjoyed widespread acceptance, partly as a common-sense theory, partly in the absence of competing theories, and partly because of Burgess's prestige and authority. Yet, some early reservations concerned the instances of declining activity without loss of morale or satisfaction, the apparent high levels of satisfaction of some individuals who had never in their lifetimes had high levels of activities, and doubts about the universality or widespread availability of economic, intellectual, or interpersonal resources needed for replacement of lost activities or roles.

Disengagement Theory

Perhaps the best-known theory in social gerontology, a theory that derives from both psychological developmental ideas and considerations and sociological structural-functional approaches and principles, is the disengagement theory. This theory was presented, argued, and defended by E. Cumming and W. Henry in the early 1960s (Cumming et al., 1960; Cumming and Henry, 1961; Cumming, 1964), partly as an attack on the implicit assumption (of activity theory) that happiness and success in old age are the result of continuing the activities and involvements of one's middle years without interruption, and that successful aging consists in being as much like a middle-aged person as possible. According to this theory, old age differs markedly from middle age, with change and adaptation functionally necessary both for the individual and society.

As formulated by Cumming and Henry in their book *Growing Old: The Process of Disengagement:*

> ...aging is an inevitable mutual withdrawal or disengagement, resulting in decreased interaction between the aging person and others in the social system he or she belongs to. The process may be initiated by the individual or by others in the situation. The aging person may withdraw [from some] while remaining relatively close in others. His withdrawal may be accompanied from the outset by an increased preoccupation with himself; certain institutions in society may make this withdrawal easy for him. When the aging process is complete, the equilibrium which existed in middle life between the individual and his society has given way to a new equilibrium characterized by a greater distance and an altered type of relationship...(Cumming and Henry, 1961, pp. 14–15)

Because of the inevitability of death, the declining abilities in later life, the value placed on youth, as well as the need to assure that roles are filled and tasks efficiently completed, both individuals and society demand disengagement, according to the theory. Disengagement is thus the mechanism enabling young persons to enter employment and advance in their careers, allowing roles to be filled by the more competent, and preventing disruption of the functioning of the social system due to deaths among the elderly.

Old people prepare for their deaths by divesting themselves of social relationships and social functions. Society, in turn, encourages its members to do this so that their deaths will not be disruptive to its equilibrium. Thus disengagement is, according to its formulators and supporters, a universal and inevitable two-way process whereby the individual withdraws from society and society withdraws from the individual. While normally aging is perceived and accepted as a functional and voluntary process, in fact many forms of disengagement are not voluntary, for example widowhood and mandatory retirement. When the process is complete the individual has shifted from being preoccupied with society to fully legitimated self-preoccupation.

Disengagement, which results in decreased interaction between an elderly individual and others in society, is hypothesized to be not only a universal process, but also one that is satisfying to both the individual and society. Disengagement is believed to be satisfying to the individual because it provides release from normative constraints. The individual is released from pressures to behave as expected (for example, in jobs), and is given more freedom to deviate from societal expectation without negative sanctions being invoked. What is ordinarily viewed as deviant, eccentric, unacceptable behavior is considered socially acceptable among the elderly.

From the perspective of society, disengagement permits younger members to enter functional roles, thereby facilitating turnover without intergenerational conflict. It also ensures that equilibrium and stability will be maintained, since members are replaced in the functional roles of society before their death. For example, without mandatory retirement more leaders and workers would die while still employed, and the social system would lose equilibrium until they were replaced. In short, disengagement is seen as a process wherein individuals, supported by societal norms and customs, voluntarily and gradually withdraw from social roles and decrease their social interaction. As a result, the individual is thought to experience a high level of satisfaction, well-being, and morale in the later years of life.

Disengagement theory is a functionalist theory in that it assumes that society is a system in balance that seeks stability or equilibrium. Disengagement is a process that contributes to that equilibrium by making the exit of its members predictable and therefore less disruptive. Like other processes that are functional for society, disengagement has become institutionalized in laws allowing for mandatory retirement.

Since disengagement is proposed as a mutual process, the theory allows for two types of disengagement—societal and individual. Societal disengagement is evident in the retreat of the environment from the individual. Examples are the departure of one's children from the family, retirement from one's occupation, and possibly the deaths of spouse, friends, and relatives. Individual disengagement appears in the loss of many of an individual's contacts and job-related activities, and turning one's attention toward internal, personal, rather than external concerns.

According to disengagement theory, when the individual and society are mutually engaged (both desiring such involvement), balance is maintained.

Similarly, when both society and the individual wish to disengage, there is balance. The problems occur when either the individual wishes to disengage, but the society does not wish him or her to do so. As would be predicted in a struggle between individual and societal forces, Cumming and Henry suggest that society will prevail in either situation. Later formulations and addenda to the theory by Cumming and Henry individually added emphasis upon individual characteristics and psychological attributes rather than social mechanisms as proximate causes and determinants of rates and styles of individual disengagement.

Obviously the rather dismal and depressing analysis of disengagement theory, and its assertion of universal applicability, have brought forth fairly vigorous critique and attack.

Continuity Theory

A theory of aging in later life that draws upon some of the motifs of activity theory but also incorporates an assumption of individual tendency to seek and maintain role stability has been connoted the continuity theory. This theory is associated with the research of R. Atchley (1971). Individuals learn and internalize habits, commitments, dispositions, preferences, and behaviors in the course of early life and, indeed, in lifelong socialization processes. These persist in later life, remaining prominent factors in social interaction. According to the continuity theory, individuals strive to maintain continuity of roles and life styles as they age. They adapt most successfully to the changes of old age to the extent that they are successful in maintaining the life style developed in early and middle years of life. It is unreasonable to expect the person who enjoys and protects privacy all his life to become a gregarious social butterfly in old age. Conversely, the individual active in family or community activities and relationships is not likely to disengage in the absence of some compelling reason (such as failing health).

Thus, the continuity theory incorporates part of the attack on disengagement theory as a central hypothesis: Individual disengagement does not take place except under compelling circumstances. But, in turn, critics of continuity theory have pointed out that its hypotheses assume, implicitly, that individual aging in the later years occurs almost in a social vacuum. In fact the social structure impinges heavily upon the very possibility, not to say desirability and success, of continuity of the elderly's life styles. Empty nests, widowhood, mandatory retirement, the death of friends, and changing values, attitudes, behaviors, and organizational features may all conspire to render impossible the putative continuity of life styles and role stability in advanced age.

Reference Group Theory

Reference group theory in sociology describes the manner in which individuals assess their own behavior, attitudes, and values by comparison with groups or individuals who are perceived as related or otherwise adopted as standards, criteria, or models. The theory was developed and received great prominence in studies of satisfaction and morale among American soldiers in World War II. People may be influenced not only by the groups to which they belong, but also by groups to which they do not belong. Any group or social category that we use as a standard of comparison and with which we measure our accomplishments and failures is called a reference group. Such groups or categories may include friends, immediate family members, occupational group, or social class. A reference group may also provide a person with a set of norms, attitudes, and values. For example, a person who aspires to move ahead socially may begin to pattern behavior after a higher status group and acquire its tastes.

The theory has been invoked and adapted to account for personal adaptation in later life. Thus Streib and Schneider (1972) studied preretirement attitudes and retirement adjustment as related to reference group identification with families, work peer groups, and friendship groups. They found that all these groups are significant in the work and retirement decisions and in adjustment thereafter. In studying changes in age identity that occur in middle and later years of life, Blau (1973, 1981) uses reference group theory to account for major variations. While the elderly in general often judge themselves by the standards of middle age (with the disadvantages such reference groups imply for comparison with their own behavior and achievements), the very oldest among the elderly have effectively outlived all their reference groups. For the centegenarian, loss to death of his last close friends nearly a generation earlier implies not only loss of friends, confidants, and intimates, but also the loss of reference group: To what group can such a person refer to gauge the appropriateness of his behavior and reinforce his identity?

Socialization and Social Learning Theory

As mentioned earlier, socialization is the fundamental mechanism for system preservation and stability in the structural-functional and conflict paradigms of social organization. It is the process by which individuals learn and internalize the norms, attitudes, and expected behaviors and relationships associated with each social role. In the earliest paragraphs of this book, socialization is mentioned as one of the central processes for assuring societal and social group continuity in the face of population turnover.

Traditionally most attention to socialization has concerned the socialization of children. These are the processes by which children learn the society's norms and values and learn the behaviors appropriate to progressively more social roles over progressively broader spheres and domains of social interaction. There has been some attention to socialization at later points in life: socialization at adolescence, upon leaving home for college or a new community, into military service, in a new job, and so forth. More generally, there has recently been systematic attention to the processes of socialization throughout the life span. These have included the concept of socialization in old age.

The elements of the socialization process have been identified as including (1) the social structure, (2) the stages and techniques of socialization, and (3) the socializing agents or significant others. Social structural features can lead to different socialization outcomes. The features include the capacity of social organizations to establish clear goals and expectations, provide facilities and resources for role performance, and control performances through positive and negative sanctions. From the side of the individual, socialization involves the ability to learn the required norms, behaviors and values, perform as required or expected, and be motivated to perform. The socialization settings are typically the family, school, and neighborhood in early life, but may be work settings, the mass media of communications, peer groups, voluntary organizations, or other settings in adult life.

In infancy and childhood techniques of socialization tend to be formal and codified. The individual is a passive actor, learning directly or indirectly the values, skills, and behaviors in the course of formal instruction or explicit teaching as well as by imitation of nearby examples. By late childhood and adolescence, however, the individual becomes a more active participant in his own socialization. He even makes decisions concerning what values and behaviors are to be internalized.

Throughout the adult years the process becomes progressively more informal, voluntary, and specific. In the structural-functional view, the process remains one in which the individual is characterized by passive role taking: The role is there and defined. The behaviors, norms, values, attitudes, and expected patterns of interaction are there and associated with the role. They are to be learned and internalized by the individual in his transition to that role. In the symbolic interactionist view, the process becomes one in which the adult individual is characterized by more active role-making, negotiation, and accommodation. He is more likely to shape the norms to which he will adhere through a continuous process of negotiation and accommodation with others in specific social situations.

The socialization processes include anticipatory socialization, desocialization, and resocialization. Anticipatory socialization is said to occur when an individual accepts the beliefs, norms, values of a status position that he does not yet hold, but to which he wishes to belong, expects to belong, or will belong in the future. In this way the individual is prepared for the new status. Marshall (1980) has invoked this concept in indicating how some individuals learn to cope with the prospect of their own death: There is an indirect process of anticipatory socialization wherein they "bury their peers."

Desocialization occurs when an individual experiences role loss or role emptying, as in retirement or the emptying of the family nest. In Rosow's analysis (1974), desocialization is said often to lead to devalued social positions characterized by ambiguous norms, role discontinuity, and status loss. Resocialization involves the change in life style when an individual enters a new social status, such as retiree or widow or widower, or a new social situation, such as a long-term care institution. The individual must then learn the new expectations, behaviors, and values associated with the new status.

Social Exchange Theory

A portrayal of social interaction as relationships in which those involved attempt to maximize gains or social rewards and minimize the losses or costs, has been developed and advanced under the name of social exchange theory. Social rewards refer to both material and nonmaterial rewards (for example, friendship, assistance, deference, care). Social interaction involves reciprocity, with each actor attempting, in the relationship, to achieve a favorable or acceptable balance of costs and rewards. As developed for social interaction generally by Blau (1964) and Emerson (1976), the process involves continued interaction as long as it is rewarding to both parties, even if the rewards attained are not necessarily equal. In the course of relationships characterized by unequal rewards, the actor for whom the cost is greater is said to incur debt, while the advantaged actor accrues power. Most social relationships are characterized by some measure of imbalance in rewards attained, such that one side cannot reciprocate identically or equally. That side becomes dependent and is obligated to try to redress the balance in the future.

In most exchange relationships participants try to maximize power while maintaining a fair outcome. Status characteristics can bear upon the terms or rates of exchange in a relationship. Having valued characteristics (for example, high occupational status, high education, wealth, youth, beauty) strengthens the individual's position in the bargaining or negotiation process. Conversely, being nonwhite, female, without valued skills, or being old places one at a disadvantage in social interaction. Having two types of status disadvantages, for example, being a woman and being an immigrant, leads to double jeopardy in social exchange relationships. Having several types of status disadvantages leads to multiple jeopardy in social negotiations. Thus, elderly women are subject to double jeopardy in the job market. Elderly men of the visible minorities are also subject to double jeopardy.

Use of the social exchange theory in explanation of aging behavior in old age has been prominent in the work of Dowd (1975, 1978, 1980). In his analysis,

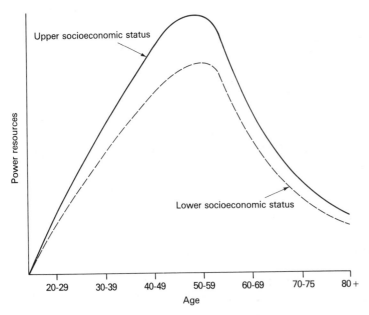

Figure 10.2 Hypothesized Relationship between Control of Power Resources and Age, within Categories of Socioeconomic Status.
Source: Dowd, 1975. Copyright The Gerontological Society of America, used with permission.

the decreased social interaction observed at advanced ages reflects a series of exchange relationships across the life course, rather than any universal process of disengagement. Relative social power diminishes in later life as a result of the exchange relationships. This leads to compliance and unbalanced relationships wherein the elderly experience greater costs and fewer rewards.

As individuals enter the later years, they have fewer resources, other than experience, available for exchange. This leads them to more conforming behavior and fewer interactions. The retirement process is readily cast in this form: As the occupational skills of the elderly worker become obsolete, he is more readily pressured into accepting retirement in return for a pension. When individuals are perceived as no longer able to care for themselves, they may be cared for by their families or institutionalized and cared for by way of restitution and repayment of past obligations and debts.

More generally, old people are often subject to loneliness, prestige loss, and social and economic discrimination after years of social investment in the form of work, commitment to their families, and citizenship. The elderly themselves perceive and experience these losses in different ways. Some are unaware of any injustice or inequity. Some are aware of injustice in the process, but powerless to achieve any improvements. But some elderly persons do actively seek to restore a more equitable distribution of resources. They perceive that the injustice is a source of lower life satisfaction, if not always distress, and that greater age consciousness is needed to restore equity (Dowd, 1978).

Labeling Theory

A sociological theory that accords central importance to the evaluations and labels that are imputed to individuals by others with whom they are interacting in various social settings has come to be identified under the name labeling theory. The labels can be positive or negative, explicit or unspoken. They are informally recognized by a variety of significant others with whom the individual maintains interaction as describing some of his or her qualities, personality traits, or behavior patterns. The theory has been used in explaining deviant behavior and mental disorders, thus developing a distinction between primary labeling and secondary labeling.

Primary labeling occurs when significant others perceive a person's behavior to differ in quality or type from normative standards, so that the person is labeled as, say, delinquent, unstable, or senile. The labeling is a social judgment, represents an interpretation of the behavior patterns, and is not an inherent property of the behavior. Nonetheless, it often enters the social interaction that follows, for example, as diagnoses for treatment or intervention, or reasons to give or deny employment to a person. If the process of labeling is repeated, it may be internalized within the individual's self-concept. Individuals become dependent upon socially induced labels to understand and demonstrate who they are, resulting in secondary labeling. The individual accepts the label and is indirectly socialized into playing the role of the delinquent, unstable, or senile person, and reinforcing the cycle of socially induced behavior.

The theory has been used by some researchers in accounting for the behavior of the elderly, most prominently by Kuypers and Bengtson (1973). In a social breakdown model, the elderly are labeled as deficient, obsolete, or incompetent. Due to role loss, vague normative standards, and diminishing reference groups as they age, the elderly turn to societal sources for a definition of the self. That is, the elderly are particularly subject to secondary labeling. For its part, society propagates negative views of the elderly and they are labeled useless, helpless, incompetent, and so forth. Elderly people may, in turn, accept these negative labels and become socialized to such roles. But alongside the social breakdown model, Kuypers and Bengtson indicate as well a social reconstruction model wherein the individual, helped by significant others in the various relevant social systems, can also enhance actual and perceived competence and improve adaptive capacity and coping skills, invoking a kind of positive labeling to assist this process.

The theory has been attacked on the grounds that such social breakdown processes are relatively infrequent among the elderly. For negative self-evaluation in later life is very much the exception rather than the rule (George, 1980). Most older people have sufficient personal resources and coping skills to maintain a positive self-image, and to adjust to role transitions as they age. In particular, it is unlikely that such a social breakdown process, induced via labeling, would occur in age-homogeneous environments (for example, senior citizens' housing developments or retirement communities) where an elderly subculture fosters positive rather than negative labels.

THE BEARING OF SOCIAL STRUCTURE AND SOCIAL CHANGE ON ADAPTATION, AGE GRADING, AND SOCIAL STATUS IN OLD AGE

Age Stratification Theory

In the theory of age stratification, the elderly are studied explicitly in relation to all the other age groups, or to the age strata in the society. The theory views the age groupings in a society as hierarchically organized age strata, and examines the differences between the age strata. It examines, however, only parenthetically the potential or actual conflicts between them. According to this theory, chronological age determines not only genetic, physiological, and psychological maturation and development. Rather, societies allocate the opportunity to play specific social roles, and their accompanying rights, privileges, status, power, and entitlements on the basis of age. That is, there is social age grading. Therefore, society is divided into age strata, each comprising individuals with similar characteristics because they are at the same stage in the life course. These consist as well of persons who have had similar experiences because they have shared a common history. Changing social environments produces different patterns of adaptation by the successive age cohorts (Foner, 1986; Riley, 1976; Riley, Johnson, and Foner, 1972).

Discussion of the age strata and their interrelationships parallels, to a certain extent, the discussion of hierarchically organized social strata generally. The basic flow into the respective strata is by virtue of birth and survival to each of the respective age groups, but mobility among the strata is unidirectional and irreversible, in contrast to interstrata social mobility generally. Interaction between individuals of the different strata may be characterized by cooperation or conflict, and various degrees of perceived or actual inequality may exist. Age conflicts may arise and be enhanced when members of the successive birth cohorts have unique attitudes, experiences, opportunities, and beliefs based on their particular social and historical experiences, and the age strata may develop corresponding expressions of solidarity.

The theory has always been controversial. Parkin (1971) has attacked the analogy of age strata to social strata on the grounds that (1) membership in the respective age strata is, for all except the very oldest, temporary and all anticipate mobility to older age strata; and (2) various axes of interage-strata relationships, commonalities, and solidarities (for example, family or social class relationships) are more permanent, have deeper historical roots and cultural features, and generally will supercede and override the age-strata ties. Much of the appeal of this theory rests upon its combining the principles of age grading in the life course with the sociodemographic principles of cohort succession.

Modernization and the Status of the Elderly

As the main themes of the theory of modernization and the status of the elderly were presented in the previous chapter, it is appropriate here to review them only briefly. In this theory, modernization brings, in the first place, an increase in the number and proportion of the elderly, thus eroding the scarcity value of the elderly in high-mortality societies. Widespread literacy and new modes of information storage and processing as well as rapidly changing technologies render the knowledge of the elderly redundant and their skills obsolete. These developments segregate the elderly intellectually and morally, and diminish their functional value to their families, communities, and to society generally. High rates of residential mobility, the establishment of households by younger persons away from the extended family household, and the rise of individualism that accompany modernization all tend to reduce the authority and control of resources and power, hence the social status of older people in modern societies by comparison with preliterate, preindustrial, or traditional societies (Cowgill and Holmes, 1972).

The modernization theory has been criticized on the grounds of oversimplification both of concepts of modern and modernization and of the concept of social status of the aged. Also, examples of modern industrial societies in which some or all of the facets of eroded social status of the elderly are clearly contradicted have been invoked by way of critique of the modernization theory. Similarly, the assertion of high status of the elderly in premodern societies has been widely questioned, criticized, qualified, and in some cases categorically disproved. Finally, even those supporting the theory relating modernization to lower status of the elderly have tended to modify it in the direction of acknowledging the contribution of the welfare state's institutions in raising important dimensions of the status of the elderly in modern societies.

Socioeconomic and Class Variations

Considering its centrality in the social sciences generally and in sociology in particular, it is remarkable that the topic of social class divisions and class differentiation seems to have entered the theoretical discussion of the variations in the adaptation and status of the elderly only quite tangentially. Longevity itself varies by social class: The rich live longer than the poor, and they are healthier than the poor in old age as well as throughout life. The well-educated, regardless of origins or income, also enjoy higher survival probabilities and better health than the less educated. They are more likely to delay retirement, have higher incomes in old age, and be more active participants in their communities (Habib and Matras, 1987). Self-employed men and men in high prestige occupations are more likely to continue in employment past conventional retirement ages than employees generally and, especially, those in low occupational status jobs. They have higher incomes and are more likely to report themselves in good health.

Because of the more favorable survival and longevity of their husbands, widowhood occurs later among rich women than among poor. They are also much better able to manage independently as widows than the poor. On the other hand, the fertility of the poor has until recently been substantially higher than among the middle or upper-middle classes. The availability of kin is greater at all ages in the life course. Thus we know that there are some very basic and important social class and socioeconomic status differences in dimensions of adaptation and social status in old age.

Moreover, we know that old age as a life stage has been historically infrequent in the lower classes or socioeconomic groups. The transmitted culture concerning the elderly, their integration in society, and their relations with non-elderly kin and others has been a culture primarily of the more advantaged socioeconomic groupings and classes. In the past, in the infrequent event that lower-class adults survived to old age, for the most part neither they nor their kin had the material, educational, or other social resources to sustain much in the way of social relations, life styles, or options beyond sheer survival and sustenance. Thus the different class groupings have quite different *histories* of aging in old age.

It should follow that these contemporary and historical social class differences in both objective situations and in historical patterns and norms governing the position of the elderly, combined with social class differences in (1) education, careers, and work histories; (2) sources, levels, and stability of income; (3) family formation and household arrangements and histories; and (4) patterns of community participation and of leisure time use, would result in quite dissimilar patterns of adaptation and status in old age. Systematic investigation of these variations must be a part of a future research agenda, although perhaps some synthesis of existing knowledge may be possible already.

Subcultural Differentiation

The growth in the number and proportion of the elderly in contemporary societies, and their improved health, income maintenance arrangements, education, and participation in voluntary and community organizations, is frequently viewed as having taken place alongside tendencies toward enhanced interaction among the elderly and diminished dependency and interaction between the elderly and the nonelderly. These trends and conditions have been viewed by Rose (1965) as ingredients of the formation of an elderly subculture. Growth of aged ghettoes and retirement communities, political action and lobby groups, mutual assistance activity on the part of the elderly organized on their own behalf, and widespread adoption of common symbols, reference groups, and age-consciousness (for example, senior citizens, retired, grandparenting, leisure styles) are all consistent with the idea of the emergent subculture of the aged.

In particular, formally established (by law, administrative practice, collective agreements) retirement policies and age grading now common in most industrialized societies have prevented many older people from retaining important connections with the larger society and prevented their integration in contemporary society. Social services are frequently designed for and restricted to helping elderly people. Such restriction also tends to prompt recognition and acknowledgment of their common situation at a time when many have an opportunity to engage in wide-ranging, non-work-related activities for the first time. Thus the elderly are naturally encouraged in the direction of greater identification with an aged peer group.

In the aged subculture, good health and physical mobility confer status, while occupational, educational, or economic prestige tend to be redefined as somewhat less influential than they were in earlier years. Individual involvement in the aged subculture is partially dependent upon the size, characteristics, and solidarilty of the aged subgroup itself. It is also partly dependent upon the nature and the extent of the links with the larger society retained by each elderly individual through families, employment, or the media.

The absence of a sense of group identification among the elderly is frequently cited in argument against the theory of emergence of an identifiable elderly subculture; it is argued that older people do not in fact actually develop a life style based on the concrete realities of old age. Nor is there so much systematic or overt prejudice or discrimination attributable to old age itself, as distinct from that attributable to qualities, characteristics, or capacities perceived to be correlated with old age. Finally, at least one critic (Streib, 1965) has argued that an essential feature of the evolvement of a distinct cultural grouping is that it be based on some *ascribed* social status, but that age is *not* actually an ascribed status.

The Aged as a Minority Group

Closely related to the theory of the aged as a subculture is the analysis viewing the elderly as a minority group. In common with other minority groups in contemporary societies, the aged are a deprived group. The elderly are frequently marginalized and victims of differential and unequal treatment compared to the nonelderly in that they are labeled old, obsolete, or dysfunctional.

In this view, age, like race, sex or national origin, is an ascribed criterion of stratification. People become older not by their own choice, and on the basis of this ascribed criterion they encounter descrimination in society. Thus older people come to resemble minority groups such as blacks or Mexican-Americans (Barron, 1953; Palmore, 1969; Palmore and Whittington, 1971; Levin and Levin, 1980). Both early (Streib, 1965) and more recent (Abu-Laban and Abu-Laban, 1980) critiques of this analysis stress the weakness of age as an ascribed status characteristic and the ambiguity of age-group consciousness and solidarity, as well as the elusiveness of the evidence of concrete discrimination on grounds of old age per se. Finally, the critics of this analysis have pointed out that it has arisen primarily out of advocacy-related considerations, to draw attention to the plight and deprivations of the elderly. They note that there is little if any concrete evidence to support the view that the aged, in general, comprise a minority group (Streib, 1976; McPherson, 1983).

AGING IN OLD AGE AND ITS EFFECTS ON SOCIAL STRUCTURE

Families of the Elderly

We have already noted some of the ways in which population aging and its underlying causes—declining mortality and declining fertility—have affected the family life cycle, the availability of kin, and patterns of dependency, obligations, and entitlements at various ages, stages, and junctures in the individual life course and in the family cycle. Our concern now is with analysis of specific ways in which aging at older ages affects the families of the elderly and, possibly, families in general.

Despite the centrality of the family as a topic in anthropology, sociology, psychology, economics and related disciplines, and even more attention to the family in social work and in social gerontology, theoretical development of this inquiry is only beginning. We consider, first, the families of the elderly themselves and then turn to families of the adult children and grandchildren of the elderly. The central questions in each case are: How do patterns of survival, health, income, income maintenance, social activity, and functioning in old age bear on the key facets of family life? How do they affect residence, division of labor and authority, sexual relations, material and emotional support, physical care, autonomy and dependency, extrafamily activities and relations, and perceived well-being and satisfaction? In many instances the answer will be: We don't yet know very credibly or in much detail.

The Elderly and Their Next of Kin   The elderly themselves have parents, siblings, spouses, and children in varying combinations (Shanas, 1980) and in varying patterns of co-residence and geographic distance. Indeed sorting out, classifying, and enumerating these combinations and patterns have only very rarely been attempted for any identifiable population group (see Shmueli, 1986). Yet, some *major* categories of family units—unattached individuals, husband-wife-only, and husband-wife + own-children only families—are routinely identified,

Table 10.1.   Persons 65 Years Old and Over—Characteristics, by Sex: 1960 to 1986

CHARACTERISTIC	MALE					FEMALE				
Percent Distribution	1960	1970	1980	1985	1986	1960	1970	1980	1985	1986
Marital status:										
Single	7.3	7.5	4.9	5.3	5.1	8.5	7.7	5.9	5.1	5.2
Married	71.7	73.1	78.0	77.2	77.2	36.8	35.6	39.5	39.9	40.0
Spouse present	69.0	69.9	76.1	75.0	75.3	35.0	33.9	37.9	38.3	38.3
Spouse absent	2.7	3.2	1.9	2.2	1.9	1.8	1.7	1.7	1.6	1.7
Widowed	19.4	17.1	13.5	13.8	13.7	53.1	54.4	51.2	50.7	50.5
Divorced	1.7	2.3	3.6	3.7	4.0	1.5	2.3	3.4	4.3	4.4
Family status:										
In families	82.3	79.2	83.0	82.4	82.6	67.7	58.5	56.8	56.7	56.6
Nonfamily householders	12.8	14.9	15.7	15.4	15.6	2.68	35.2	42.0	42.1	2.2
Secondary individuals	2.4	2.4	1.3	2.2	1.8	3.0	1.9	1.1	1.1	1.2
Residents of institutions	2.5	3.6	(N/A)	(N/A)	(N/A)	2.4	4.4	(N/A)	(N/A)	N/A
Living arrangements:										
Living in household	97.4	95.5	99.9	99.5	99.5	97.0	95.0	99.7	99.6	99.6
Living alone	(NA)	14.1	14.9	14.7	14.9	(N/A)	33.8	41.0	41.1	41.3
Spouse present	73.2	69.9	76.1	75.0	75.3	36.9	33.9	37.9	38.3	38.3
Living with someone else	(NA)	11.5	8.9	9.8	9.3	(N/A)	27.4	20.8	20.2	19.9
Not in household	2.6	4.5	.1	.5	.5	3.0	5.0	.3	.4	.4

Source: U.S. Bureau of the Census, *Statistical Abstract of the United States, 1988*, 108th ed. (Washington, D.C.: Government Printing Office, 1988), Table 40.

counted, and classified in national population censuses and surveys. We know that recent trends in mortality, fertility, marriage, and divorce have resulted in relatively more elderly persons in empty-nest (husband-wife-only) settings and relatively fewer in husband-wife + dependent-children families. We know, too, that the empty-nest stage is longer now than it was in the past. For example, the data of Table 10.1 show a moderate increase for elderly women, and a substantial increase among elderly men, between 1960 and 1986 in the percent "married with spouse present" among the total elderly population.

We know also that there are many more elderly unattached individuals, especially women, maintaining their own households than in the past. A dramatic growth (from less than 27 percent to more than 42 percent in 1986) in the percent of elderly women who are "nonfamily householders" (that is, they head single-person or other nonfamily households) is also shown in Table 10.1. The growth in the corresponding percent among elderly men is a more modest, but still notable, one.

As noted in an earlier chapter, we know from calculations based on mortality and fertility probabilities that many more elderly persons now than in the past have even more elderly surviving parents. We also know that the average number of surviving siblings is lower than in the past. We don't actually know if the number with *any* (at least one) or with *no* surviving siblings is higher or lower than in the past. And although the average number of surviving children is somewhat lower, on the whole, among the elderly today than in the past, the numbers of elderly with *no* surviving children or with *any* surviving children vary among the different cohorts within the elderly population.

Most of the elderly have living adult children, although the probability of an elderly person having at least one surviving child has declined substantially among recent cohorts. According to Wolf (1983) the probability of having at least one surviving child when reaching age 65 was about 0.833 percent for the cohort born between 1906 and 1910, and increased in the wake of the post-World War II baby boom. It will reach a peak of about 0.912 percent for the 1931 to 1935 cohort when it reaches age 65 around the year 2000. A decline is projected thereafter, to about 0.845 percent for the cohort born 1946 to 1950 and reaching age 65 around the year 2015.

In a national health survey carried out in 1984, the U.S. National Center for Health Statistics also inquired about children and siblings of elderly respondents. Among the elderly population of the United States in 1984, more than 81 percent had at least one living child (estimates are for the noninstitutionalized elderly, about 95 percent of the total). Indeed, just under 39 percent have three or more living children (Table 10.2) Just over 79 percent of the elderly have at least one living brother or sister, and 39 percent have three or more living living siblings. Of the total elderly population, less than 5 percent reported having *neither* a living child *nor* a living sibling, while almost two-thirds (65.3 percent) reported having *both* living children *and* living siblings (Table 10.2). Among elderly persons living alone, almost three-fourths (73 percent) have at least one living child, three-fourths (75 percent) have at least one living sibling, and about 56 percent have *both* a living child *and* a living sibling.

Table 10.2.   Persons 65 Years Old and Over—Family Characteristics by Living Arrangements: 1984

	LIVING				LIVING		
	Total	Alone	With others		Total	Alone	With others
Total (1,000)	26,433	8,397	18,036	Number of living siblings:			
Percent Distribution				None	20.6	25.0	18.5
				One	21.5	23.6	20.6
				Two	18.7	16.7	19.6
Total	100.0	100.0	100.0	Three	13.8	12.5	14.4
Number of living children:				Four or more	25.4	22.2	26.9
None	18.7	26.9	15.0	Living children or siblings:			
One	17.7	19.3	17.0	Neither	4.6	7.8	3.2
Two	24.7	22.6	25.6	Children only	15.9	17.2	15.3
Three	15.4	13.5	16.4	Siblings only	14.1	19.1	11.8
Four or more	23.4	17.7	26.1	Both	65.3	55.9	69.7

Source: U.S. Bureau of the Census, *Statistical Abstract of the United States, 1988*, 108th ed. (Washington, D.C.: Government Printing Office, 1987), Table 41.

The conjectures we are able to make on the basis of calculations from mortality and fertility rates and probabilities do not tell us much about the closeness or distance between the elderly and their parents, siblings, or children. Nor do they tell us about the needs or resources of the parents, siblings, or children respectively, or about the actual relationships between members of these varying kin groupings and constellations. But the same National Health Interview Survey has provided some data on distances between elderly respondents and their living children and on the intensity of contacts with children not residing in the same household.

About 83 percent of the elderly respondents reported that they see or speak with one of their children weekly at least, including almost two-thirds (63 percent) who reported seeing or speaking with a child daily or twice weekly or more. Only 5 percent reported less than monthly contact with children. Speaking with children is more frequent than seeing children. In general, the older the respondents the more frequently they reported seeing or speaking with their children. Those living alone reported seeing or speaking with their children slightly more frequently than did the elderly who reside with others (U.S. Bureau of the Census, *Statistical Abstract of the United States, 1988,* Table 42).

The great majority of the elderly in the United States with children who do not live together in the same household report living very close to at least one child. More than half (54 percent) reported having a child living less than thirty minutes' travel distance away. An additional 12 percent reported that the closest-residing child lives less than one hour's travel time (that is, between thirty and fifty-nine minutes) away. Only 7 percent report that the closest child lives more than a day's travel time away (U.S. Bureau of the Census, 1987, Table 42). The older the respondents in the survey the shorter reported distances (travel time) to their children. Those residing alone tend to report shorter distances to their children somewhat more frequently than those residing with others.

Child-Parenting and Adult-Parenting in Old Age   Some of the children of the elderly are young. Men with wives, say, five or more years younger who have borne children at later ages, say, after age forty, have dependent children. Even more have children who are young adults but not yet economically independent. Others have adult children who are impaired or disabled and dependent. Thus, a certain number of elderly individuals or couples must parent dependent children well into old age. Yet quite little is known about the special problems of parenting dependent children late in life, beyond the problems arising out of unemployment or mandatory retirement and associated loss of income or poverty. The elderly whose children are all independent can more readily agree to, or indeed look forward to, early retirement since their needs for income diminish as their children leave parental homes. Those still burdened with support of dependent children are more likely to try to delay retirement, and they suffer greater hardship under unemployment or mandatory retirement.

Even parents of independent adult children continue to parent well into old age in roles akin to the roles of parenting young or dependent children (Streib and Thompson, 1960; Habib and Matras, 1987). Elderly parents visit, provide financial, emotional, and general assistance to children, take part in socialization and care of grandchildren, and, in many settings, provide either direct employment or business opportunities or ongoing contacts enhancing the employment opportunities of their children. They often provide the childcare services enabling daughters or daughters-in-law to enter or remain in the labor force, generally contingent on their own health (Habib and Matras, 1987).

Parent-Childing, Brothering, and Sistering in Old Age   Many elderly persons or couples still have living parents to whom they give care (Cherlin, 1983). In fact, one of the central roles of the young-old is that of caregivers to their old-old parents (Brody, 1985). Among the cohort born 1906 to 1910 and passing age 65 in the late 1970s, only about 7 percent had a living parent in 1975; it is projected that for the cohort born 1946 to 1950 and reaching old age in about the year 2015, more than 28 percent will at that time still have at least one living parent (Wolf, 1983).

Both from the results of mathematical modeling and simulation and from empirical studies, we know that the numbers of siblings of the elderly have fluctuated somewhat in this century. This has been due to declining mortality offset by generally declining fertility except for the post-World War II baby boom. The great majority of the elderly have at least one surviving sibling, although there is not much information available about location, patterns of contiguity, or distance between siblings. Sibling interaction has been found to increase in later years, after declining beginning in early adulthood and family formation. Presumably the sibling interaction is renewed as their own children begin to leave home, when siblings jointly contribute to the care of ailing, impaired, or disabled parents, or sometimes upon the death of one or both parents (McPherson, 1983).

Sister-to-sister relationships are said to be stronger than sister-to-brother relationships; brother-to-brother relationships are weaker than those involving a sister, who may sometimes serve as surrogate wife or mother for a surviving lone brother (Troll, 1971). The theoretical and empirical materials on sibling relationships, and even the numbers of households comprising siblings, have not been extensively developed thus far.

Marriage and Marital Relationships   There is fairly extensive discussion of marriage, marital relationships, and marital satisfaction among the elderly (not infrequently under the Sex-in-old-age? rubric). In modern societies most marriages, and especially most first marriages, involve brides and grooms of roughly similar age, with roughly concomitant life histories, and reaching old age chronologically close to one another.

Longitudinal studies of marital relationships and of marital satisfaction suggest a prevalent pattern of decline in satisfaction and its components after marriage and the birth of first children. Some studies have found continuing decline in relationships and satisfaction throughout marriage, while others have identified upturns in relationships and satisfaction beginning at various junctures in the family cycle. Such upturns have been found or conjectured to take place after the last child is born, after the last child has left home (transition to empty-nest stage), or just prior to or at retirement of the husband (McPherson, 1983). All of the latter scenarios indicate *continuously improving* marital relationships, marital satisfaction, and specific components of relationships and satisfaction (for example, sexual relations, financial security, time to pursue joint and separate interests) throughout the elderly years and the last stages of the marriage.

Children and Grandchildren of the Elderly   One of the central implications of the aging of populations is that more and more nonelderly adults have two or one surviving parents. More and more families of nonelderly adults and their offspring are taken up in one measure or another with the care and well-being of elderly parents and grandparents. Remarkably, there is very little quantitative documentation of this trend; three-generation families are recorded in population censuses and surveys almost exclusively if they are co-resident in the same household or dwelling unit. And, as noted above, the increase in the numbers of elderly empty-nest couples and single-person households tends to *reduce* the proportions of three-generation *households* reported in censuses and surveys, confounding somewhat the quantitative portrayal of the actual increase in survival of parents and grandparents.

The lives, activities, and social relationships and arrangements of the children, and often the grandchildren, of the elderly are probably only quite rarely indifferent to or unaffected by situations, needs, wishes, and activities of the elderly themselves. If the elderly are young-old or well elderly, the relationships may be much as suggested above in connection with continuing parenting and continuing assistance, care, and socialization of grandchildren. Surviving elderly parents or grandparents are, under these circumstances, important resources for the adult children and for their own offspring, important parts of their social and emotional networks, and in effect continue, with some modifications, the patterns of lifelong childing to their lifelong parents.

But as elderly parents become frail, ill, impaired, or disabled, or otherwise dependent in their daily lives, their needs and the demands upon the adult children and their own offspring, and the responses, may change radically. The families of the elderly, primarily their children and grandchildren, typically become the locus of direct support—whether economic, instrumental, or emotional support—for the elderly.

In the previous chapter we have already mentioned the view that in modern societies the status of the elderly in their families as elsewhere has declined relative to premodern societies. Such a view implies, of course, that contemporary adult children do not take care of their elderly parents as they did in the good old days. D.P. Kent (1965) has characterized the image of the idyllic three-generation household of earlier times as the "illusion of the Golden Past," and mention was made in the previous chapter of Laslett's critique of such comparisons.

Recent research has shown quite definitively that adult children continue to be the major source of care and support for elderly parents today. Indeed, as Brody (1985) has pointed out, adult children now provide more care and more difficult care to more parents over much longer periods of time than they did in the past. They provide more emotional support to the elderly than in the past as well. The caregivers are primarily women: daughters and daughters-in-law, but sons also provide support and affection, carry out gender-defined tasks, and are often the responsible relatives for those elderly who have no daughters or daughters-in-law at all, or none close by (Brody, 1985). The elderly mother-adult daughter relationship has received special attention in the literature (Noam, 1987).

The discussion of implications of development and use of extrafamily services—private, for-profit, market or the state or public sectors—for individual well-being and family functioning and solidarity was reviewed briefly in Chapter 5. Explicit mention was made there about the extrafamily services and care for the elderly. An interesting theoretical and empirical approach to the continuing importance, but changing functions, of families of the elderly in this connection points to the centrality of adult children and other family members of the elderly as the mediators in the bureaucratic arrangements for access to and use of extrafamily services by the elderly (Sussman, 1985; Shanas and Sussman, 1977). Families have now become the links of the old-old, the frail or impaired elderly, to the wider society *as well as* or *in addition* to being the direct caregivers and support-providers.

Quality of Intergenerational Relations   An important new frontier in the discussion of implications of aging in old age for family life and organization has focused on the *quality* of intergenerational relationships and, in particular, on the bearing of the quality of parent-offspring relationships for the nature, extent, and quality of informal care provided within families (Cherlin, 1983). Noam (1987) has pointed out that the investigation has been elusive due to conceptual and methodological difficulties, but she is able to propose four observable dimensions of the quality of interpersonal relationships.

1. sentiments and emotions generated by another family member, for example, affection, love, understanding;
2. conscious assessment of the other's attributes, for example, respect, approval, esteem;
3. the nature of communication between two family members, for example, its openness, the scope of its content; and finally
4. degrees of consensus or conflict in the relationships, for example, specific opinions, basic values and beliefs, or general world view.

Noam hypothesizes, for example, that the quality of elderly mother-adult daughter relationships described in terms of these dimensions will vary among different population subgroups. In particular, it varies in accordance with changing patterns of intergenerational similarities and gaps in the life-course events, experiences, and trajectories. Moreover, these variations bear strongly, in her view, on the propensities and capabilities of daughters, and their willingness or ability to provide care. They also bear on the daughters' sense of burden, and ultimately on the well-being of the elderly mothers (Noam, 1987, p. 69).

Finally, there has been some discussion of the problems entailed for families by extended caregiving and mediation activity, including burnout, stress, and impairment of other family functions, especially in connection with the proposal to assist or compensate families in their caregiving activity. However, these studies are in their early stages. We return to these issues in the chapters that follow.

Firms and Employers

A relatively recent development in modern aging population is the decline in economic activity among elderly men. Rates of labor force participation among the elderly are low and falling dramatically in recent decades. Yet many elderly men wish to continue, and many do continue, in employment beyond the conventional retirement ages. They may do so because of their need to maintain the income levels attained in middle ages, absence of pensions or nonemployment income entitlements, their interest in work, desire to maintain the social status or social network associated with employment, or other reasons. A variety of considerations point to efforts on the part of government and employers to encourage delay of retirement or reentry into employment following retirement. Many of these efforts entail a variety of schemes for adjusting jobs, production processes, hours of work, remuneration and benefit arrangements, and so forth, to the needs, health, and capabilities of elderly workers.

The extent to which such schemes and arrangements have been adopted by employers is not well known. Most of the information and analyses are based upon case studies in individual organizations or communities. It is also not generally known how many firms have large numbers or proportions of elderly workers, what characterizes such firms, or, in particular, how the employment of elderly workers affects the rest of the work setting. Robinson, Coberly, and Paul (1985) have noted that in the United States around 1980, employed men over 65 were concentrated in services, trade, and agriculture. Most working women in these ages were employed in services and trade. This is not surprising inasmuch as there is comparatively much self-employment in agriculture while the services and trade sectors offer, in addition to self-employment opportunities, more part-time, easy-entry, and flexible-work-schedule jobs than, say, manufacturing. Older workers are also concentrated in smaller firms, possibly because smaller firms have generally lower pension coverage and their employees need to continue beyond normal retirement age because of inadequate retirement income.

Several kinds of individual aging processes take place within firms. First, there are career processes entailing mobility among work roles, tasks, responsibilities and authority, and rewards within firms. These are typically presumed to have an upward direction as individuals remain in a firm and level off at, or even decline after, some career peak. Second, there are biological and psychological processes affecting work interest, capabilities, and performance associated with chronological aging. In addition, there are organizational aging processes involving development, evolution, or changes in production, marketing, accounting and management, remuneration, size of the organization, and so forth, as the organization ages. Finally, there are processes of aging, hiring, dismissal, retirement, and succession and turnover of the cohorts of employees and labor forces of the organizations as a whole. Chapter 4 alluded to discussions and studies of productivity of older workers and the general finding that older workers are not less productive than younger workers. There remain, however, large gaps in knowledge and discussion of other effects of aging at later ages on work organization and work relations, income, reward, and gratification structures, and attitudes, perceptions, and well-being of employees of *all* ages (Schrank and Waring, 1983).

Community Organization

The issues surrounding organization of public and social services in the wake of the aging of populations were outlined and discussed in Chapter 5. Adjustment of public expenditure priorities, on the one hand, and the development of extrafamily care services were mentioned, in connection with both the changing age composition of the populations and the changes in individual life course and family life cycle and associated microdependency constellations and resources for addressing them. The transitions into old age imply additional community organizational contingencies and implications for community interaction, neighborhood relations, physical security, voluntary organization and political participation, and perceptions of community order, well-being, and quality of life. Variations in these community features and their relationships to patterns of aging in later life have so far been considered only speculatively and tentatively.

A first type of community organization variable concerns patterns of residence and housing. The location of the various population subgroups in a community, and, in particular, patterns of concentration and segregation or integration, bear strongly on virtually all facets of social interaction and participation. Within cities and metropolitan areas, the elderly do tend to be concentrated and segregated. In part this is due to migration: It is typically the younger individuals, and families of young couples, who tend to move to newer areas of a community, with the elderly more stable and left behind disproportionately in the older neighborhoods. Lower income of the elderly also inhibits migration or their moving to newer and more expensive residences. Established homeownership and reluctance or inability to undertake new mortgage commitments tend, similarly, to inhibit migration. Finally, the elderly often prefer familiar surroundings, social relationships, and services of the old neighborhoods, and have relatively less need for the newer school and recreational facilities of newer neighborhoods.

At a different level, there have been a number of well-publicized flows of elderly migrants and concentration of elderly in so-called Sunbelt areas—Florida, California, and some of the Southwestern states—leading to relatively high percentages of elderly throughout those areas compared to the total U.S. population. Other countries have similar net flows of elderly to areas of favorable climates. In the areas of more severe climate the population is somewhat younger than average, and the remaining elderly include higher proportions in lower income groups. Finally, there has been the highly publicized emergence of retirement communities. These are comprised entirely of elderly members and contain only quite small numbers in professional, maintenance, and service industries and occupations who can directly address the needs of the elderly communities.

The issue of age segregation or age integration in residence and community life has received a certain amount of speculative discussion. It is a relatively straightforward task to *measure* age integration or age segregation for geographic areas of varying scope or dimensions. However, the actual *effects* or outcomes that may be convincingly imputed to age integration or segregation—for the community, the elderly, the families of the elderly, the nonelderly, and so forth—remain quite obscure. The questions concerning the optimal locations for the elderly, from the point of view of their own, their families', or community well-being are barely formulated, much less investigated and resolved.

The housing arrangements of the elderly are also widely understood to be a critical facet of both their own well-being and the organization of their communities. The overwhelming majority of elderly persons live in private households, whether alone, with spouses, adult children, sometimes siblings or other relations, and sometimes in private households with nonrelatives. A small proportion of the elderly live in noninstitutional group housing, such as hotels, rooming houses, or communal arrangements either spontaneously organized or with organizational sponsorship. A small proportion, at any moment in time, live in institutions of one type or another: hospitals, nursing homes, rest or old-age homes, and the like. These may be government-sponsored and financed, private nonprofit institutions, or private for-profit nursing or convalescent homes.

The distribution of the elderly by alternative types of housing arrangements, and the factors affecting that distribution, bear upon community organization in at least two distinct ways. First, the analysis of the relationships of the elderly to the community—their activities, interaction, and social participation in the community setting, contributions to community economy, social life, and solidarity, and needs for community services and arrangements—are closely related to their housing arrangements. Individuals living alone, in family settings, or in institutional settings respectively have differing patterns of participation, interaction, and needs. Second, it is increasingly recognized, however, that community organization, services, facilities, and patterns of support and interaction bear very strongly on the ability of the elderly to remain independent in their own homes, and, for that matter, upon the capabilities of the children and families of the elderly to be both supportive of their aging members *and* to carry on with their own activities, life course, and family cycle.

Patterns of aging in later life, then, bear on community interaction, neighborhood relations, physical security, voluntary organizations, and political participation. The questions of organization of acceptable services, amenities to the aged and nonaged alike, and satisfaction from community and housing in the face of increasing numbers of elderly and, especially, of the long-term care needs of the old-old pose both practical and theoretical challenges.

Perhaps the most explosive community organizational question surrounding aging in later life concerns the extent to which the elderly form distinctive electoral blocs, political lobbies, and pressure groups. This issue hinges
primarily around that of age-consciousness, the salience of age identity, age
solidarity, and age-based issues for the elderly (and, possibly for their families) as
citizens and voters. The increasing numbers of young-old, their own awareness of
age status by virtue at least of their increasing retirement from active labor force
participation, their income and health care entitlements, and the attacks on their
status and entitlements, alongside their increasing educational credentials, financial resources, and organizational experience seem already to have engendered one
of the largest and strongest political constituencies and coalitions ever in American
politics. Similar developments are being observed elsewhere as well.

For the time being, the meaning of this emerging constituency and coalition has been cast primarily in terms of numbers of voters and influence on political
climate relating to issues directly affecting the health and material well-being of
older voters. There have also been instances of spillover into other issues, for
example, organization of older voters against nuclear weaponry. If, as Laslett
(1985) has asserted, the large numbers, longevity, good health, and general status
of the elderly in modern Western societies are historically unprecedented, even
more unprecedented is the emergence of an elderly political coalition whose
potential influence and direction are yet to be charted.

ROLE TRANSITIONS THROUGH THE LIFE COURSE REVISITED

Normative versus Interpretive Explanations
of Role Transitions

In the early sections of this chapter it was noted that virtually all the
sociological theories of well-being, satisfaction, and adaptation in later life are
actually theories of roles, role-transitions, and socialization and resocialization.
This is so whether our focus is upon the individual elderly person, the families of
the elderly, or their communities. It was mentioned as well that sociological
theories of aging in later years bear very close relationships to contemporary
general sociological theory. In particular they are closely related to the normative
or socialization-driven explanations of social relations and social organization. We
mentioned only briefly a competing approach to sociological explanation in contemporary sociological theory. This is the interpretive explanation—less well-
known, less frequently invoked, and, indeed, something of an underdog or
anti-Establishment sociological approach.

The central motif of the normative paradigm accounts of role transitions
generally, and of role transitions late in life in particular, is that societies recognize and
take into account the age-related capacities or incapacities, abilities or disabilities, of
their members and map out, as it were, trajectories across successive age-based roles.
The individual's task is to learn, internalize, or be socialized in the succession of roles

and to perform them adequately and satisfactorily. Explanations for changes in trajectories, in timing of role transitions or their directions, or in role contents are to be sought in the various historical, demographic, ideological or ideational, technological, economic, factors and forces bearing upon social organization.

Increasingly, theorists addressing the questions of role transitions in old age are seeking explanations and accounts for the fact, timing, and directions of change in the framework of the interpretive sociological paradigm (Neugarten, 1985; Marshall, 1986; Ryff, 1984, 1986; Kohli, 1986). In this view, the elderly do not simply respond to the cues of their own declining powers, senescence, and disability on the one hand, and to those of their families, employers, and communities, on the other hand, in giving up middle-age roles and in moving into old-age roles. Rather, they design new constellations of activities, relationships, meanings, rewards, and gratifications for themselves.

An implication of this approach is that descriptions of roles, status, and relationships of the elderly must be reviewed, revised, and reformulated on an ongoing basis. Failure to do so, and insistence on casting the role transitions in old age simply as flows of successive cohorts across recognized roles and role trajectories, risks misunderstanding of the social and individual processes taking place *and* misguided social intervention and policy that can promote the ill-being, rather than the well-being, of the elderly, their families, and their communities.

The Bearing of Early Life-Course Experience on Role Transitions in Old Age

In Chapter 6 it was noted as one of the special contributions of the life-span development group of investigators of the life course the attention to questions of the relations of early life-course experience to the content, timing, and directions of subsequent life-course events and transitions. That contribution is relevant as well in consideration of role transitions in old age. Whether or not individuals retire from employment, and when they do so, are affected by earlier events: schooling, occupational histories, family and household events, and so forth, as well as by personal age-related characteristics and job or firm characteristics or rules. Whether or not elderly individuals remain in their own homes or turn to other living arrangements depends, to be sure, upon their personal situations and the available options. There may also be effects of the examples of their own parental or grandparental living arrangements, factors in their own household and residential histories, and earlier parent-child or sibling relationships.

It is probably the psychoanalytic literature and case materials that are most suggestive of hypotheses concerning relationships between events in disparate parts of the life course and the family life cycle. There is an increasing number of more broadly based investigations illustrating such relationships. What is called for at this point is more systematic conceptualization and theorizing about relationships between life-course events and later-life transitions and their mechanisms. The technical apparatus for testing such hypotheses and elucidating such theories is increasingly in place and awaits appropriate substantive challenges.

Dependency, Obligations, Entitlements, and Role Transitions in Later Years

We have earlier made the distinction between phenomena and measures of macrodependency and microdependency. Macrodependency refers to the broad quantitative ratios or relationships between those in the population of ages or statuses rendering them potentially or actually dependent on the productive activity of others (that is, children, the elderly or infirm, or those prevented from such organized activity by childrearing or household commitments) and those of ages or statuses rendering them potential or actual participants in the regime of material production (that is, the employed, entrepreneurs, property owners, or the like). Classical and refined dependency ratios, as illustrated in Chapter 4, are frequently used to measure important aspects of macrodependency.

Microdependency refers to an individual's inability to carry out the ordinary activities of sustenance and daily life without assistance of some other person or agency. Familiar measures of microdependency include rates of dependency in instrumental activities in daily life (IADL), measures of use of certain services (for example, meals-on-wheels, housekeeping services). Obligations are requirements of individuals to act in response to needs or address and resolve microdependencies of other individuals in some given social relationship to them, for example, obligations to parents, children, other kin, neighbors, or sometimes community or wider society. Entitlements are legitimate claims that individuals have on other individuals, groups, agencies, or social units to resources or services that can address their needs or microdependencies.

In Part II it was noted that each individual has, at each juncture in his life course, or at each age, some constellation of dependencies, obligations, and entitlements. It was argued that much of the individual's behavior and social relationships is organized around bringing dependencies, obligations, and entitlements into some acceptable and reasonably stable balance. It was argued, also, that the fact, frequency, timing, and directions of important life-course transitions are strongly influenced by the constellation, at that age or life-course juncture, of dependency, obligations, and entitlements. We argued that changes in these constellations—occasioned by demographic trends, technological or economic factors, or sociohistorical circumstances—engender changes in broad patterns of life-course and family life-cycle trajectories and derivative social organizational features.

Patterns of life-course transitions in later life are simply a special case of the general relationship. For the middle-aged and the elderly, constellations of dependency, obligations, and entitlements bear very strongly upon transitions such as retirement, residential stability or change, social participation, family activity, and on adaptation to transitions such as widowhood, bereavement, illness and impairment. Marital and household status, on the one hand, and pension entitlements, on the other hand, affect the timing of retirement. Income, employment, kin relations, and availability of community services are all believed to bear upon housing decisions made by or for the elderly.

These relationships, too, need systematic conceptual and theoretical development, especially since so much of social intervention is cast in terms of matching entitlements to dependencies and obligations for individuals and families of the various types and at the various points or stages in the life course or family cycle. Elaboration of the bearing of dependency, obligations, and entitlements thus remains one of the frontiers of sociological theories of aging in later life.

11

ROLE TRANSITIONS
IN MIDDLE AND LATE LIFE

the contraction of social networks

INTRODUCTION

In earlier chapters dealing with the life course, we have seen that from a sociological point of view the critical process that the individual undergoes in aging at all stages and ages, and in middle and old age as well, is one of role transitions. In the preceding chapter it was noted that some theories and analyses assert or hypothesize that such transitions in later life inevitably entail role loss, while others point to a process of exchange or substitution of roles. Still others see even an increase in the numbers and varieties of roles in old age. All of the approaches and theories, however, are in agreement about the occurrence of role *changes* and *transitions* at middle or old age.

Without necessarily adopting a position concerning *the* characteristic pattern of role transitions in middle or old age, in this chapter we identify and review some of the features of five types of role transitions that are very frequent, even if not necessarily dominant to the point of characterizing the transitions into old age. They all involve some contraction of social networks. (In the final chapter we shall identify and discuss some types of role transitions that imply *expansion* of social networks.) The five types of role transitions are

1. Shifts in the nature, quality, and characteristic relationships of parenthood associated with the departure of children from the parental home (the emptying of the nest transition);
2. Retirement from paid employment;
3. Widowhood, loss of spouse through death;

4. Loss of friends, relatives, or intimates through death;
5. Loss of health, impairment, disability, or acute or chronic illness.

These role transitions have been identified by some writers as universally associated with stress and issues of identity. However these characterizations are not always sustained by empirical findings. In particular, they may or may not entail dependency. A major research challenge is the measurement of the changing independence and dependency associated with these role transitions in later life and the factors and correlates of variation in such dependency shifts. A major challenge to public policy is the creation of conditions, arrangements, and institutions that may substitute or compensate for the contraction of social networks and which diminish or alleviate the dependency associated with such transitions.

More generally, we will pose the following questions about these transitions that have the effect of contracting social networks:

1. What are the variations and changes we can identify in the frequency and the timing of such transitions in the later life course? What are the factors and correlates of such variations?
2. How do these transitions affect the patterns of dependency, obligations, and entitlements of the elderly?
3. What are the characteristic—positive or negative—responses, adjustments, or adaptations of individuals to the transitions?
4. What are the characteristic—positive or negative—responses, adjustments, or adaptations of related individuals, families, and other social units related to those undergoing the late life transitions?

The first three types of questions are addressed in this chapter; the last type of question is considered in Chapter 12.

CHILD-LAUNCHING AND THE EMPTY NEST

While the concept of the empty nest as a stage in the family cycle has been familiar at least since the earliest discussions of the size and structural transformations of nuclear families over time, there are remarkably few details of the process well documented. In general, our quantitative information about family structure is more often than not based upon household statistics. These include information about whether or not the households include married couples, whether or not there are children of the couple in the household, and the ages, marital status, and sometimes employment status of children.

An individual householder or a couple without children may or may not have had children in the past. Yet our major source of estimates of the numbers, ages, and characteristics of individuals or couples in empty nests is generally based on such household statistics. In 1981, about 12 percent of nonelderly (under 65 years of age) men and 13 percent of nonelderly women in Canada lived in husband-wife households without children; these included both young couples prior to childbirth and middle-aged couples whose children have left the parental home. In the same year, 53 percent of elderly (65 or over) men and 30 percent of elderly women in Canada lived in and shared private households with only their spouses; of these, some had never had children. A national survey of family histories in Canada carried out in 1984 and a national survey of family histories in the United States now being conducted will provide many more details on the frequency and timing of child-launching and the empty-nest transitions in the near future.

The actual launching of children from the household can be very gradual or very abrupt. The exact pattern depends upon the number of children and their ages, whether their departure is connected with marriage and immediate formation of their own households, or for other reasons, such as employment, schooling, or military service. In the latter case, child-launching may be gradual or take place in fits and starts. There may be frequent returns to the nest for visits or for longer or shorter periods of renewed residence in the parental home. As noted earlier, research into the timing and characteristics of departure from parental home from the point of view of the young persons in their transitions to adulthood is only beginning.

From the point of view of middle-aged or elderly parental couples experiencing child-launching and transition to the empty nest, the focus of research has been primarily upon the marital and life satisfaction of one or both members of the couple in its aftermath. As Clausen (1986) has pointed out, prior to the availability of systematic research evidence on marital and life satisfaction at the various life-course junctures, the prevailing view about the empty nest was that it was a time of emotional depression for most mothers. Research evidence has largely disproved this earlier view (George, 1980). It indicates that neither the departure of children nor the physiological transitions (menopause), often occurring close in time, are typically cause for despair or depression among mothers. Rather, most mothers are glad to see their children launched, despite regrets of losses or changing nature of some relationships, and especially of the mother-daughter relationship (Atchley, 1980). Counteracting the departure of children is the greater freedom that parents can enjoy, including greater economic freedom.

For some couples the empty nest is indeed symbolic of an emptying of meaning of their marriages and joint lives. If they share little or nothing else beyond the interest in and responsibility for children, the child-launching and empty nest may indeed be translated into marital crises. For women with no interests outside the home and childcare, the empty nest confronts them with the problem of what to do with the rest of their lives.

But this is primarily a problem of transitional couples and families. Transitional couples are those themselves socialized in settings emphasizing lifelong dense intergenerational and extended family relations and interaction, but (1) who have effected in their own lives the transition to smaller nuclear families and (2) whose children are socialized with stronger orientation to extrafamily interaction, activities, and resources. The modern couples and individuals, themselves already socialized in the small nuclear family regime, are more likely to have had lifelong extrafamily interests and activities. Our concrete knowledge of these variations and cohort trends remains quite limited.

In any event, the empty nest typically does not represent an *end* to parenting and the parent roles. Rather it sets in motion a sequence of changes probably more extreme than the previous lifetime change and development in the parenting roles (Palmore, 1981). Probably the critical shift associated with the end of co-residence in the parental household is the end, or at least the very substantial cutback, in parental authority over the child. Continued economic support, advice, cooperation, health care, and emotional support very frequently take place either in the parent-to-child direction or in the child-to-parent direction or both. These are clothed in strong norms of mutual obligation and often of children's traditional respect and deference to parents. The departure of children from the parental household introduces and legitimates a new dimension of voluntarism, on the one hand, and diminished accountability, on the other hand, into the child-parent relationships and interaction.

RETIREMENT FROM PAID EMPLOYMENT

A definition of retirement proposed by Atchley (1980) as the "institutionalized separation of individuals from their occupational positions with a continuation of income based on prior years of service," has enjoyed wide currency and acceptance among North American social gerontologists and other researchers and writers on related topics. Yet the concept of retirement remains elusive; it is not at all easy to identify the retired population of a community or of an entire society. Do housewives "retire"? Are persons employed after separation from previous jobs with pension entitlements "retired"? Are nonemployed elderly persons with no job-related pension entitlements "retired"? Can self-employed persons "retire"?

In their statistical descriptions of the elderly in the United States, Canada, and elsewhere, national statistical agencies and bureaus typically present no estimate of the number or percentage retired among the elderly. Rather, they show the numbers and percentages of elderly "in the labor force" and the distribution of the elderly by major sources of income. In the United States almost three-fourths of men and 86 percent of women aged 65 to 69 were reported *not* in the labor force in 1983; all but about 12 percent of the men and 5 percent of the women aged 70 and over were also not in the labor force.

In Canada, government pensions and transfer payments and private pensions and annuities were the main sources of income for some 72 percent of elderly (aged 65+) Canadian men and for about 79 percent of elderly Canadian women in 1980. For most of the women and for many of the men these sources of income are not related to their own occupational experience or histories. Yet, from the point of view of their age combined with nonparticipation in the labor force, their nonemployment-related income entitlements, and the range of life styles that these conditions engender we would probably wish to consider them retired.

What is discussed in the literature as the retirement experience, or the role transition conventionally denoted retirement is in fact associated with the termination of a career, a job, or a sequence of jobs and employment for pay or profit in a labor market. Such termination of employment may be permanent or temporary. Indeed, it may occur with the expectation that it will be permanent and subsequently turn out to have been temporary. Probably more frequently, it may occur with the expectation that it will be temporary and subsequently turn out to be permanent.

Termination of employment may be gradual or abrupt; it may be voluntary or involuntary. Its proximate causes may rest with the individual—his age, wishes and preferences, competence and capabilities, or health. Or it may rest with the employer, the employer's overall economic health and prospects, or the employer's demand for labor; or it may rest with collective agreements or legislation. Finally, it may rest with general economic conditions and the level and composition of demand for labor.

History of Retirement

It is important to recognize that historically the conception, formulation, and implementation of retirement schemes had as their objective not so much the welfare of the aged or elderly no longer able to work in paid employment. Rather, its focus was the regulation of the labor market and the attempt to assure or enhance employment opportunities for younger adult men, and means and legitimation for employers to rid themselves of older workers (Johnson and Williamson, 1987; Graebner, 1980). More active participation and involvement of the elderly themselves in the politics of retirement is quite recent.

In the United States only public sector employers had superannuation schemes, although in Germany and elsewhere in Europe modest income maintenance arrangements were introduced for all retired employees late in the nineteenth century. Public welfare and pension schemes were put together to address problems of poverty and destitution among elderly no longer employed and deemed no longer employable. In North America Social Security and income maintenance schemes were adopted relatively late as improvements on income-tested welfare schemes (Myles, 1986).

Labor unions became more favorable to retirement to preserve jobs for prime-age employees, especially during and following the Great Depression of the 1930s. They worked to introduce and improve universal Social Security benefits. Employers have tended to welcome retirement scheme opportunities to replace older, frequently higher-waged (because of seniority) employees perceived to be less able to maintain productivity with advancing age, or else perceived less able to adapt to new technologies. Governments have tended to favor retirement arrangements both as measures supporting employment opportunities for younger adult workers and as measures improving efficiency, higher productivity, and improved competitive position for industries.

Especially since World War II, Social Security and similar types of retirement income maintenance schemes have increasingly replaced job earnings, thus permitting and encouraging more universal and earlier retirement. There has also been an explosion of private market pension schemes, company-sponsored pension plans, and pension arrangements negotiated on a firm, occupational, or industry-wide basis in collective agreements. For their part, older workers could more easily forgo full employment earnings in later years as numbers of dependent children declined and as wives were increasingly engaged in paid employment as well. In effect, employers, government, and unions have colluded and converged in support of retirement-tested income maintenance schemes and earlier retirement. Throughout the industrialized Western world, the labor force participation rates of elderly men, and of late middle-aged men as well, have fallen dramatically.

Variations in the Timing of Retirement

There has been some attention in the literature to the decision to retire—the considerations leading the individual to leave paid employment, and when and under what circumstances such decisions are made. Any *group* of elderly persons no longer employed—retired—typically report having left employment over some *range* of ages or dates, and because of some *range* of reasons. In the United States the age range reported usually centers on 62 to 65 years of age (Figure 11.1). There are two peaks in the retirement curve: a first lower peak at age 62 and a second sharp peak at age 65. These peaks correspond to ages at early retirement and conventional retirement entitlements under Social Security regulations. Reasons reported retrospectively usually include primarily wishing or planning to retire, poor health or disability. Also

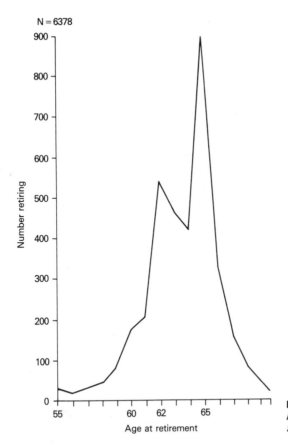

Figure 11.1 Age at Retirement, United States Males Aged 58-63 in 1969.
Source: Burtless and Moffit, 1984.

reported, but less frequently, are mandatory retirement provisions of the employer or layoff, unemployment, and inability to find new employment.

Retirement from paid employment in modern societies is often an act that is completely voluntary on the part of the employee and may be entirely unaffected by conditions and contingencies apart from the preferences, welfare, and well-being of the employee and his closest family and dependents. When this is the case the delay, or for that matter the precocity, of retirement does not require schemes or special arrangements. The individual simply works as much as he or she wishes or can for as long as he or she wishes, and withdraws fully or partially, gradually or at once, from employment in accordance with his personal needs and timetable.

Increasingly in modern societies both employment and retirement from employment are organized and structured by factors external to the individual employee as well as private and individual considerations. External factors include:

1. Employers' understandings, calculations, and determinations concerning the labor market, the alternative employee recruitment options it affords, and their costs and utilities;
2. The understandings, calculations, and determinations of trade unions and government bodies concerning the supply of jobs and demand for employment and the ways in which these understandings inform collective agreements and legislation; and
3. The available income maintenance arrangements, social status options, and legitimate roles and activities outside of employment.

Thus the timing of retirement most typically takes place in the context of a firm or employer's rules, negotiated collective agreements and pension arrangements, or legislation governing work, disability contingencies, and income entitlements after partial or full withdrawal from paid employment. These, in turn, have typically offered—or imposed—retirement arrangements and timing that have become conventional and more or less rigidly formalized and prescribed by the respective firms, occupational groups, private and public sectors, trade unions or federations, or other worker or employee groupings.

While individual deviations from these rules, conventions, and prescriptions are possible and tolerated—whether in the direction of earlier or later retirement—the numbers of such deviations have been small. In order to legitimize and institutionalize deviations—especially in the direction of delayed retirement—from conventional prescribed timing and forms of retirement, schemes for work adjustment and legislative or pension and benefit innovations have been proposed, developed, and implemented in Western countries. It is increasingly clear that the main trends in the timing of retirement are governed by public pension provisions and labor market and legislative arrangements and forces—largely outside the decisions and control of individual employees (Sheppard, 1976; Pampel, 1981; 1983; Pampel and Weiss, 1983).

Life Years in Retirement

In earlier chapters we presented and discussed age-specific rates of labor force participation and some of their changes over time. Included were the declines in rates of labor force participation among older men. Chapter 3 introduced the concepts of survival and life years associated with mortality rates, and it was noted that it is useful and suggestive to consider how total life years are partitioned among activities in various life domains; for example, parenting, employment, and schooling. Applying age-specific rates of labor force participation to total numbers of a cohort's life years at each age yields estimates of the numbers of cohort life years in the labor force or outside the labor force at each age.

In a calculation carried out for Canada for 1951 and 1981 (Matras, forthcoming) it was found that under 1951 mortality and labor force participation rates about 81 percent of male life years at ages fifteen and over were life years in the labor force. These included, also, about 59 percent of life years in the labor force at older ages, 55 or over. But under the mortality and labor force participation rates characterizing Canadian men, only 76 percent of total life years at ages 15 or over, and less than 40 percent of life years at ages 55+, are devoted to employment (Table 11.1). Thus for the cohort characterized by 1951 mortality and labor force participation, there would be

Table 11.1.   Estimates of Male Life Years in the Labor Force, by Age. Canada—1951 and 1981

AGE GROUP	1951		1981	
	Labor Force Partic. Rate	Life Years in Labor Force	Labor Force Partic. Rate	Life Years in Labor Force
15–19	58.4	274058	58.2	285318
20–24	92.4	430071	86.5	420941
25–34	96.4	887912	95.3	917588
35–44	96.7	866906	96.1	910194
45–54	94.5	802623	92.8	845878
55–59	89.6	348970	}	
60–64	81.4	286543	} 75.1	616709
65–69	60.1	182343	21.9	76196
70+	23.4	134180	8.9	65951
Total all ages		4213606		4138775
Total life years at ages 15 and over		5217074		5708285
Percent of life years at ages 15+ in the labor force		80.8		75.7
Total life years at ages 55 and over		1618313		1910136
In the labor force		952036		758856
Not in the labor force		666277		1151280
Percent of life years at ages 55+ in the labor force		58.8		39.7

Source: J. Matras, "Demographic Trends, Life Course, and Family Cycle—The Canadian Example: Part II. Employment, Parenting, and Their Alternatives," *Canadian Studies in Population,* forthcoming b. Table 1.

a total of 666,277 life years at ages 55+ *not* in the labor force, that is, in retirement. This represents an average of 6.6 years of retirement per newborn male in the cohort. For the cohort characterized by 1981 mortality and labor force participation, there would be a total of 1,151,280 life years at ages 55+ not in the labor force, or in retirement, representing 11.5 years of retirement per newborn male in the cohort (see Figure 11.2).

As mentioned earlier, labor force participation rates of older men have declined dramatically in recent decades. There has also been some decline in labor force participation rates of young adult men in their early twenties. Despite these declines in rates of labor force participation between 1951 and 1981, the total life years of cohorts devoted to labor force activity declined only very little in the period. Cohort life years in the labor force total 4,213,606 under 1951 conditions; under the 1981 rates the number of labor force life years is estimated as 4,138,775, only slightly less than the 1951 figure. The reason for the apparent stability in the total number of labor force life years despite the declining *rates* of labor force participation is, of course, the decline in mortality during the period, a decline that resulted in a substantial increase in *total* life years lived by the cohort.

Attacking and Defending Retirement

Retirement as a social institution and as a personal life situation has always been viewed in mixed ways. Most individuals who have retired report satisfaction with their situations; there is very broad and very strong support for public and private provisions for retirement as an institution. Yet retirement is a cause of personal and family distress, economic hardship, or reduced social status for many individuals. There has been growing concern about the costs and strains to the economy and society of both increasingly widespread and progressively earlier and longer-lasting retirement of a large segment of the population. Especially since the economic slowdowns experienced in the Western industrialized countries in the 1970s and 1980s and since the rise to power of conservative governments in several of the major industrialized countries, retirement provisions have come under scrutiny and attack on economic grounds.

At the same time, as the numbers of well, active, and politically experienced and sophisticated young-old have increased, retirement arrangements and provisions excluding them from continued employment have been attacked. Both types of attack have given rise to increasing discussion of the virtues and possibilities of extending employment in middle and later life. They have also given rise to the proposal of schemes for work adjustment and for legislative or pension and benefit innovations involving (1) delay in retirement or withdrawal from employment, or (2) reemployment of persons who have in effect once retired or withdrawn from paid employment.

In the United States, but not yet in other Western countries, these schemes and innovations have been accompanied by legislation proscribing mandatory retirement rules by firms or in collective agreements prior to age 70. The legislation also proscribes age discrimination in hiring or dismissal of employees and prescribes equal wages and fringe (other than pension) benefits and equal training and promotion opportunities for older workers (U.S. Department of Labor, 1981;

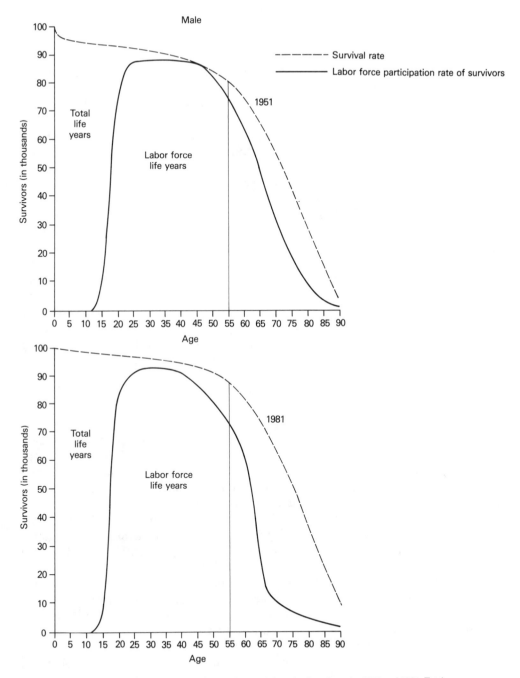

Figure 11.2 Survivors Out of 100,000 Born Alive at Selected Ages by Sex, Canada, 1951 and 1981. Total
Life Years in the Labor Force.

1982; McConnell, 1983). In the Government of Canada and in a number of large Canadian firms, rigid fixed retirement at age 65 has been abandoned. Even though mandatory retirement at age 65 is prevalent, extensions are granted to individuals on the basis of efficiency upon recommendation of the employing department and following examination and appraisal of skill and fitness to work (Koyl, 1970). The concept of functional criteria instead of chronological age in individual and collective retirement decisions and arrangements has received a certain amount of attention and support elsewhere as well (U.S. Department of Labor, 1979; Special Committee on Aging, 1982).

Attacks on eligibility provisions and retirement benefit levels have taken various forms and have had a certain amount of success. Age at eligibility for benefits in the United States is being gradually raised, and other changes are likely. On the other hand, the enhanced political power of the elderly population has been demonstrated both in the United States and in Canada in powerful defense of the indexing provisions of retirement benefits.

In the early 1980s federal administrations in both the United States and in Canada had sought to curtail the price-indexing provisions for public pension benefits; in both countries the proposals were set aside in the face of strong organized opposition by the elderly and their various political allies. Similarly, the trade unions and, especially, the powerful national trade unions in certain of the Western European countries that have long been involved in so-called corporatist social and economic policy concertation and package deals together with governments and with employer organizations (Goldthorpe, 1986; Casey and Bruche, 1983), have been steadfast in their support of retirement options and view the income maintenance provisions sustaining them fundamental to maintenance of full employment.

Retirement as Transition, Role, and Life Style

When people leave their occupations or employment, many changes typically occur in their lives: Their daily routines and physical surroundings change, their work-related social networks disappear for the most part, their incomes are usually substantially reduced, and for some there are crises or changes of identity and self-image. Reorganization of time budgets can be either attractive and favorable opportunities or dreaded misfortunes. More generally, the retirement transition is recognized as having the potential for both positive and negative meanings and outcomes on well-being and the quality of life. The meanings and outcomes are dependent, at least partly, upon the personal characteristics, health, income entitlements, preparation for, and attitudes toward retirement. They may depend as well upon a range of social support opportunities and arrangements as well as on the nature, skill levels, tasks, prestige, and other characteristics of the career or job being terminated and on the individual's lifetime work, job, or career attitudes, commitments and orientations (Minkler, 1981).

There has been an explosion of literature and studies on retirement and adaptation to retirement. It is clear that retirement represents for most persons a severe contraction of activity, social networks, and sometimes of social status and peer support. But altogether, the most recent and technically most sophisticated findings suggest that most middle-aged and elderly workers look forward to retirement, provided a reasonably adequate income is assured. They adjust very positively to retirement, express satisfaction with retirement and their retirement situations, do not seek additional employment and report disinclination to accept employment even if it is offered, provided they have reasonably good health and reasonably adequate income. Postretirement problems are typically problems of health and inadequate income, and only rarely do retired persons report missing the job.

Analyzing results of a longitudinal study, Palmore (1981) concluded that:

> The event of retirement by itself does not usually produce enough stress to result in long-term negative adjustment. Retirement does not appear to increase overall morbidity or mortality, although sick people retire more than healthy people. It does not appear to cause an increase in mental illness, at least among those with moderate to high income and education. Retirement does not usually cause a decrease in life satisfaction, and those who are less satisfied after retirement tend to be balanced by those who are more satisfied. However, *mandatory* retirement tends to have negative effects on life satisfaction, adjustment, and activity; while return to work tended to have positive effects. When retirement is accompanied by sharp declines in adequacy of income or illness and disability, the result is often decreased life satisfaction; but this decrease may be more the result of the declines in income and health than the result of retirement as such. Spouse's retirement appears to have no significant negative effects (Palmore, 1981, p.111).

These findings and this interpretation are consistent with those of other studies (Parnes, 1981; National Council on Aging, 1981) reporting overall satisfaction of retirees with retirement and positive outcomes of retirement for individual well-being in later life. They are, of course, consistent also with the increasing popularity and precocity of retirement and the strong defense of retirement and retirement benefits even as schemes for enhancing employment opportunities for those among the elderly who wish them also receive increasing support.

Women in Retirement

It is probably not unfair to assert that research and discussion of retirement has been decidedly sexist in focus. If the very definition of retirement poses difficulties for men, this is doubly the case for women. There are still many middle-aged and elderly women in the population who have *never* been employed outside the home, and even more who have been employed only part time, sporadically, or cyclically. A large part of the discussion of women in retirement has centered upon the relationship of women to the retirement of their *husbands*, with an explicit or implied presumption that wives of retired husbands are themselves retired. McPherson (1983) has noted that concerns of researchers have centered upon (1) how wives reacted to the retirement of their husbands, (2) how retirement affected the marital relationships, and (3) how the adjustment of husbands to retirement is facilitated by supportive wives.

Increasingly, studies have examined the retirement of women as transitions out of their own paid-labor-force employment and into nonemployment, separately from their marital status and from the employment or retirement status of their husbands. As Zopf (1986) has noted, the involvement of women in the labor force has increased substantially since 1950 and the percentages of participants aged 45 to 64 are now much higher than in the past. Women workers are more likely than men to retire early, and the retirement rate of women in their fifties is substantially higher than that of men. Married women have higher retirement rates than single, widowed, or divorced women. This may be partly due to their retirement in tandem with their husbands, but is more likely due to economic pressures on the nonmarried women (Zopf, 1986). Married women often report retirement to care for ailing husbands, and women of all marital statuses frequently report retirement to care for older parents (Foner, 1986; Gee and Kimball, 1987).

Some researchers have conjectured that as lifetime patterns of women's worklife converge with those experienced by men, it is likely that sex differences in retirement patterns will diminish. Zopf (1986) contends that the gradual shift toward equality of men and women in the workplace, the increasing numbers of women in the labor force and working fulltime and without long interruptions, and changing attitudes of men toward working women together with improved job, wage, and tenure opportunities for women all operate to render the timing and age patterns of women's retirement increasingly similar to those of men. At the same time, more men are retiring earlier and their retirement rates are moving toward those of women.

However, these conjectures may be somewhat premature. It is true that women increasingly have Social Security retirement benefit entitlements based on *their own* earnings records rather than as beneficiaries of entitlements based (as spouses or as survivors) upon their husbands' earnings records (O'Rand, 1984). These changes do reflect the long-term shift from the M-shaped curve of lifetime labor force participation (high rates of participation before the childbearing period, a drop between ages 25 to 35, and a rise again until retirement age; see Chapter 7) to high rates of labor force participation across all ages. Also, by and large, men and women alike tend to follow orderly labor force status patterns, with continuous work followed by permanent withdrawal from employment.

Working women, whether wives or single women, retire somewhat later than husbands, and they are more likely to return to paid employment later. In the view of O'Rand (1984) it is economic need that propels women back into the labor market to augment their incomes from earnings. Indeed a wide variety of indicators point to continuing economic hardship and poverty among older women, especially among those not married. Older women evidently retire for largely the same reasons as men: health and pension availability. They tend, however, to indicate negative subjective responses to retirement more frequently (O'Rand and Henretta, 1982). Although the presence of children has little or no effect on the adjustment of men in retirement, the presence has a positive effect of women's retirement adjustments (O'Rand, 1984).

Noting that a larger proportion of Canadian women than men live out their last years in poverty and poor health, McDaniel (1986) notes also that women, unlike men, become more politically active with increasing age. She has conjectured the emergence of more militant women pensioners' rights groups in Canada patterned on the Gray Panthers in the United States.

More generally, the evidence for convergence of women's and men's lifetime employment patterns not withstanding, there is so far little evidence for convergence of women's and men's lifetime patterns of care and nurturance. Women continue to be biological and social mothers, and indeed they continue to be wives, sisters, daughters, and daughters-in-law. Also, women continue to live longer than men and widowhood is and will remain much more prevalent among older women than among men. Thus the conjectured model of convergence of women's retirement patterns to those of men seems very unlikely. Rather, the meanings and outcomes of retirement of women must be studied and understood separately and in their own right.

WIDOWHOOD

It is the fate of every married couple ultimately to be dissolved by separation, divorce, or death of a spouse. All persons in intact marriages must either predecease their spouses or else survive them as widows or widowers. Thus widowhood is both familiar and frequent in every society. Yet its personal and social meanings have only begun to be explored by social scientists. Most of the attention has had a psychological focus, examining the nature of grief and bereavement, feelings such as loneliness, anger, guilt, sense of abandonment, and so forth among the widowed, and their adaptation under varying circumstances (see, especially, Glick, Weiss, and Parkes, 1974). It is only more recently that systematic attention has been paid to distinctly social dimensions of widowhood: living arrangements, income maintenance, economic dependency or independence, physical and instrumental assistance and support, companionship, and social participation (George, 1980).

Changes in the Extent and Timing of Widowhood

The percentages widowed in the population 55 and over in the United States in 1984 are shown in Table 11.2. Widowhood is very much more prevalent among elderly women than among men.

Table 11.2   Percent widowed, by sex, race, and age, United States, 1984

AGE GROUP	MALES			FEMALES		
	Total	Whites	Blacks	Total	Whites	Blacks
55–64	4	3	8	17	16	27
65–74	9	8	17	39	38	53
75+	24	23	35	67	66	72

Source: U.S. Bureau of the Census, *Current Population Survey,* Series P–20, No. 389. Washington, D.C.; Government Printing Office, 1985

1. Because of sex differences in mortality at every age (women at any given age have lower mortality rates, hence are more likely to survive husbands the same age than be survived by their husbands),
2. Because brides tend to marry grooms somewhat older than themselves (rendering it more likely for the women to survive and become widows as their husbands, somewhat older on the average, predecease them), and
3. Because widowers at any given age are very much more likely to remarry than are widows the same age.

Widowhood is also much more prevalent among black women and men alike than among whites. This difference reflects both higher mortality in the black population and lower rates of remarriage.

In the present century the proportions of both widows and widowers in the elderly (65+) population of the United States have been falling (Figure 11.3). The decline has been much faster for men than for women, and corresponds to the more rapid growth in the percent married among elderly men. It must be recalled that the mortality differences render the men aged over 65 years both a smaller and a younger population than the women aged 65 or over.

The changing patterns of widowhood reflect changes in mortality and in marriage, divorce, and remarriage that have taken place in this century. R. Schoen and his associates have constructed marital status life tables to describe the

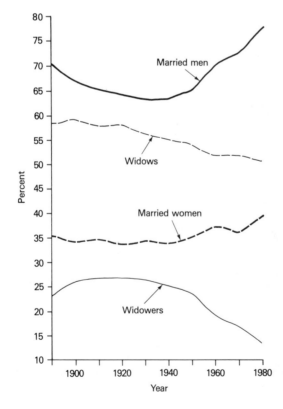

Figure 11.3 Percentages of People Aged 65 and Older Classified as Married or Widowed, by Sex, 1890-1980. *Sources:* U.S. Bureau of the Census, *U.S. Census of Population: 1960. Characteristics of the Population, U.S. Summary* (1964), Table 177; *U.S. Census of Population: 1970. Detailed Characteristics, U.S. Summary* (1973), Table 203; "Marital Status and Living Arrangements: March 1980," *Current Population Reports*, P-20, no 365 (1981), Table 1.

composition by marital status of cohorts from birth to the death of their last members for American female cohorts in the twentieth century based on observed marriage, divorce, and death rates (Schoen et al., 1985). Selected measures from the Schoen marital status life tables are shown in Table 11.3 for actual American female cohorts born late in the nineteenth century (1888 to 92), at the turn of the twentieth century (1903 to 07), in the mid-1920s (1923 to 27), in the mid-1930s Depression (1933 to 37), in the early post-World War II years (1948 to 50), and for synthetic cohorts subject to 1980 rates.

The proportion ever marrying peaked for the 1933 to 37 cohort and declined somewhat thereafter. Age at first marriage declined from 23.0 years

Table 11.3. Selected Measures from U.S. Marital Status Life Tables for Female Cohorts Born 1888 to 1950 and for 1980 Period

ITEM	1888–1892	1903–1907	1923–1927	1933–1937	1948–1950	YEAR 1980
Expectation of life at birth	54.2	60.7	70.7	73.0	76.0	77.6
Proportion ever marrying	.712	.751	.873	.903	.919	.893
Proportion ever marrying among survivors to age 15	.919	.920	.965	.973	.954	.908
Average age at first marriage	23.0	22.9	21.8	21.0	21.8	24.1
Proportion of marriages ending in divorce	.167	.223	.301	.338	.421	.429
Proportion of marriages ending in widowhood	.541	.532	.485	.463	.406	.400
Proportion of marriages ending in death	.292	.246	.213	.199	.173	.171
Average age at widowhood	61.1	64.1	66.7	67.0	67.6	67.9
Proportion of widows remarrying	.143	.136	.096.	.090	.081	.076
Average age at remarriage for widows	50.2	51.0	52.8	53.2	54.5	56.0
Average duration of widowhood	15.2	15.2	15.1	15.1	15.0	15.0
Proportion of life spent widowed	.135	.132	.124	.121	.114	.109

Source: Adapted from R. Schoen, et al., "Marriage and Divorce in Twentieth-Century American Cohorts." *Demography* 22. 1985 (1):101–114, Table 2.

among the 1888 to 92 cohort to 21.0 years for the 1933 to 37 cohort that began to marry in the early 1950s. In more recent years the average age at first marriage has gone up sharply. The proportion of marriages ending in divorce has gone up steadily from 16.7 percent (one in six) in the 1888 to 92 cohort to 42.9 percent (about three in seven) for those marrying under 1980 conditions. At the same time, the percent of marriages ending in death (of the woman) declined from 29.2 percent among the earliest cohort to 17.1 percent for the latest year, 1980.

The percent of marriages ending in widowhood declined from 54 percent among the 1888 to 92 cohort to 40 percent for the 1980 year. Average age at widowhood has increased, the proportion of widows remarrying decreased by about one-half, and the age at remarriage of widows increased as well. Although age at widowhood is now much higher, the average *duration* of widowhood has remained about the same. Since total life years has increased, the proportion of life spent in widowhood has declined.

Widowhood as Crisis and Condition

There is a traditional image of widowed persons, and especially of widows, as dependent upon surviving family members for material and instrumental as well as emotional support. The great majority of widowed persons in contemporary urban industrial societies now live alone, and a substantial fraction (about one-fifth, in the United States) are heads of households still supporting or caring for other family members. The evidence suggests that there has been in the present century a very notable transformation in the life styles and individual and social settings of widows, and to a much lesser extent of widowers. This transformation has been connected to both the development and expansion of public and private pension and income maintenance arrangements and, not less, to changing patterns of education, labor force participation, and work histories of women (Lopata, 1979; Palmore, 1981).

Along with the elements of grief and bereavement associated with widowhood, the newly widowed typically experience serious disorganization of social networks and support systems. In the first place, the very identities of individuals are embedded in their marital roles, although some researchers have felt that this is considerably more the case for women than for men. Second, living arrangements and household economies are typically based upon the marital couple and its arrangements for division of labor, sharing of income and consumption, and organization of relationships with other household members. Among elderly couples this will often include physical care and mutual assistance in instrumental activities of daily living: dressing, washing, feeding, mobility, personal care, and so forth. Finally, most extrahousehold leisure and social activities are organized for participation of couples as couples (although of course in many circles involving widowed elderly participants this will no longer be the case). Inevitably these arrangements are upset and disorganized by the death of a spouse. The surviving spouse is forced to make adjustments.

More than half of the elderly widows live alone or with nonrelatives (Carp, 1976). The older the widow the more likely she is to live alone. Elderly widows constitute a large part of the population below the poverty line and very frequently have very small budgets for housing and other services. They may live in dilapidated, isolated, or unsafe environments. In the largest cities they are often concentrated in public housing with kitchen facilities in areas that then tend to become occupied preponderately by older women. Widowers and other unattached older men are more likely to find accommodations in rooming houses, hotels, or facilities with some availability of meals.

Social Disruption in Widowhood

Widows vary in the types and amounts of social disruption they suffer following the loss of spouse. Personal characteristics, social class, and the nature and the histories of the marital relationships themselves all bear on the manner and extent to which social networks contract or change in widowhood. The age of the widows, their education, and their previous employment attachments and histories affect the adjustments made in widowhood. Younger women experiencing death of husbands are generally less prepared themselves for widowhood, have had fewer friends already widowed as examples and role models. They are more likely to have been part of more exclusively couple- and family-oriented social circles than the older widows. It is the older women who may lose their spouse after several, or even most, of their friends have already experienced such losses.

Women with more education and those with more or higher-level employment experience are better able to take up additional or alternative extrafamily roles following widowhood. They are less dependent upon their children and kin for support of all types than women with fewer personal human capital resources. Middle-class women are more likely than working-class women to have perceived themselves as part of a husband-wife team. Thus their involvement in a wide variety of roles and activities is more seriously impaired by death of their husbands (Troll, Miller, and Atchley, 1979).

The first and most immediate impact of widowhood is generally on the family roles and activities. According to Lopata (1973), the contacts with adult children initially increase, but they diminish later as widows typically withdraw to their own private households and try to maintain some distance from their children's if they are healthy and reasonably independent economically. According to Adams (1968), mutual aid and closeness between widows and their daughters is enhanced over time, but the relationships with sons diminish in intensity.

Relationships with siblings and with extended family also become somewhat more intense immediately after the death of the husband, but taper off over time. Contacts with in-laws diminish or even disappear, especially if children are all grown (Glick, Weiss, and Parkes, 1974). If the widow is frail, impaired, ill, or economically destitute, the relationships with children, siblings, or other family members are rendered both more intense and more complex over time. These involve now the delicate patterns of the widow's dependency, on the one hand, and the obligations of her family members, on the other hand.

Friendship groups consisting entirely of couples are initially supportive of members experiencing widowhood, but eventually the continued participation and integration of the widow or the widower in such groups become awkward (Glick, Weiss, and Parkes, 1974). On the other hand, the friendship groups already comprising mostly, or many, widows or widowers are continuing sources of comfort, interaction, and support for the newly widowed. Indeed, as Troll, Miller, and Atchley (1979) suggest, it may happen that as a group of women friends grows older, those who are still married may sometimes feel left out because their widowed friends do many things as a group that they do not feel free to join. Widowhood may, for these people, bring some compensation of being among old friends again.

Sex-segregated groups and organizations, for example, church groups, ladies' charitable activity clubs, men's bowling and card-playing groups, or other groups organized around interests, often provide avenues of social contacts for widows, although less often for widowers, since they do not usually depend upon having a spouse or being accompanied by someone of opposite sex. Thus, sex-segregated groups can be more comfortable and hospitable for widows and widowers since they do not confront them with being the lone single person.

Working-class widows are more likely to be isolated and suffer extended loneliness than middle-class widows. It is true that middle-class women are more likely than working-class women to have had close companionship relations with husbands. For them the loss of husbands as comrades and companions is probably, on the average, more traumatic. But working-class women, in emphasizing the mother role relatively more and the wife role relatively less than middle-class women, may be less vulnerable to the personal loss associated with transitions to widowhood. The middle-class women are generally in better health, have much more secure income, more education and job skills, and more social options. They have nonfamily friends, organizational experience and activity, and more personal resources accessible.

Age at Widowhood

In a number of studies of widowhood, sharp distinctions appear between the situations, transitions, adaptations, and resocialization of those experiencing widowhood at relatively young ages, say, in middle age, and those undergoing this transition in old age. In her detailed study of widows in the Chicago area, Lopata (1979) analyzed "age as resource" of widows, pointing out that the age at widowhood both influences the manner and degree of disorganization of past social networks and support systems *as well as* the content of the new networks and support systems developed subsequent to widowhood.

Very young widows with no children revert to a kind of singlehood and eligibility for early remarriage. Young mothers and younger middle-aged women, say, those aged 30 to 54 at the death of the husbands, are hardest hit by the event of widowhood: They usually have dependent children. They experience what Lopata calls "widowhood off-time with most friends still married." They face loss of husbands' income and the need to make severe changes in life styles (see, also, Glick, Weiss, and Parkes, 1974). On the other hand, women widowed in these ages may be able to remain in or reenter the labor force and benefit from the status and support that employment provides. Those widowed in their early or mid-fifties typically have the highest average income (except for the younger women who remarry). But often they have the problem of dealing with the grief of their children in addition to their own.

Women who are widowed at ages 55 to 65 are likely to be without dependent children, but they may be in serious economic straits in that they may qualify for full Social Security benefits only at age 65 and for only reduced benefits at age 60. For women in this age group, the income drop forces reorganization of life styles. This occurs while their relationships with still-married friends and the possibilities of male companionship may be limited or strained. The elderly (65+) women experiencing widowhood are most likely to experience social isolation and loss of husband's companionship and links to other people, even if their income and other social roles remain relatively intact. In fact, the elderly widows are the most highly dependent upon Social Security. They have fewer other sources of income than the middle-aged or younger widows, and they have the least well-developed support networks, having had least opportunity to develop or draw involvement of significant others into a support system (Lopata, 1979, Chapter 8).

Summarizing findings of a longitudinal study of aging in the United States carried out over some three decades from 1950 through 1977, Palmore (1981) notes that the event of widowhood appears to be more stressful in middle age than in old age. Widowhood appears to produce lower morale, lower income, more institutionalization, and higher morbidity and mortality rates. Widowhood in old age appeared to have no measurable long-term negative effects. Even among the middle-aged, the long-term effects of the transitions to widowhood appeared to be relatively small. Indeed, death of spouse in late life appeared to bring relief and improved adjustment for those elderly persons who had been caring for a spouse during disability or terminal illness.

The somewhat surprising conclusion that widowhood experienced in old age has no measurable long-term effects on morale, income, institutionalization, morbidity, or mortality is probably best understood in the light of the fact that the longitudinal studies reported introduced statistical controls for a long list of variables characterizing respondents in the initial studies (Palmore, 1981, Appendix). Typical comparisons of elderly widowed and married persons may confound the effects of age, health, income, or other variables correlated with widowhood with those of the event of widowhood. With these and other factors controlled, the findings of the longitudinal studies suggest that the event of widowhood and its accompanying social disruptions and contraction of social networks may be less traumatic and stressful than commonly perceived. Alternatively, the trauma and stress are overcome in the aftermath of the widowhood transition by mechanisms of role substitution, resocialization, or other adaptations. Good health and adequate income are, as in the case of retirement from employment, probably central factors in the ability of individuals to make appropriate and acceptable adaptations to the contraction of social networks implied by the widowhood transition in old age.

LOSS OF FRIENDS, CONFIDANTS, AND INTIMATES THROUGH DEATH, IMPAIRMENT AND DISABILITY, AND UNCOORDINATED ROLE TRANSITIONS

An important type of transition experienced by persons at any age is the gain or loss of friends, intimates, and confidants. This occurs in the course of social encounters and interaction, development of school, work, neighborhood, voluntary organizational, or other contacts and friendships, and movement into or out of residential, work, or social settings of every type. The development of friendship networks during the life course is itself very complex. Presumably the friendship network in early childhood is very limited and circumscribed by home and neighborhood. Later it is expanded to include the school setting. Ultimately the friendship networks of some individuals may range worldwide and be based on a wide variety of axes of contact and interaction. Those of other individuals may be quite circumscribed in numbers of friends, geographic space, and content. The actual study of friendship networks has many difficulties, not least of which is that of arriving at operational definitions of the concept "friend."

However, it seems reasonable to presume that the friendship networks of most individuals grow and expand early in the life course. They come to include kin, confidants, and intimates of one degree or another. Among some individuals, the friendship networks might stabilize at some point fairly early in the life course. Among others the networks might expand virtually throughout the entire life course. We may presume that, among most individuals, there is some age, or some stage in the life course, or some life-course juncture at which the size and complexity of the friendship network stabilizes. Probably for most individuals, it even declines thereafter. In particular, as individuals survive into old age, their friendship networks increasingly decline and are decimated by deaths, impairment, or disability of friends, neighbors, kin, or intimates and confidants.

Loss of friends, intimates, and confidants by death can be as traumatic and as disruptive as the loss of spouse or of other close kin. Obviously the severity of the loss is related to the nature and intensity of the initial relationship. It seems reasonable to surmise that responses of distress and loneliness, and even grief and bereavement, to the deaths of close friends are not uncommon. Moreover, the contraction of the elderly individual's social network renders him with proportionately less social support and interaction at about the same time in which he may be undergoing other kinds of contractions of social networks and support, for example, retirement, widowhood, or child-launching.

In a discussion of formation, duration, and disruption of friendship over the life course, Hess (1972) has pointed out that friendships tend to be homophilous—that is, among persons of similar characteristics—generally. In particular they tend to be homophilous with respect to age. To be sure, some friendships form across age strata, but these are exceptions to the general pattern. Age homogeneity is explicitly endorsed in preadult years, when parents and adult socializing agents widely recognize the peer group as an important auxiliary in the socialization process.

Whether friendships persist or are lost depend upon exigencies affecting both partners in a friendship. Especially in old age, the age-related exigencies working to dissolve a friendship are not matters of personal decision. Rather they are outside the control of the persons involved. Obviously the limiting case is the death of one of the partners, a likelihood that increases with age. Disability or illness can also interfere with the homophilous character of the friendship. Death of close friends has long been recognized as a stressful life event (Dohrenwend and Dohrenwend, 1974; Holmes and Masuda, 1974); in the Duke Longitudinal Studies of aging (Palmore, 1981; Wilson, 1985), death of a close friend was indeed found to affect psychophysiological health outcomes significantly.

Hess points out (1972, p. 381), homophily can also be disturbed, although less abruptly, when *roles* to which the friendships are fused are themselves relinquished. For example, with the relinquishment by one or both friends of parental, work, marital, or community roles, consequent discrepancies in activities and status can increase the cost of interaction. The new inequality of the friends can threaten their relationships unless the shared satisfactions of contact can compensate. On the other hand, the nearly simultaneous role transitions in old age of old friends may, in turn, fortify the friendship and render it even more enduring over time. It is this relationship between *other* role transitions in late life and friendship that has been explored by Blau (1973; 1981), Rosow (1967), and others and discussed in a very important public policy context.

The bearing of role transitions in later life on friendship relationships has been studied and reformulated somewhat by Blau in terms of "role exits":

> The effect of major role exits on older people's friendships depends upon the *prevalence* of these exits among their peers. An exit that places the individual in a deviant position in his or her age or sex group interferes with opportunities to maintain old friendships. For an exit from a major role that places an individual in a minority position among his or her peers differentiates his or her interests from theirs, and thereby reduces the basis of formation and persistence of friendships. But if the same status change becomes predominant in a social group, then the individual who retains the earlier role becomes the deviant one, and it is his or her social participation that suffers (Blau, 1981, p. 77).

This type of finding and discussion amplifies and elucidates the social-network-contracting effects of role transitions discussed earlier in this chapter, to be sure. Beyond this point, the analysis has been drawn upon first by Rosow (1967) and subsequently by Blau and others (Stephens and Bernstein, 1984) to argue the merits of age-segregated housing and account for the success of retirement communities. If the effects of retirement, widowhood, and other late life role transitions on the friendships, friendship formation and duration, and friendship networks depend upon the *prevalence* of such role transitions in the group, then dispersion of older people in a community in effect promotes their social isolation. Such dispersion renders those undergoing role exits, or late life role transitions, small minorities in their communities and residential settings. Concentrating elderly persons in retirement communities or in other relatively age-segregated residential settings also concentrates the field of potential friends and maximizes the prospect of friendship formation and group embeddedness. It is this process, in Rosow's view (1967, 1974), that explains the success of so many retirement communities and which justifies the promotion and encouragement of such communities in public policy.

LOSS OF HEALTH

A very substantial proportion of the elderly, 21 percent of those aged 65 and over in the United States in 1981, reported poor health as a "very serious problem" for them. Moreover, almost half the nonelderly adult population (47 percent and some 40 percent of those themselves aged 65 and over) attributed "very serious problems" of poor health to most people 65 and over (National Council on Aging, 1981; see also Foner, 1986; Kart, 1985; and Burdman, 1986). Thus poor health is both an actual condition for many of the elderly and widely perceived to be a serious problem for the elderly by elderly and nonelderly alike.

Older people are afflicted relatively less often than the young with acute conditions, such as infectious diseases, injuries, or common colds (see, for example, *Statistical Abstract of the U.S., 1988,* Table 167). They are much more often afflicted with chronic conditions, such as heart trouble or deafness (Table 11.4). They are much more likely to suffer impairments and disability restrictions on activities. More than three-fourths of the elderly suffer from at least one chronic condition, and about one-half report two or more such conditions. Almost one-half report some type of impairment, such as hearing impairments (the most frequent), blindness and other visual impairments, mental or nervous conditions, or paralysis or impairment of limbs or extremities. About 24 percent of the elderly report chronic conditions severe enough to prevent them entirely from carrying on one or more major activities. An additional 16 percent report chronic conditions serious enough to cause limitation in amount or kind of some major activity (Table 11.4).

Of course the percentages afflicted among the elderly are higher the more advanced the age, although there are exceptions (for example, hay fever, asthma, hemorrhoids; see Table 11.4). Rates of morbidity and major illness, as well as rates of mortality, are higher at successively higher ages. At the extreme, some 5 percent of the elderly in the United States are residents of institutions at any moment in time. And Palmore (1985) has estimated that about 25 percent of the population will ultimately experience institutionalization at some time in their lives due to frailty, impaired health, or disability.

Among those retiring by their own decision, poor health is the most frequently reported reason. A variety of studies have shown that objective health

Table 11.4.   Persons with Selected Chronic Conditions and with Activity Limitations: Rates and Percents by Age and Sex, United States, 1985

CONDITION	AGE							
	Total	<18	18–44	45–64	65–74	75+	Male	Female
Chronic Conditions Rates per 1000								
Heart condition	82.6	21.2	40.1	129.0	276.8	349.1	78.5	86.4
High blood pressure (hypertension)	125.1	2.3	64.1	258.9	426.8	394.6	114.8	134.8
Varicose veins of lower extremities	30.6	.3	26.4	55.1	68.1	87.9	14.2	45.8
Hemorrhoids	44.3	1.4	54.7	71.0	66.7	53.9	40.2	48.2
Chronic bronchitis	49.7	55.5	40.5	54.3	67.0	55.9	38.3	60.3
Asthma	36.8	47.8	33.4	28.2	48.3	22.2	34.2	39.3
Chronic sinusitis	139.0	59.6	164.4	184.8	151.2	160.0	120.5	156.3
Hay fever, allergic rhinitis w/o asthma	84.0	50.3	111.2	90.2	50.8	55.0	77.0	90.6
Dermatitis, including eczema	39.0	44.5	44.2	28.4	27.3	19.8	31.6	45.9
Arthritis	128.6	2.2	52.1	268.5	459.3	494.7	89.7	164.9
Diabetes	26.2	1.9	9.1	51.9	108.9	95.5	24.0	28.3
Migraine	35.6	12.7	52.9	41.1	20.6	8.5	18.8	51.3
Diseases of urinary system	31.3	5.7	30.0	44.9	61.8	92.0	15.7	45.9
Visual impairments	36.4	10.8	32.8	43.7	76.4	128.8	47.6	25.8
Hearing impairments	90.7	19.8	49.8	159.0	261.9	346.9	107.4	75.1
Deformities orthopedic impairments	112.6	33.2	125.3	160.6	167.9	175.5	108.7	116.2
Persons w/activity Limitations-Percent								
Heart condition	17.4		4.7	21.5		27.1	18.2	16.7
Arthritis and rheumatism	18.9		5.4	22.8		29.7	12.4	24.6
Hypertension	10.5		2.9	15.2		14.2	7.9	12.8
Impairment of back or spine	9.2		12.5	10.4		4.4	8.9	9.4
Impairment of lower extremities, hips	8.9		10.7	8.2		7.8	9.4	8.5
Percent with								
No activity limitation	86.0		92.8	76.6		60.4	86.4	85.6
Activity limitation	14.0		7.2	23.4		39.6	13.6	14.4
in major activity	9.5		4.9	17.5		24.1	9.7	9.4

Source: Adapted from *Statistical Abstract of the United States, 1988,* Tables 172, 173.

conditions and subjectively assessed health are important factors in levels and nature of virtually the entire range of social participation and social relations of the elderly (Palmore, 1981; Habib and Matras, 1987) as well as in levels of life satisfaction. It is in these senses that poor health, illness, and impairment are seen as roles among the elderly; *becoming* ill or impaired is an important category of role transition in late life.

Survival Curves and Morbidity Curves: Disability-Free Life Years

In earlier chapters we discussed the concept of life years lived by a cohort, the idea that the total and average numbers of life years lived have changed over time as mortality has fallen and survival rates increased. By *partitioning the total life years* in various ways, it was possible also to develop and illustrate the idea that the composition of total life years with respect to activities such as work, parenting, and marital states has also changed. All these have important consequences for the individual life course and life course transitions, the family cycle, and patterns of dependency, obligations, and entitlements through the life course. They also have important implications for social, economic, and political organization. In this chapter we have already invoked some of these ideas with reference to transitions to the empty nest, retirement, and widowhood, and to their timing and durations.

In a corresponding vein, it is useful and illuminating to partition the life years lived by cohorts and individuals into those characterized by full health and those characterized by impairment, disability, or illness. There are some serious conceptual and technical difficulties in estimation of healthy and nonhealthy life years. Data on morbidity and disability gleaned from national surveys of health have provided opportunities for some pioneering efforts toward such measurement and estimation.

Using data from the 1978 Canada Health Survey on short-term disability and on long-term activity restriction, Wilkins and Adams (1983a; 1983b) were able to partition life years at each age by categories of health restrictions. They were able to calculate "health expectancy," that is, average numbers of life years remaining, at birth and at subsequent years in each of the health categories. For example, they estimated that total life expectancy at birth for Canadian males and females based on 1978 mortality and disability conditions can be described as follows:

	MALES	*FEMALES*
Total life expectancy	70.8	78.3
Long-term institutionalization	0.8	1.5
Major activity impossible	3.0	1.3
Major activity restricted	5.4	8.7
Minor activity restricted	1.3	2.2
Short-term disability only	1.1	1.8
Activities not restricted = Disability-Free Life Expectancy	59.2	62.8

Thus of the total life expectancy at birth of 70.8 years for Canadian males, 59.2 years (84 percent) are estimated to be "disability-free" years. Of the total life expectancy at birth of 78.3 years for Canadian women, 62.8 years (80 percent) are estimated to be "disability-free" years. That a smaller percentage of the women's total life years are "disability-free" is, of course, not surprising in view of the fact that a larger proportion of total women's life years are life years lived at older ages (see Chapter 3). Wilkins and Adams also found variations by socioeconomic group and by geographic region in Canada.

The broad partitioning of life years at each age by health status is shown in Figure 11.4. The top curves show survival probabilities, and the areas under the top curves show total life years lived by Canadian males and females, under 1978 mortality conditions. Note that these are the same curves first shown in Figure 3.1 in introducing the concepts of survival and life years. The bottom curves, which we may denote morbidity curves, show estimated probabilities of survival in good health, that is, not restricted in activities due to health impairment. The areas under the bottom curves in Figure 11.4, then, represent healthy life years lived by a cohort at each age and altogether until all cohort members die. The shaded area between the total survival and the morbidity curves represents the total "impaired" life years lived by the cohort.

Health expectancy at selected ages for Canadian males and females in the late 1970s is shown in Table 11.5. The table shows total life expectancy, an estimate of "disability-free life" as discussed and illustrated above, and an estimate of "quality-adjusted life" at birth and at selected ages. "Quality-adjusted life" years are taken as weighted sums of restricted life years involving institutionalization (weight = 0.3), restricted life years not involving institutionalization (weight = 0.5), and life years free of restrictions (weight = 1.0). Thus "quality adjusted" life years may be viewed as life years

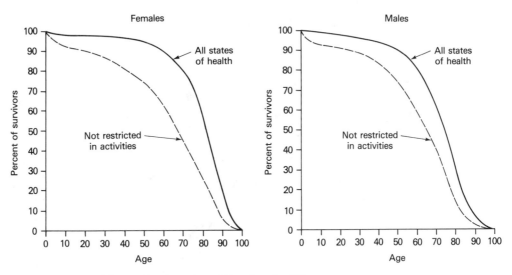

Figure 11.4   Health Status of Survivors, Age and Sex, Canada, 1978.
Source: Wilkens and Adams, 1983a.

Table 11.5.   Health Expectancy by Sex and Age. Canada. Late 1970's

Age	TOTAL LIFE EXPECTANCY		DISABILITY-FREE LIFE EXPECTANCY		QUALITY-ADJUSTED LIFE EXPECTANCY	
	Males	Females	Males	Females	Males	Females
At Birth	70.8	78.3	59.2	62.8	65.8	71.7
15 years	57.2	64.5	46.2	49.4	52.4	58.1
25 years	48.1	54.8	37.6	40.4	43.5	48.7
45 years	29.6	35.7	20.6	23.6	25.6	30.5
65 years	14.4	18.7	8.2	9.9	11.5	14.7
75 years	8.9	11.7	4.6	5.2	6.9	8.6

Source: R. Wilkins and O.B. Adams, "Health Expectancy in Canada, Late 1970's: Demographic, Regional, and Social Dimensions," *American Journal of Public Health,* 73. 1983(9):1073–80. Table 3.

unimpaired or only mildly impaired. In the table, we note again that total life expectancy of women at birth exceeds that of men by 7.5 years. The difference is reduced by half if only years free of health-related restrictions are considered. As Wilkins and Adams (1983a) note, "death undoubtedly eliminated many men who, had they survived, might well have been impaired or perhaps institutionalized."

For both males and females at birth, quality-adjusted life expectancy amounted to more than 90 percent of total life expectancy. Even in old age quality-adjusted life expectancy constitutes a large proportion of remaining life years, although by age 65 nearly half of all remaining years were expected to be lived with at least some degree of activity-restricting health impairment (Table 11.5).

It is appropriate to mention here again the concept of rectangularization of the survival curve, the historical extension of survival to later ages and expansion of total life years that have accompanied the long-term declines in mortality (Figure 11.5). Each survival curve is, theoretically at least, associated with a

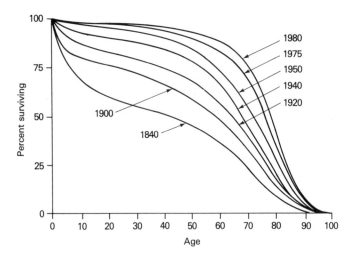

Figure 11.5   Changes in Survivorship Curves in the United States in the Twentieth Century.
Source: Fries, 1984.

morbidity curve of the kind illustrated for Canada in Figure 11.4. A very important question concerns the shifts in the morbidity curve in relationship to the total survival curve. To the extent that the morbidity curve is fixed and unchanging over time, the rectangularization of the survival curve implies expansion of the impaired life years, represented by the expanding area between the survival and morbidity curves. To the extent that the morbidity curve also undergoes rectangularization, then improved survival and increasing total life years imply no change, or even reduction, in impaired life years.

As mentioned in Chapter 1, the actual trends in the morbidity curve relative to the survival curve are a matter of considerable controversy among researchers. One view holds that there is compression or rectangularization of the morbidity curve already taking place or in sight in the near future (Fries, 1980, 1983). An opposite view suggests that increasing longevity has not been accompanied by health improvements sufficient to prevent great growth in the numbers of impaired and disabled persons and life years (Verbrugge, 1984).

Illness and Other Role Transitions

Among events and role transitions in late life, major illness is *not* the most frequent. In the Duke Longitudinal Studies of aging, among respondents initially aged 45 to 69 years of age and studied over periods totaling about six years, the most frequently reported life events were the transition to empty nest. Retirement was the next most frequent event. Widowhood was the least frequent (just under 8 percent of the respondents initially married and, thus, at risk during the period of the study) among life events reported. Major illness was reported by some 26 percent of the respondents, and some reported *several* major illnesses in the period (Palmore, 1985).

An important finding of the Duke Longitudinal Study was that most life events have only minor negative effects on either physical adaptation or on social-psychological adaptation. Major medical events (major illnesses) do have the expected negative effects on physical adaptation, but they have little effect on social-psychological adaptation. The researchers concluded that this finding seems to indicate that most seriously ill persons manage to limit any social-psychological reactions to a short period after the illness and tend to return to baseline condition within a few months.

When several such events occurred to the same individual during the study they tended to cumulate in their impact, most clearly on the measures of satisfaction. Those respondents with the least personal and social resources had more difficulty adapting to these events. Most people with the resources normally available can adapt successfully to any single one of the life events within a short time. However, the occurrence of several events simultaneously or consecutively tends to have long-term negative effects, especially for those with least resources (Palmore, 1985). The frail elderly or those most at risk are those who have experienced several of the late life transitions within a short period of time and those with poor physical, psychological, or social resources for coping with the events.

Thus, loss of health is a late life role transition and operates to reduce the scope and intensity of social relations in two ways. First, it is a factor in the frequency and timing of other late life role transitions, particularly in retirement and in loss of friends. Second, it circumscribes the activity and the social relationships of ill, impaired, or disabled elderly generally, and for some, to the extent of institutionalization and nearly complete dependency.

SUMMARY

As we have seen in earlier chapters, role transitions and resocialization take place at many junctures in the life course. For the most part, these entail the expansion of social participation and networks of individuals at the various junctures. Sometimes they entail replacement of one role or activity pattern with another. It is in old age where the role transitions are frequently associated with contraction of social networks and diminution of social participation. Yet the most sophisticated studies of changes over time in both scope and density of social networks and the frequency and intensity of social participation suggest that the life events and role transitions in old age do not inevitably entail severe contraction of networks. Thus Palmore (1981) writing of the empty-nest transition reported, that there is no clear evidence that children leaving home produces any substantial negative effects. On the contrary, the Duke Longitudinal Study of aging data suggest rather that the last child's leaving home tended to increase life satisfaction and to increase "affect balance" for elderly respondents.

Similarly, retirement was found to produce no significant changes in self-rated health, physician-rated health, or a number of other measures of health or illness. Retirement was related to some decrease in numbers of persons with whom interaction takes place, but not in attendance at religious services, other meetings, and the like, nor to any significant change in the number of friends visited. Indeed, there was some increase in the numbers of neighbors known well enough to visit.

On the other hand, retirement is consistently found to be associated with a substantial loss (on the average, 28 percent decline, in the Duke Longitudinal Study) of family income. Retirees consistently report declines in the adequacy (as well as in the amount) of their incomes. Those retiring due to mandatory retirement provisions were typically lower in activity levels, adjustment ratings, and levels of life satisfaction reported than other retirees. Elderly persons returning to full-time employment after retirement, however, were higher than all others on activity, adjustment, and life satisfaction scales.

Widowhood has been cast as the most traumatic of all life events and transitions in late life. To be sure, there are a variety of research findings pointing to lower morale, lower incomes, higher rates of institutionalization, higher mortality, and higher suicide rates among widows than among those married. Widows do usually increase contact with their children, especially daughters, and both widows and widowers are somewhat more likely than married parents to move in with children. They increase contacts temporarily with other relatives, although these diminish ultimately.

Widowhood's effects on the number and nature of friendships are related to the marital status of the friends; widowhood tends to increase interaction with widowed friends, but to decrease interaction with married friends. In the Duke Longitudinal Study, however, it was found that widowhood produced a small decline in measures of life satisfaction and some minor increase in psychosomatic symptoms. There are no other measurable negative effects on health or adjustment.

Having friends is evidently not only a source of pleasure and satisfaction in and of itself. It is also a buffer against the traumas of widowhood, retirement, illness, or reduction of various aspects of functioning and activity. There is some cross-sectional evidence suggesting that the number and intensity of friendships and interaction with friends in various social activities and settings are less frequent among the old-old than among the young-old. At least one study (Habib and Matras, 1987b) relates this age variation to perceived health conditions which, on the average, are lower among the old-old. The extent to which the loss of friends is directly implicated in reduction of social interaction and contraction of social networks remains obscure.

Finally, the major medical events (those requiring hospitalization) entailing loss of health produce some decline in activity. According to Palmore's report of findings of the Duke Longitudinal study, they also do not entail significant long-term decline of other facets of adjustment. More generally, the *single* life events or role transitions, by themselves, do not appear to be sufficiently stressful to produce long-term negative effects on adjustment. There is no clear evidence to impute to them any severe contraction of social networks or social support.

The role transitions are *additive* over the later part of the life course; the larger the number of stressful events and role transitions the greater the negative effects on adjustment, functioning, and activity. Personal and psychological resources (intelligence and mental health) and social resources (high income, high socioeconomic status, large initial social networks) help maintain health, happiness, and life satisfaction. They do not, however, affect other measures of social-psychological adjustment. Greater health resources appear to help in maintaining health after such role transitions, but they do not appear to help in social-psychological adaptation (Palmore, 1981). In the next chapter we turn to family and societal resources, processes, and mechanisms for addressing the needs and dependencies of the elderly.

12

DEPENDENCY, OBLIGATIONS, AND ENTITLEMENTS

the changing mix of family,
market, and societal responses

INTRODUCTION

In the review of sociological theories of aging late in the life course of the preceding chapters, the central motif was the characteristic role transitions. These generally entail at least some contraction of social networks. Only exceptionally do the elderly maintain their peak patterns of social participation, exchange, and interaction until the end of life. Whether we agree to call it disengagement or something else, and whether or not there are role substitutions and partially compensatory transitions, the kinds of role transitions discussed—child-launching, retirement, widowhood and loss of intimates, and physical or mental health impairment—are indeed frequently accompanied by quite marked and sometimes dramatic decline in social participation and exchange.

Two of the variables mentioned in the role transition processes of old age—(1) the nature and severity of the dependency associated with these transitions, and (2) their timing in the life course—are of particular salience for public policy. This is because the very necessity or appropriateness of public policy responses is generally gauged with reference to the perceived severity of need or dependency along with the absence or inadequacy of private responses. The volume or quantity of public input required is a function of the life-course timing. Put in another familiar way, the requirements are a function of the numbers or proportions of life years in need or dependency that must be addressed. As a crude example, if *all* the surviving elderly were to become completely helpless and dependent exactly one week prior to death, this would pose a certain kind of problem for provision of care and attention that societies would have to address.

If all were to become completely helpless and dependent much earlier, say, fifteen years prior to death (that is, if all the elderly became completely helpless and dependent and survive for fifteen helpless and dependent years thereafter) a quite different type of problem would be posed for societies.

In fact, as we noted earlier, we do not yet have very satisfactory ways of measuring, estimating, or even describing the types and severities of dependency and need associated with these transitions. Our measurement of their timing in the life course is only in its earliest stages. Retrospective and longitudinal studies, synthetic cohort studies, and mathematical modeling are only beginning to show us some of the patterns of ages and volumes of life years in retirement, empty nest states, widowhood, or impaired health or disability. Probably no less important, they are also beginning to show us the volume of life years in the later stages of the life course that are *free* of impairment or dependency.

Perhaps it is more accurate to say that we are learning to recognize the volumes of life years in middle and old age that have *become* free of impairment or dependency for more recent cohorts in consequence of (1) improved income, levels of living, and health earlier in the life course and (2) improved arrangements for income maintenance, health care, and social support later in the life course. In all events, there has been great increase in the numbers of elderly persons in Western populations, the absolute and relative numbers of life years lived in later life, and the patterns of need and dependency characterizing significant parts of those populations and those life years. These have posed continuing challenges to families and primary social groups as well as to societal private market and public sector institutions.

A number of types of changes and trends have been noted throughout this book. These included increased total longevity and life years, diminishing life years in paid employment and parenting, declining fertility and increasing population aging, increasing productivity and per capita income, and improved communications, access to information and knowledge, and mutual visibility. These changes and trends have rendered many of the responses—whether traditional or innovative—very controversial philosophically, economically, and politically as well as strongly laden with emotion. We examine next some of the types of responses to issues of income maintenance, health care, and social support of the elderly.

INCOME MAINTENANCE: SELF-RELIANCE, RUGGED INDIVIDUALISM, FILIAL PIETY, AND THE POLITICAL ECONOMY OF PUBLIC PENSIONS

The image of elderly parents financially supported and cared for in their later years by loving, grateful, dutiful, and unselfish children and grandchildren in a more traditional and perhaps more humane and ordered past is often projected in stark contrast to that of present-day elderly. Today's elderly, it is often asserted, are forced to find sustenance from public pensions, live in households apart from their unappreciative children, and buy or receive the care they need in old age from commercial or public purveyors of services and welfare.

Self-Reliance and Filial Piety

There is indeed evidence to support the presence of a variety of arrangements for intergenerational transfer of resources, wealth, and care and support obligations among parents and children in nonindustrial and preindustrial societies (Goody, 1976). There are also studies of such transfers and exchanges in contemporary societies (Sussman, 1976). The portrayal of surviving elders sharing households and incomes of their adult children has been attacked and shown to have been grossly exaggerated in modern European history (Laslett, 1985). It seems quite clear that the numbers surviving to old age were relatively much smaller. Elderly men sought and held on to self- or wage-employment as long as they were physically able. There was very extensive poverty among the elderly.

There does not seem to be much evidence showing the actual frequency or extent of direct financial support of elderly persons by their own children in contemporary Western societies. There have, however, been frequent *assertions* of traditional patterns of middle-aged persons supporting their elderly parents even by sophisticated economists (Boulding, 1961; Kreps, 1976). There do remain significant numbers of elderly sharing households, and presumably household income whatever its sources, with their unmarried and married children. Intergenerational income transfers are now being mediated, in effect, by the tax and public pension systems (Myles, 1984, pp. 25–26).

Some of the elderly continue to have income from earnings in paid employment; some have income from private employee pensions; a small proportion have income from privately owned assets. The large majority of the elderly in the Western capitalist democracies, however, have public pensions as their primary sources of income. In the United States, Social Security retirement income is the major source of income for the majority of the elderly.

The admonition to save and look after one's material needs in old age and retirement during active working life has been unrealistic for all wage and salary earners except the minority with highest earnings. Both the relative numbers of landowning self-employed farmers, proprietors, and property-owners in the past *and* their ability to convert intergenerational transfer of their property rights into schemes for income maintenance and support in old age have probably been exaggerated. What does seem clear is that prior to the introduction and universalization of public health care and pension schemes, neither personal savings nor support by children have sufficed to prevent widespread poverty, low levels of living, and inability to cover the costs of medical care among the elderly retired from (dismissed or otherwise unable to continue in) paid employment.

Early Pension Schemes

The growth of private and trade union pension and annuity schemes has been very recent and is still largely restricted to a minority with either relatively high incomes or in employment protected and covered by collective agreements including such arrangements. Indeed, these have also been publicly supported or tax-subsidized in considerable measure, since their growth has been largely contingent upon a variety of tax deferrals and deductions to individuals, employers, or both.

Early public pension schemes in Europe in the late nineteenth century and in North America in the first half of this century were primarily extensions of provisions for public assistance to the indigent elderly. They were designed to ease the extreme poverty of the least privileged members of society (Myles, 1984, 1986). Their benefits were low and of a subsistence character rather than representing any intent to provide retirement income in place of employment income. A major departure from the social assistance programs of the countries in which they were adopted was their universality of coverage and entitlements. They extended benefits to all citizens as a matter of right. This was a departure from, or more often in addition to, the means-tested availability of benefits of the earlier social assistance schemes.

Modern Universalized Public Pension Schemes

It was largely after World War II that the social insurance schemes evolved and were transformed from social assistance benefits for the indigent into a retirement wage for workers. In some countries, where a universal flat benefit system had been in place, this was achieved by addition of a second tier of earnings-related pensions. Canada, for example, had had a flat benefit Old Age Security scheme in place since 1927. Canada universalized the program with the passage of the Old Age Security Act in 1951 while leaving benefit levels quite low. A second tier, the Canada Pension Plan, was introduced in 1965, providing for additional earnings-related benefits.

In other countries, where the initial universal public pension scheme was of a social insurance type, the transition to a retirement wage was effected by increasing benefit entitlements at all income levels and by raising the income ceiling of covered earnings. In the United States this took place primarily during the 1968 to 1972 period. It culminated in the 1972 reforms that extended coverage, introduced medical coverage (in July 1966) and full index of pension benefits to consumer price levels, and liberalized retirement options.

Thus the modern public old-age pension systems benefit not just the poor. Rather, they benefit also the middle class when confronting the threat of poverty of old age. They obviously benefit not just the elderly but also their middle-aged or younger offspring who would otherwise carry or share the direct support of the elderly.

Financing Pension Plans

There are basically four ways of financing pension plans. Three of them involve financing the income entitlements over the later, generally postemployment, life years of *cohorts*. Only one involves *personal* savings and dissavings over the employment and the nonemployment years respectively of the individual life course.

Personal Savings   The *personal savings* type of financing involves simply accumulation of savings or assets, and their accumulated compound interest, over some period of life in which earnings suffice to allow such saving. The allocation or expenditure, or dissaving, of these funds and assets takes place in later life. The unused or unspent remainder if any is transferred to heirs upon the death of the individual.

It is this type of saving or pension scheme that is generally implicit in the idea of saving for old age. Many such schemes currently enjoy certain kinds of public encouragement and subsidy through tax deferrals, as in Individual Retirement Accounts (IRAs) or Keogh plans in the United States and Recognized Retirement Savings Plan (RRSP) and Recognized Retirement Income Fund (RRIF) plans in Canada. In the United States about 17 percent of all employees held IRAs in 1983 (*Statistical Abstract of the U.S., 1988,* Table 567). Less directly, there are various tax deferral options for certain kinds of investments, but they remain primarily options available only to those earning relatively high incomes.

Most savings schemes accessible to lower-income earners have been vulnerable to very serious erosion of their value by inflation. Yet the rhetoric and normative encouragement of self-reliance and savings continue to support high levels of such saving. In fact, though, they have had only minimal benefits for income maintenance in later life, often wiped out either by inflation or by sudden massive expenditures or need.

Fully Funded Pension Plans　The type of pension insurance scheme under which a *cohort* accumulates savings during its working years and makes benefit payments upon withdrawal from employment only to those of the cohort surviving in retirement for as long as they survive is called a *fully funded* pension plan. Like a life insurance scheme, the fully funded pension plan invests the savings, or contributions to the plan, of the participants and beneficiaries themselves, accumulated while most or all are alive and employed. The plan uses these funds to make annual payouts for each of the participant's remaining life years following retirement.

Obviously not all participants will live the same number of years following retirement, although all may have had the same or nearly the same numbers of years of employment and contributions accumulated. Those surviving only briefly after retirement receive relatively small total payouts or benefits. Those surviving longer receive benefits over the longer period and so a greater total payout. Yet in such a fully funded pension scheme each cohort does assure that each participant in the plan receives income and pension benefits for as long as he or she survives. Each cohort finances its pension benefits from its own accumulated savings and contributions.

Most private, that is, nongovernment-sponsored pension plans including private firm- and trade union-sponsored plans, are fully funded plans. Again, they may be not entirely private in that (1) they are regulated by legislation and government regulatory agencies, and (2) they may receive certain government or tax concessions or subsidies. In some situations they may also not be strictly fully funded. Supplemental funds may be infused to assure promised or contracted payouts and benefits or to raise the benefits beyond those initially promised.

Participation of American employees in private pension plans has been increasing in recent decades. In 1985 about 43 percent of American employees under conventional retirement age (below age 65) were covered by such plans (Table 12.1). Coverage of male employees is overall more extensive than for female employees. The youngest employees (under 25) of both sexes are only infrequently covered by private

Table 12.1. Pension Plan Coverage of Civilian Workers by Wage or Salary Income: 1985

SEX, AGE	NUMBER WITH COVERAGE (1,000)					PERCENT OF TOTAL CIVILIAN WORKERS				
	Total[a]	$5,000– $9,999	$10,000– $14,999	$15,000– $19,999	$20,000– and over	Total[a]	$5,000– $9,999	$10,000– $14,999	$15,000– $19,999	$20,000– and over
Total	**48,959**	**3,930**	**7,147**	**8,491**	**27,826**	**42.8**	**21.9**	**40.9**	**59.4**	**73.4**
Male[a]	20,083	1,190	2,508	4,046	20,787	47.5	16.8	33.0	54.6	72.8
15–24 years old	1,861	320	404	488	488	14.0	12.3	22.1	47.0	53.7
25–34 years old	8,346	322	900	1,436	5,582	46.9	15.8	30.9	49.7	65.6
35–44 years old	8,330	174	465	926	6,708	63.4	18.9	37.3	59.4	76.1
45–64 years old	10,064	297	691	1,132	7,778	66.4	26.3	46.2	62.9	78.8
Female[b]	19,876	2,740	4,639	4,445	7,037	37.4	25.3	46.9	64.6	75.1
15–24 years old	1,729	442	629	304	157	13.9	17.2	35.5	50.3	49.7
25–34 years old	6,158	687	1,463	1,563	2,179	40.9	23.2	45.9	62.0	68.6
35–44 years old	5,415	612	1,093	1,179	2,333	46.7	26.7	48.8	66.2	78.6
45–64 years old	6,254	920	1,400	1,358	2,304	49.3	34.0	54.5	71.6	82.0

[a]Includes workers with income under $5,000, not shown separately.
[b]Includes persons 65 years old and over, not shown separately.
Source: U.S. Bureau of the Census, *Statistical Abstract of the United States, 1988* (Washington, D.C.: Government Printing Office, 1987), Table 568.

pension plans. Almost two-thirds of male employees aged 35 to 64 years are covered, compared to less than half of the men aged 25 to 34 and less than half the women in any of the age groups between 25 and 64.

Private pension coverage is much lower among employees in the low wage and salary level groups and higher among the much larger middle- and higher-income groups, reflecting also differences between full-time and part-time employees. Most of the male-female disparities in private pension coverage are due to the earnings and full-time and part-time differences between male and female employees. Within each of the income groupings private pension coverage is more frequent among women employees than among men (Table 12.1).

Pay-as-you-go Pension Plans Pension schemes that create and maintain funds *into which* currently employed persons pay savings, contributions, or taxes and *out of which* currently retired persons are paid retirement benefits are called *pay-as-you-go* pension plans. In such plans current outlays for those entitled to benefits are financed by taxes and contributions of those currently employed and whose own entitlement to benefits and payouts will begin only at some future date. In the United States, the Social Security Act, and in Canada, the Canada Pension Plan and the Quebec Pension Plan, are of this form. Funds collected from employees and employers as the Social Security tax are *earmarked* for payment as benefits to contributors and participants in these plans. Depending upon the actual financial situation of the plans, beneficiaries typically do not receive benefits from funds which they (or their cohorts) save directly. Rather, they receive benefits financed by Social Security payments, taxes, and contributions of current employees, savers, and contributors into the fund.

Pay-as-you-go pension plans have become the largest public pension plans and have the most extensive and complex provisions of benefits and eligibility. In the United States, the Social Security system is by far the largest public pension scheme. It is the main source of income and economic security for millions of retired, disabled, or surviving elderly persons and couples. It is the main source of public funding for health care. At the same time it is a major source of stability in the economy, guaranteeing directly the purchasing power, consumption, and demand generated by the part of the population—the elderly—directly supported. It indirectly aids the consumption and demand generated by the part of the population that would otherwise have to bear or share in support of the elderly.

Between 1960 and 1985, while the total U.S. labor force grew by about 61 percent as the baby boom generation entered employment, the number covered by public social insurance plans, primarily Social Security, increased by about 75 percent (Table 12.2). About 91 percent of the total labor force of 117.5 million was covered by public retirement programs. Almost as many were also covered by unemployment insurance and by workers' compensation programs as well.

The Social Security system, and other pay-as-you-go public pension plans, are not insurance or savings schemes, even though they may have been cast or sold as such to legislators or a public taken up with self-reliance rhetorics and ideologies. In the United States the Social Security program is named *Old Age, Survivors, Disability, and Health Insurance* (OASDHI). To be sure benefits are typically linked

Table 12.2.   Estimated Workers Under Social Insurance Programs: 1960 to 1985 (In millions, except percent. As of December, except as noted.)

EMPLOYMENT AND COVERAGE STATUS	1960	1970	1975	1980	1985
Total labor force[a, b]	73.1	86.2	96.2	109.1	117.5
Paid civilian population	64.6	77.6	86.0	98.9	107.7
Wage and salary workers	55.3	70.8	78.7	90.2	98.5
Self-employed	9.3	6.9	7.3	8.7	9.2
Unpaid family workers	1.4	.8	.7	.6	.4
Unemployed	4.5	2.6	7.3	7.4	7.7
Armed Forces[b]	2.5	3.4	2.2	2.1	1.7
Civilian population covered by					
Public retirement programs	**60.9**	**75.3**	**83.7**	**96.4**	**106.9**
OASDHI[c]	55.4	69.2	77.0	89.3	99.7
Wage and salary workers	48.0	63.4	70.6	81.8	91.2
Percent of all wage and salary workers	86.8	89.5	89.7	90.7	92.6
Self-employed	7.4	5.8	6.4	7.5	8.5
Railroad retirement	.9	.6	.5	.5	.3
Public employees retirement[d]	4.6	5.5	6.2	6.6	6.9
Unemployment insurance	**43.7**	**55.8**	**69.7**	**87.2**	**98.2**
Workers' compensation	**44.6**	**59.0**	**68.6**	**79.1**	**87.0**
Temporary disability insurance	**11.3**	**14.6**	**15.7**	**18.4**	**19.8**

[a]Data from U.S. Bureau of Labor Statistics and based on U.S. Bureau of the Census' Current Population Survey; see text, section 1, and Appendix III. [b]Excludes Armed Forces overseas beginning 1983.
[c]OASDHI = Old-age, survivors, disability, and health insurance. Excludes members of Armed Forces and railroad employees.
[d]Data represent yearly averages. Excludes State and local government employees covered by both OASDHI and their own retirement program.
Source: U.S. Bureau of the Census, Statistical Abstract of the United States 1988 (Washington, D.C.: Government Printing Office, 1987), Table 559.

to past earnings levels and to levels and durations of employee and employer taxes or contributions. But, the relationships between payments into the fund and benefits received is neither based on principles of savings and compounded interest calculations nor on principles of insurance and actuarial calculations. Rather, they are based entirely on legislative determination and decision.

It is the actual or anticipated shortages of money in these funds, relative to promised benefits for current and future retirees and claimants, that have been the cause of fiscal concern and, as some would have it, the coming financial crisis facing welfare states and their income maintenance programs. Initially these funds receive payments from many young and middle-aged participants, have few claims and low levels of payouts because of the small numbers in the retirement ages and the low eligibility for benefits among survivors and retirees. Thus they actually generate surpluses of funds.

As the system matures, the numbers of claimants as well as the levels of benefits have grown. Indeed as the numbers of Social Security claimants, the levels of benefits, and the total payout grow, there are fears and calculations that the level of Social Security taxes and payments received from current and new employees and participants will not suffice to cover the outlays. Resolution of such problems is possible either by reducing benefits or eligibility, by increasing Social Security taxes, or financing benefits from other sources. We return to this issue later.

General Revenue-Financed Pension Plans   The final type of financing for public pension plans is one drawing on general state or governmental revenues for covering the costs of pension benefits and outlays. In Canada the Old Age Security program is financed by general revenues. In the United States the pensions of government employees are financed by general revenues, as are the pensions of retired military personnel (through the defense budget), although many are covered by Social Security as well. Similarly, other income maintenance programs are financed in the United States by general revenues, generally under the Health, Education, and Welfare budgets.

Earmarked Funds versus General Revenue Financing   The creation of special earmarked funds for financing public pension plans has both historical and political facets, at least in the United States. The original Social Security Act of 1935 was enacted in an ideological and rhetorical climate quite intolerant of the principle of government transfers or subsidies to individuals or families except in most exceptional distress. The act was cast as a compulsory savings and insurance scheme out of which eligible beneficiaries were to be repaid their earlier forced savings. In fact, the Social Security contributions are equivalent to an additional income tax for covered individuals, except that the tax is distinctly regressive rather than progressive like most income taxes. Social Security benefits are legislated entitlements, rather than either insurance payments or savings returned with interest. A variety of considerations combine to press for continuation of the distinct earmarked pension funds rather than their merger with general revenues. They include the historical inertia, the vested interests of administrators of the funds, the favored tax position of the higher income groups, and the availability of a separate pension-contribution-based pool of capital. Sometimes they include the fears that pension funds deposited into general revenues could be used for general purposes and depleted with no means of meeting pension obligations.

Ongoing Issues Surrounding Public Pension Plans

The failure of recent attacks of conservative governments in North America and Europe on various features of the eligibility and benefit levels of public pension plans has highlighted the broad public support that these programs enjoy. Yet there remain political, ideological, and practical issues surrounding public pension plans that continue to evoke lively debate and, indeed, are close to the heart of the major social, political, and ideological cleavages of modern societies.

Benefit Levels   A major issue surrounds the level of benefits that should be paid by public pension plans to fully retired persons. This issue is also the question of whether public pensions should suffice simply to assure subsistence of retired persons or whether they should replace employment earnings. If the latter, in what relationship should they be to the levels of previous employment earnings? (The relationship between total pension benefits and preretirement earnings, that is, the ratio of benefits to earnings, is conventionally called the *replacement rate*.)

A low level of public pension benefits is generally perceived to cost less to the economy, taxpayers, and current contributors to pay-as-you-go pension plans. It also discourages, or encourages, postponement of retirement of employees who are not disabled and do not have additional or alternative sources of income support. Low benefit levels also encourage and sustain alternative, private, pension plans and schemes for those wishing or able to pay for higher retirement benefits than provided by the public plans.

Private sector financial circles, including the banks, insurance companies, and large corporations, have always viewed accumulated pension funds as a major source of investment capital and have been very strongly opposed to state control or even regulation of such funds. They have, accordingly, always viewed public pension schemes as competing unfairly with the private pension plans whose funds are retained in control of private sector financial institutions and, hence, have a long and reasonably successful history of combatting the expansion of public pension coverage and benefits.

Low levels of pension benefits also leave those not employed and without other sources of income impoverished and often dependent upon family or public assistance. Low universal levels of benefits, supplemented by means-tested assistance to those without other income, however, are often viewed as morally and philosophically more acceptable than are high public pension benefits, or perhaps more acceptable than *any* public benefits to those not in need. The latter should, after all, be self-reliant and sufficiently prudent and provident to look after their retirement needs themselves, in this view.

The considerations favoring high levels of public pension benefits include, of course, concern for the needs, well-being, independence, and dignity of the elderly themselves. This concern is also combined with the concern for the freedom from possibly oppressive obligations and for the well-being of the children and families of the elderly. For both the elderly and their offspring, adequate public pension benefit levels are often the only alternative to stigmatization associated with means-tested public assistance.

Another, and perhaps more broadly compelling, consideration favoring high levels of benefits is the perceived effects of high benefit levels in encouraging retirement, discouraging reentry of the elderly into the labor market, and improving the employment and career prospects for younger and middle-aged employees. It is this facet of retirement in general, and of high retirement benefits in particular, which has drawn the support of trade unions and sometimes of business and government as well. The interests of all three converge in favor of earlier and more universal retirement. Trade unions seek to assure employment for prime working age membership. Business firms seek younger, cheaper, and putatively more able or more efficient employees. And governments seek to reduce redundancy and unemployment in the labor market.

In 1986 the number of retired workers receiving Social Security benefits reached almost 23 million; the average U.S. Social Security monthly benefit was $488 to individual retired workers and $831 to retired couples (Table 12.3). Table 12.3 shows

Table 12.3. Social Security (OASDI)–Benefits, by Type of Beneficiary: 1970 to 1986 (A person eligible to receive more than one type of benefit is generally classified or counted only once as a retired-worker beneficiary. OASDI = Old-age, survivors, and disability insurance.)

TYPE OF BENEFICIARY	1970	1975	1980	1985	1986
	Benefits in Current-Payment Status[a] (end of year)				
Number of benefits (1,000)	**26,229**	**32,086**	**35,585**	**37,058**	**37,708**
Retired workers[b] (1,000)	13,349	16,588	19,562	22,432	22,987
Disabled workers[c] (1,000)	1,493	2,489	2,859	2,657	2,727
Wives and husbands[b, d] (1,000)	2,952	3,320	3,477	3,375	3,388
Children (1,000)	4,122	4,972	4,607	3,319	3,291
Under age 18	3,315	3,835	3,423	2,699	2,661
Disabled children[e]	271	362	450	526	545
Students[f]	537	774	733	94	84
Of retired workers	546	643	639	457	450
Of deceased workers	2,688	2,919	2,610	1,917	1,875
Of disabled workers	889	1,411	1,358	945	965
Widowed mothers[g] (1,000)	523	582	562	372	350
Widows and widowers[b, h] (1,000)	3,227	3,889	4,411	4,863	4,931
Parents[b] (1,000)	29	21	15	10	7
Special benefits[h] (1,000)	534	224	93	32	25
Average monthly benefit, current dollars					
Retired workers[b]	118	207	341	479	488
Retired worker and wife[b]	199	344	567	814	831
Disabled workers[c]	131	226	371	484	488
Wives and husbands[b, d]	59	100	164	236	241
Children of retired workers	45	77	140	198	204
Children of deceased workers	82	139	240	330	337
Children of disabled workers	39	62	110	142	141
Widowed mothers[g]	87	147	246	332	338
Widows and widowers, nondisabled[b]	102	194	311	433	444
Parents[b]	103	172	276	378	387
Special benefits[i]	45	69	105	138	140
Average monthly benefit, constant (1986) dollars					
Retired workers[b]	328	412	437	484	488
Retired worker and wife[b]	553	685	726	823	831
Disabled workers[c]	364	450	475	489	488
Wives and husbands[b, d]	164	199	210	239	241
Children of deceased workers	228	277	307	335	337
Widowed mothers[g]	242	293	315	336	338
Widows and widowers, nondisabled[b]	284	386	398	438	444

Table 12.3. Social Security (OASDI)–Benefits, by Type of Beneficiary: 1970 to 1986 (A person eligible to receive more than one type of benefit is generally classified or counted only once as a retired-worker beneficiary. OASDI = Old-age, survivors, and disability insurance.)(*cont.*)

TYPE OF BENEFICIARY	1970	1975	1980	1985	1986
	Benefits Awarded During Year (1,000)				
Number of benefits	**3,722**	**4,427**	**4,215**	**3,796**	**3,853**
Retired workers[b]	1,338	1,506	1,620	1,690	1,734
Disabled workers[c]	350	592	389	377	417
Wives and husbands[b, d]	436	499	469	440	441
Children	1,091	1,332	1,174	714	701
Widowed mothers[g]	112	116	108	72	69
Widows and widowers[b, h]	363	377	452	502	491
Parents[b]	2	1	1	(z)	(z)
Special benefits[i]	30	4	1	1	(z)
	Benefit Payments During Year (mil. dol.)				
Total amount[j]	**31,863**	**66,923**	**120,472**	**186,195**	**196,692**
Monthly benefits[l]	31,570	66,586	120,118	185,988	196,489
Retired workers[b]	18,437	38,078	70,359	116,823	123,584
Disabled workers[c]	2,448	6,908	12,817	16,483	17,409
Wives and husbands[b, d]	2,194	4,104	7,043	11,061	11,700
Children	3,517	6,643	10,514	10,710	10,899
Under age 18	2,701	4,823	7,374	8,502	8,687
Disabled children[e]	250	537	1,048	1,760	1,961
Students[f]	566	1,283	2,093	447	251
Of retired workers	303	634	1,142	1,140	1,166
Of deceased workers	2,760	4,888	7,389	7,762	7,843
Of disabled workers	454	1,121	1,982	1,809	1,890
Widowed mothers[g]	574	1,009	1,572	1,474	1,457
Widows and widowers[b, h]	4,055	9,596	17,638	29,330	31,345
Parents[b]	39	50	55	51	48
Special benefits[i]	306	198	119	57	47
Lump sum	294	337	355	207	203

[a]Benefit payment actually being made at a specified time with no deductions or with deductions amounting to less than a month's benefits; i.e., the benefits actually being received. [b]62 years and over. [c]Disabled workers under age 65. [d]Includes wife beneficiaries with entitled children in their care and entitled divorced wives. [e]18 years old and over. Disability began before age 18 and, beginning 1973, before age 22. [f]Full-time students aged 18–21 through 1984 and aged 18 and 19 beginning 1985. [g]Includes surviving divorced mothers with entitled children in their care and, beginning June 1975, widowed fathers with entitled children in their care. [h]Includes widows aged 60–61, surviving divorced wives aged 60 and over, disabled widows and widowers aged 50 and over; and beginning Jan. 1973, widowers aged 60–61. [i]Benefits for persons aged 72 and over not insured under regular or transitional provisions of Social Security Act. [j]Constant dollar figures are based on the consumer price index published by the U.S. Bureau of Labor Statistics; see table 738. [k]Represents total disbursements of benefit checks by the U.S. Dept. of the Treasury during the years specified. [l]Distribution by type estimated.

Sources: U.S. Social Security Administration, *Annual Statistical Supplement to the Social Security Bulletin,* and unpublished data; U.S. Bureau of the Census, *Statistical Abstract of the U.S. 1988* (Washington, D.C.: Government Printing Office, 1987), Table 560.

the numbers of beneficiaries of the different categories, the average levels of benefits in absolute terms, and the benefits in constant dollars (that is, corrected for inflation and expressed in terms of 1986 valued dollars) from 1970 to 1986. In this period the total number of persons receiving benefits rose from 26.2 million to 37.7 million, while the number of retired workers rose from 13.3 million to 23 million. Average benefits for retired workers and their wives rose from $199 in 1970 to $831 in 1986 in absolute terms, and from $553 to $831 in terms of 1986 dollars. Thus benefits for couples rose in real terms by about 50 percent. The total amount of benefits paid out by the U.S. Social Security system rose from 31.9 billion in 1970 to about 196.7 billion in 1986 (Table 12.3).

Coverage and Eligibility   Another major issue concerns coverage and eligibility for public pension plan benefits. The expansion of coverage of pension schemes has taken place in fits and starts and progressively more and more industrial sectors, economic branches, and occupational categories have become included in the coverage. Employers, however, have typically viewed coverage of their employees in public pension plans, as in other benefit schemes, as fundamentally adding to the wage bill that they are obliged to pay per unit of labor. They have resisted individually and collectively the extension of coverage at virtually every juncture.

Fiscal conservatives have viewed expansion of coverage as likely to lead ultimately to increased public expenditures and, minimally, to expansion of the publicly employed staff required to administer the additional coverage. Traditional opponents of government or state initiatives or responsibilities have opposed extension of coverage on the same grounds on which they oppose the initial programs: That such programs erode individual and family responsibility and subvert private initiative, self-reliance, and the values of rugged individualism.

In fact, coverage of the Social Security system in the United States has expanded throughout its existence. The system now largely covers all employees, whether full- or part-time, and most self-employed persons. The controversial new frontier of Social Security coverage is that of persons not themselves employed, such as housewives and students. These may often have entitlements to Social Security benefits as dependents or survivors of covered employees, but they are not now contributors or covered by Social Security provisions in their own right.

Probably not less controversial is the issue of age at eligibility for partial and full retirement benefits and the so-called retirement test for full benefits. The basic eligibility for full retirement benefits under Social Security is at age 65, but for those under 72 years of age, employed, and earning more than an earnings ceiling, benefits are reduced by $1.00 for every $2.00 earned over the ceiling. Thus, for those under 72 years of age, receipt of full Social Security pension benefits is contingent on full or nearly full retirement, hence the retirement test appellation. Early retirement, at age 62 or thereafter, is possible and qualifies such retirees for pension benefits reduced by 5 percent for each year prior to age 65. Finally, disability benefits may be claimed at any age prior to the retirement ages and are contingent upon meeting established criteria. In 1986 benefits were paid to about

2.7 million disabled workers and to about 965,000 children of disabled workers (Table 12.3).

These eligibility criteria are topics of debate and controversy in several respects. First, many view both the early retirement provisions and the retirement test as strong financial disincentives to continued employment for persons otherwise able and willing to work. For those looking to retirement as a means of assuring employment and job opportunities for younger persons, this is a favorable result. Others have viewed this loss of employment as representing loss of skills, labor, and productive capacity and an unnecessary burden on the Social Security system.

Second, many favor a change in eligibility provisions to delay entitlement to full pension benefits until a later age—ages 67 or 68 are frequently mentioned—allowing retirement at age 65 only as an early retirement option with reduced benefits. They support this position by citing, on the one hand, the improved health and physical capacities of the elderly that enable them to continue in employment beyond age 65, and on the other hand the savings in expenditures and outlays on pension benefits that would result from such a delay. Indeed, recently passed legislation in the United States provides for delay of full retirement eligibility to age 67, to be introduced gradually beginning in the year 2000.

Income Inequality and Redistribution Finally, an important issue in the debates about public pension schemes concerns the extent to which benefits and their differentials should preserve preretirement income inequality or, conversely, should have the effect of diminishing income inequality in old age and retirement. This issue is related, but not identical, to the issue of the replacement rate or the relationships between retirement benefits and preretirement income.

The earliest public pension schemes did in fact provide equal benefits to all retirees, that is, they were flat benefit systems. The uniform benefits were also very low benefits, resulting in what Myles (1984) has called the "equal but poor" retired workers. The inadequacy of the benefits of flat-benefit public pensions left the least advantaged employees in or near poverty upon retirement. The more advantaged or better organized found or created alternative private or employer or trade union sponsored earnings-related pension schemes as a second tier of retirement income maintenance. In most countries this led to demand for, and eventual realization, of government organized second tiers of pension schemes. These are typically earnings related in part, thus preserving preretirement income inequality into the postretirement benefit schemes.

Nonetheless, overall benefit formulas have been redistributive despite incorporation of labor-market based inequalities. The wage-based benefit formulas typically provide a higher return on past contributions to low-income groups than to high-income groups (Myles, 1984). Moreover, most of the pension schemes provide supplements and benefit adjustments to take need and adequacy into account through family allowance, housing benefits, and special credits to compensate for periods outside the labor force.

The American Social Security system is an example of a single-tiered system that combines income redistribution with benefits that are related to previous earnings. It has a progressive benefits structure that pays out proportionately more to those who earned less prior to age 65, with the consequence that income inequality diminishes somewhat after age 65 (Fuchs, 1983). These redistributive provisions are frequently attacked as violating the principle of equity in provision of benefits (benefits in strict relation to past contributions). They are also attacked for not going far enough in the direction of equality in provision of benefits (benefits in relation to needs).

EMPLOYMENT IN LATER YEARS

Only a minority of the elderly in modern industrialized societies continue in or return to paid employment after reaching the conventional retirement ages. They are mostly employed in part-time employment. Yet, there has been growing interest in and demand for expansion of employment opportunities for the elderly to (1) preserve civil rights; (2) address income, and social and psychological, needs of the elderly; (3) conserve, mobilize, and use available work skills and experience which the elderly have; and (4) render the retirement benefit programs financially less tenuous and ensure future viability. While many of the employed elderly continue in jobs and tasks similar to those performed by younger adults, there have been many proposals for defining and designing jobs to accommodate the skills, capabilities, and special needs of elderly workers.

Extension of Employment and Delay of Retirement

Work Adjustment Through Changed Working Conditions The first major category of schemes for promoting extension of employment and delay of retirement addresses the supposed or actual decline in performance and diminished ability of middle-aged and elderly workers to adjust to the new demands made on them by technological changes. They do so by providing for a better match between work demands and worker capabilities. Following Casey and Bruche (1983), we may distinguish among three approaches to effecting change in the working conditions for this purpose.

1. Organizational and technical adjustment of work to adapt it to the abilities of older workers. In the literature this is often denoted job redesign (Barkin, 1970; Buchman, 1983; Jacobson, 1980; Doering, Rhodes, and Schuster, 1983).
2. Training programs intended to adjust the older workers' qualifications to the changing requirements of their work, or to the requirements of the new works in case of transfers (Barkin, 1970; Copperman and Keast, 1983). Such programs are often denoted continuing education in the literature.

3. Reduction of work demands or alteration of working conditions. The older worker remains at the same or an equivalent work place but, for example, is no longer obligated to work on piecework or in shifts (Casey and Bruche, 1983).

Work Adjustment Through Job Transfers   A second major category of work adjustment to allow continuing employment is through job transfers. This typically involves the transfer of older employees whose performance is reduced or whose health is in jeopardy to lighter work. In the literature, this approach is often termed "job reassignment," (e.g., Buchmann, 1983) or "redeployment" (Jacobson, 1980). These transfers typically involve moves within the employing firm and often represent some form of voluntary demotion, downgrading of responsibilities, scope, and earnings (Copperman and Keast, 1983).

Work Adjustment Through Reduction in Working Time   A third, and quantitatively probably the most important approach to work adjustment to allow continuing employment or delay of retirement, comprises the range of schemes included under the rubric of work-time reductions. Ordinary part-time work is probably the most familiar arrangement, but other work-time reduction schemes include as well:

1. Flextime, or flexitime: A scheme wherein employees may choose their starting and stopping times. Generally they must agree to be present during a core period of the day and work a previously agreed number of hours (Copperman and Keast, 1983).
2. Job-sharing: An agreement in which two people have responsibilities for one full-time position. (Jacobson, 1980; Buchmann, 1983).
3. Compressed work week: Work is compressed to less than the traditional five-day week. The common pattern is to compress the forty-hour week into four ten-hour days, the so-called 4/40. (Copperman and Keast, 1983).
4. Cottage industry: Job assignments are undertaken or completed at home rather than at a traditional work site.
5. Sabbatical, non-linear career: Somewhat akin to arrangements in the academic world, but new and rare in business and industry, this arrangement permits time away from the job to pursue education, public service, avocational, and other interests, or to take temporary employment in another firm or organization (Best and Stern, 1977; McConnell, 1980).
6. Phased retirement: Gradual reduction of work-time prior to retirement, but culminating ultimately in complete separation from the job. (Buchmann, 1983; Copperman and Keast, 1983; Jacobson, 1980; Casey and Bruche, 1983). Employees nearing retirement gradually decrease their hours and responsibilities over a period as long as several years.
7. Rehearsal retirement: Employees take an unpaid leave of absence to "test the waters" of retirement without losing their jobs. At the end of this time the employee may either return to the job and resume full seniority credit, or he may retire. (Buchmann, 1983).

Remuneration, Pension, and Benefit Option Innovations   A long, complex list of legislative, employer, and collective agreement innovations has been adopted or proposed in support of continuing employment of middle-aged and elderly workers or to effect delay of retirement. These are basically policies or options affecting wage, benefit, or pension rights and entitlements of workers under varying schemes and contingencies of continuation in employment or withdrawal from employment.

In the view of many analysts, the availability and levels of alternative income sources—in particular, retirement pensions—is as important as, or more important than, employment compensation in determining willingness to continue in employment and to delay retirement (Doering, Rhodes, and Schuster, 1983; DeViney and O'Rand, n.d.). Historically it has been the expansion of retirement income entitlement that has been the main factor invoked to account for declining labor force participation of males in late-middle and old age (Pampel and Weiss, 1983; Schulz, 1985; Kingson, 1984; Easterlin, Crimmins, and Ohanian, 1984). Accordingly a range of proposals for encouraging extension of employment among the middle-aged and elderly involve reform or alterations of arrangements for provision of retirement income (Meier, 1980). These include:

1. Change in the retirement age. Deferral of the age of eligibility for full or partial retirement income and benefits would encourage, or indeed force, many middle-aged and older workers to remain in paid employment and delay retirement in the absence of alternative sources of income.
2. Liberalization or abolishment of retirement tests for pension income in private and public pension plans. Retirement tests imply reduction of retirement benefits to those who have passed the formal retirement age but have not retired, or have only partly retired, from employment. They are viewed as strong disincentives to continued employment of those reaching or past normal retirement age.
3. Adjustment of early and deferred retirement options. Some pension plans allow early retirement with actuarial reduction of pension income rendering the benefits of equal or even greater value to the workers (Tracy, 1978; Schulz, 1985), while the actuarial credit to pension income of those deferring retirement renders the benefit of lower value generating disincentives to continued employment. Revision of these options would reward and promote continued employment and delay of retirement.

Re-Employment Schemes

According to the L.Harris and Associates' national survey findings, an overwhelming majority of the U.S. working population (75 percent) report the desire to continue some kind of paid part-time work after retirement. Among those wishing part-time work after retirement, the majority (54 percent) of the younger persons, those 18 to 54, prefer switching to a different *kind* of job. A large majority of the older employed individuals, those 65 and over, who wish to work after retirement would rather continue in the *same* kind of work. Of those aged 55 to 64 just over half (52 percent) say they wish to continue in the same kind of work (National Council on Aging, 1981).

In fact only just over one-third of those retired do actually work for pay at some point after retirement. Of these most experience some measure of change or mobility between pre- and post-retirement occupations (Beck, 1986). The arrangements for post-retirement employment fall into four basic types: (1) re-employment with the preretirement employer, (2) employment in a new firm or organization, (3) self-employment or contracting, and (4) so-called sheltered employment. For the most part the work or job design and remuneration arrangements are similar to the schemes for extending employment and delaying retirement reported above.

Same Job, Same Employer Re-employment Schemes   A frequent pattern of postretirement re-employment is that of firms and organizations rehiring their own annuitants or employing them for varying periods, usually under some arrangement not inconsistent with their respective pension plan rules (Rosow and Zager, 1980). These can include use of annuitant banks, self-employment and independent contracting arrangements, and indirect hiring of annuitants through temporary employee firms and organizations (Jacobson, 1980, Chap. 5; Copperman and Keast, 1983).

New Employer Schemes   Probably the most important avenue of promotion and availment of new employment opportunities and second careers for retired persons is that of the organized placement service. An enormous number of such organizations and agencies have emerged in recent years in North America, including voluntary and nonprofit organizations, commercial for-profit agencies, in-house and outside placement services of firms for their own retiring employees, and personnel offices and units of large employers (Buchmann, 1983; Rosow and Zager, 1980; Jacobson, 1980, Chap. 3; Copperman and Keast, Chap. 5). These in turn include skill-bank placement services and retraining and subsequent placement services.

Self-Employment Schemes   Establishing one's own business is a familiar dream, and indeed many individuals actually do so in the course of their work lives, some successfully and many unsuccessfully. A variant on the dream of one's own business is the dream of starting one's own business after retirement from a job or career. This is a dream whose fulfillment is rather less risky for individuals or families with pension income entitlements, since there is a measure of income protection in the event of the failure of a business venture.

Protected, Subsidized Employment Schemes   Since the Great Depression of the 1930s there have been schemes initiated to provide employment for persons wishing to work, but unable to find or compete for employment in the private labor market. These programs have been motivated and informed primarily by considerations of provision of income to unemployed persons and their families and as an alternative to other nonwork-based income maintenance or assistance. More recently, however, such programs have also incorporated training or retraining objectives, or job seeking or job mobility objectives. They have often taken the form of subsidies to private employers to create jobs for or hire otherwise unemployed persons of various categories of hardship, disadvantage, attributes, or entitlements.

An outcome, and in some periods a secondary objective, of some types of subsidized employment has been the creation or enhancement of certain kinds of public facilities, or provision or enhancement of certain kinds of public services, not otherwise available in the context of private enterprise and the private labor market. Probably the best known examples of such objectives and outcomes are the projects of the Public Works Administration (PWA), the Civil Works Administration, and the Works Progress Administration (WPA) in the United States in the 1930s under the Roosevelt administration's New Deal.

Thus, there is a history of using public funds to support and subsidize employment, and there is a history of combining subsidized employment with provision or enhancement of public facilities and services. More recently, there is a history of public support or subsidy of private sector employment whether in the form of direct subsidy for job creation, protection of industries and their employment from foreign competition, guaranteeing markets for products or services of protected industries, or grants or loans under favorable conditions to private sector firms whose survival and employment are threatened by mishap, mismanagement, or adverse economic conditions.

Such programs are most frequently targeted on the unemployed generally and, if age is at all a criterion, more frequently to the younger unemployed. Only infrequently do they address the retired seeking to return to employment. Casey and Bruche (1983) survey a number of such programs in Western European countries and impute very little significance or impact to them with respect to employment of older workers. They accord more weight to the Swedish national work accords and agreements whereby employers are deemed responsible not only for recruitment in accordance with the needs and cost effectiveness of their production regimes, but for participation in maintenance of full or near-full employment in the society. Even in Sweden, however, the impact of these arrangements on employment of older workers is minimal.

An American example of a program combining subsidized employment of *older* workers and provision of public services or services not readily available or affordable on a private market basis is the Senior Community Service Employment Program (SCSEP), first developed in the late 1960s. The program is administered primarily by eight national voluntary organizations that organize jobs and services in the areas of (1) general community services, including education, health, hospitals, housing, home rehabilitation, employment assistance, recreation, parks, forests, environmental quality, public works, transportation, social and other services; and (2) services to the elderly, including health, home care, housing, home rehabilitation, employment assistance, senior citizens' recreation, nutrition programs, transportation, and outreach, referral, and other services (Special Committee on Aging, 1981, Table 5). The program provides jobs and income to the elderly poor, and it yields other individual and social rewards to participants. The jobs and services also meet many community service needs. The program has been generally applauded and viewed as effective and successful. Like other U.S. federal programs, however, the SCSEP has recently been curtailed by funding cuts.

It has been and remains extremely difficult to assess the impact of programs, policies, and innovations for extension of worklife upon the actual patterns of employment in middle and later life. Information upon which analysis of labor force participation and employment in entire communities is based typically does not include the details of retirement status or pension income entitlements. It is, therefore, difficult to associate persons employed with some specific program or category of employment programs or policies. Older employees *may* be working under some such plan, or they may simply be employed in jobs just as workers of any age are employed throughout the labor market. Finally, the choice and measurement of the outcome criteria that are to be adopted for assessment of such programs is inherently difficult and controversial. Such assessment, and policy discussion and activity based on it, requires some minimal consensus concerning the purposes of the programs and the *needs* (whether of the elderly, employers, the economy and pension system, the employment opportunities for younger employees, and so forth, to which they are to be addressed.

HEALTH CARE AND HEALTH CARE-GIVERS

As we saw in the previous chapter, impaired health and physical and mental deterioration can impinge upon virtually every facet of personal and social life. Most of the elderly population report themselves in good or satisfactory health or better. Yet a large majority report themselves as having *some* chronic condition, including more than half with some limitation on activity. However, the elderly include persons in a wide age range, with age itself highly correlated with health impairment. The health conditions among the elderly range from complete absence of disease or impairment through impairments or disabilities of varying gravity to complete inability to engage in either major activities or personal functions and care.

The transition to the sick role, whether in acute or in chronic illness, typically constrains and contracts the scope and domains of social interaction and participation very drastically. In effect, such transitions *mean* and are *defined by* movement into states of physical, and often emotional, dependency. In this section we consider the types, availability, and social locations of responses to the social and physiological exigencies and predicaments of illness, chronically impaired health, or other deviations from physiological and mental health and well-being.

Sources, Types and Sites of Health Care

Most people—whether children, adults, or elderly persons—are well most of the time. When they are not well they usually care for themselves or are cared for by their parents, spouses, children, other family members, or sometimes by neighbors or friends. A large variety of services, products, and institutions support these arrangements for addressing the minor or short-term deviations from health or being not well. They include visits and professional consultations with physicians, nurses, and other practitioners; home remedies and patent and prescription medicines; home care appliances and equipment; and arrangements for absence or rest from normal activities.

Of course, many disorders and illnesses are more serious and require more complex or extended or highly skilled treatment and care, and often over extended periods of time; they engender much more elaborate, and costly, arrangements for care. Moreover many individuals with even minor disorders and illnesses are not able to care for themselves, nor do they have close kin, friends, or neighbors able to provide needed care. Informal self-care or care by family members or friends cannot suffice to deal effectively with such disorders and illnesses.

Acute and Chronic Conditions   In the discussion of such disorders and illnesses, a distinction is conventionally made between acute and chronic conditions. Acute conditions are generally presumed to have causes outside the body, such as infectious microorganisms. They typically have a beginning, some peak or crisis, and some limited recovery period.

Chronic conditions are frequently presumed to have internal causes. They develop slowly without a marked peak or crisis and linger for extended periods. Limitation of activity is a frequent and distinct feature of age-related chronic conditions; care of chronic conditions makes up the bulk of the institutional health care for the elderly. Hospital services are primarily oriented to addressing of acute health conditions.

Informal and Open and Closed Formal Care   Self-care and family care of ailments, disorders, and illnesses is usually denoted informal care, or care in informal settings. The care available in formal settings may be given in closed or institutional settings: primarily acute care hospitals, psychiatric hospitals, or nursing homes. Or formal care may be available in open or community settings: primarily health services, out-patient facilities, doctors' offices, adult day care centers, mental health centers, board and care homes such as domiciliary, residential group, or other private homes or hotels (Estes et al., 1984). A distinction is often made between the preventive care and the remedial care available. The consensus has been that most attention and resources of formal care systems have been devoted primarily to remedial care.

Long-term Care   Finally, among persons with chronic illnesses and disorders, the great majority—including the elderly—are able to look after themselves on a day-to-day basis. They do so even if many suffer some disabilities and may be prevented from engaging in work or homemaking activities. A small minority, however, suffers from functional incapacities and have not developed, or have lost, some capacity for self-care to the extent that they require long-term care for their very survival or safety.

Long-term care consists of the range of services that address the health, social, and personal care needs of such individuals. The services may be continuous or intermittent, but it is generally presumed that they will be delivered for the long term, that is, indefinitely to individuals with such demonstrated need. Long-term care incorporates a wide variety of dependency needs that differ for individuals and may include provisions for income maintenance, health, housing, personal care, and social services. It may encompass preventive care or acute care as well as continuous or chronic care over a long period of time. It may also be provided informally or in community-based or institution-based care settings.

Health Care Systems

It is useful to develop a concept of health care system to refer to

1. The entire set of institutions, arrangements, and services addressing health care needs and health-related social needs of a given or identified population,
2. The manner in which the set of institutions and services responds to these needs, and
3. The relationship of these to the social, economic, and political organization and features of the society.

The concept is very general, and we can understand that each community, each region, or each national society may have its particular health care system. Thus health care systems vary across communities and societies. They change over time with respect to attributes such as their physical settings, their personnel composition, their financing, the mix of services offered, the mix of clients or needs addressed, and so forth. They also vary in their mix of formal and informal services, their mix of attention to preventive, acute, and chronic and long-term care, and the extent to which they are planned, coordinated, and centralized or, conversely, operate diffusely or as collections of independent and uncoordinated actors and elements.

For example, the health care system of Britain is dominated by the legislation, financing, services, and personnel of the National Health Service, a genuine national system of health care charged with assessment of health care needs of the entire population and provision of services to address them. The health care system of the United States, although increasingly influenced by federal legislation and financing, is based largely on private market offerings of services on the part of health care professionals and private health care organizations, with very diffused centers of control and accountability. Judged in terms of the proportion of gross national product allocated to health care needs, the American health care system is probably more costly than that of any other major advanced industrial capitalist country's, with somewhat over 10 percent of gross national product spent on health care. Judged in terms of conventional population health indicators, such as life expectancy, infant mortality rates, or workdays lost due to illness, the American health care system is not more effective than other advanced industrial countries and, indeed, less effective than some.

The characteristics of health care systems are very important for the welfare and well-being of societies and individuals of every age and every stage in the life course. The nature, availability, mix and quality of care and services provided in health care systems are particularly pertinent to the well-being of the elderly and their families. This is so because of their high rates of illness, morbidity, impairment, and disability, because of the adverse effects of simultaneous or densely occurring stressful life events and transitions in old age, and because of their reduced incomes and consumption capabilities and choices. The topic is fairly complex, and we can review it here only briefly. Yet, together with income maintenance arrangements, the health care system and its operations in any given community and society are the most important set of social institutions governing the lives and well-being of the elderly.

Health Care Systems and the Needs of the Elderly

The ideological and organizational features, and the ways in which health care systems allocate resources to deal with the different types of health needs, result in an array of different types of health care systems and an array of responses to the health care needs of the elderly. In this section we mention only four types of health care system differentiation:

1. Organizational and service entitlement bases;
2. Relative weights of the different types of health disorders addressed;
3. Relative weights of the alternative physical environments in which care is offered;
4. Methods of payment for, or otherwise financing, services offered.

We will next illustrate how these affect access to service and health outcomes among the elderly.

Organizational and Service Entitlement Bases The American health care system centers around the private fee-for-service practice of medicine by licensed physicians, government, nonprofit, and proprietary for-profit hospitals, laboratories, and related services, and proprietary for-profit nursing homes. There has recently emerged a category of health maintenance organizations (HMOs) that are sometimes under sponsorship of cooperatives and nonprofit organizations and sometimes organized privately on a for-profit basis. There are also recently emerging proprietary home-care services. Generally access is through referral by physicians on a fee-for-service basis. Sometimes there is means-tested fee reduction or subsidization by charitable organizations or public bodies. Access to HMO services is through membership and insurance coverage.

Some local governments—municipalities or state or county governments—operate medical services including hospital, outpatient, and ambulatory services; some operate nursing homes, other long-term care facilities, and community and home services. Each of these initiate and operate their own services, subject to state licensing and regulation. Residents and citizens typically are entitled to services on either a straight fee-for-service basis or on the basis of means-tested reduced fees as welfare medicine care systems, frequently financed by federal funds.

The British National Health Service, by contrast, is a public, comprehensive health care service to which all residents have free access as a matter of right. In the United Kingdom, the Ministry of Health has responsibility for organization and administration of the service. Its mandate is to address *all* of the health care needs—acute care, chronic and long-term care, and preventive care—for all citizens and residents of all ages and in all places. In principle, health care of all types is tax supported and free to all residents. Recently, however, some nominal fee schedules have been introduced in an attempt to curtail overuse or related abuse of access to services. The national and local governments initiate and organize services in response to perceived needs in the population. They obviously must do so within the bounds of planning and budgeting and reporting and accountability. In the United States, the Veteran's Administration health services have in effect long been organized on a similar basis, except that entitlement to services is restricted to veterans and their families.

The organizational bases of health care systems in other countries vary from universal mandatory health insurance that covers costs of privately organized fee-for-service medical practice and public and proprietary hospitals (as in Canada) to systems of very large health maintenance organizations (HMOs) or sick funds organized by trade union federations, philanthropic or cooperative organizations, or private entrepreneurs (as in Israel). These typically encompass virtually the entire population and are frequently subsidized by government funding.

Every health care system apparently has its own openings, opportunities, and temptations for abuse and corruption by patients, physicians and health care personnel, entrepreneurs, politicians, or others. This seems to be the case whether the system is market- and competition-driven or planned and administered. Fortunately, however, the analysis of health care needs is both increasingly sophisticated and accessible to public scrutiny. Hopefully the flaunting of abuses and corruption in alternative health care systems in public discussion will increasingly be replaced by information and comparisons of their actual experiences in terms of access, costs, benefits and services provided, and indicators of health and well-being.

The Mix of Acute, Chronic, and Preventive Care   In the American health care system medical and care services have emerged in response to opportunities for earnings for physicians and profits for the health-related industries and economic branches; public funding of health care has developed largely as a means of paying for privately offered and privately initiated services. These arrangements and organizational features have historically given the health care system a strong orientation favoring a medical model of health care and service. It features a strong bias towards acute care and relative neglect of chronic and long-term care. There is also relative neglect of preventive care. Of national expenditures on health care in 1983, more than three-fifths was spent on hospitals and physicians, reflecting largely acute care expenditures for medical attention.

By contrast, the British and other Western European health care systems have been able to organize and implement programs to address chronic disorders, disabilities, and long-term care needs, often with much less weight to the physician and the hospital facility elements. Day-care programs, home help arrangements, physiotherapy, meal delivery, nutrition services, and transportation programs have all been part of the organized health care system in Britain, for example, rather than being relegated to voluntary and charitable organizations or permitted to be market and profit opportunities for private firms, as so often occurs in North America.

Health Care Settings and Environments   The most frequent setting and environment for health care is the informal, unorganized, private home. Most elderly men in need of care receive it from their wives. Widowers receive care from their daughters; elderly married women receive care from their husbands and daughters; elderly widows receive care from their daughters.

Most health care systems recognize this by default. They relegate certain kinds of care and attention, or the care and attention of certain kinds of individuals, to the private home with no particular ado or recognition, much less help or support. They are able to focus their own attention, resources, and arrangements on those whose care must and can take place outside their homes. The health care in such settings is often self-care, or it may be provided by spouse, children, other family members, or sometimes by neighbors or friends.

Formal, organized health care is generally viewed as having either an open community setting or a closed institutional setting. The open community settings typically include the professional physician's office services and other professional health services, adult day care, mental health center services. They also include a list of social services, such as senior centers, nutrition sites, transportation, home-maker services, board and care homes, and other residential arrangements. The closed institutional settings include acute care hospitals, psychiatric and mental hospitals, and nursing homes (Estes et al., 1984).

The American health care system has frequently been described as heavily favoring closed institutional settings. There has been relatively little development of open community settings and virtually no support for home or informal care arrangements. Thus, emphasis on hospital services and their related technologies—and very high cost—and emphasis on hospital-like nursing home solutions to long-term care needs of the elderly are characteristics of the health care system in the United States. The insistence on viewing the increased longevity and absolute and relative growth of the aged population primarily in terms of the increased burden—or, opportunities, in the view of some—on the medical profession, illness and disability, and the formal health care system has been termed the "medicalization" of old age.

By contrast, open or community care facilities are relatively underdeveloped in the American health care system, although they are much more familiar and developed in Great Britain, Scandinavia, and other Western European countries. The emerging interest in community care facilities in the United States probably derives more from concern over the costs of institutional care and the conjecture that community care may offer some acceptable and less costly substitute for institutional care. Services and programs in the community settings are designed to help the elderly maintain themselves independently as far as possible, exercise control over their own lives and activities, and participate in family and community life in accordance with their wishes and abilities.

On the other hand institutionalization, primarily in nursing homes, has been the dominant solution invoked to address not only chronic illness, but also general illness in the presence of poverty, loss of social status, and absence of social support. Older people generally make more use of medical facilities and services than younger people. Only about 4 percent reside in long-term institutions in the United States (7 percent in Canada). However, about a quarter of the population age 85 or over resides in such institutions.

Older people with spouses or living children and adequate financial resources can usually (but not always) delay or avoid entering a nursing or personal care facility. Widowhood and loss of residence are two events that often precipitate a move into an institution. Most older people view nursing homes negatively, but enter them if necessary. The inability of our system to develop a way to finance genuinely adequate long-term health care means that most nursing homes are lacking in staff and facilities. It also results in an organizational structure that must stress efficiency and profitability. Not inevitably, but all too often, it may neglect the socioemotional needs of the residents.

In 1985, approximately 1.3 million persons over 65 years of age living resided in nursing homes in the United States. The overwhelming majority, about 982,000, are women. All but 212,000 are old-old persons, that is, aged 75 or over (Table 12.4). The majority came to nursing homes after hospitalization (38 percent) or from another nursing home (12 percent), but a large minority (40 percent) moved to nursing homes from previous private residence, mostly alone. Only 19 percent came to nursing homes from previous residence with other family members. About half are supported in nursing homes by their own income or family support, with the other half supported primarily by Medicare or Medicaid programs.

The overwhelming majority of nursing home residents are severely impaired and dependent in their activities of daily life (ADL), with the number and severity of the dependencies obviously higher the older the residents. More than 91 percent require assistance for bathing, about 78 percent need help dressing, and somewhat lower proportions—although still the majority—

require assistance in using toilets, getting in or out of bed or chairs, and continence (Table 12.4).

Table 12.4.   Nursing Home Residents by Sex, Age, and Selected Characteristics, United States, 1985

	TOTAL	AGE			SEX	
		65–74 years	75-84 years	85 years and over	Male	Female
All residents (1,000)	**1,315.8**	**212.1**	**509.0**	**594.7**	**334.0**	**981.9**
Living Arrangements— Percent Distribution						
Total[a]	100.0	100.0	100.0	100.0	100.0	100.0
Private or semiprivate residence[a]	40.0	29.2	40.5	43.3	36.3	41.2
Alone	14.7	8.2	14.7	17.0	11.6	15.8
With family members	18.9	16.0	19.8	19.2	19.3	18.8
Another health facility[a]	57.0	67.7	56.5	53.6	60.4	55.9
Another nursing home	12.2	12.9	12.6	11.5	13.1	11.8
General or short-stay hospital[b]	38.7	39.5	38.2	38.9	35.2	40.0
Primary source of payment— percent distribution						
Total[a, c]	100.0	100.0	100.0	100.0	100.0	100.0
Own income or family support	49.8	39.0	51.2	52.4	50.9	49.5
Medicare	4.9	4.7	5.2	4.6	4.8	4.9
Medicaid payment for—						
Skilled nursing	13.9	13.9	13.5	14.3	11.9	14.6
Intermediate care	26.2	31.5	25.3	25.1	23.7	27.0
Dependency Status						
Average number of dependencies	3.9	3.4	3.8	4.2	3.6	4.0
Percent of nursing home population requiring assistance in						
Bathing	91.2	84.8	90.3	94.1	86.9	92.6
Dressing	77.7	70.2	75.9	81.9	71.5	79.7
Using toilet room	63.3	56.6	60.3	68.2	56.2	65.7
Transferring[d]	62.7	52.1	59.7	69.0	55.3	65.2
Eating	40.4	33.4	39.1	44.0	34.8	42.3
Continence	54.5	42.9	55.0	58.1	51.9	55.3

[a]Includes other living arrangements and payment sources, not shown separately. [b]Excludes psychiatric units of hospitals. [c]For persons who were residents for one month or more. [d]Getting in or out of a bed or a chair.
Source: U.S. Bureau of the Census, *Statistical Abstract of the U.S., 1988* (Washington, D.C.: Government Printing Office, 1987).

Adjustment to nursing homes is made difficult by the negative stereotype most people hold, the isolation of the nursing home from the community, the weakened conditions of the residents, loss of independence, and often widowhood. In addition many institutions have policies that unnecessarily segregate their residents from the outside world. They often stress congregate solutions to individual needs, and seek to control even the most minute aspects of the patients' lives. The systematic consideration of these issues and the development of standards for comparison and assessment of long-term care facilities are in early development stages (Fleishman, et al., 1988).

Financing Health Care Services   Discussion of the financing of health care services almost inevitably centers upon expenditures for formal medical care, nursing home care, and drugs, medications, and appliances. It rarely takes into account the costs to family members and care-givers, of the large proportion of health care and support that is provided informally in homes and family settings. It is primarily in connection with the proposal to encourage and subsidize informal home care as substitute for formal medical care and, especially for institutionalization, that some attention has been given to estimation of the actual costs or foregone earnings associated with informal home care (Shanas and Maddox, 1985).

There is a fairly wide range of schemes for covering costs of the various types of health services offered in the different health care systems. They extend from a fee-for-services paid privately to physicians, health care professionals, proprietary hospitals, and nursing homes to publicly supported services financed by general revenues or by earmarked taxes to funding by voluntary or philanthropic organizations. Western European countries have tended to view health care primarily as a societal responsibility to be financed or insured with public funds, while the United States has stressed health care as a personal responsibility to be financed or insured by private funds. The American health care system has historically been dominated by fee-for-service arrangements, but increasingly these, in turn, have been covered by private insurance arrangements.

Since 1965, costs of physicians, hospitals, and certain other health care services to the elderly in the United States are covered by Medicare, an insurance program enacted as Title XVIII under the Social Security Act. A further provision, Medicaid (Title XIX under the Social Security Act) extended the coverage and federal financial participation in costs of health care under joint federal-state programs for the poor. Insofar as Medicare and Medicaid have recognized and undertaken coverage of costs of certain health care services and not others, they have of course been factors in the emergence and development of those services. The Medicare and Medicaid programs do not, however, in any way purport to assess health needs of the population or address them by initiation or organization of health care services. Rather, they are designed only to cover costs to the elderly population of privately initiated and controlled services.

The number of elderly persons *using* Medicare coverage was about 12 million in 1975, representing about 53 percent of the total number covered. By 1984 the number served reached more than 18.9 million, representing more than two-thirds (68.9 percent) of the total enrolled elderly population (Table 12.5). There has been, to be sure, dramatic growth in numbers of persons served and expenditures for "home health" services (covered under the "hospital insurance" category after 1982). But the (1) inpatient and outpatient hospital services and (2) physicians and other medical services categories overwhelmingly represent the major part of services covered.

Matching Health Care Systems and Care Needs of the Elderly   A long list of studies has documented mismatches between the health care needs of the elderly and the services and facilities available. One category of mismatch involves the numbers of well elderly who are placed in hospital or nursing home facilities in the absence of alternative support systems. Another category of mismatch involves the retention of frail or chronically ill elderly in hospital acute care facilities while awaiting placement or access to nursing home or other long-term care facilities.

A third type of mismatch occurs when impaired or disabled persons, who could continue independent lives in their own households if certain kinds of nonmedical assistance, for example, home help, shopping, transportation, were available, are forced into dependency, and often institutionalization, in the absence of such assistance. Perhaps the most massive mismatches derive from *either* lack of awareness or information about available care services and entitlements *or* from inability to afford those services available only on a market basis.

The growth in the numbers of elderly population, on the one hand, and the slowdown in economic growth and the perceived fiscal strains on governments, on the other hand, have led to more intensive examination of the areas of match and mismatch between the health care needs of the elderly and the existing health care systems. The examination and analysis are themselves burdened by a variety of difficulties. First, as indicated in Chapter 5, analysis of the health care needs of the elderly presents conceptual and empirical difficulties. Definition and measurement of health, illness, and types and levels of impairments and disabilities have undergone rapid development in recent years. There remain, however, many problems of adequacy and comparability of measures. Perhaps more important, the interaction between social, psychological, and physiological states, functioning, and impairment is not well understood. Well designed longitudinal studies of such interactions have been few, and even theoretical development is in its infancy.

Second, the existing health care systems have built-in rigidities and strong protection of vested interests. Many of them are only tangentially related to the well-being of the elderly and their families. In the United States, and to a somewhat lesser extent in Canada, the health care industry and the medical-industrial complex, accounting for nearly 10 percent of the gross national product, is to be sure increasingly financed from public sources (Estes et al., 1984). Nonetheless, it has a long, successful history of preserving its fee-for-services basis, and it has

Table 12.5.   Use of Medicare Coverage and Reimbursements Among Persons 65 and Over, United States, 1975–1984

TYPE OF COVERAGE AND SERVICE	UNIT	PERSONS 65 YEARS OLD AND OVER		
		1975	1980	1984
Persons served, total[a]	1,000	12,032	16,271	18,904
Hospital insurance[a]	1,000	4,963	6,024	6,496
Inpatient hospital	1,000	4,913	5,951	6,195
Skilled-nursing services	1,000	260	248	290
Home health services[b]	1,000	329	675	1,398
Supplementary medical insurance[a]	1,000	11,762	16,099	18,706
Physicians' and other medical services	1,000	11,396	15,627	18,128
Outpatient services	1,000	3,768	6,629	8,743
Home health services[b]	1,000	161	302	24
Persons served per 1,000 enrollees, total[a]	Rate	528	638	686
Hospital insurance[a]	Rate	221	240	240
Inpatient hospital	Rate	219	237	229
Skilled-nursing services	Rate	12	10	11
Home health services[b]	Rate	15	27	52
Supplementary medical insurance[a]	Rate	536	652	699
Physicians' and other medical services	Rate	519	633	677
Outpatient services	Rate	172	269	327
Home health services[b]	Rate	7	12	1
Reimbursements, total	Mil. dol	12,689	29,134	(NA)
Hospital insurance	Mil. dol	9,209	20,353	(NA)
Inpatient hospital	Mil. dol	8,840	19,583	(NA)
Skilled-nursing services	Mil. dol	233	331	(NA)
Home health services[b]	Mil. dol	136	440	(NA)
Supplementary medical insurance	Mil. dol	3,481	8,781	(NA)
Physicians' and other medical services	Mil. dol	3,050	7,361	(NA)
Outpatient services	Mil. dol	374	1,261	(NA)
Home health services[b]	Mil. dol	56	159	(NA)
Reimbursements, per person served, total	Dollars	1,055	1,791	(NA)
Hospital insurance	Dollars	1,855	3,379	(NA)
Inpatient hospital	Dollars	1,799	3,291	(NA)
Skilled-nursing services	Dollars	896	1,336	(NA)
Home health services[b]	Dollars	413	652	(NA)
Supplementary medical insurance	Dollars	296	545	(NA)
Physicians' and other medical services	Dollars	268	471	(NA)
Outpatient services	Dollars	99	190	(NA)
Home health services[b]	Dollars	347	526	(NA)

NA Not available.

[a]Persons are counted once for each type of covered service used, but are not double counted in totals. [b]Beginning 1982, a change in legislation resulted in virtually all home health services being paid under hospital insurance.

Source: U.S. Bureau of the Census, *Statistical Abstract of the U.S., 1988* (Washington, D.C.: Government Printing Office, 1987), Table 576.

been able to direct increments in the public commitment to health care overwhelmingly to the control and profit of medical practitioners and the industries and services related to formal and largely institutional-setting medicine. Elsewhere, bureaucratic rigidities and vested interests in publicly sponsored health care schemes have slowed initiatives and reforms aimed at changing the mix of services available. Often trade unions and labor federations, employers organizations, and governments have found it convenient, necessary, or appropriate to enmesh health care schemes and their proposed reforms in broader negotiations surrounding wage policies and social pacts.

Finally, the role of families in health care of the elderly *and* the role of health care of the elderly in the functioning and well-being of families and the family as a social institution, also mentioned in Chapter 5, remain topics of considerable ideological and theoretical debate. However, they are still obscure empirically. The elderly clearly wish to remain independent and look after their own health care needs as long as they can. There are recurring and consistent findings indicating that, to the extent that they are unable to look after their own needs, the elderly do prefer the interest, commitment, and care of family members (Shanas and Sussman, 1977).

Of the more than 26.4 million elderly living in private residences (not in nursing homes or institutions) in the United States in 1984, a large percentage reported one or more difficulties in activities of daily life (ADL) due to a health or physical problem. Almost one-fourth (23.8 percent) reported difficulties in doing heavy housework and nearly 10 percent reported not doing heavy housework at all. About 19 percent reported difficulty in walking, almost 10 percent reported difficulties in getting outside, and about 10 percent reported difficulties in bathing or showering. More than 11 percent reported difficulties in shopping for personal items, and 2 percent reported that they do not do so at all. Again, these limitations are fairly infrequent among the young-old, those aged 65 to 74, but very much more frequent among the old-old (Table 12.6).

Quite large proportions of those living in private residences and reporting physical or health limitations and difficulties in ADL report also that they receive help in such activities as walking, getting outside, or in bathing or showering (Table 12.6). Part of this help is provided by paid persons and some by unpaid nonfamily volunteers. The great part of such assistance is provided by spouses, daughters, and other family members. Such assistance is, of course, much more readily available for elderly living together with others. Many of the elderly living alone (12 percent of those with difficulty walking, 42 percent of those with difficulty getting outside, and 36.5 percent of those with difficulty bathing or showering) also report receiving help in performing these activities. Probably a larger part of this help to elderly living alone is paid or volunteer help. However, recalling from the data shown in Chapter 9 that most of the elderly have children residing close by, it is reasonable to conjecture that most of this help, too, is provided by family members.

The effectiveness of home-care and care by family members exclusively or primarily may often be far less than optimal. Shanas and Maddox (1985) report

Table 12.6. Functional Limitations of the Elderly Residing in Communities (Not in Nursing Homes or Institutions), United States 1984 (In thousands, except percent. Covers persons 65 years old and over who were living in communities outside of nursing homes or other institutions (civilian noninstitutional population).

FUNCTIONAL LIMITATION	PERSONS 65 YEARS AND OVER Total	AGE 65–74 years old Total	Male	Female	75–84 years old Total	Male	Female	85 years and over	LIVING Alone	With others
Total, 65 years and over	**26,433**	**16,288**	**7,075**	**9,213**	**8,249**	**3,128**	**5,121**	**1,897**	**8,397**	**18,036**
Percent with difficulty[a] in										
Walking	18.7	14.2	12.9	15.1	22.9	18.3	25.7	39.9	20.4	17.9
Getting outside	9.6	5.6	4.5	6.5	12.3	7.5	15.3	31.3	9.7	9.5
Bathing or showering	9.8	6.4	5.7	6.9	12.3	9.2	14.2	27.9	9.9	9.7
Transferring[b]	8.0	6.1	4.8	7.0	9.2	6.0	11.2	19.3	8.8	7.6
Dressing	6.2	4.3	4.4	4.2	7.6	7.3	7.7	16.6	5.0	6.8
Using toilet	4.3	2.6	2.4	2.7	5.4	3.6	6.5	14.1	3.4	4.7
Eating	1.8	1.2	1.5	.9	2.5	2.5	2.4	4.4	1.2	2.1
Preparing meals	7.1	4.0	3.0	4.8	8.8	6.0	10.5	26.1	6.0	7.6
Shopping for personal items	11.3	6.4	4.6	7.8	15.0	9.6	18.4	37.0	11.9	11.0
Managing money	5.1	2.2	2.8	1.8	6.3	5.4	6.8	24.0	4.0	5.5
Using the telephone	4.8	2.7	3.5	2.0	6.0	7.9	4.8	17.5	2.6	5.8
Doing heavy housework	23.8	18.6	11.2	24.3	28.7	15.9	36.4	47.8	28.0	21.9
Doing light housework	7.1	4.3	3.5	5.0	8.9	6.2	10.5	23.6	6.6	7.4
Percent not performing activity										
Preparing meals	5.2	4.6	9.8	.5	5.5	12.0	1.6	8.9	1.1	7.1
Shopping for personal items	2.0	1.1	1.9	.5	2.5	2.9	2.3	7.5	2.2	1.9
Managing money	1.9	1.3	1.6	1.1	2.2	2.1	2.2	5.9	.8	2.4
Using the telephone	.8	.5	.8	.3	.9	1.4	.6	2.1	.8	.7
Doing heavy housework	9.7	8.1	12.7	4.6	11.5	16.3	8.6	15.9	7.1	11.0
Doing light housework	3.5	2.8	6.1	.3	4.0	7.8	1.7	7.1	.7	4.8

Table 12.6. Functional Limitations of the Elderly Residing in Communities (Not in Nursing Homes or Institutions), United States 1984 (In thousands, except percent. Covers persons 65 years old and over who were living in communities outside of nursing homes or other institutions (civilian noninstitutional population). (cont.)

FUNCTIONAL LIMITATION	PERSONS 65 YEARS AND OVER	AGE							LIVING	
		65–74 years old			75–84 years old			85 years and over	Alone	With others
		Total	Male	Female	Total	Male	Female			
Percent of total receiving help										
Walking	4.7	2.9	2.8	2.9	5.7	3.7	6.9	15.3	2.4	5.7
Getting outside	5.3	2.7	2.2	3.1	6.9	3.7	8.8	21.2	4.1	5.9
Bathing or showering	6.0	3.3	3.3	3.3	7.7	6.6	8.4	21.0	3.6	7.0
Transferring[b]	2.8	1.8	1.7	1.8	3.6	2.7	4.1	9.0	1.0	3.7
Dressing	4.3	2.9	3.3	2.7	5.1	5.7	4.7	13.3	1.7	5.6
Using toilet	2.2	1.2	1.4	1.1	2.9	2.3	3.2	8.2	.7	3.0
Eating	1.1	.6	.9	.5	1.5	1.8	1.4	2.7	.3	1.4
Preparing meals	6.0	3.3	2.8	3.7	7.1	5.4	8.2	23.7	3.6	7.0
Shopping for personal items	10.5	5.8	4.3	6.9	14.1	8.9	17.2	35.9	10.4	10.6
Managing money	4.8	2.1	2.6	1.7	5.8	5.0	6.3	23.5	3.6	5.3
Using the telephone	3.0	1.5	2.0	1.1	3.9	5.0	3.2	11.7	.9	3.9
Doing heavy housework	19.3	14.5	9.3	18.5	23.1	12.7	29.4	44.1	20.1	18.9
Doing light housework	6.2	3.6	3.2	4.0	7.6	5.7	8.7	21.6	4.5	6.9
Percent of those with difficulty receiving help[c]										
Walking	24.8	20.4	21.8	19.4	24.9	20.2	26.9	38.3	11.8	31.7
Getting outside	55.8	48.0	49.4	47.3	55.7	49.4	57.5	68.0	42.0	62.4
Bathing or showering	60.9	51.9	58.4	47.9	62.6	71.6	59.1	75.1	36.5	72.5

[a]Difficulty due to a health or physical problem.
[b]Getting in or out of a bed or chair.
[c]Receiving help due to a health-related problem with the specified difficulty.
Source: U.S. Bureau of the Census, *Statistical Abstract of the United States, 1988,* (Washington, D.C.: Government Printing Office, 1987), Table 174.

findings of a American national survey indicating that a large proportion of bedridden elderly in their own, their children's, or other family members' homes do not receive adequate medical attention. The costs of home-care and care by family members include direct costs and foregone income of family members engaged in the care of the elderly. Other costs reckoned in terms of welfare, satisfaction, leisure, deprivation, and so forth are very difficult to estimate in their own right. It is especially difficult to compare private and alternative public costs for putatively equivalent care and services (Shanas and Maddox, 1985; Habib, 1985).

The bearing of family care and commitment on the very nature of family relationships, stability, and on the viability of the family as an institution is frequently cited in the political debate surrounding alternative care arrangements. Empirical materials bearing on this point seem few; the very design of studies bearing on this point seems problematic. But an interesting line of analysis emerging recently has cast the family in a new, bureaucratic-intermediary role on behalf of the elderly. This has taken the form of (1) seeing to the arrangements of extrafamily care and entitlements on behalf of the elderly (Sussman, 1985; Shanas and Susman, 1977); and (2) continuing support and interaction of families with their elderly members, even when health care is basically anchored outside the families. For example, there is typically fairly intensive visiting of institutionalized elderly (Shanas and Maddox, 1985). In the view of some analysts these emerging family roles operate partly to replace more traditional modes of family care for the elderly (to the extent that in fact they were common). Perhaps more important, they may fortify the family as an institution under changing health care systems and arrangements.

SOCIAL PARTICIPATION OF THE ELDERLY

A theme of this book has been the challenge to social organization of the individual life course, the family life cycle, and social, economic, and political arrangements that is posed by the important historical trends in mortality and longevity, fertility and lifetime parenting, and productivity and lifetime employment. The increase in average length of life and the decrease in the numbers of life years devoted to parenting and paid employment have heralded major changes in the organization of personal, family, and social and economic life. Lifetime social participation has historically been dominated by employment, parenting, and the relations associated with the organizational and community settings in which they take place.

There has been a reduction of time and life years devoted to employment and to child-parenting at virtually all adult ages. The change is most prominent among the elderly, who have both increased total life years and diminished employment and parenthood years in the later ages. However interesting or attractive some dimensions of privacy may be, there is universal agreement that continued social participation, as opposed to withdrawal from social life, is critical for the well-being of both the elderly and their families. We have already mentioned in the previous chapter and in this chapter the continuation of parenting and of employment past retirement age among many of the elderly. However, there are important additional avenues of social participation for the elderly. The most important of these are church and religious organizations, volunteer activities, senior citizens clubs and centers, and continuing education.

Church and religious participation are by far the most frequent extrahome and extraemployment activities of the elderly, just as it is at other ages (McPherson, 1983; Atchley, 1988). Data cited by Atchley indicate that more than one-third of the young-old (aged 65 to 74) and close to half of the old-old (aged 75+) report membership in church-related organizations. There is no evidence of any special increase in such activity with advancing age. Although the old-old tend to report church and religious organization membership and activity more frequently than younger persons, most researchers agree that this reflects cohort effects, that is, greater lifelong attachment to church activities among the oldest cohorts than among younger groups. For their part, churches have frequently been at the forefront of organization of activities, senior centers, and the advocacy of programs and causes related to the elderly.

There does not yet seem to be any strong indication that church and church-related activities and participation reflect any fundamental change in the organization of the later life course or social relations of the elderly. Nor has there been much indication that religious and church leadership has adopted any great pretensions or visions of revolutionizing the lives of senior citizens. In particular, there seems to be no obvious rhetoric developing the theme of church or religious activity as substitute or replacement for previous employment, family roles, and activities. On the contrary, these activities seem by and large to reflect continuity with traditional patterns of religious belief, worship, and activity, with senior citizens having now more time and opportunity to engage in such activity and avail themselves of their social as well as spiritual benefits.

The opposite seems to hold for newly emerging types of activities such as volunteer activity, senior citizens centers and clubs, and continuing education. Strictly speaking none of these is novel in conception or operation. Yet the numbers and varieties of these activities have grown very rapidly in recent decades, and they have been increasingly *promoted* and *sold* to the elderly and the public generally as the new wave, the new options for the elderly. Very frequently they are viewed as social and legitimate *replacements* for relinquished earlier family and employment roles and activities.

The growth in the number and variety of such opportunities and activities notwithstanding, for the time being only quite small minorities of the elderly population report participation in volunteer, senior citizens centers, or continuing education. Many of these activities already are, or are likely in the future to be, combined with senior citizen political activity and advocacy. It seems clear that they do have an impact on the personal and social lives of those participating, although the numbers and percentages are small.

It is probably not the case that these activities are actually *replacements* for employment or family activity. There is, on the contrary, some evidence that such activities are, rather, complementary and conjoint with employment and family involvement and activity. Data from a national sample of persons aged 60 and over in Israel indicate clearly that the elderly still active in employment and family involvement (parenting their adult children and grandparenting) are much more likely also to be involved in volunteer activity, continuing education, or senior citizens clubs than those no longer employed or free of parenting activity (Habib and Matras, 1987). The relationship holds even when education and health status are taken into account.

Thus it remains to be seen how and to what extent new extrafamily and extraworkplace social activity options in later life will affect the life course, social relations, and well-being of the elderly and their families. It is clear that the increasing numbers of elderly, their improved health and economic resources, and their new patterns of family and extrafamily dependency, obligations, and entitlements open new opportunities for personal and social activities in later life. There are many public, private voluntary, and commercial bodies and agencies offering to structure and restructure the new opportunities for the elderly, each with its own activity or product. Although it is premature to pass judgment on the responses and directions of the elderly, both social scientific inquiry and public policy require continuing monitoring, study, and analysis.

13

AFTER THE BABY BOOM

the new aging, life course, and family cycle

In the earlier parts of this book we have introduced the ideas and description of the aging of populations and its demographic, social, and economic factors and correlates. We have discussed the life course and family cycle and how they are shaped and altered by the same demographic and social trends that have been associated with population aging. We have also described the elderly population, growing so dramatically and with important social and economic consequences, but whose lives and situations are largely shaped by life-course and family-cycle factors and transitions in old age just as at earlier ages. In this concluding chapter we try to draw upon the ideas, descriptions, and analyses of the previous chapters to indicate some implications of the recent social, economic, and demographic trends and some individual, family, and social organizational responses that it seems reasonable to anticipate in the near future.

AGING OF POPULATIONS

Projections of future populations in the Western countries anticipate some leveling off of the population aging trends, at levels comprising about 15 to 20 percent aged 65 years and over in the populations, and about 20 to 25 percent aged under 15 years. To the extent that employment and career opportunities for women remain circumscribed either by slow economic growth or by labor market constraints, and to the extent that governments learn and adopt measures to compensate women for foregone employment earnings or otherwise reward them for childbearing, some mild upward inflection in fertility in Western countries seems likely. However, the recent demographic experience of the Northern and Western European countries seems, basically, likely to be the pattern that will characterize most of the Western world. In the not too distant future, it will be commonplace in Eastern Europe as well. Eventually much of the so-called third world will move in similar directions demographically, if not necessarily socially, politically, or economically.

Even if there should be an upturn in fertility, parenting will take up a relatively small part of total life years. An upturn in fertility will probably result in increased parenting in only part of the population. Much of the population will continue with very limited time spans, or none at all, devoted to parenting. More women will be available for paid employment in patterns similar to those of men's work histories and trajectories. Almost all women will have had at least some labor force attachments during most of their young- and middle-adult lives. The numbers and proportions of adult men who are sole earners and breadwinners in their families will continue to diminish, and the men's expectations and commitments to work and careers throughout the adult life will erode at least partially.

The production of goods and services will make some further adjustments to the needs and consumption patterns of old populations. These will include the development of housing, transportation services, educational and cultural packages, health, and personal services addressing the needs of the large elderly subgroups in the populations. Some employment opportunities are likely also to be reorganized and redesigned to accommodate older workers. Length of worklife will continue to shrink for men especially, and eventually for women as well. Unemployment in one guise or another—that is, the absence of full-time jobs available in a labor market in the conventional sense in capitalist economies—will continue and is likely to be even more pervasive than in the 1970s and 1980s, despite the baby bust or diminished fertility after the mid-1960s. There is likely to be considerable movement in the direction of nonlinear patterns of work life; that is, deviations from the conventional schooling-full-time employment-retirement sequence, although the conventional sequence familiar in the life course now is likely to remain the norm and the most frequent pattern.

Governments, or the state, will have to be even more deeply involved in the economies of modern Western capitalist societies in at least three different ways. First, in the absence of labor-market-generated full employment for persons of all ages and both sexes, the state will have to redistribute national wealth and incomes and guarantee minimum incomes for all regardless of sex, age, or past or present employment status. It will assure income entitlements to those who have completed their lifetime employment histories and are retired. It will also assure income entitlements and training opportunities to those who have not yet begun their lifetime employment trajectories. Second, the state will probably have to arrange to organize, support, or subsidize employment opportunities for some for whom nonemployment-based income entitlements and guarantees do not suffice or are unsatisfactory but for whom there is, nonetheless no satisfactory employment available in the private labor market. Third, the state will have to continue not only to finance, but also to organize and provide, and indeed to enhance, health, welfare, and educational services available only partially, or not at all, in private markets. Income transfer and income maintenance schemes will have to be extended to the population of all ages not only as a measure of assuring minimum subsistence levels for the population under widespread unemployment or diminished working life, but to assure stable markets for goods and services produced in the economy. In turn, schemes such as guaranteed annual incomes (GAI) will have very fundamental effects upon the various dimensions of the life course and the family cycle generally, and on life-course and family-cycle transitions and relationships in old age in particular.

SMALL FAMILIES, DEPENDENCY, AND OBLIGATIONS

Low-mortality and low-fertility societies are for the most part small-family societies. Although we have not yet learned all their properties and nuances, it seems clear that the nature of "parenting" and of "childing" and patterns of parent-child as well as sibling- and other-kin dependency and obligations are distinctly different in small-family societies than in larger-family societies. First, parents are parents to dependent children for much less of their lifetimes, and children are adult social supporters of parents for much more of *their* lifetimes than in larger-family, higher-fertility settings and environments. Second, per capita parental income, parental time, and other parental resources are higher for children in small-family societies, while per capita adult child income, adult child time, and other adult child resources are lower for parents in small-family societies.

In the literature and public discussions of provisions and financing of services to the elderly population, the extent of continuing intergenerational mutual responsibility, dependency, and obligations has typically been understated. The implications of declining mortality, extended longevity, and lower fertility for these intrafamily patterns have not yet been fully studied and understood. Thus the small-family society, an outcome of aging of populations, undergoes a certain reversal of the patterns of intergenerational dependency and obligations. Child dependency on adult parents is circumscribed or cut short, while adult-child obligations to parents are extended in scope and over time. These changes result not only in new patterns of individual and family behavior and relationships, but in shifts in the interrelationships between individuals, families, and community and societal institutions.

THE LIFE COURSE OF POST-BABY-BOOM SMALL-FAMILY OFFSPRING

The outstanding features of the life course of small-family offspring have been, on the one hand, extended schooling and delay of worklife, career beginnings, marriage and family formation. On the other hand, they are likely to include adults' later extended obligations to elderly parents, often without the possibility of sharing them with siblings and even while still bearing obligations to their own dependent children. Middle-aged adults increasingly become the *sandwich generation*, that is, sandwiched between the dependency of their own children and dependency and obligations to their aging parents.

More than in earlier cohorts, women of the post-baby-boom birth cohorts will have high educational attainments, universal employment experience, and relatively frequent and strong career orientations and commitments. Their marriage prospects are relatively good, as the size of the male cohorts two to five years older are somewhat larger, due to the downward inflection in fertility in the years surrounding their own births. They are likely to marry somewhat earlier, on the average, than did women of the baby-boom cohorts; in early middle age they are likely to be caught in a care-squeeze between needs of their own dependent children and those of their elderly parents.

Both men and women of the post-baby-boom cohorts are likely to enjoy very favorable employment prospects throughout most of their work histories. On entrance into the labor force they will be replacing the much larger baby-boom cohorts, and they are relatively well credentialed. Later in their work histories they will be obliged to compete with somewhat older and more experienced workers of the very large baby-boom cohorts, but toward the end of their worklife they will encounter less pressure to retire and, indeed, will have many options for flexible retirement or continuing employment.

SMALL-FAMILY LIFE CYCLES

As indicated earlier, the characteristics of the life cycle of the family are basically retained in small-family sociodemographic regimes. But there are important changes in the timing of family events and transitions, and changes in the time spans characterizing the major stages of the family cycle. Dissolution of the marital couple takes place much more frequently because of divorce and less frequently because of mortality and widowhood. Within each family-cycle stage, the number of children present and the total family size are smaller, and there is much greater likelihood that wives will be employed.

Increasing numbers of women have employment experience not only prior and subsequent to childbearing and childrearing, but simultaneously. There are increasing numbers of dual career families. The division of activities and attentions of wives, and sometimes of husbands, between employment and childrearing generates both new intrafamily patterns of division of labor, authority, and solidarity and new extrafamily support arrangements. Childbearing and childrearing are completed earlier in small families than in the past. This occurs despite the more frequent delays and longer intervals between marriages and first births. To be sure, schooling is much longer than in the past, and, along with delay of marriage, this has operated to delay the departure of individual children from the parental homes. Altogether the smaller numbers of children have resulted in earlier *completion* of child-launching. Moreover, the earlier transition into the empty-nest stage of the family cycle along with the delay of mortality, widowhood, and the resulting dissolution of the marital couples have rendered the empty-nest stage of the family cycle a major part of married life for intact couples in stable marriages. Investigation of the empty nest is probably one of the frontiers of family research.

Finally, the small family and the reduced intensity of dependency and obligations within nuclear families have contributed to the trend toward retirement generally, and toward early retirement in particular. The labor force activity of wives in small family societies, the early completion of child-launching and the transition to the empty nest, and the reduced numbers of child, adolescent, or young adult dependents have allowed many middle-aged and young-old male breadwinners to accept early retirement options even under reduced levels of pension benefits.

THE ELDERLY IN SMALL-FAMILY SOCIETIES

The convenience of controlled, low fertility and very small families in early and middle adulthood is widely conjectured to have a price exacted in old age. The elderly in the small family society already have fewer adult children, and this will be even more widely true of the baby-boom cohorts upon reaching old age. In the near future those themselves brought up in the small family society, say the post-baby-boom cohorts, will have fewer siblings, cousins, and other relatives throughout their lives as well as fewer adult children when they reach old age. Moreover, the adult daughters and the female relatives of the elderly, those traditionally fulfilling the caregiving roles in informal and family settings, are much more likely than in the past to be taken up with their own employment and careers.

Just what the price of these trends and changes will be to the elderly, or for that matter how much actual change in the situations and well-being of the elderly they may entail, has been difficult to assess. It is not a matter of simple calculus of tradeoffs to evaluate the degree to which new and emerging extrafamily arrangements for the material support, health care, and social support of the elderly replace or improve upon those of the presmall-family society. By many measures and criteria, the actual social and economic status of the elderly is much improved compared to the recent past, but it is not clear that such measures capture effectively the nuances, qualities, or quantities of family relationships late in life.

THE REORGANIZATION OF EMPLOYMENT AND INCOME

In an earlier chapter we mentioned the familiar point that employment is not only the way in which individuals are organized to participate in the production of goods and services. Rather, employment also provides through wages and salaries the main mechanism for arranging, regulating, and legitimating the claims of individual participants and their families and dependents upon some part of the total product. If, hypothetically, very large quantities of goods and services could be produced without the participation of individual workers, some rules or mechanisms for allocating goods and services to those not participating in their production and thus not earning anything that could be consumed directly or exchanged for goods and services would have to be devised.

One possibility includes allocating goods and services, or income to buy them, to every individual or every family with no conditions attached. Another possibility might involve demanding some publicly beneficial activity or service in return for allocation of nonemployment-based income. Another possibility might be to require or allow such individuals either to share some of the work or employment of others who *are* regularly employed in the production of goods and services, or to provide some services to employed persons directly or indirectly. The first option—providing income with no conditions attached—is simply carrying out income transfers, while the other possibilities and schemes all generate new employment in some sense, even if that employment would not have emerged in a strictly private market setting.

In fact, the most advanced Western industrial capitalist societies *are* faced with situations in which goods and services sufficient to saturate the normal markets can be produced without fully employing all those who wish employment or need to have income in the private labor markets. Entrepreneurs have competitive interests in *reducing* employment requirements for the production and marketing of their products as far as possible. They have only quite indirect interests in maintaining overall employment and income levels to sustain demand for their products and services. Thus governments intervene to effect income transfers and to generate new employment.

State and government intervention to effect income transfers or to generate new employment has always been a matter of considerable ideological, political, and economic controversy. The amount or the part of the national product controlled or redistributed by the state, the manner in which such control or redistribution are effected, the specific parts of the potential labor markets that are subsidized, the specific types of consumption subsidized, the specific population groups to which income is transferred or for whom employment is offered are inevitably matters that erode the interests, profits, or perceived freedoms or well-being of other groups in the populations.

Yet, one way or another, modern states and governments of capitalist democracies *have* intervened and adopted policies and programs designed to harmonize production of wealth and its distribution, generally in the context of welfare state measures and strategies (Myles, 1987). These policies frequently cause industrial strife and struggle, but are also frequently topics of negotiations and ultimately cooperation, agreements, and social compacts or package deals involving both organized labor and organized employers (Goldthorpe, 1986).

There have been basically two directions, alone or in combination, for such state intervention: The guarantee of a job that provides a livelihood, or the direct guarantee of income and livelihood (Handy, 1984). These alternate directions have different implications for different groups and economic actors (Myles, 1987), but basically they both serve to guarantee minimum incomes for all citizen or members of a society when total private labor market employment volume is diminishing *unequally*. This process leaves some persons fully employed, others partially employed, some employed in well-paying jobs, others employed in inadequately paying jobs, and still others not employed at all. The general movement is in the direction of guaranteed citizen incomes, whether through provision of jobs, income maintenance schemes and Social Security measures for the unemployed and retired, elderly, or disabled, or means-tested public assistance or employment-wage-tested income supplements. The impact of this general movement will be to legitimate and de-stigmatize guaranteed citizen incomes of all types.

GUARANTEED INCOMES AND THE LIFE COURSE

As we have tried to point out in earlier chapters, the changing patterns of dependency, obligations, and entitlements have already had important effects upon the life course and family cycle. Length of schooling, the timing of departure from parental households, the formation of independent households, timing of marriage and childbearing, timing and directions of work, career patterns, and retirement are all affected by the constellations of dependency, obligations, and entitlements at the respective life course junctures. In a similar vein, we may expect that guaranteed incomes will have important impacts on various facets and dimensions of the life course.

Life-course patterns, decisions, and behavior are very often informed by the inherent *insecurity* of income and by the wish and intention of stabilizing and assuring future income flows and entitlements. This is probably the most prominent factor in social class variations in life-course patterns. Those in the middle and upper classes are generally already assured some measure of income stability, while those in the working or lower classes must consider always the potential interruption or serious fall in income. Thus schooling, studies, and pre-employment training are frequently guided by understandings, hopes, or expectations concerning future earnings and income returns. Remaining in the parental home or leaving, employment decisions, courtship and marriage choices, numbers and timing of children, and timing and directions of other life-course transitions and their related decisions are frequently informed by income considerations.

Guaranteed lifetime incomes, in whatever form and at whatever levels, are likely to render many life-course patterns and transitions much more flexible than they have been historically and even more flexible than they are presently or have been in the recent past (see various findings of the Seattle, Denver, and New Jersey income experiments cited earlier). When individuals can make decisions about schooling, marriage or divorce, or having children, and try employment and career paths relatively unclouded by considerations of expected income payoffs, it is likely that the range and variation of behavior, sequences of activity, and directions and timing of transitions will expand considerably.

GUARANTEED INCOMES AND THE FAMILY CYCLE

In a similar vein, guaranteed incomes will probably allow very much more flexibility in the family cycle generally, and in intrafamily interpersonal relationships, in particular. Not only are the numbers and timing of children likely to be affected by some new measure of freedom from the foregone incomes associated with childbearing, but the quality of children, styles of socialization, and patterns of intrafamily dependency, obligations, and care are likely to be affected. On the one hand, it will be easier for family members to forgo income in favor of childcare in the home, care of elderly family members in the home, and maintaining or renewing other activities and relationships in the home. On the other hand, it will also be easier to afford the purchase of attention and services from outside the home.

The increasing ability of married women to enter and maintain their own employment and career trajectories has long been imputed to be a factor in the rise in divorce in Western countries. In a not entirely dissimilar vein, the access to Aid to Families with Dependent Children (AFDC) benefits has been asserted to constitute a disincentive for unwed mothers to marry, stay married, or for divorced mothers to remarry (Hacker, 1988). More generally, the mutually independent incomes and earnings opportunities for men and women have been viewed as constituting a disincentive for investment in marriage or its stability. The same types of consideration as well as research findings on the impact of guaranteed incomes (Hannan, Tuma, and Groeneveld, 1977; Groeneveld, Tuma, and Hannan, 1980) lead to the conjecture that guaranteed incomes are likely to render marriages less stable over time, contribute to increasing divorce rates, and fortify patterns of serial monogamy, especially in the lower-income groups and in higher-fertility groups in Western societies. The latter have been groups where, in the past, considerations of income security, or perhaps more correctly the fear of income insecurity have been factors in sustaining fragile or unhappy marriages intact.

Guaranteed incomes are probably supportive of childbearing in that they render easier the decision to have an additional child. They diminish the amount of income foregone by women in pregnancies, childbirth, and childrearing. In addition, they are likely to affect the timing of childbearing. They may encourage a longer spread over the family cycle, possibly earlier beginnings and earlier first pregnancies and births, and very likely longer intervals between births. Again, these changes may be expected because of the diminution of income losses under guaranteed income schemes.

Child-launching and the transitions of couples into the empty-nest stage of the family cycle will likely, for the most part, take place earlier than in the past under guaranteed income schemes. This is expected because young persons will have their *own* income entitlements and, indeed, assurance of stable incomes that will encourage them to make independent housing arrangements and commitments at ages earlier than before. The changes will probably be least prominent in the highest class or highest income groups, where high and secure parental incomes have already contributed to early departure of late adolescents and young adults from parental homes.

We hypothesized earlier that retirement decisions have been strongly affected by the changing constellations of family dependency, obligations, and entitlements. Retirement can take place earlier, and with lower or less favorable pension benefits, when there are no dependent children still in the household or when there are employed persons in the household, especially spouses, in addition to the person contemplating retirement. More generally, to the extent that other household members enjoy guaranteed incomes in their own right, the retirement process and decisions of major earners are rendered more flexible.

We have already noted in a previous chapter that the meaning of widowhood, and the impact of the transition to widowhood on activity and well-being, have been transformed by improvement in health and, especially, in income maintenance of widows. The numbers of widows able to maintain their own living arrangements and the range and scope of their activities and social relationships are related to the incomes that widows have. Guaranteed incomes will, of course, improve the income situations of most widows and, for some, will permit remarriage without the threat of loss of widowhood or survivor benefits. More than that, guaranteed incomes will allow those in the social networks of widows, including especially daughters, but other family members, friends, and neighbors as well, to relate to widows under less onerous dependency and obligation constellations of their own. Because of their own guaranteed incomes, they will be less influenced by the calculus of foregone income and will have freedom to allocate their time.

GUARANTEED INCOMES, CHILD CARE, AND HEALTH CARE SYSTEMS

The last point made in the previous paragraph is central to the likely effects of guaranteed incomes on care arrangements and the division of care within families and outside of families. Guaranteed incomes will allow individuals and families freedoms and options to continue and assume additional care functions under less stringent foregone income calculations and tradeoffs. This type of point is often made, but in an unfavorable light, in connection with the assertion that Aid to Families with Dependent Children (AFDC) and other benefits to unwed mothers and dependent children constitute disincentives for the mothers to seek or accept paid employment. The same point could be made somewhat more favorably if cast as an assertion that AFDC and other benefits to unwed mothers and dependent children allow the mothers to care for their own children rather than turn them out to extrafamily care.

In the same way, guaranteed incomes will help at least some mothers choose to care for their children and forgo employment. They will help at least some daughters care for their parents or parents-in-law and forgo employment. Indeed they will help many men not necessarily enamoured with employment and careers to spend all or part of their time freed from employment in care-giving activities as well. As noted in the previous chapters, a very substantial part of health care as well as of custodial and protective and socialization-type care is already to be found in informal settings of private homes and families.

Although a vast literature is published every year on how to care for children, parents, spouses, friends, and pets, there are all manner of fee-for-service consultants and therapists to help carers care, the organized private or public services to family and other informal caregivers are not well developed in North America; they are much more advanced in Western Europe. Guaranteed incomes are likely to give great impetus to organization and development of services to such caregivers. These will include day-care services, home cleaning and maintenance help, provision of medical appliances and devices, home examination and therapy services, food preparation and transportation assistance, and recreational and educational services. Altogether, guaranteed incomes are likely to have the effect of expanding greatly the informal and open community parts of health care systems, possibly even regardless of the costs of such services relative to those of privately and competitively organized institutional (private nursing home) long-term care for the elderly requiring it.

THE GRAY POWER BOTTOM LINE

The demographic, social, and economic trends viewed in this book as behind and accompanying the aging of populations and changes in life course and family cycle have been accompanied by a revolution in knowledge, communication, access to information, and mutual visibility of the various social groupings. As knowledge, information, mutual visibility, and shared social, economic, and political analyses and understandings proliferate, there is increasing demand for equality. The rhetoric of equality increases in volume and power, and social inequality becomes less tolerable as a permanent societal feature. The demands for resolution of social inequality may take the form of demands for individual increments or collective increments, and they may find partial resolution in measures promoting equality of opportunity or seek resolution in measures promoting equality of condition.

The elderly in modern industrialized societies have become increasingly organized and articulate, due both to their rapidly increasing numbers and electoral leverage, and to their increased levels of information, skills, and political experience and sophistication. In North America, it is probably the elderly, through their various associations and groupings, who have come closest to recognition that resolution of problems of inequality of opportunity and condition are fundamentally problems of powerlessness, and that their resolution must take the form of collective increments achieved by political means. Their successes in recent decades show that they still have very much to teach their children and succeeding cohorts in modern society.

REFERENCES

ABELES, R.P., L. STEEL, AND L.L. WISE 1980. "Patterns and Implications of Life-Course Organization: Studies from Project TALENT." in P.B. Baltes and O.G. Brim, Jr., eds., *Life-Span Development and Behavior*, Vol. 3. New York: Academic Press.

ABU-LABAN, S. AND B. ABU-LABAN, 1980. "Women and the Aged as Minority Groups."in V. Marshall, ed., *Aging in Canada: Social Perspectives*, Don Mills, Out.: Fitahenry and Whiteside.

ACHENBAUM, W.A., 1978. *Old Age in the New Land*. Baltimore: Johns Hopkins University Press.

ACHENBAUM, W.A., 1974. "The Obsolescence of Old Age in America, 1865-1914."*Journal of Social History*, 8:45-64

ACHENBAUM, W. A. 1985. "Societal Perceptions of the Aging and the Aged" in R.H. Binstock and E. Shanas, eds., *Handbook of Aging and the Social Sciences*. 2d ed., New York: Van Nostrand Reinhold.

ADAMS, B.N. 1968. *Kinship in an Urban Setting*. Chicago: Markham Publ. Co.

ALBRECHT, S.L., AND P.R. KUNZ, 1980. "The Decision to Divorce, A Social Exchange Perspective." *Journal of Divorce* 3(4):319-339.

ALDOUS, J., 1978. *Family Careers: Developmental Change in Families*. New York: Wiley

ALWIN D.F., P.E. CONVERSE, AND S.S. MARTIN 1986. "Living Arrangements and Social Integration" in F.M. Andrews, ed., *Research on the Quality of Life*. Ann Arbor: Institute for Social Research. Survey Research Center, University of Michigan.

ANDREWS, F.M., ed. 1986. *Research on the Quality of Life*. Ann Arbor: Institute for Social Research. Survey Research Center, University of Michigan.

ARIES, P. 1962. *Centuries of Childhood*. Translated by R. Baldick. New York: Vintage Books.

ARON, R. 1967. *Main Currents in Sociological Thought*. Vol.2 Translated by R. Howard and H. Weaver. London: Penguin Books.

ATCHLEY, R.C. 1971. "Retirement and Work Orientation." *The Gerontologist* 11: 29–32.

———. 1976. *The Sociology of Retirement*. Cambridge, Mass.: Schenkman.

———. 1988. *The Social Forces in Later Life*. 4th ed. Belmont, Calif.: Wadsworth Publishing Co.

BAKKE, E.W. 1940. *The Unemployed Worker*. New Haven, Conn.: Yale University Press.

BALTES, P.B., AND O.G. BRIM JR., eds. 1978. *Life-Span Development and Behavior*. Vols. 1–New York: Academic Press

BARKIN, S. 1970. "Retraining and Job Redesign: Positive Approaches to the Continued Employment of Older Persons." In H.L. Sheppard, ed. *Toward an Industrial Gerontology*. Cambridge, Mass.: Schenkman Publishing Co.

BARON, J.N., AND W.T. BIELBY. 1985. "Organizational Barriers to Gender Equality: Sex Segregation of Jobs and Opportunities."In A.S. Rossi, ed., *Gender and the Life Course*. New York: Aldine.

BARRON, M., 1953. "Minority Group Characteristics of the Aged in American Society." *Journal of Gerontology*. 8(3):477-82

BEATTIE, JR., W.M. 1978. "Aging and the Social Services."In R.H. Binstock and E. Shanas, eds., *Handbook of Aging and the Social Sciences*. New York: Van Nostrand Reinhold.

BECK, S.H. 1986. "Determinants of Labor Force Activity among Retired Men."*Research on Aging 7:251–80*.

BECKER, G.S. 1976. *The Economic Approach to Human Behavior*. Chicago: University of Chicago Press.

BENGTSON, V., 1979. "Ethnicity and Aging: Problems and Issues in Current Social Science Inquiry."in D. Gelfand and A. Kutzik, eds., *Ethnicity and Aging: Theory, Research, and Policy*. New York: Springer Publishing Co.

BENGTSON, V.L., AND K.D. BLACK. 1973. "Intergenerational Relations and Continuities in Socialization." In P.B. Baltes and K.W. Schaie, eds., *Life-Span Development Psychology. Personality and Socialization*. New York: Academic Press.

BERELSON, B., 1974. "World Population: Status Report 1974. A Guide for the Concerned Citizen."*Reports on Population/Family Planning*. No. 15, January.

BERG, G. AND S. GADOW. 1978. "Toward More Human Meanings of Aging: Ideals and Images from Philosophy and Art." In S.F. Spicker, K.M. Woodward, and D.D. Van Tassel, eds., *Aging and the Elderly*. Atlantic Highlands, N. J.: Humanities Press.

BEST, F., AND B. STERN. 1977. "Education, Work, and Leisure: Must They Come in That Order?"*Monthly Labor Review* July: 3–10

BINSTOCK, R.H., AND E. SHANAS, eds. 1985. *Handbook of Aging and the Social Sciences*. 2d ed. New York: Van Nostrand Reinhold.

BLAU, P.M. 1964. *Exchange and Power in Social Life*. New York: Wiley.

BLAU, P.M., AND DUNCAN, O.D. 1967. *The American Occupational Structure*. New York: Wiley.

BLAU, Z.S. 1973. *Old Age in a Changing Society*. New York: Franklin Watts.

———. 1981. *Aging in a Changing Society*. 2d ed. New York: Watts.

BLOOD, R.D., AND D.M. WOLF. 1960. *Husbands and Wives: The Dynamics of Married Living*. Glencoe: Free Press.

BLOSSFIELD, H.P., 1986. "Career Opportunities in the Federal Republic of Germany: a Dynamic Approach to the Study of Life-Course, Cohort, and Period Effects."*European Sociological Review* 2 (December) :3.

BONGAARTS, J., 1983. "The Formal Demography of Families and Households: An Overview." International Union for the Scientific Study of Populations Newsletter. No. 17, 27–42.

BONGAARTS, J., AND R.G. POTTER. 1983. *Fertility, Biology and Behavior: An Analysis of Proximate Determinants*. New York: Academic Press.

BOUDON, R., 1974. *Educational Opportunity and Social Inequality*. New York: Wiley.

BOULDING, K. 1961. "Reflections on Poverty." *The Social Welfare Forum*. New York: Columbia University Press.

BOWLES, S., AND H. GINTIS. 1976. *Schooling in Capitalist America*. New York: Basic Books.

BOYD, M. 1985. "Immigration and Occupational Attainment in Canada." In M. Boyd et al. eds., *Ascription and Achievement: Studies in Mobility and Status Attainment in Canada*. Ottawa: Carleton University Press.

BOYD, M., FEATHERMAN, D.L., AND J. MASTRAS. 1980. "Status Attainment of Immigrant and Immigrant Origin Groups in the United States, Canada, and Israel."*Comparative Studies in Sociology* 3:199–228.

BRODY, E.M. 1978, "The Aging of the Family." *The Annuls of the American Academy of Political and Social Science* 438: 13–27

———. 1985. "Parent Care as a Normative Family Stress."*The Gerontologist* 25(1):19–29.

BRUNO, M., AND J. D. SACHS, 1985. *Economics of Worldwide Stagflation*. Oxford: Basil Blackwell.

BUCHMANN, A.M. 1983. "Maximizing Post-Retirement Labor Market Opportunities." In H.S. Parnes, ed., *Policy Issues in Work and Retirement*. Kalamazoo, Mich.: Upjohn Institute for Employment Research.

BURCH, T.K., 1980. "Household Size and Structure in Demographic Transitions." *Proceedings of the Social Statistics Section, American Statistical Association*. Washington, D. C.: ASA, pp. 149–53.

———. 1981. "Interactive Decision Making in the Determination of Residence Patterns and Family Relations." Paper presented at the International Population Conference, International Union for the Scientific Study of Population, Manilla, December.

———. 1982. "Household and Family Demography."In J.A. Ross, ed., *International Encyclopedia of Population*. Vol. 1. New York: Free Press, pp. 299–307.

———. 1985a. "Changing Age-Sex roles and Household Crowding: A Theoretical Note." Paper presented at the General Conference of the International Union for the Scientific Study of Population, Florence, June.

———. 1985b. *Family History Survey: Preliminary Findings*. Ottawa: Statistics Canada. Catalogue 99–955.

BURDMAN, G.M., 1986. *Healthful Aging*. Englewood Cliffs, N. J.: Prentice-Hall, Inc.

BURGESS, E.W. 1960. "Aging in Western Culture."In E.W. Burgess, ed., *Aging in Western Societies*. Chicago: University of Chicago Press.

BURTLESS, G., AND R.A. MOFFITT. 1984. "The Effect of Social Security Benefits on the Labor Supply of the Aged."In H.J. Aaron and G. Burtless, eds., *Retirement and Economic Behavior*. Washington, D.C.: The Brookings Institution.

Business Week, Oct. 28, 1985.

Business Week, Nov. 25, 1985.

BUTLER, R.N. 1975. *Why Survive? Being Old in America*. New York: Harper and Row.

CAIN, L.D., JR. 1964. "Life Course and Social Structure."In R.E.L. Faris, ed., *Handbook of Modern Sociology*. Chicago: Rand McNally and Co.

CALDWELL, J.C., 1976. "Toward a Restatement of Demographic Transition Theory."*Population and Development Review*. 2:321–66.

CALDWELL, J.C. 1982. *Theory of Fertility Decline.* London: Academic Press.

CAMPBELL, A. 1981. *The Sense of Well-Being in America. Recent Patterns and Trends.* New York: McGraw-Hill Book Co.

CAMPBELL, A., P.E. CONVERSE, AND W.L. RODGERS, 1976. *The Quality of American Life.* New York, Russell Sage Foundation.

CAPLOW, T. 1968. *Coalitions in the Triad.* Englewood Cliffs, N. J.: Prentice Hall, Inc.

CARP, F.M. 1976. "Housing and Living Environments of Older People."In R.H. Binstock and E. Shanas, eds., *Handbook of Aging and the Social Sciences.* New York: Van Nostrand Reinhold.

CARROLL, G.R., AND K.U. MAYER. 1986. "Job-Shift Patterns in the Federal Republic of Germany: The Effects of Social Class, Industrial Sector, and Organizational Size."*American Sociological Review.* 51(3):323–341.

CARTER, H., AND P.C. GLICK. 1976. *Marriage and Divorce: A Social and Economic Study.* Cambridge, Mass.: Harvard University Press.

CASEY, B., AND G. BRUCHE. 1983. *Work or Retirement? Labor Market and Social Policy for Older Workers in France, Great Britain, The Netherlands, Sweden, and the USA.* Aldershot, England: Gower.

CHERLIN, A. 1981. *Marriage, Divorce, Remarriage.* Cambridge, Mass.: Harvard University Press.

———.1983. "Changing Family and Household: Contemporary Lessons From Historical Research."*Annual Review of Sociology* 9:51–66.

CLARK, R.L., AND J.J. SPENGLER. 1979. "Dependency Ratios: Their Use in Economic Analysis."In J.L. Simon and J. DaVanzo, eds., *Research in Population Economics.* Vol. 2, 1980. Greenwich, Conn.: JAI Press, 63–77.

CLARK, R.L., AND J.J. SPENGLER. 1980. *The Economics of Individual and Population Aging.* New York: Cambridge University Press.

CLAUSEN, J.A. 1972. "The Life Course of Individuals."In M.W. Riley et al., *Aging and Society.* Vol. 3, *A Sociology of Age Stratification.* New York: Russell Sage Foundation.

———. 1986. *The Life Course.* Englewood Cliffs: Prentice Hall, Inc.

COALE, A.J. 1956. "The Effects of Changes in Mortality and Fertility on Age Composition."*Milbank Memorial Fund Quarterly* 34:79–114.

COALE, A.J., AND E.M. HOOVER, 1958. *Population Growth and Economic Development in Low Income Countries.* Princeton, N. J.: Princeton University Press.

COLEMAN, J.S. 1984. "The Transition from School to Work."*Research in Stratification and Mobility* 3:27–59.

COLLINS, R. 1979. *The Credential Society.* New York: Academic Press.

COPPERMAN, L.F., AND F.D. KEAST 1983. *Adjusting to an Older Workforce.*New York: Van Nostrand Reinhold Co.

COTTRELL, F. 1960. "The Technological and Societal Basis of Aging."In C. Tibbitts, ed., *Handbook of Social Gerontology.* Chicago: University of Chicago Press.

COWGILL, D. O. 1974. "Aging and Modernization: A Revision of the Theory."In J.F. Gubrium, ed., *Late Life: Communities and Environmental Policy.* Springfield, Ill.: Charles C. Thomas.

———. 1974. "The Aging of Populations and Societies."*The Annals of the American Academy of Political and Social Science* 415:1–18.

COWGILL, D.O., AND L.D. HOLMES, eds. 1972. *Aging and Modernization.* New York: Appleton-Century-Crofts.

CROWN, W.H., 1985. "Some Thoughts on Reformulating the Dependency Ratio."*The Gerontologist* 25(2):166–171.

———. 1987. "The Prospective Burden of an Aging Population,"in *Economic Roles for Older People in Maturing Societies.* New York: Springer.

CUMMING, E. 1964. "New Thoughts on the Theory of Disengagement,"in R. Kastenbaum, ed., *New Thoughts on Old Age.* New York: Springer.

CUMMING, E., et al. 1960. "Disengagement—A Tentative Theory of Aging."*Sociometry* 23:23–35.

CUMMING, E., AND W. HENRY. 1961. *Growing Old: The Process of Disengagement.* New York: Basic Books.

CUTRIGHT, P. 1973. *Achievement, Mobility, and the Draft: Their Impact on the Earnings of Men.* U.S. Department of Health, Education, and Welfare, Social Security Administration, Office of Research and Statistics. Staff paper no. 14. Publication No. (SSA) 73–11854.

DAVIES, A.M., 1984. "The Epidemiology of Aging." Jerusalem: Brookdale Institute International Forum Paper IF-2-84.

DAVIS, K. 1984. "Wives and Work: The Sex Role Revolution and its Consequences."*Population and Development Review* 10:397–417.

DAVIS, K., AND P. VAN DEN OEVER. 1981. "Age Relations and Public Policy in Advanced Industrial Societies."*Population and Development Review* 7:1–18.

DAVIS, K., AND P. VAN DEN OEVER, 1982. "Demographic Foundations of New Sex Rules."*Population and Development Review* 8:495–511.

DE BEAUVOIR, S. 1972. *The Coming of Age* New York: Putnam.

DEMOS, J., AND V. DEMOS, 1969. "Adolescence in Historical Perspective."*Journal of Marriage and the Family.* 31(4): 632–8.

DENTON, F.T., AND B.G. SPENCER. 1975. *Population and the Economy.* Lexington, Mass: D.C. Heath & Co.

DEVINEY, S., AND A. O'RAND. n.d. "Retirement Policy, Economic Change, and Labor Force Participation Among Older Men and Women, 1951 to 1979." Durham, N. C.: Duke University Center for the Study of Aging and Human Development, unpub. ms.

DOERING, M., S.R. RHODES, AND M. SCHUSTER. 1983. *The Aging Worker. Research and Recommendations.* Beverly Hills, Calif.: Sage Publications.

DOHRENWEND, B.S., AND B.P. DOHRENWEND, eds. 1974. *Stressful Life Events.* New York: Wiley.

DORON, A. 1979. *Social Services for the Aged in Eight Countries. A Comparative Study.* Jerusalem: Brookdale Institute.

DOWD, J.J. 1975. "Aging as Exchange: A Preface to Theory."*The Journal of Gerontology* 30:4.
———. 1978. "Aging as Exchange: A Test of the Distributive Justice Proposition."*Pacific Sociological Review* 21:351–75.
———. 1980. *Stratification among the Aged*. Monterey, Calif.: Brooks/Cole Publishing Co.
———. 1986. "The Old Person as Stranger."In V.W. Marshall, ed., *Later Life. The Social Psychology of Aging*. Beverly Hills, Calif.: Sage Publications.
DRAGASTIN, S.E., AND G.H. ELDER, JR. 1975. *Adolescents in the Life Cycle. Psychological Change and Social Context*. New York: John Wiley & Sons.
DUNCAN, G.J. 1984. *Years of Poverty, Years of Plenty: The Changing Economic Fortunes of American Workers and Families*. Ann Arbor, Mich.: Institute for Social Research.
DUNCAN, O.D. 1964. "Social Organization and the Ecosystem." In R E.L. Faris, ed., *Handbook of Modern Sociology*. Chicago: Rand McNally.
DUNCAN, O.D., FEATHERMAN, D.L., AND B. DUNCAN. 1972. *Socioeconomic Background and Achievement*. New York: Seminar Press.
DUNN, J. 1984. "Sibling Studies and the Developmental Impact of Critical Incidents." In P.B. Baltes and O.G. Brim Jr., eds., *Life-Span Development and Behavior*. Vol. 6. New York: Academic Press.
DUVALL, E.M. 1962. *Family Development*. 2d ed. Philadelphia, Penn.: Lippincott Co.
EASTERLIN, R.A., E.M. CRIMMINS, AND L. OHANIAN. 1984. "Changes in Labor Force Participation of Persons 55 and Over Since World War II: Their Nature and Causes." In P.K. Robinson, L. Livingston, and J.E. Birren, eds., *Aging and Technological Advances*. New York: Plenum Publishing Co.
EHRLICH, P.R. 1968. *The Population Bomb*. New York: Ballantine Books.
EICHLER, M. 1983. *Families in Canada Today. Recent Changes and Their Policy Consequences*. Toronto: Gage Educational Publishing Co.
EISENSTADT, S.N. 1956. *From Generation to Generation. Age Groups and Social Structure*. Glencoe, Ill. Free Press.
ELDER, G.H., JR., 1978. "Family History and the Life Course." In T.K. Hareven, ed., *Transitions. The Family and the Life Course in Historical Perspective*. New York: Academic Press.
ELDER, G.H. JR. 1982. "Historical Experiences in the Later Years." In T.K. Hareven and K.J. Adams, eds., *Aging and Life Course Transitions: An Interdisciplinary Perspective*. New York Guilford Press.
———. ed., 1985. *Life Course Dynamics,. Trajectories and Transitions, 1968–1980*. Ithaca, N. Y.: Cornell University Press.
———.1974. *Children of the Great Depression Social Change in Life Experience*. Chicago, Ill.: University of Chicago Press.
———.1975. "Age Differentiation and the Life course." *Annual Review of Sociology*. 1:165–90.
ELDER, G.H., JR., J.K. LIKER, AND C.E. CROSS. 1984. "Parent-Child Behavior in the Great Depression: Life Course and Intergenerational Influences." In

P.B. Baltes and O.G. Brim, Jr., eds., *Life-Span Development and Behavior*. Vol. 6. New York: Academic Press.
ELDER, G.H., JR., G. DOWNEY, AND C. E. CROSS. 1986. "Family Ties and Life Changes: Hard Times and Hard Choices in Women's Lives Since the 1930s." In N. Datan, A.L. Greene, and H.W. Reese. eds., *Life-Span Development Psychology. Intergenerational Relations*. Hillsdale, N. J.: Lawrence Erlbaum Associates, Publishers.
EMERSON, R.M. 1976. "Social Exchange Theory." *Annual Review of Sociology* 2:335–62.
ENGLAND, P., AND G. FARKAS. 1986. *Households, Employment, and Gender: A Social, Economic, and Demographic View*. New York: Aldine de Gruyter.
ERIKSON, E.H. 1950. *Childhood and Society*. New York: Norton.
———. 1982. *The Life Cycle Completed: A Review*. New York: Norton.
ESTES, C.L., et al. 1983. *Fiscal Austerity and Aging: Shifting Government Responsibility for the Elderly*. Beverly Hills, Calif.: Sage.
ESTES, C.L., et al. 1984. *Long Term Care of the Elderly: Public Policy Issues*. Beverly Hills, Calif.: Sage.
EURICH, A.C. 1981. *Major Transitions in the Human Life Cycle*. Lexington, Mass.: D.C. Heath. Lexington Books.
EVERSLEY, D. 1982. "Some New Aspects of Aging in Britain."In T.K. Hareven and K.J. Adams, eds., *Aging and Life Course Transitions: An Interdisciplinary Perspective. New York,: Guilford Press.*
EVERSLEY, D., AND W. KOLLMAN. 1982. *Population Change and Social Planning*. London : Edward Arnold.
FEATHERMAN, D.L. 1971. "A Research Note: A Social Structural Model for the Socioeconomic Career." *American Journal of Sociology*. 77:293–304.
———. 1987. "Industrialization, the Life Course, and the Changing Process of Stratification." In K. Tominaga and D. Treiman, eds., *Comparative Stratification in Japan and the United States*.
———. 1985. "Life-Span Perspectives in Social Science Research." In P.B. Baltes and O.G. Brim, Jr., eds., *Life-Span Development and Behavior*. Vol. 5. New York: Academic Press.
———. 1986. "Societal Change, the Life Course, and Social Mobility."In A. Weymann, ed., *Handlungspielraume Reihe:Der Mensch als soziales und personales Wesen*. Stuttgart: Ferdinand Enke Verlag.
FEATHERMAN, D.L., AND T. PETERSEN, 1986. "Markers of Aging: Modeling the Clocks That Time Us."*Research on Aging*. 8(3):339–365.
FEATHERMAN, D.L., AND A. SORENSEN. 1983. "Societal Transformation in Norway and Change in the Life Course Transition into Adulthood."*Acta Sociologica* 26:105–26.
FEATHERMAN, D.L., D.P. HOGAN, AND A.B. SORENSEN. 1984. "Entry into Adulthood: Profiles of Young Men in the 1950s."In P.B. Baltes and O.G. Brim, Jr., eds., *Life-Span Development and Behavior*. Vol. 6. New York: Academic Press.

FEATHERMAN, D.L., AND R.M. HAUSER. 1978. *Opportunity and Change.* New York: Academic Press.

FEATHERMAN, D.L., D.P. HOGAN, AND A. SORENSEN. 1984. "Entry into Adulthood: Profiles of Young Men in the 1950s." *Life-Span Development and Behavior* 6:159–202.

FEATHERMAN, D.L., AND K. SELBEE, in press. "Class Formation and Class Mobility: A New Approach With Counts From Life History Data."In M.W. Riley and B. Huber, eds., *Social Structure and Human Lives.* Newburg Park: Sage Publications.

FEATHERMAN, D.L., AND A. SORENSEN. 1983. "Societal Transformation in Norway and Change in the Life Course Transition into Adulthood."*Acta Sociologica* 26:105–26.

FINCH, J. 1987. "Family Obligations and The Life Course." In A. Bryman et al., eds. *Rethinking the Life Cycle.* London: Macmillan Press, Ltd.

FISCHER, D.H. 1977. *Growing Old in America.* New York: Oxford University Press.

FLEISHMAN, R., et al., 1988. "Improving the Quality of Service in Long Term Care Institutions for the Elderly."*World Health Forum.* 9:327–335.

FLORA, P., AND A.J. HEIDENHEIMER. 1981. *The Development of Welfare States in Europe and America.* New Brunswick, N. J.: Transaction Books.

FONER, A. 1986. *Aging and Old Age. New Perspectives.* Englewood Cliffs: Prentice Hall, Inc.

FONER, A., AND D. KERTZER. 1978. "Transitions Over the Life Course: Lessons from Age-Set Societies." *American Journal of Sociology* 83(5):1081–1104.

FORDER, A. 1983. *Penelope Hall's Social Services of England and Wales.* 10th ed., London: Routledge and Kegan Paul.

FOURASTIE, J. 1959. "De la vie traditionelle a la vie tertiare."*Population* 143):417–432

FREEMAN, H.E., S. LEVINE, AND L.G. REEDER. 1979. *Handbook of Medical Sociology.* Englewood Cliffs: Prentice Hall, Inc.

FREEMAN, R.B. 1976. *The Overeducated American.* New York: Academic Press.

FREEMAN, R.B., 1979. "The Effect of Demographic Factors on the Age-Earnings Profile in the U. S. "*Journal of Human Resources.* Summer.

FRIEDLANDER, D. 1969. "Demographic Responses and Population Change."*Demography* 646:359–81.

FRIEDLANDER, D., 1983. "Demographic Responses and Social Economic Structure: Population Processes in England and Wales in the Nineteenth Century."- *Demography* 20:249–72.

FRIEDMAN, M., AND R. FRIEDMAN. 1980. *Free to choose: A Personal Statement.* New York: Avon Books.

FRIES, J.F., 1980. "Aging, Natural Death and the Compression of Morbidity."*New Englend Journal of Medicine.* 303:130–35.

FRIES J.F. 1983. "The Compression of Morbidity." *Milbank Memorial Fund Quarterly* 61, no. 3 (Summer): 397–419.

FUCHS, V.R. 1974. *Who Shall Live?* New York: Basic Books.

———. 1979. "Economics, Health, and Post-Industrial Society."*Milbank Memorial Fund Quarterly* 57, 2(Spring): 153–82.

———. 1983. *How We Live. An Economic Perspective on Americans from Birth to Death.* Cambridge, Mass.: Harvard University Press.

———. 1984. "Though Much is Taken: Reflections on Aging, Health, and Medical Care."*Milbank Memorial Fund Quarterly* 62, No.2(Spring): 143–66.

GEE, E.M. 1986. "The Life Course of Canadian Women: an Historical and Demographic Analysis." *Social Indicators Research* 18:263–83.

GEE, E.M., AND M.M. KIMBALL. 1987. *Women and Aging.* Toronto: Butterworths.

GELFAND, D.E. AND A.J. KUTZIK. 1979. *Ethnicity and Aging. Theory, Research, and Policy.* New York: Springer.

GENDELL, M. 1980. "Sweden Faces Zero Population Growth."*Population Bulletin* 35, No.2 (June). Washington, D.C.: Population Reference Bureau.

GEORGE, L.K. 1980. *Role Transitions in Later Life.* Monterey, Calif.: Brooks/Cole Publishing Co.

GILBERT, N. 1983. *Capitalism and the Welfare State.* New Haven, Conn.: Yale University Press.

GILBERT, N., AND H. SPECHT. 1974. *Dimensions of Social Welfare Policy.* Englewood Cliffs, N. J.: Prentice Hall, Inc.

GILLIS, J.R. 1974. *Youth and History.* New York: Academic Press.

GINZBERG, E. 1983. "Life Without Work: Does It Make Sense? In H.S. Parnes, ed., *Policy Issues in Work and Retirement.* Kalamazoo, Mich.: Upjohn Institute for Employment Research.

GLASS, D.V., AND E. GREBENIR, 1954. *The Trend and Pattern of Fertility in Great Britain,* Papers of the Royal Commission on Population. Vol.VI. Part I, Report, London: HMSO.

GLICK, P.C. 1947. "The Family Cycle."*American Sociological Review* 12:164–74.

———.1977. "Updating the Life Cycle of the Family." *Journal of Marriage and the Family* 39:5–13.

GLICK, I.O., R.S. WEISS, AND C.M. PARKES, 1974. *The First Year of Bereavement.* New York: Wiley.

GOLDSCHEIDER, F.K., AND J. DAVANZO. 1986. "Semi-autonomy and Leaving Home in Early Adulthood."*Social Forces.* 65:187–201.

GOLDTHORPE, J.H., ed. 1986. *Order and Conflict in Contemporary Capitalism. Studies in the Political Economy of Western Nations.* New York: Oxford University Press.

GOODMAN, L., N. KEYFITZ, AND T.W. PULLUM. 1974. "Family Formation and the Frequency of Various Kinship Relationships."*Theoretical Population Biology* 5:1–27.

GOODMAN, L., N. KEYFITZ, AND T.W. PULLUM. 1975. "Addendum: Family Formation and the Frequency of Various Kinship Relationships."*Theoretical Population Biology* 8: 376–81.

GOODY, J. 1976. "Aging in Nonindustrial Societies."In R.H. Binstock and E. Shanas, eds., *Handbook of Aging and the Social Sciences.* New York: Van Nostrand Reinhold.

GOVE, W.R. 1985. "The Effect of Age and Gender on Deviant Behavior: A Biopsychosocial Perspective."

In A.S. Rossi, eds., *Gender and the Life Course.* New York: Aldine.

GRAEBNER, W. 1980. *A History of Retirement.* New Haven, Conn.: Yale University Press.

GREELEY, A. 1974. *Ethnicity in the United States: A Preliminary Reconnaissance.* New York: Wiley.

GREENE, A.L., AND A.M. BOXER. 1986. "Daughters and Sons as Young Adults: Restructuring the Ties that Bind." In N. Datan, A.L. Greene, and H.W. Reese, eds., *Life-Span Psychology. Intergenerational Relations.* Hillsdale, N.J., Lawrence Erlbaum Associates, Publishers.

GRIGSBY, J., AND J.B. McGOWAN. 1986. "Still in the Nest: Adult Children Living with Their Parents." *Sociology and Social Research* 70(2):146–8.

GROENEVELD L.P., N.B. TUMA, AND M.T. HANNAN. 1980. "The Effect of Negative Income Tax Programs on Marital Dissolution." *Journal of Human Resources* 15: 654–74.

GRUMAN., G.J. 1978. "Cultural Origins of Present-day Age-ism: The Modernization of the Life Cycle."In S.F. Spicker, K.M. Woodward, and D.D. Van Tassell, eds., *Aging and the Elderly.* Atlantic Highlands, N. J.: Humanities Press.

GUILLEMARD, A.M. 1982. "Old Age, Retirement, and the Social Class Structure: Toward an Analysis of the Structural Dynamics of the Latter Stage of Life."In T.K. Hareven and K.J. Adams, eds., *Aging and Life Course Transitions: An Interdisciplinary Perspective.* New York: Guilford Press.

GUTTENTAG, M., AND P.F. SECORD. 1983. *Too Many Women? The Sex Ratio Question.* Beverly Hills, Calif.: Sage.

HABIB, J., 1985. "The Economy and the Aged." In R.H. Binstock and E. Shanas, eds., Handbook of Aging and the Social Sciences. 2d. ed. New York: Van Nostrand Reinhold Co.

HABIB, J., AND J. MATRAS. 1987a. "On Trends in Retirement in Israel."In K.S. Markides and C.L. Cooper, eds., *Retirement in Industrialized Societies.* London: John Wiley & Sons.

HABIB J., AND J. MATRAS. 1987b. "Role and Activity Profiles of Middle-Aged and Elderly Israelis: First Findings of a National Survey."Paper Presented to Future of Adult Life, First International Conference. Leeuwenhorst, Netherlands, April.

HACKER, A., 1988. "Getting Rough on the Poor."*The New York Review of Books.* 35(15):12–17.

HANDY, C., 1984. *The Future of Work.* Oxford: Basil Blackwell.

HANNAN, M.T., N.B. TUMA, AND L.P. GROENEVELD. 1977. "Income and Marital Events: Evidence From an Income-Maintenance Experiment."*American Journal of Sociology* 82:1186–1211.

HAREVEN, T.K. 1975. "Family Time and Industrial Time: The Family and Work in a Planned Corporation Town, 1900–1924." *Journal of Urban History* 1:365–89.

———. 1978. *Transitions: The Family and the Life Course in Historical Perspective.* New York: Academic Press.

———. 1981. "Historical Changes in the Timing of Family Transitions: Their Impact on Generational Relations."

In R.W. Fogel, et al., eds., *Aging, Stability, and Change in the Family.* New York: Academic Press.

———. 1982. *Family Time and Industrial Time.* Cambridge, England: Cambridge University Press.

———. 1982. "The Life Course and Aging in Historical Perspective." In T.K. Hareven and K.J. Adams, eds., *Aging and Life Course Transitions: An Interdisciplinary Perspective.* New York: Guilford Press.

HAREVEN, T.K., AND K.J. ADAMS, eds. 1982. *Aging and Life Course Transitions: An Interdisciplinary Perspective.* New York: Guilford Press.

HASTINGS, D.W., AND L.G. BERRY. eds. 1979. *Cohort Analysis: A Collection of Interdisciplinary Readings* Oxford, Ohio: Scripps Foundation.

HAUSER, R.M., AND D.L. FEATHERMAN. 1977. *The Process of Stratification: Trends and Analysis.* New York: Academic Press.

HAUSER, R.M., W.H. SEWELL, AND B.R. CLARRIDGE. 1982. "The Influence of Family Structure on Socioeconomic Achievement: A Progress Report."CDE Working Paper 82–59. Madison, Wisc.: Center for Demography and Ecology, University of Wisconsin.

HEER, D.M., R.W. HODGE, AND M. FELSON. 1985. "The Cluttered Nest: Evidence That Young Adults Are More Likely to Live At Home Now Than in the Recent Past."*Sociology and Social Research* 69(3):436–41.

HELLER, P.S.,et al. 1985. *Aging and Social Expenditure in the Major Industrial Countries, 1980–2025.* Washington, D.C.: International.

HENDRICKS, J., AND C. HENDRICKS, 1981. *Aging in Mass Society.* 2d ed. Cambridge, Mass.: Winthrop Publishers.

HENRETTA, J.C., AND A.M. O' RAND. 1980. "Labor Force Participation of Older Married Women." *Social Security Bulletin* 43(8):10–16.

HENRIPIN, J. 1968. *Trends and Factors of Fertility in Canada.* Ottawa: Queen's Printer.

HESS, B. 1972. "Friendship."In M.W. Riley, M. Johnson, and A. Foner, eds., *Aging and Society.* Vol. 3, *A Sociology of Age Stratification.* New York: Russell Sage Foundation.

HILL, D., AND M. HILL. 1976. "Older Children and Splitting Off."In G. Duncan and J. M. Morgan, eds., *Five Thousand Families—Patterns of Economic Progress.* Ann Arbor, Mich.: Survey Research Center, Institute for Social Research, University of Michigan, pp.117–154.

HIRSCHMAN, C. 1975. *Ethnic and Social Stratification in Peninsular Malaysia.* ASA Rose Monograph Series. Washington, D. C.: American Sociological Association.

HIRSCHMAN, C. 1988. "Minorities in the Labor Market, Cyclical Patterns and Secular Trends in Joblessness." In G.D. Sandefur and M. Tienda, eds., *Divided Opportunities.* New York: Plenum Publishing Corp.

HOGAN, D.P. 1978. "The Variable Order of Events in the Life Course."*American Sociological Review* 43:573–86.

———. 1981. *Transitions and Social Change. The Early Lives of American Men.* New York: Academic.

———. 1982. "Subgroup Variations in Early Life Transitions." In M.W. Riley, R.P. Abeles, and M. Teitelbaum, eds., *Aging from Birth to Death.* Vol.2, *Sociotemporal Perspectives.* AAAS Symposium 79. Boulder, Colo.: Westview Press.

———. 1985. "The Demography of Life-Span Transitions: Temporal and Gender Comparisons." In A.S. Rossi, ed., *Gender and the Life Course.* New York: Aldine.

HOLMES T.H. AND M. MASUDA. 1974. "Life Change and Illness Susceptibility." In B.S. Dorhrenwend and B.P. Dohrenwend, eds., *Stressful Life Events.* New York: Wiley.

HUBER, J. AND G. SPITZE. 1983. *Sex Stratification: Children, Housework, and Jobs.* New York: Academic Press.

INBAR, M. 1976. *The Vulnerable Age Phenomenon.* New York: Russell Sage Foundation.

JACKSON, J.J. 1985. "Race, National Origin, Ethnicity, and Aging," in R.H. Binstock and E. Shanas, eds., *Handbook of Aging and the Social Sciences.* 2d ed. New York: Van Nostrand Reinhold.

JACOBSON B. 1980. *Young Programs for Older Workers. Case Studies in Progressive Personnel Policies.* New York: Van Nostrand Reinhold.

JAFFE, A.J., AND C.D. STEWART. 1951. *Manpower Resources and Utilization.* New York: Wiley.

JAHODA, M., P. LAZARSFELD, AND H. ZEISEL. 1971. *Marienthal: The Sociography of an Unemployed Community.* Chicago: Aldine–Atherton.

JENCKS, C., et al. 1972. *Inequality. A Reassessment of the Effect of Family and Schooling in America.* New York: Basic Books.

JENKINS, C., AND B. SHERMAN. 1979. *The Collapse of Work.* London : Eyre Methuen.

JOHNSON, E.S., AND J.B. WILLIAMSON. 1987. "Retirement in the United States." In K.S. Markides and L. Cooper, eds., *Retirement in Industrialized Societies.* Chichester, England: John Wiley & Sons Ltd.

JOHNSTON, J., AND J.G. BACHMAN. 1972. *Youth in Transition.* Vol.5, *Young Men and Military Service.* Ann Arbor, Mich.: Institute for Social Research, Survey Research Center.

KAHN, R.L. 1979. "Aging and Social Support". In M.W. Riley, ed., *Aging from Birth to Death. Interdisciplinary Perspectives.* AAAS Selected Symposium 30. Boulder, Colo.: Westview Press.

KAHN, R.L., AND T.C. ANTONUCCI. 1980. "Convoys over the Life Course: Attachment, Roles, and Social Support." In P.B. Baltes and O.G. Brim, Jr., eds., *Life Span Development and Behavior,* Vol. 3. New York: Van Nostrand Reinhold.

KALISH, R.A. 1976. "Death and Dying in a Social Context." In R. Binstock and E. Shanas, eds., - *Handbook of Aging and the Social Sciences.* New York: Van Nostrand Reinhold.

KAMERMAN, S.B., AND A.J. KAHN. 1976. *Social Services in the United States. Policies and Programs.* Philadelphia: Temple University Press.

KART, C.S. 1985. *The Realities of Aging.* New York: Allyn and Bacon.

KATZ, M.B. 1975. *The People of Hamilton Canada West.* Cambridge, Mass.: Harvard University Press.

———. 1982. "Families and Early Industrialization: Cycle, Structure, and Economy." In M.W. Riley, R.P. Abeles, and M.S. Teitelbaum, eds., *Aging From Birth to Death.* Vol.2, *Sociotemporal Perspectives.* AAAS Selected Symposium 79. Boulder, Colo.: Westview Press.

KEITH, J. 1982. *Old People as People. Social and Cultural Influences on Aging and Old Age.* Boston: Little, Brown and Co.

———. 1985. "Age In Anthropological Research." In R.H. Binstock and E. Shanas, eds., *Handbook of Aging and the Social Sciences.* 2d ed. New York: Van Nostrand Reinhold.

KENT, D.P. 1965. "Aging—Fact or Fancy." *The Gerontologist.* 5:2.

KEYFITZ, N. 1973. "Individual Mobility in a Stationary Population." *Population Studies* 27: 335–32.

———. 1986. "Canadian Kinship Patterns Based on 1971 and 1981 Data." *Canadian Studies in Population* 13(2):123–50.

KINGSON, E.R. 1984. "Current Retirement Trends." In M.H. Morrison, ed., *Economics of Aging. The Future of Retirement.* New York: Van Nostrand Reinhold.

KITANO, H.H.L. 1969. *Japanese Americans. The Evolution of a Subculture.* Englewood Cliffs, N. J.: Prentice Hall, Inc.

KLEINMAN, D.S. 1980. *Human Adaptation and Population Growth.* Montclair, N. J.: Allanheld, Osmun, and Co.

KLEINBERGER A.F. 1969. *Society, Schools, and Progress in Israel.* London: Pergamon Press.

KNOWLES, D.E. 1983. "Keeping Older Workers on the Job: Methods and Inducements." In H.S. Parnes, ed., *Policy Issues in Work and Retirement.* Kalamazoo, Mich: Upjohn Institute for Employment Research.

KOBRIN, F.L. 1976. "The Fall in Household Size and the Rise of the Primary Individual in the United States." *Demography* (February): 13:127–38.

KOBRIN, F.L. 1980. "Children and the Household Economy: Ethnic Differences in Leaving Home." Paper presented at Social Science History Association Meeting, Rochester, N. Y., Nov.6–9.

KOHLI, M. 1986. "The World We Forgot: A Historical Review of the Life Course." In V.W. Marshall, ed., *Later Life. The Social Psychology of Aging.* Beverly Hills, Calif.: Sage Publications.

———. 1987. "Social Organization and Subjective Construction of the Life Course." In A.B. Sorensen, F.E. Weinert, and L.R. Sherrod, eds., *Human Development and the Life Course: Multidisciplinary Perspectives.* Hillsdale, N.J.: Erlbaum.

KOYL, L.F. 1970. "A Technique for Measuring Functional Criteria in Placement and Retirement Practices." In H.L. Sheppard, ed., *Toward An Industrial Gerontology.* Cambridge, Mass.: Schenkman Publishing Co.

———. 1974. *Employing the Older Worker. Matching the Employee to the Job.* Fairfax, Va.: National Publications Center.

KREPS, J.M. 1971. *Lifetime Allocation of Work and Income.* Durham, N.C.: Duke University Press.

———. 1976. "Social Security in the Coming Decade: Questions for a Mature System." *Social Security Bulletin* 39, No.3 (March):21–29.

KUPER, L. 1974. *Race, Class, and Power: Ideology and Revolutionary Change in Plural Societies.* Chicago: Aldine.

KUYPERS, J., AND V.L. BENGSTON. 1972. "Social Breakdown and Competence: A Social Psychological View of Aging." *Human Development* 16:181–201.

LASLETT, P. 1985. "Societal Development and Aging." In R.H. Binstock and E. Shanas, eds., - *Handbook of Aging and the Social Sciences.* 2d ed. New York: Van Nostrand Reinhold.

———. 1983. *The World We Have Lost, Further Explored.* London: Methuen.

LAUFFER A. 1978. *Social Planning at the Community Level.* Englewood Cliffs, N.J.: Prentice Hall, Inc.

LE BOURDAIS, C. AND F.K. GOLDSCHEIDER. 1986. "The Falling Age at Leaving Home, 1920–1979." *Sociology and Social Research.* 70:99–102.

LEFF, N.H. 1979. "Dependency Rates and Savings Rates: A New Look." In J.L. Simon and J. DaVanzo, eds., *Research in Population Economics.* Vol.2, 1980. Greenwich, Conn.: JAI Press pp.205–14.

LEHRER, E., AND M. NERLOVE. 1986. "Female Labor Force and Fertility in the United States." *Annual Review of Sociology* 12:181–202.

LEONTIEF, W. 1983. "Technological Advance, Economic Growth, and Income Distribution." *Population and Development Review* 9, no.3 (September): 403–10

LEVIN, J., AND W.C. LEVIN. 1980. *Ageism: Prejudice and Discrimination against the Elderly.* Belmont, Calif.: Wadsworth Publishing Co.

LIEBERSON, S. 1980. *A Piece of the Pie: Black and White Immigrants since 1880.* Berkeley.: University of California Press.

LILLIENFELD, A.M., AND D.E. LILLIENFELD. 1980. *Foundations of Epidemiology.* New York: Oxford University Press.

LOPATA, H.N. 1973. *Widowhood in an American City.* Cambridge, Mass.: Shenkman Publishing Co.

———.1979. *Women as Widows.* New York: Elsevier North Holland Inc.

MADDOX, G.L., AND J. WILEY. 1976. "Scope, Concepts, and Methods in the Study of Aging." In R.H. Binstock and E. Shanas, eds., *Handbook of Aging and the Social Sciences.* New York: Van Nostrand Reinhold.

MADDOX, G.L. AND R.T. CAMPBELL. 1985. "Scope, Concepts, and Methods in the Study of Aging." In R.H. Binstock and E. Shanas, eds., *Handbook of Aging and the Social Sciences.* 2d ed New York: Van Nostrand Reinhold.

MANSKI, C.F., AND D.A. WISE. 1983. *College Choice in America.* Cambridge, Mass.: Harvard University Press.

MANUEL, R.C., ed. 1982. *Minority Aging: Sociological and Social Psychological Issues.* Westport, Conn.: Greenwood Press.

MARCH, J.G., ed. 1981. *Aging.* Vol.1, *Social Change,* edited by S.B. Kiesler et al. Vol.2, *Stability and Change in the Family,* edited by R.W. Fogel et al. New York: Academic Press.

MARINI, M. 1978. "The Transition to Adulthood." *American Sociological Review* 43:483–507.

MARKIDES, K.S., AND C.H. MINDEL. 1987. *Aging and Ethnicity.* Newbury Park, Calif.: Sage.

MARSHALL, V.W. 1980. *Last Chapters: A Sociology of Death and Dying.* Belmont, Calif.: Wadsworth Publ. Co.

———. ed. 1986. *Later Life. The Social Psychology of Aging.* Beverly Hills, Calif.: Sage Publications.

———. 1986. "Dominant and Emerging Paradigms in the Social Psychology of Aging." In V.W. Marshall, ed., *Later Life. The Social Psychology of Aging.* Beverly Hills, Calif.: Sage Publications.

MATRAS, J. 1973. *Populations and Societies.* Englewood Cliffs, N.J.: Prentice Hall, Inc.

———. 1977. *Introduction to Population. A Sociological Approach.* Englewood Cliffs, N. J.: Prentice Hall, Inc.

———. 1984. *Social Inequality, Stratification, and Mobility.* 2d ed. Englewood Cliffs, N.J.: Prentice Hall, Inc.

———. forthcoming, a."Demographic Trends, Life Course, and Family Cycle-The Canadian Example: Part I. Changing Longevity, Parenting, and Kin Availability." *Canadian Studies in Population.*

———. forthcoming, b."Demographic Trends, Life Course, and Family Cycle-The Canadian Example: Part II. Employment, Parenting, and Their Alternatives." *Canadian Studies in Population.*

MATRAS, J., G. NOAM AND I. BAR-HAIM, 1984. *Young Israelis on the Threshold: A Study of the 1954 Cohort of Israeli Men.* In Hebrew, with English summary. Jerusalem: Brookdale Institute Discussion Paper D, pp.102–84.

MAYER, K.U. 1986. "Structural Constraints on the Life Course." *Human Development* 29: 163–70.

MAYER, K.U. AND W. MULLER. 1986. "The State and the Structure of the Life Course." In A.B. Sorensen, F.E. Weinert, and L. Sherrod, eds., *Human Development and the Life Course. Multidisciplinary Perspectives.* Hillsdale, N.J.: Erlbaum.

MAYER, K.U., AND G.R. CARROLL. 1987. "Jobs and Classes: Structural Constraints on Career Mobility." *European Sociological Review* 3(1): 14-38.

MAYER, K. U., et al. 1987. "Class Mobility During the Working Life- A Cross-National Comparison Between Germany and Norway." Paper presented at 1987 Annual Meeting, American Sociological Association, Chicago, August.

MAYS, J., A. FORDER, AND O. KEIDAN, eds. 1983. *Penelope Hall's Social Services of England and Wales.* London: Routledge & Kegan Paul.

McCONNELL S.R. 1980. "Alternative Work Patterns for an Aging Labor Force." In P.K. Ragan, ed., *Work and Retirement: Policy Issues.* Los Angeles: Andrus Gerontology Center, University of Southern California.

———. 1983. "Age Discrimination in Employment." In H.S. Parnes, ed., *Policy Issues in Work and Retirement*. Kalamazoo, Mich.: Upjohn Institute for Employment Research.

McDANIEL, S.A. 1986. *Canada's Aging Population*. Toronto: Butterworths.

McDONALD, J. AND S.P. STEPHENSON, JR. 1979. "The Effect of Income Maintenance on the School Enrollment and Labor Supply Decisions of Teenagers." *Journal of Human Resources* 14:488–506.

McLANAHAN, S.S., AND A.B. SORENSEN. 1985. "Life Events and Psychological Well-Being Over the Life Course." In G.H. Elder, Jr., ed., *Life Course Dynamics. Trajectories and Transitions, 1968–1980*. Ithaca, N.Y.: Cornell University Press.

McPHERSON, B.D. 1983. *Aging as a Social Process* Toronto: Butterworths.

MEAD, M. 1961. *Coming of Age in Samoa. A Psychological Study of Primitive Youth for Western Civilization*. New York: Morrow.

MEIER, E.L. 1980. "Employment of Older Workers. Disincentives and Incentives." President's Commission of Pension Policy. Working Papers. Washington, D.C.: President's Committee on Pension Policy.

MICHAEL, R.T., AND N.B. TUMA. 1985. "Entry into Marriage and Parenthood by Young Men and Women: The Influence of Family Background." *Demography* 23(4): 515–43.

MIDLARSKY, E.S., AND E. KAHANA 1983. "Helping by the Elderly: Conceptual and Empirical Considerations," in M.B.Kleiman, *Social Gerontology. Interdisciplinary Topics in Gerontology*. Vol.17. Basel: Karger.

MILBANK MEMORIAL FUND QUARTERLY, 1979. 57, no.4 (Fall). Issue on Deinstitutionalization: The Evolution and Evaluation of Health Care Policy in the United States and Great Britain.

MINKLER, M. 1981. "Research on the Health Effects of Retirement: An Uncertain Legacy." *Journal of Health and Social Behavior* 22(2):117–30.

MODELL, J., F.E. FURSTENBERG, JR., AND T. HERSCHBERG. 1976. "Social Change and Transitions to Adulthood in Historical Perspective." *Journal of Family History* 1:7–32.

MORGAN, J.N., et al. 1974–1983. *Five Thousand American Families—Patterns of Economic Progress*. Vols.1–10. Ann Arbor: Institute for Social Research.

MORGAN, L.A. 1982. "Social Roles in Later Life: Some Recent Research Trends." In C. Eisdorfer, ed., *Annual Review of Gerontology and Geriatrics*. Vol.3. New York: Springer.

MORONEY, R.M. 1976. *Family and the State*. London: Longman.

———. 1986. *Shared Responsibility. Families and Social Policy*. New York: Aldine de Gruyter.

MUSCROVE, P. 1980. *Effects of Income and Demographic Change on the Structure of Household Consumption, 1975–2025*. Washington, D. C.: Resources for the Future.

MYLES, J. 1984. *Old Age in the Welfare State. The Political Economy of Public Pensions*. Boston: Little, Brown and Co.

———. 1986. "Social Security and Support for the Elderly: The Western Experience." Ottawa: Carleton University, Department of Sociology and Anthropology Working Paper v.86–03.

———. 1987. "Decline or Impasse? The Current State of the Welfare State, Manuscript, Department of Sociology and Anthropology, Carleton University, Ottawa.

NAGNUR, D. 1986. *Longevity and Historical Life Tables, 1921–1981, Canada and the Provinces* (abridged). Ottawa: Statistics Canada. Catalogue 89–506.

NAM, C.B., AND S.O.GUSTAVAS. 1976. *Population. The Dynamics of Demographic Change*. Boston: Houghton Mifflin Co.

NATIONAL CENTER FOR HEALTH STATISTICS, P.M.GORDON. 1985. *Charting the Nation's Health: Trends Since 1960* DHHS Pub. No. (PHS) 85–1251. Public Health Service. Washington: Government Printing Office, August.

NATIONAL COUNCIL ON THE AGING. 1981. *Aging in the Eighties: America in Transition*. A survey by Louis Harris and Associates, Inc. Washington, D.C.: The National Council on the Aging, Inc.

NEUGARTEN, B.L. 1985. "Interpretive Social Science and Research on Aging." In A.S.Rossi, ed., *Gender and the Life Course*. New York: Aldine.

NEUGARTEN, B.L., AND N. DATAN. 1973. "Sociological Perspectives on the Life Cycle." In P.B.Baltes and K.W. Schaie, eds., *Life-Span Developmental Psychology. Personality and Socialization*. New York: Academic Press.

NEUGARTEN, B.L., AND G.O. HAGESTAD. 1976. "Age and the Life Course." In R.H.Binstock and E. Shanas, eds., *Handbook of Aging and the Social Sciences*. New York: Van Nostrand Reinhold.

NEUGARTEN, B.L., AND G.O. HAGESTAD. 1985."Age and the Life Course." In R.H.Binstock and E.Shanas, eds., *Handbook of Aging and the Social Sciences*. 2d ed. New York: Van Nostrand Reinhold.

NEW YORK TIMES."America's Army of Non-Workers," Sept. 27, 1987.

NOAM, G. 1986. "The Elderly Mother-Adult Daughter Relationship: A Survey of Recent Literature." Jerusalem: Brookdale Institute Discussion Paper D–141–86.

———. 1987. "Issues in the Study of the Quality of the Elderly Mother-Adult Daughter Relationship." *Comprehensive Gerontology B* 1:68–71.

OFFE, C. 1984. *Contradictions of the Welfare State*. London: Hutchinson.

ONTARIO ECONOMIC COUNCIL. 1981. "User Charges in the Social Services: An Economic Theory of Need and Inability." Toronto: Ontario Economic Council Research Studies, no. 22.

OPPENHEIMER, V.K. 1974. "The Life Cycle Squeeze: The Interaction of Men's Occupational and Family Life Cycles." *Demography* 11:227–45.

———. 1982. *Work and the Family: A Study in Social Demography*. New York: Academic Press.

O'RAND, A. 1984. "Women." In E. Palmore, ed., *Handbook on the Aged in the United States*. Westport, Conn: Greenwood Press.

O'RAND, A. AND J. HENRIETTA, 1982. "Delayed Career Entry, Industrial Pension Structure, and Early Retirement in a Cohort of Unmarried Women." *American Sociological Review*. 47(3): 365–73.

PALMORE, E.B., 1969. "Sociological Aspects of Aging." in E. Busse and E. Pfeiffer, eds., *Behavior and Adaptation in Later Life*. Boston: Little Brown.

———. 1975. "The Status and Integration of the Aged in Japanese Society." *The Journal of Gerontology* 30:2.

———. 1975. *The Honorable Elders. A Cross-Cultural Analysis of Aging in Japan*. Durham, N.C. Duke University Press.

———. 1981. *Social Patterns in Normal Aging: Findings from the Duke Longitudinal Study*. Durham, N.C.: Duke University Press.

PALMORE, E., et al. 1985. *Retirement. Causes and Consequences*. New York: Springer Publishing Co.

PALMORE, E., AND F. WHITTINGTON. 1971. "Trends in the Relative Status of the Aged." *Social Forces* 50:84–91.

PAMPEL, F. 1981. *Social Change and the Aged. Recent Trends in the United States*. Lexington, Mass.: D.C.Heath.

———. 1983. "Changes in Propensity to Live Alone." *Demography* 20: 433–48.

PAMPEL, F.C., AND J.A. WEISS. 1983. "Economic Development, Pension Policies, and the Labor Force Participation of Aged Males: A Cross-National, Longitudinal Approach." *American Journal of Sociology* 89(2):350–72.

PARKER, R.A. 1980. "The State of Care," Jerusalem: Brookdale Institute, The Richard M. Titmuss Memorial Lecture 1979–80. Paper S–3–80.

———. 1981. "Tending and Social Policy." In E.M. Goldberg and S. Hatch, eds., *A New Look at the Personal Social Services*. London: Policy Studies Institute, Discussion Paper 4.

PARKER, S. 1982. *Work and Retirement*. London: George Allen & Unwin.

PARKES, C.M., 1964. "Effects of Bereavement on Physical and Mental Health: A Study of the Medical Records of Widows." *British Medical Journal*. 2:274–279.

PARKIN, F. 1971. *Class Inequality and Political Order*. London: McGibbon & Kee.

———. 1979. *Marxism and Class Theory: A Bourgeois Critique*. New York: Columbia University Press.

PARNES, H.S. 1981. ""From the Middle to the Later Years: Longitudinal Studies of Pre- and Post-retirement Experiences of Men." *Research on Aging* 4:387–402.

———. 1983. "Introduction and Overview." In H.S. Parnes, ed., *Policy Issues in Work and Retirement*. Kalamazoo, Mich.: Upjohn Institute for Employment Research.

PARNES, H.S., et al. 1985. *Retirement Among American Men*. Lexington, Mass.: D.C. Heath and Co., Lexington Books.

PARSONS, T. AND N.J. SMELSER. 1956. *Economy and Society. A Study in the Integration of Economic and Social Theory*. London: Routledge & Kegan Paul Ltd.

PERLMAN, M. 1981. "Some Economic Consequences of the New Patterns of Population Growth." In W. Fellner, project director, *Essays in Contemporary Economic Problems. Demand, Productivity, and Population*. Washington, D.C.: American Enterprise Institute for Public Policy Research.

PIVEN, F.F., AND R.A. CLOWARD. 1971. *Regulating the Poor: The Functions of Public Welfare*. New York: Pantheon.

POOL, I. 1985. *Family History Survey: New Perspectives on Lone-Parents*. Ottawa: Statistics Canada. Catalogue 99–948.

POPULATION REFERENCE BUREAU. 1987. *World Population Data Sheet* Washington, D.C.: Population Reference Bureau.

PORTER, J. 1979. *The Measure of Canadian Society*. Agincourt, Ont.:Gage.

PRESSAT, R. 1972. *Demographic Analysis*. Chicago: Aldine Publ. Co.

PRESTON, S.H. 1984. "Children and the Elderly: Divergent Paths for America's Dependents." *Demography* 21:435–57.

———. 1982. "Relations Between Individual Life Cycles and Population Characteristics." *American Sociological Review*. 47:253–264.

PULLUM, T.W. 1982. "The Eventual Frequencies of Kin in a Stable Population." *Demography* 19(4):549–65.

REIN, M. 1977. "Social Planning: The Search for Legitimacy. In N. Gilbert and H. Specht, eds., *Planning for Social Welfare. Issues, Models, and Tasks*. Englewood Cliffs, N.J.: Prentice Hall, Inc.

RICE, D.P., AND J.J. FELDMAN. 1983. "Living Longer in the United States: Demographic Changes and Health Needs of the Elderly." *Milbank Memorial Quarterly/Health and Society* 61:362–396.

RILEY, J.W., JR. 1983. "Dying and Meanings of Death." *Annual Review of Sociology* 9:191–216.

RILEY, M.W. 1976. "Age Strata in Social Systems." In R.H.Binstock and E. Shanas, eds., *Handbook of Aging and the Social Sciences*. New York: Van Nostrand Reinhold.

———. 1985. "Age Strata in Social Systems." In R.H.Binstock and E.Shanas, eds., *Handbook of Aging and the Social Sciences*. 2d ed., New York: Van Nostrand Reinhold.

RILEY, M.W. AND A. FONER, 1968. *Aging and Society*. Vol. I, *An Inventory of Research Findings*. New York: Russell Sage Foundation.

RILEY, M.W., M. JOHNSON, AND A. FONER EDS.. 1972. *Aging and Society*. Vol.3, *A Sociology of Age Stratification*. New York: Russell Sage Foundation.

RILEY, M.W., R.P. ABELES, AND M.S.TEITELBAUM, EDS. 1982. *Aging From Birth to Death*. Vol.2, *Sociotemporal Perspectives*. AAAS Selected Symposium 79. Boulder, Colo.: Westview Press.

RINDFUSS, R.R., S.P. MORGAN, AND C.G. SWICEGOOD, 1984. "The Transition to Motherhood: The Intersection of

Structural and Temporal Dimensions." *American Sociological Review.* 49(3): 359–372.

———.1988. *First Births in America: Changes in the Timing of Parenthood.* Berkeley, Calif.: University of California Press.

ROBINS, P.K., N.B. TUMA, AND K.E. YAEGER. 1980. "Effects of SIME/DIME on Change in Employment in Employment Status." *Journal of Human Resources* 15:544–73.

ROBINSON, P. 1987. *Women's Work Interruptions: Results From the 1984 Family History Survey.* Statistics Canada. Ottawa: Ministry of Supply and Services.

ROBINSON, P.K., S. COBERLY, AND C.E.PAUL. 1985. "Work and Retirement." In R.H. Binstock and E. Shanas, eds., *Handbook of Aging and the Social Sciences.* 2d. ed. New York: Van Nostrand Reinhold.

ROSE, A.M. 1965. "Group Consciousness Among the Aging." In A.M. Rose and W.A. Peterson, eds., *Older People and Their Social World.* Philadelphia: F.A.Davis.

ROSENMAYER, L. 1968. "Family Relations of the Elderly." *Marriage and the Family* (November): 30:672–680.

———. 1981. "Objective and Subjective Perspectives of Life Span Research." *Aging and Society* 1(1):29–45.

ROSENWAIKE, I. 1985. *The Extreme Aged in America. A Portrait of an Expanding Population.* Westport, Conn.: Greenwood Press.

ROSOW, I. 1967. *Social Integration of the Aged.* New York: The Free Press.

———. 1974. *Socialization to Old Age.* Berkeley,Calif.: University of California Press.

———. 1976. "Status and Role Change through the Life Span." In R.H.Binstock and E. Shanas, eds., *Handbook of Aging and the Social Sciences.* New York: Van Nostrand Reinhold.

———. 1985. "Status and Role Change through the Life Span." In R.H.Binstock and E. Shanas, eds., *Handbook of Aging and the Social Sciences.* 2d ed. New York: Van Nostrand Reinhold.

ROSOW, J.M., AND R. ZAGER. 1980. *The Future of Older Workers in America. New Options for an Extended Working Life.* Scarsdale, N.Y.: Work in America Institute, Inc.

ROSSI, A.S. 1980. "Aging and Parenthood in the Middle Years." In P.B. Baltes and O.G. Brim, Jr., eds., *Life Span Development and Behavior.* Vol.3. New York: Academic Press.

ROSSI, A.S., 1968. "Transition to Parenthood." *Journal of Marriage and the Family.* 32:20–28.

———. ed. 1985. *Gender and the Life Course.* New York: Aldine Publ.Co.

ROSSI, P. 1955. *Why Families Move.* New York: Free Press.

RUBIN, L. 1976. *Worlds of Pain: Life in the Working Class Family.* New York: Basic Books.

RUSSELL, C.S. 1974. "Transition to Parenthood: Problems and Gratifications." *Journal of Marriage and the Family* 36: 244–303.

RYDER, N.B. 1975. "Reproductive Behavior and the Family Life Cycle." in *The Population Debate: Dimensions and Perspectives.* Vol.2. New York: United Nations, Department of Economic and Social Affairs, pp.278–88.

RYFF, C.D. 1984. "Personality Development from the Inside: The Subjective Experience of Change in Adulthood and Aging." In P.B.Baltes and O.G.Brim, Jr., eds., *Life-Span Development and Behavior.* Vol.6. New York: Academic Press.

———. 1985. "The Subjective Experience of Life-Span Transitions." In A.S.Rossi, ed., *Gender and the Life Course.* New York: Aldine.

———. 1986. "The Subjective Construction of Self and Society: An Agenda for Life-Span Research." In V.W. Marshall, ed., *Later Life. The Social Psychology of Aging.* Beverly Hills, Calif.: Sage Publications.

SAUVY, A. 1954. *Theorie generale de la population.* 2 vols. Paris: Presses Universitaires de France.

SCHNEIDER, D., AND R. SMITH, 1973. *Class Differences and Sex Roles in American Kinship and Family Structure.* Englewood Cliffs, N.J.: Prentice Hall, Inc.

SHOEN, R., et al. 1985. "Marriage and Divorce in Twentieth Century American Cohorts." *Demography* 22(1):101–114.

SCHRANK, H.T., AND J.M. WARING, 1983. "Aging and Work Organizations," in M.W. Riley, B.B. Hess, and K. Bond, eds., *Aging in Society: Selected Reviews of Recent Research.* Hillsdale, N.J.: Erlbaum Associates.

SCHULZ, J.J. 1985. *The Economics of Aging.* 3d ed. New York: Van Nostrand Reinhold Co.

SEWELL, W.H., R.M. HAUSER, AND W.C. WOLF, 1980. "Sex, Schooling, and Occupational Status," *American Journal of Sociology.* 86:551–583

SHANAS, E. 1980. "Older People and Their Families. The New Pioneers." *Journal of Marriage and the Family* 42:9–15.

SHANAS, E. AND G.L. MADDOX, 1985 "Health, Health Resources, and the Utilization of Care," in R. Binstock and E. Shanas, eds., *Handbook of Aging and The Social Sciences,* 2d ed. New York: Van Nostrand Reinhold.

SHANAS, E., AND M.B. SUSSMAN. 1977. *Family, Bureaucracy, and the Elderly.* Durham, N.C.: Duke University Press.

SHAPIRO, D. AND F.L. MOTT, 1979. "Labor Supply Behavior of Prospective and New Mothers," *Demography* 16(2):199–209.

SHAVIT, Y., 1984. "Tracking and Ethnicity in Israeli Secondary Education." *American Sociological Review.* 49(2):210–220.

SHAVIT, Y., J. MATRAS, AND D.L. FEATHERMAN. 1987. "Job-shifts in the Career Beginnings of Israeli Men." In K.U.Mayer and N.B Tuma, eds., *Applications of Event History Analysis in Life Course Research.* Berlin: Max-Planck-Institut. Materialien aus der Bildungsforschung Nr.30.

SHEPPARD, H.L. 1976. "Work and Retirement." In R.H.Binstock and E. Shanas, eds. *Handbook of Aging and the Social Sciences.* New York: Van Nostrand Reinhold Co.

SHMUELI, A. 1985. "The Demography of Kinship in Israel, 1960–1980,"(in Hebrew). Discussion Paper 116–85. Jerusalem: Brookdale Institute.

———. 1986. "Kinship Networks in Israel" (in Hebrew). Jerusalem: Brookdale Institute. Mimeo'd.

SIMMONS, L.W. 1945. *The Role of the Aged in Primitive Society.* New Haven, Conn.: Yale University Press.

———. 1960. "Aging in Preindustrial Societies." In C.Tibbets, ed., *Handbook of Social Gerontology.* Chicago: University of Chicago Press. © 1960 by The University of Chicago. All rights reserved.

SIMON, J.L. 1977. *The Economics of Population.* Princeton, N.J.: Princeton University Press.

———. 1981. *The Ultimate Resource.* Princeton, N.J.: Princeton University Press.

SMITH, S.J. 1982. "New Worklife Estimates Reflect Changing Profile of Labor Force." *Monthly Labor Review* (March):15–20.

SOLDO, B.J. 1980. "America's Elderly in the 1980's." *Population Bulletin* 35 (November):4. Washington, D.C.: Population Reference Bureau.

SORENSEN, A. 1983a. "Women's Employment Patterns After Marriage." *Journal of Marriage and the Family.* 45: 311-21.

———. 1983b. "Family Effects of Life Course Patterns in Early Adulthood: The Mediating Effect of Adolescent Status." Madison Wis.: CDE Working Paper 83–24. University of Wisconsin Center for Demography and Ecology.

———. 1983. "Role Transitions in Young Men's Lives: Reversibility, Time Between Events, and Age Grading of Transitions." Madison, Wis.: CDE Working Paper 83–24. University of Wisconsin Center for Demography and Ecology.

SORENSEN, A., AND A.B. SORENSEN. 1983. "An Event History Analysis of the Process of Entry into First Marriage." Madison, Wis.: CDE Working Paper 83–26. University of Wisconsin Center for Demography and Ecology.

SPECIAL COMMITTEE ON AGING. 1981. "Toward a National Older Worker Policy." Special Committee on Aging, U.S. Senate. Washington, D.C: Government Printing Office.

SPECIAL COMMITTEE ON AGING. 1982. "Aging and the Work Force: Human Resource Strategies." Special Committee on Aging, U.S. Senate. Washington, D.C.: Government Printing Office.

SPENGLER, J.J. 1972. "Declining Population: Economic Effects." Economic Aspects of Population Change." U.S. Commission on Population Growth and the American Future research papers. Vol. 2. Washington, D.C.: Government Printing Office.

———.ed. 1975. *Zero Population Growth: Implications.* Chapel Hill N.C.: Carolina Population Center.

———. 1978. *Facing Zero Population Growth. Reactions and Interpretations, Past and Present.* Durham, N.C.: Duke University Press.

SPICKER, S.F., K.M. WOODWARD, AND D.D. VAN TASSEL. 1978. *Aging and the Elderly: Humanistic Perspectives in Gerontology.* Atlantic Highlands, N.J.: Humanities Press.

SPILERMAN, S. 1977. "Careers, Labor Market Structure, and Socioeconomic Achievement." *American Journal of Sociology* 83:551–93.

SPROAT, K.V., H. CHURCHILL, AND C. SHEETS. 1985. *The National Longitudinal Surveys of Labor Market Experience. An Annotated Bibliography of Research.* Lexington, Mass.: D.C. Heath & Co.

STAHMER, H.M. 1978. "The Aged in Two Ancient Oral Cultures: The Ancient Hebrews and Homeric Greece." In S.F. Spicker, K.M. Woodward, and D.D. Van Tassel, eds., *Aging and the Elderly.* Atlantic Highlands, N.J.: Humanities Press.

STATISTICS CANADA. 1985. *Family History Survey.* Public Use Micro-data Documentation. Special Surveys Program, September.

———. 1984. *The Elderly in Canada.* Ottawa: Minister of Supply and Services.

STEINER, G.Y., 1981. *The Futility of Family Policy.* Washington, D.C.: Brookings Institution.

STEPHENS, M.A.P., AND M.D. BERNSTEIN. 1984. "Social Support and Well-Being Among Residents of Planned Housing." *The Gerontologist* 24:144–148.

STOCK, C. 1974. *All Our Kin.* New York: Harper and Row.

STONE, D.A. 1984. *The Disabled State.* Philadelphia: Temple University Press.

STRAUS, M.A., AND G.T. HOTALING. 1980. *The Social Causes of Husband-Wife Violence.* Minneapolis: University of Minnesota Press.

STREIB, G.F. 1965. "Are the Aged a Minority Group?" In A.W. Gouldner and S.M. Miller, eds., *Applied Sociology.* Glencoe, Ill.: Free Press.

———. 1976. "Social Stratification and Aging." In R.H. Binstock and E. Shanas, eds., *Handbook of Aging and the Social Sciences.* New York: Van Nostrand Reinhold.

STREIB, G.F., AND C.J. SCHNEIDER, 1972. *Retirement in American Society.* Ithaca, N.Y.: Cornell University Press.

STREIB, G.F., AND W.E. THOMPSON. 1960. "The Older Person in a Family Context." In C. Tibbets, ed., *Handbook of Social Gerontology.* Chicago: University of Chicago Press.

SUSSER, M., 1973. *Causal Thinking in the Health Sciences.* New York: Oxford University Press.

SUSSMAN, M.B. 1976. "The Family Life of Old People." In R.H. Binstock and E. Shanas, eds., *Handbook of Aging and the Social Sciences.* New York: Van Nostrand Reinhold.

———. 1985. "The Family Life of Old People." In R.H. Binstock and E. Shanas, eds., *Handbook of Aging and the Social Sciences.* 2d.ed. New York: Van Nostrand Reinhold.

SWEET, J.A. 1977. "Demography and the Family." *Annual Review of Sociology* 3:363–405.

———. 1979a. "Changes in the Allocation of Time of Young Women Among Schooling, Marriage, Work and Childrearing: 1960–1976." CDE Working Paper

79–15. Madison, Wis.: Center for Demography and Ecology, University of Wisconsin.

———. 1979b. "Changes in the Allocation of Time of Young Men Among Schooling, Marriage, Work and Childrearing: 1960–1976." CDE Working Paper 79–28. Madison, Wis.: Center for Demography and Ecology, University of Wisconsin.

———. 1979c. "Ethnic Differences in the Allocation of the Young Adult Years: Comparisons Among White, Black, and Mexican-American Men and Women." CDE Working Paper 79–31. Madison, Wis.: Center for Demography and Ecology, University of Wisconsin.

SWEET J.A., AND BUMPASS L.L. 1984. "Living Arrangements of the Elderly in the United States." CDE Working Paper 84–11. Madison, Wis.: Center for Demography and Ecology, University of Wisconsin.

TEDRICK, T. 1985. *Aging. Issues and Policies for the 1980s.* New York: Praeger.

TIBBETTS, C., ed., 1960. *Handbook of Social Gerontology.* Chicago: The University of Chicago Press.

TOLKE, A. 1987. "Family Development and Labor Force Participation—A Dynamic Analysis of Job Leaving." Paper presented at the first International Conference on the Future of Adult Life, Leeuwenhorst, Netherlands, April.

TRACY, M.B. 1978. "Flexible Retirement Features Abroad." *Social Security Bulletin* (May)

TREIMAN, D.J. 1985. "The Work Histories of Women and Men: What We Know and What We Need to Find Out." In A.S. Rossi, ed., *Gender and the Life Course.* New York: Aldine de Gruyer. Copyright © 1985 by the American Sociological Association.

TROLL, L.E. 1971. "The Family of Later Life: A Decade Review," *Journal of Marriage and the Family* 33:263–290.

TROLL, L.E. 1985. *Early and Middle Adulthood.* 2d ed. Monterey, Calif.: Brooks/Cole.

TROLL, L.E., S.J. MILLER, AND R.C. ATCHLEY. 1979. *Families in Later Life.* Belmont, Calif.: Wadsworth Publishing Co., Inc.

TUMA, N.B., AND M.T. HANNAN. 1984. *Social Dynamics: Models and Methods.* New York: Academic Press.

UHLENBERG, P. 1969. "A Study of Cohort Life Cycles: Cohorts of Native Born Massachusetts Women, 1830–1920." *Population Studies* 23(3):284–92.

———. 1974. "Cohort Variations in the Family Life Cycle Experiences of U.S. Females." *Journal of Marriage and the Family* 36:284–94.

UNITED NATIONS. 1973. *The Determinants and Consequences of Population Trends.* 2d ed. Population Studies No.50. New York: United Nations.

———. 1987. *Demographic Yearbook, 1986.* New York: United Nations.

U.S. BUREAU OF THE CENSUS, 1987. *Statistical Abstract of the United States, 1988.* Washington, D.C.: Government Printing Office.

U.S. DEPARTMENT OF LABOR. 1979. *Employment-Related Problems of Older Workers: A Research Strategy.* R & D Monograph 73. Washington, D.C.: Government Printing Office.

———. 1981. *Interim Report on Age Discrimination in Employment Act Studies.* Employment Standards Administration. Washington, D.C.: Government Printing Office.

———. 1982. *Final Report to Congress on Age Discrimination in Employment Act Studies.* Washington, D.C.: Government Printing Office.

VAN GENNEP, A. 1960 (1908). *Rites of Passage.* Chicago: University of Chicago Press.

VERBRUGGE, L.M. 1984. "Longer Life but Worsening Health? Trends in Health and Mortality of Middle-aged and Older Persons." *Milbank Memorial Fund Quarterly/Health and Society* 62, No.3 (Summer): 475–519.

WALKER, A. 1982. "Dependency and Old Age." *Social Policy and Administration* 16(2):115–35.

WATKINS, S.C., J.A. MENKEN, AND J. BONGAARTS, 1987. "Demographic Foundations of Family Change." *American Sociological Review.* 52:346-358.

WELLMAN, B., AND A. HALL. 1986. "Social Networks and Social Support: Implications for Later Life." In V.W. Marshall, ed., *Later Life. The Social Psychology of Aging.* Beverly Hills, Calif.: Sage Publications.

WEST, R.W. 1980. "The Effects of SIME/DIME on the Labor Supply of Young Non-heads of Households." *Journal of Human Resources* 15:574–96.

WILENSKY, H.L. 1961. "Orderly Careers and Social Participation: The Impact of Work History on Social Integration in the Middle Class." *American Sociological Review* 26:521–539.

———. 1975. *The Welfare State and Equality.* Berkeley, Calif.: University of California Press.

WILKINS, R., AND O.B. ADAMS. 1983a. "Health Expectancy in Canada, Late 1970's: Demographic, Regional, and Social Dimensions." *American Journal of Public Health* 73(9):1073–80.

———. 1983b. *Healthfulness of Life.* Montreal: Institute for Research on Public Policy.

WILLIAMS, J.A., AND R. STOCKTON. 1973. "Black Family Structure and Functions: An Empirical Examination of Some Suggestions Made by Billingsly." *Journal of Marriage and the Family* 35:39–49.

WILSON, R.W., 1985. "Assessing the Impact of Life Change Events" in E.B. Palmore et al., eds., *Normal Aging III.* Durham, N.C.: Duke University Press.

WINSBOROUGH, H.H. 1978. "Statistical Histories of the Life Cycle of Birth Cohorts: The Transition from Schoolboy to Adult Male." In K.E. Taeuber, et al., eds., *Social Demography.* New York: Academic Press.

———. 1979. "Changes in the Transition to Adulthood," in M.W. Riley, ed., *Aging from Birth to Death.* Boulder, Colo.: Westview Press.

WOLF, D.A. 1983. "Kinship and Living Arrangements of Older Americans. Washington, D.C.: The Urban Institute.

THE WORLD BANK. 1985. *Population Change and Economic Development.* Reprinted from World Development Report 1984. New York: Oxford University Press.

YOUNG, C.M. 1974. "Ages, Reasons, and Sex Differences for Children Leaving Home. Observations from Survey Data for Australia." *Journal of Marriage and the Family* 36:769–78.

———. 1975. "Factors Associated with Timing and Duration of the Leaving Home Stage of the Family Life." *Population Studies* 29:61–73.

YOUNG, C. 1977. *The Family Life Cycle*. Australian *Family Formation Project Monograph No.6*. Canberra: Australian National University Press.

ZOPF, P.E. JR. 1986. *America's Older Population*. Houston: Cap and Gown.

INDEX